JFK AND THE MASCULINE MYSTIQUE

Also by Steven Watts

Self-Help Messiah:
Dale Carnegie and Success in Modern America

Mr. Playboy:
Hugh Hefner and the American Dream

The People's Tycoon:
Henry Ford and the American Century

The Magic Kingdom:
Walt Disney and the American Way of Life

The Romance of Real Life:
Charles Brockden Brown and the Origins of American Culture

The Republic Reborn:
War and the Making of Liberal America, 1790–1820

JFK AND THE MASCULINE MYSTIQUE

SEX AND POWER ON THE NEW FRONTIER

STEVEN WATTS

THOMAS DUNNE BOOKS
ST. MARTIN'S PRESS ≋ NEW YORK

THOMAS DUNNE BOOKS.
An imprint of St. Martin's Press.

JFK AND THE MASCULINE MYSTIQUE. Copyright © 2016 by Steven Watts.
All rights reserved. Printed in the United States of America. For information,
address St. Martin's Press, 175 Fifth Avenue, New York, N.Y. 10010.

www.thomasdunnebooks.com
www.stmartins.com

The Library of Congress Cataloging-in-Publication Data is available upon request.

ISBN 978-1-250-04998-8 (hardcover)
ISBN 978-1-4668-5115-3 (e-book)

Our books may be purchased in bulk for promotional, educational, or business use.
Please contact your local bookseller or the Macmillan Corporate and Premium Sales
Department at 1-800-221-7945, extension 5442, or by e-mail at MacmillanSpecial
Markets@macmillan.com.

First Edition: November 2016

10 9 8 7 6 5 4 3 2 1

For the University of Missouri, my professional home for many years, and a humane, tolerant, and distinguished institution of higher learning that has provided an excellent education to many generations of the state's young people.

CONTENTS

Acknowledgments   *ix*

Introduction: Kennedy Adonais   *1*

One   The Crisis of Masculinity in 1950s America   11

Two   Style Makes the Man: Candidate John F. Kennedy   39

Three   Hollywood Cool: Frank Sinatra and the Jack Pack   72

Four   Existential Tough Guy: Norman Mailer   104

Five   Secret Agent Men: Ian Fleming and James Bond   132

Six   A Philosophy for Playboys: Hugh Hefner   162

Seven   Vigor and Virility: President John F. Kennedy   186

Eight   Celebrity Journalist: Ben Bradlee   227

Nine   Modern Warriors: Maxwell Taylor and Edward Lansdale   260

Ten   The Spartacus Syndrome: Kirk Douglas and Tony Curtis   289

Eleven   Mercury Macho: Alan Shepard and John Glenn   323

Epilogue: The Masculine Mystique   *356*

Notes   *369*

Index   *403*

ACKNOWLEDGMENTS

I t is a pleasure to acknowledge the many people who have contributed to the making of this book. Several colleagues from the Department of History at the University of Missouri read the manuscript and generously offered a wealth of suggestions and criticisms: Robert Collins, Victor McFarland, Jonathan Root, Jonathan Sperber, and John Wigger. Another colleague, Catherine Rymph, led me to a number of insights in a couple of interesting discussions about *Mad Men* and the Kennedy ethos, while Melinda Lockwood assisted with numerous technical issues in preparing the manuscript and images. Another circle of friends—Armando Favazza, Ann Korschgen, Cindy Sheltmire, Marty Townsend, Steve Weinberg—critiqued the manuscript, corrected mistakes, and made many useful suggestions for improvement.

The Kinder Institute for Constitutional Democracy at the University of Missouri provided a lecture forum for trying out some of my ideas about JFK, masculinity, and politics. In Ellis Library at MU, several librarians— Dorothy Carner, Dolores Fischer, Gwen Gray, Sandy Schiefer—deployed their considerable skills to help locate and procure elusive research sources. Steve Martinez, archivist at the Playboy Mansion in Los Angeles, kindly assisted me with locating some key items regarding Hugh Hefner and Kennedy. The JFK Library proved invaluable with its massive collection of online source material on Kennedy's life and career. At Thomas Dunne Books, Emily Angell skillfully edited the manuscript while making some shrewd suggestions about trimming and tightening the original submission, while Jennifer Letwack assisted with a host of tasks as the book moved to completion.

Cassandra Yacovazzi, first a student and then a colleague at the University of Missouri, provided invaluable service as a research assistant. She chased down many hard-to-locate source materials, made numerous suggestions about new avenues of research and interpretation, and read the entire manuscript with a keen and discerning eye. My friend and agent, Ronald Goldfarb, himself a recruit for the New Frontier many years ago, not only did his usual outstanding job on the business end of things but convinced me I had something new and interesting to say about JFK.

My greatest thanks go to my wife, Patti, and daughter, Olivia, both of whom probably heard more than they ever wanted to about Kennedy and his circle over the last few years. The former provided a sounding board for my reflections on JFK's life and career and contributed her usual intelligence and perception to helping me make sense of things. The latter often asked me how the book was coming along on our daily rides home from her grade school, and displayed great patience as her father watched far too many films and videos from the "olden times" of the 1950s and 1960s on the family television. Their love and support was indispensable.

It seemed to me that men weren't really the enemy—they were fellow victims, suffering from an outmoded masculine mystique that made them feel unnecessarily inadequate when there were no bears to kill.

—BETTY FRIEDAN, *The Feminine Mystique*

Thou wert the morning star among the living,
Ere thy fair light had fled;
Now, having died, thou art as Hesperus, giving
New splendor to the dead.

—PERCY SHELLEY, *Adonais: An Elegy on the Death of John Keats*

The Washington landscape seemed to me littered with male widows [after JFK's assassination].

—JOSEPH ALSOP, *I've Seen the Best of It*

JFK AND THE MASCULINE MYSTIQUE

INTRODUCTION

Kennedy Adonais

Coming to terms with John F. Kennedy is no easy matter, although it is certainly not from a lack of effort. Hundreds of books and articles have been written on the thirty-fifth president since he moved into the public spotlight in the mid-1950s. On the fiftieth anniversary of his assassination several years ago, for example, a tidal wave of volumes swept over the reading public treating various aspects of his life, death, administration, and legacy. Yet these many efforts have been strangely unsatisfying. Neither the human being nor the historical import of his endeavors has ever quite come into focus. As an article in *The New York Times* observed of the multiplying volumes on Kennedy, "To explore the enormous literature is to be struck not by what's there but by what's missing. Readers can choose from many books but surprisingly few good ones." There remains, argued the author, a fundamental "elusive detachment" about JFK that foils the biographers and the historians and the political scientists just as "even during his lifetime, Kennedy defeated or outwitted the most powerfully analytical and intuitive minds." Both the man and his meaning have avoided capture.[1]

Part of this elusiveness stems from the devastating impact of Kennedy's assassination in November 1963. He has been frozen in time, in our mind's eye forever young and vigorous, cool and witty. It is simply impossible to imagine JFK as a decrepit old man with a receded hairline, clouded vision, halting gait, and quaking voice. We can never know how his story would have ended. Thus, after the tragedy in Dallas and the images burned into the national consciousness—Walter Cronkite's breaking voice and brimming eyes as he announced the president's death on national television, Jackie Kennedy's blood-splattered pink suit as she returned to Washington, D.C., with her husband's body, three-year-old John Kennedy Jr.'s heartbreaking salute to his father's casket as it moved by on its horse-drawn caisson, the slow parade of dignitaries and political leaders walking the broad avenues of Washington, D.C., in a mournful procession—it seemed only natural to embrace the Camelot myth. Its portrait of the heroic, idealistic young leader struck down in his prime performed the double task of all mythology: inspiration and emotional sustenance, on the one hand, obfuscation and self-delusion, on the other.

But Kennedy's elusiveness stems not from tragedy and sentiment alone. It also flows from his profound internal contradictions. For in the storied symbolism of Camelot, ironies abounded. Kennedy's image as a youthful advocate of vigor and physical fitness carefully screened from the public his nearly crippled condition from Addison's disease and spinal degeneration that required a back brace and extensive drug regimen to function on a daily basis. His image as a peace advocate masked a career trajectory as a stern anti-Communist who supported Joseph McCarthy in the 1950s and a fervent cold warrior who ran to the right of Richard Nixon on foreign affairs in the 1960 election. His image as a civil rights crusader concealed that he had voted against the 1957 Civil Rights Act, dragged his feet for years over desegregating federal housing, and found Martin Luther King Jr.'s crusade to be an annoying distraction from foreign affairs in the early 1960s. His image as a cosmopolitan sophisticate ignored his penchant for dozing off at the ballet and the symphony and his personal preference for books such as the gossipy treatment of the English aristocracy *The Young Melbourne,* songs such as "Won't You Come Home, Bill Bailey," romantic landscape paintings of the Old West, and cowboy movies.

But perhaps the greatest irony—it certainly has become the most controversial, and perhaps the most revealing in terms of American values—

involves the image of JFK as a family man. During his rise to the presidency and his occupation of that office, millions of Americans warmed to depictions of the youthful leader, his beautiful wife, Jacqueline, and their two adorable children, Caroline and John Jr., as they encased the White House in a bright domestic glow. Photographs of the First Family became mainstays of the Camelot myth as magazines and newspapers depicted the handsome chief executive at the side of his radiant wife at social events or in the Oval Office playing with his young children as they peeked out from under his desk or romped around the room.

But as many knew at the time—and in subsequent years the confirming evidence has become mountainous—JFK womanized relentlessly with a staggering array of female acquaintances, actresses, secretaries, interns, call girls, and mistresses both before and during his term as president. This schizophrenic portrait of JFK causes deeply conflicted feelings. As one critic has admitted, each new revelation of yet another Kennedy paramour "makes me realize anew what a patsy I've been" about the family image "that plays on the very sentiment—an essential bourgeois regard for what is nowadays called 'the sanctity of marriage'—for which JFK himself had such obvious contempt." But then she sees another Camelot family photograph, and the revelations from "the aging hookers and cast-aside girlfriends" fly out the window: "JFK is more important to us than you can ever be, so you might as well keep quiet. The cause endures, sweetheart. The hope still lives. And the dream will never die."[2]

So how does one resolve the contradictions and cut through the mythological underbrush to reach a fuller reckoning? Kennedy's politics certainly offer little in the way of clues to understanding the enthusiasm he generated and the popularity he enjoyed. For the historically informed, JFK's political position has never really been in question: he was a centrist "Cold War liberal" who endorsed the basic tenets of the New Deal on the domestic front while embracing a determined anti-Communism in foreign policy. Sometimes he tacked a bit to the right, as in his refusal to abandon Joseph McCarthy in the 1950s or in the 1960 presidential election when he denounced a fictitious "missile gap" vis-à-vis the Russians and nuclear capability; sometimes he tacked a bit to the left, as when he urged American support for the peaceful economic development of third world countries as a senator or advocated a nuclear test ban treaty as president. Despite attempts to capture him posthumously for antiwar radicalism or antigovernment conservatism by eager activists in later decades, Kennedy in his own time floated in the broad mainstream of Cold War liberalism like countless others in the Democratic Party or even in the liberal wing of the Republican Party. His politics, in other words, provided no special cause for reverence or near mania, no special foundation for immortality.[3]

Much greater insight into the excitement and the significance of Kennedy's ascension in our national life comes from another strategy: approaching him from the outset as a cultural figure rather than as a political one. It seems clear that his appeal, from early in his career, was more about his image than his political ideology, more about the emotions he represented and the yearnings he fulfilled than the policies he advocated or the great ideas he embodied. As many observers have noted, Kennedy generated an enthusiasm and an allure that was more akin to a movie star or a popular singer than a candidate for office. Like theirs, his appeal was at the same time intensely personal and wildly popular, rooted both in the attractions of his personality and in the fascination of his celebrity. But even granting this, a bigger question remains unanswered: *Why* were Americans so attracted to Kennedy's package of attributes in the late 1950s and early 1960s—his glamorous image, good looks, cool and elegant style, tough-minded rhetoric, sex appeal? The answer lay embedded in the realm of culture rather than ideological exhortation or electoral tactics. It requires excavation.

Some decades ago, the historian and critic Garry Wills offered a brilliant cultural analysis of JFK's graceless, tormented opponent, Richard Nixon, in *Nixon Agonistes: The Crisis of the Self-Made Man*. Wills contended that the Republican had instigated his own tragic demise through his devotion to a frayed American tradition of self-made success. Nixon's loyalty to various, older market conceptions of life—the moral market of Ralph Waldo Emerson, the economic market of Adam Smith, the intellectual market of John Stuart Mill, the political market of Woodrow Wilson—made him the last gasp of this tradition that was rapidly evaporating in mid-twentieth-century America. He entered the presidential lists as a knight defending an archaic creed of liberal individualism, an impulse that made his life a constant struggle for success and for acceptance. Nixon, in Wills's words, was "always the lone man testing himself and others in a battle for survival." Wills chose *agonistes,* the ancient Greek word for "the struggler" or "the combatant," a term John Milton had employed in his famous tragic poem *Samson Agonistes,* to symbolize Nixon's anguished, never-ending battle for achievement and recognition.[4]

Similarly, JFK can be understood as a cultural figure, in this case one who captured the American imagination as the country moved into a new age. The youthful senator, and then president, embodied many of the modern values of his time that were rapidly replacing an older Victorian creed of self-denial and upright moral character. With the powerful development of a consumer economy after 1945, a mainstream value system based on the attractions of personality (rather than the traditional virtues of character) and expectations of self-fulfillment (rather than the old-fashioned restrictions of self-denial) emerged full blown. Kennedy, with his handsome demeanor, confident manner, and elegant style, was tailor-made for such a cultural atmosphere.[5]

More immediately, JFK benefited enormously from a crisis of manhood that had welled up in postwar America. By the late 1950s, according to a host of contemporary critics and observers, the American male seemed to be degenerating. Wandering through frustrating mazes of bureaucracy, drifting in endless cul-de-sacs of suburban life, physically weakened by consumer comfort, and entangled in social webs spun by newly aggressive women, many men, it was feared, had lost their identity and vitality. This resulting torpor had undermined their roles in both private and public life. Kennedy promised redemption, appearing at the forefront of a movement to revive the modern American man as youthful and individualist, cool and vigorous, masculine and urbane, tough-minded and athletic, and a sexual conquistador. Advocates eagerly juxtaposed this dynamic, manly image with an older Eisenhower-era portrait of the stodgy, unimaginative, timid, conforming, often aging "organization man."

Thus John F. Kennedy generated a powerful "masculine mystique" that became central to his remarkable public appeal. While representing a vibrant postwar culture of personality and self-fulfillment in America, it also offered a solution to festering concerns about the weakened condition of its males. Like Wills's *agonistes* with Nixon, another ancient trope captures the quintessential Kennedy appeal. The Greek legend of Adonis portrayed the god of male beauty and desire whose virile attractiveness led to great prominence, but also to jealous entanglements and a premature death. The seductive young deity became the icon of a spiritual cult celebrating his immortal, inspirational spirit. In 1821, Percy Shelley had penned *Adonais,* an elegy on the death of his close friend the young romantic poet John Keats. Now Kennedy Adonais, like Shelley's portrait of Keats, appears through the mists of Camelot as a handsome, charismatic, alluring young man—"Thou wert the morning star among the living"—who survives in American memory as the stuff of legend. His relentless masculine mystique, like Nixon's fanatical drive for self-made success, both drove him forward and hamstrung many of his best efforts.[6]

But this cultural crusade to regenerate masculinity, while led by JFK, involved other prominent figures in what might be called the Kennedy Circle. This does not refer to Kennedy's team of White House advisers who interacted with him on a daily basis and helped shape his political program, men such as Ted Sorensen, McGeorge Bundy, Pierre Salinger, Robert McNamara, Walt Rostow, Dave Powers, and Kenneth O'Donnell. Instead, the Kennedy Circle consisted of public figures, famous in their own right, who associated with the senator from Massachusetts, and later president, and who shared a broader set of values and impulses. It included Frank Sinatra and his Hollywood Rat Pack; the novelist and journalist Norman Mailer; the author Ian Fleming and his popular fictional character James Bond; the publisher Hugh Hefner and his magazine, *Playboy;* the charismatic political journalist Ben Bradlee; the military officers Maxwell Taylor and Edward Lansdale; the movie actors Kirk Douglas and Tony Curtis; and the astronauts Alan Shepard and John Glenn.[7]

This group maintained an intriguing web of interconnections—they supported and identified with Kennedy, he associated with them in various ways, and they maintained ties with one another—and collectively shaped a revived masculine image that had garnered tremendous public attention by the early 1960s. This new ideal promised to liberate men from old-fashioned restraints, push them forward into new frontiers of experience, and replace a standard of sober industriousness and social conformity with one of physical vigor, individualist ethics, cool elegance, tough-minded intelligence, and sexual adventure. Symbolized by JFK and sharpened in various ways by others in the Kennedy Circle, this fresh masculine model changed how American culture viewed men and how they viewed themselves. As a result, both the attitudes and the policies of the New Frontier were shaped by an agenda of manly revitalization. And it would have a profound historical impact by importing celebrity standards into the political process, nourishing the angry rebellions of the later 1960s, and weakening traditional attachments to the family and standards of male responsibility.

Yet a focus on Kennedy's masculine mystique demands facing up to certain complexities and limitations. Time provides one cautionary constraint. Clearly, we now know much more about the youthful president's private life and sexual escapades than did many of his contemporaries. Given the fact that much of this personal activity was hidden from sight during his meteoric ascendancy and domination of the national landscape, one may fairly ask, how could JFK successfully promote an ethos of sexual conquest, male assertion, and antibourgeois sophistication? The answer lies in the vagaries of culture. Unlike elections, where votes can be counted, or social experience, where population trends and family structure can be gauged, or the economy, where incomes and growth statistics can be assessed, values and attitudes provide a more tenuous, slippery subject for the historian. Kennedy's masculine mystique, in its time, was often a product of image and implication rather than public knowledge of specific actions. While his sexual adventures were more a matter of rumor than fact during his life, many journalists clearly knew about them, and these escapades influenced their shaping of his persona as the nation's sexy leading man. Moreover, the Kennedy Circle—Sinatra, Fleming and Bond, Hefner, Mailer, and others—performed as cultural surrogates who embodied the assertive sexual derring-do that the political leader could only imply. Through standing as an icon of masculine vigor, rather than through widespread public knowledge of his private life per se, JFK established a new atmosphere, a new attitude, a new set of aspirations, that helped reshape the mind-set of early 1960s America.

Scope offers a second restraint. Clearly, Kennedy's masculine mystique illuminates more about his popularity than about his policies. One should never forget, of course, that myriad, pragmatic calculations of strategic maneuver, political advantage, and national progress play paramount roles in any president's formulation of policy. At the same time, however, it would be myopic to ignore the vibrant masculine mystique that informed JFK's very approach to pressing issues. Its imprint can be seen in his decision making about Castro's Cuba, the Cold War struggle against Communism, the physical fitness program, the space program, counterinsurgency, and even the Peace Corps, for example. Correctly seen, a cultural analysis supplements, rather than supplants, a political approach in reaching a broader understanding of John F. Kennedy's historical significance.

Thus this analysis offers a fresh perspective based on something hiding in plain sight: a little-understood, but extremely important, set of cultural ideals focused on manhood that explains much about JFK's meteoric rise to leadership, the nature of his programs, and the subsequent unraveling of traditional social values in the 1960s. *JFK and the Masculine Mystique* is not just another standard biography of the youthful president. It resituates JFK in his cultural milieu and suggests a new understanding of how and why, in concert with a supporting cadre of cultural figures, he generated such a powerful appeal. Even more, it presents a snapshot of a key moment in modern American history that lay midway between the conventions of the Eisenhower era and the angry divisions of the late 1960s. By examining Kennedy in the context of certain books, movies, social critiques, music, and cultural discussions that framed his ascendancy, we open a window on the excitement and sense of possibility, the optimism and aspirations, that accompanied the dawn of a new age in America. At the same time, such a perspective also illuminates many of the darker impulses and implications of JFK's unfettered masculine assertion, celebrity politics, and cavalier social attitudes that undermined many vital social traditions.

What follows also attempts to overcome a striking dichotomy in the usual understanding of John F. Kennedy the human being. He often appears as almost two different people. There is the public man, challenging his countrymen to put aside selfish, mundane concerns and "pay any price, bear any burden" to promote the cause of freedom around the world, the youthful leader inspiring them to "ask not what your country can do for you; ask what you can do for your country." Then there is the private man, the tireless sexual adventurer who womanized relentlessly, recklessly, and with a guilt-free conscience. For most people—this includes ordinary citizens as well as historians and biographers—the response is to focus on the first man and interpret his actions and policies and political principles while downplaying or even dismissing the second man as an irrelevant figure whose unfortunate personal peccadilloes deserve a sorrowful shake of the head and relegation to the scandal sheets. The problem with this strategy, of course, is that the public figure and the private figure were actually one and the same. The task remains: to try to grasp what bound together those two sets of impulses into a coherent human being. Kennedy's masculine mystique, which permeated both his public and his private endeavors and attracted the loyalty of influential adherents, provides that coherence. It brings the whole man into focus.

ONE

THE CRISIS OF MASCULINITY
IN 1950s AMERICA

In November 1958, Arthur Schlesinger Jr. published an urgent essay in *Esquire*. This influential man of letters had ranged widely through American public life over the previous twenty years. A Pulitzer Prize–winning historian at Harvard, he had made his mark with massive presidential studies, *The Age of Jackson* (1945) and *The Age of Roosevelt* (1957–1960). A political writer, social critic, and political activist, he had published magazine pieces on a host of contemporary issues as well as polemical books about contemporary politics such as *The Vital Center* (1949) and *What About Communism?* (1950). An operator in the Democratic Party, he had led the liberal anti-Communist movement that purged the party of leftist radicals in the late 1940s, helped found Americans for Democratic Action shortly thereafter, and played a key role advising the presidential candidacies of Adlai Stevenson in 1952 and 1956.

In other words, when this public intellectual spoke, people tended to listen. Intelligent, articulate, ambitious, and effervescent, with his oval-shaped glasses and jaunty bow tie, Schlesinger was firmly ensconced among the American intelligentsia and had his finger on the pulse of the country's public life. Now, he insisted, the United States stood in the throes of a crisis. But this was no emergency involving the Cold War, or civil rights, or a floundering national economy. Instead, according to the title of his piece, it involved a "crisis of American masculinity."

By the middle of the twentieth century, Schlesinger argued, "the male role had plainly lost its clarity of outline. Today men are more and more conscious of maleness not as a fact but as a problem." Men were now performing tasks once relegated to women—"changing diapers, washing dishes, cooking meals"—while growing numbers of females were becoming doctors, lawyers, bankers, and executives. In this scene where a "blurring of function" had become the norm, women had emerged as an "expanding, aggressive force, seizing new domains like a conquering army," while men adopted a defensive posture "hardly able to hold their own and gratefully accepting assignments from their new rulers." In addition, it was no accident "that homosexuality, that incarnation of sexual ambiguity, should be enjoying a cultural boom new in our history." Thus an important question loomed: "What has unmanned the American man?"

Schlesinger noted that the fashionable answer to this question pointed to the aggressive nature of modern women and a growing "feminization of American society." But such an explanation was too pat, too simplistic, too unrealistic, he contended. Instead, an understanding of male malaise could only be reached by digging deeper. In Schlesinger's words, "Why is the American man so unsure today about his masculine identity? The basic answer to this is surely because he is so unsure about his identity in general." He explained that the growth of a democratic society had steadily substituted opportunity and fluidity for traditional community and stable social roles; that postwar technological development and economic growth had fostered bureaucracies and the ideal of the "organization man"; that modern suburban life had elevated "adjustment" into the greatest social ideal. This cluster of developments, the author lamented, had created a process wherein people felt uprooted and adrift, and the "loss of a sense of identity is obviously a fundamental step in the decay of masculinity."[1]

Schlesinger was no lone voice crying in the wilderness. In fact, during the late 1950s a chorus of complaints about masculine degeneration sounded from all corners of American life. Many of them picked up on themes identified by Schlesinger, while others pointed to different culprits in the social, cultural, and economic circumstances defining the contemporary scene. But they all agreed on a central point: the modern American man was in trouble.

Look, for example, a very popular middle-class magazine of the period, presented an extensive and gloomy analysis in a three-part series in early 1958 titled "The American Male." It unfolded one long tale of woe. *Look*'s essential argument was that "in the years since the end of World War II he has changed radically and dangerously; that he is no longer the masculine, strong-minded man who pioneered the continent and built America's greatness." The first installment detailed the growing domination of women over men in family life, the workplace, and society and pointed to a resulting flurry of problems—fatigue, passivity, anxiety, impotency, lesser life span—that laid men low. It inspired a plaintive warning from a female psychiatrist, Dr. Irene Josselyn: "We are drifting toward a social structure made up of he-women and she-men."[2]

The second installment explored the pressures for conformity that pressed in upon millions of middle-class males as they labored in a milieu that stressed the virtues of fitting in. Working for a corporation or other large entity, likely living in a suburb, probably attending a comfortable middle-class church, the American male faced daily an overarching standard: "If the individual does not fit the mold, he is 'maladjusted.'" In postwar America, such social pressures (reinforced by the scientific vogue for psychology) made clear that the modern man "had his single duty: adjust." As a result, the American male "was not really happy. . . . He had lost his individuality." The third installment examined men's work life and the contemporary "rat race." The frantic pursuit of productivity and advancement during the workday, and equally frantic pursuit of leisure in the off-hours, had enlisted nearly every life activity in the service of getting ahead. In this pressurized atmosphere, escalating stress was inevitable: "The American male is working much of the time he is not sleeping. And judging from the growing consumption of tranquilizers, barbiturates, and alcohol—to say nothing of the sale of how-to-relax books—he seems to be working pretty hard at sleeping too."[3]

Look offered no dramatic solution to this masculine crisis, only advising men to slow down, relax, and search for perspective and equilibrium in their endeavors. "The answer," it concluded rather haltingly, "is for the

American male to grow up emotionally so that he can learn to live with the pressures of this society and balance the demands of job, community, and home without ruining his health and disposition. This is a large order." It was indeed, and strikingly short on specifics.[4]

Other publications sounded similar warnings about the degeneration of modern manhood. In a special issue of May 1957, *Cosmopolitan,* a popular family magazine in the 1950s, noted that many critics viewed modern men as "worried, harried, and insecure, and they base their arguments on the very factors that have taken him so far on the road to success—his drive to get ahead, his urge to do everything better, his inability to relax easily." Modern American males, the magazine posited, were caught between an old-fashioned model of male behavior based on "brawn, bravado, toughness, sternness, and stoicism" and modern demands for gentler qualities such as "sympathy, kindness, tenderness, softness, sentimentality and refinement." The modern male life cycle, it concluded, had become a depressing series of crises ranging from adolescent torment over girls and future career to middle-aged restlessness over the restraints of family and job to old-age depression over retirement and vanishing usefulness.[5]

Woman's Home Companion, in an article titled "Uncertain Hero: The Paradox of the American Male," argued that many contemporary men had been denied a sphere of vigorous action and had become "uncertain and ill at ease in a world that robs [them] of [their] chance of heroism." Sitting behind his office desk or sprawled in an easy chair at home, he yearned to somehow recapture the robust masculinity of a younger America when men were building railroads, draining swamps, erecting cabins and fencing the land, and protecting their families with firearms when necessary. It would be wise, the article concluded, if modern society would quit inhibiting "certain deep and perfectly normal masculine drives." This rhetoric of male crisis, in fact, became a mainstay in a wide range of publications. *Today's Health* offered grave warnings about "the suicidal cult of manliness," while *The New York Times Magazine,* in a piece by the noted anthropologist Margaret Mead, warned that modern social arrangements had "hamstrung the men." The professional journal *Marriage and Family Living* explored "the new burdens of masculinity" that had arisen from the disjuncture between traditional expectations regarding male behavior and new conditions, and the subsequent "difficulties in establishing a satisfying new role."[6]

Hollywood contributed to the portrait of modern male malaise in a parade of popular films that featured lost, degenerate masculine figures. In *Rebel Without a Cause* (1955), an anguished adolescent, James Dean, yearns for a model of male behavior as he confronts his emasculated father, Jim Backus, tongue-tied and memorably outfitted in a frilly apron, and pleads, "What can you do when you have to be a man?" In *Cat on a Hot Tin Roof* (1958), Tennessee Williams created in Brick Pollitt a memorable protagonist who refuses to embrace any of the standard male roles— father, husband, son—and takes to alcohol as he wrestles with the "unnatural love" of homosexual urges. *Some Like It Hot* (1959) offered a comedic version of male disarray in a clever story starring Tony Curtis, Jack Lemmon, and Marilyn Monroe. This male masquerade of gender role-playing features Lemmon and Curtis pretending to be women, complete with dresses and makeup and vampy gestures, to save themselves from mobsters after witnessing a gangland killing. The pair subsequently, and hilariously, become entangled in various difficulties and romances with both men and women as they scramble to avoid detection. Drifting wildly atop these crosscurrents of gender confusion, Lemmon and Curtis represented a marked, if humorous, decline from the strong, masculine image of an earlier era.[7]

What were the underlying causes of this festering social problem? Analysts pointed to several sources. For many critics, the roots of masculine degeneration lay entangled in what was perhaps the distinguishing structure of modern American life: the large, complex organizations that increasingly dominated business, labor, education, and government by the mid-twentieth century. Bureaucracies, many commentators feared, while undergirding much of the productivity and prosperity of contemporary society, had also emerged as a scourge of modern manhood.

As part of its series "The American Male" in 1958, *Look* magazine took a hard look at the work life of the typical modern, middle-class man. Most men now worked a forty-hour week in an office or organization in a job that, admittedly, seemed leisurely compared with the physical grind of farm labor, craft production, or assembly-line toil of an earlier generation. But at the same time, work in postwar America had taken on a new burden as it became the foundation for both a "career" and an abundant standard of living. Taking into account commuting time, entertaining for business rather than enjoyment, honing your "personality" for white-collar advancement, serving on committees and boards to maintain your community reputation, laboring to be a good husband and father, and embracing the "active leisure" that denoted a worthwhile and fulfilled life, the very idea of work had broadened dramatically. And it seemed to never stop. When one considered "the sum total of energy-consuming, tension-building activities to which he devotes himself," concluded *Look,* the "American male is working at something much of the time he is not sleeping."[8]

The magazine put its finger on an issue that troubled many who were proclaiming a masculinity crisis in the late 1950s. For many men in postwar America, the nature and quality of modern work had emerged as a powerful problem in daily life. The key influence, of course, was the increasing domination of large bureaucracies in industry, marketing, retail business, government, education, and medicine that provided the bulk of white-collar, executive-style jobs. Millions of middle-class men, whose families were flocking to the suburbs of America's cities, were now laboring in these bureaucratic structures and enjoying the fruits of a generous salary. Moreover, their earnings had become the basis of a booming consumer economy as postwar America turned its massive capacities from the war effort to peacetime abundance. But it soon became clear that the material blessings of bureaucratic labor had come at a heavy emotional price. Unfamiliar burdens emerged that prompted resentment and unhappiness among many men and fear among some.

The characteristic of modern work that most obviously troubled men was its frantic, unrelenting pace. A mid-decade study of white-collar workers gave form to such an impression. It examined several hundred executives and concluded that the great majority worked between fifty and sixty hours a week; when they did go home, it was often to a "branch office"; and pursuit of leisure hobbies was often measured by "a yardstick of business relevance." Such an unrelenting pace escalated tension, fatigue, and poor health. In *Today's Health,* a physician concluded that many men were killing themselves because of a work compulsion. According to another observer, "because of the cult of manliness" men "drive themselves to the point of exhaustion."[9]

Equally corrosive to men's well-being, if more subtly so, was the nature of the success code in modern bureaucracies. In the corporations or law firms or hospitals or insurance agencies or public universities dominating the work life of postwar America, advancement no longer followed the traditional trail of hard work, individual skill and expertise, relentless effort, and firm moral character. In a modern bureaucratic setting, the employee was defined as a team player whose success depended on smoothly interacting with others, deploying a sparkling "personality," and gaining consensus and cooperation from one's fellow laborers in the organization. As one analyst noted, successful white-collar workers were "now expected to demonstrate manipulative skill in interpersonal relations. . . . [They] must be free with the glad hand, they must impress others with their warmth and sincerity (rather than as formerly with their courage and honesty and industry), they must be trouble shooters on all fronts."[10]

Two popular and influential books added breadth and depth to this discussion. The sociologist David Riesman, in his magisterial *The Lonely Crowd: A Study of the Changing American Character* (1950), provided postwar Americans with a vocabulary for talking about bureaucracy and male decline. This book so captured the public imagination that its author, an academic at the University of Chicago, appeared on the cover of *Time* magazine. The volume identified the modern male as an "other-directed personality," a character type that reflected the demands of a bureaucratic society. Instead of listening to his own voice and following a set of embedded moral principles, he cultivated "an exceptional sensitivity to the actions and wishes of others. . . . While all people want and need to be liked by some of the people some of the time, it is only the modern other-directed types who make this their chief source of direction and chief area of sensitivity." This type picked up signals of approval or disapproval, enthusiasm or resentment, from a wide circle of colleagues and plotted his course accordingly. Thus the management, or manipulation, of self and of others had become the key skill for individual advancement in a bureaucratic atmosphere.[11]

But a problem lurked within the other-directed ethos, *The Lonely Crowd* noted. Bureaucratic men with their facile personalities had no hard core of self but instead donned a series of masks as they adapted to circumstances with glad-handing and false bonhomie. A specter of inauthenticity haunted the proceedings. The other-directed individual, wrote Riesman, "is, in a sense, at home everywhere and nowhere, capable of a rapid if sometimes superficial intimacy with and response to everyone." Yet he was never quite sure he was reading the signals correctly. Thus he was characteristically beset by "anxiety" as he constantly struggled to gauge his own impact and the intentions of others. *Look* picked up on this theme of other-directed manipulation, noting that in modern bureaucracies "teamwork and personal relations reigned over all. This meant you had to like everyone, give careful consideration to every proposal, no matter how trivial, handle every employee with the velvet gloves of insincerity. . . . It meant you put aside personal convictions and developed instead a personal radar, sensitive to the moods of others who made up The Group. Everyone ended up groping for the right way, the Group way, while phony politeness and synthetic good intentions resounded through the corridors." Such pressures forced men to be inauthentic. Manly assertion and sturdy principle had given way to milquetoast maneuvering.[12]

Another much-discussed book, William H. Whyte Jr.'s *Organization Man* (1956), focused on an additional consequence of bureaucracy: the pressures to conform emanating from large-scale organizations. Such demands to fit a common mold were eroding men's individual capacity for judgment and action. An editor of *Fortune* magazine, Whyte had studied white-collar managers, corporations, and suburban communities over the previous few years and concluded that bureaucratization had nearly obliterated individual initiative. Instead, organization men paid homage to the "Social Ethic" and its key tenets: creativity came from group collaboration; "belongingness" was the ultimate human need; human relations held the key to promoting one's happiness. This impulse was surging through nearly every channel of modern work life. In Whyte's words, "Blood brother to the business trainee off to join DuPont is the seminary student who will end up in the church hierarchy, the doctor headed for the corporate clinic, the physics Ph.D. in a government laboratory, the intellectual on the foundation-sponsored team project, the engineering graduate in the huge drafting room at Lockheed, the young apprentice in a Wall Street law factory." Suburban life, with its kaffeeklatsches, bridge parties, golf clubs, and rash of school-related activities, further reinforced the importance of "belonging" and "adjustment." The "suburbanites' group-mindedness" emerged as a close cousin to the Social Ethic of the bureaucratic workplace, and both enervated men.[13]

In fact, anxiety about the conforming organization man had become a staple of masculinity-in-crisis rhetoric by the late 1950s. Variations on the theme appeared everywhere. In popular culture, *The Man in the Gray Flannel Suit* (1955), a novel by Sloan Wilson then made into a 1956 movie starring Gregory Peck, examined a fictional businessman struggling to find happiness as a public relations executive in a big New York media firm. The title quickly entered the national vocabulary as a shorthand phrase for the modern male whose individual vitality was threatened by the bureaucratic leviathan. "Even the quietest Sunday gardener or the most efficient man in the gray flannel suit may have his indestructible dream of greatness and adventure," proclaimed *Woman's Home Companion*. "Before the day is out, the gray flannel suit has become a straitjacket and the dream has been nibbled away by confidential memos." In the words of *Look,* when a man allowed the company to do "his choosing for him, he can lose pride in himself as an individual; to be a truly masculine, independent individual is the deepest of psychic needs."[14]

From this litany of complaints about bureaucratic work—its relentless pace, pallid other-directedness, enervating conformity—emerged a troubling composite of the modern American male. Many feared that he had become an affable yet stressed-out organization drone, a plump, conforming popularity seeker who attended countless meetings and sat behind a desk pushing paper in pursuit of salary and security. Such a dispiriting image paled in comparison to earlier heroic generations of tough-minded American men who had succeeded by dint of hard work, firm convictions, and decisive action.

But warnings about modern work and masculine decline were matched by a fear emanating from another prominent social development. One of the hallmarks of postwar America—the vaunted consumer prosperity that had made the country's elevated standard of living the envy of the world— seemed to nourish the seeds of male decline. Many observers believed that the average American man, wallowing in prosperity, had become soft.

Consumer abundance had become nearly synonymous with American-ism during the 1950s, and most citizens viewed it as a pillar of national strength. In the years after World War II, the United States had recovered from the economic travails of the Great Depression and the economic sac-rifices of World War II to embrace a flourishing consumer economy. In rapidly multiplying suburban developments, a host of white-collar work-ers and their families settled in to enjoy the fruits of material abundance: eight-cylinder chrome-and-tail-fin automobiles from Detroit, barbecue grills and patio furniture, televisions and gleaming refrigerators, vacuums and rec rooms, Barbie dolls and credit cards. Moreover, this cornucopia of goods seemed to spill outward from the middle class into the working class, so much so that the historian David Potter dubbed Americans a "people of plenty." In fact, consumer prosperity became a key weapon in the Cold War struggle against Communism. In his 1959 impromptu "kitchen debate" with the Soviet premier, Nikita Khrushchev, while tour-ing an exhibition of an American home in Moscow, Vice President Richard Nixon insisted that its widespread affluence guaranteed the victory of mod-ern capitalism over Communism. With the great mass of ordinary citizens already enjoying the fruits of comfort, leisure, and prosperity, why would they turn to Bolshevik doctrine?[15]

At the same time, however, persistent fears about the consumer ethic lay just beneath the surface of American culture. Commentators frequently voiced a nagging suspicion that the very material abundance of postwar society was destroying the fiber of masculinity. It was a devilish process. First, as *Look*'s "American Male" series explained, a man scrambled and worked compulsively "to keep on buying and consuming the things his family is expected (and incessantly urged) to buy and consume. . . . [E]very possession becomes doubly important, not only for its own use and beauty, but as a palpable symbol of its owner's or purchaser's relative position in the competition of life." This unremitting struggle proved mentally and emotionally exhausting. Then, however, the successful accumulation of the consumer comforts—television and easy chairs, automobiles and power lawn mowers, the creature comforts of suburbia—compounded the problem by removing men from vigorous activity and weakening them. "Anxieties about an erosion of masculinity," a historian of the era has noted, "were inextricably bound up with the growing dread of the 'soft,' malleable American psyche. . . . A society of abundance, social critics charged, had created a nation of overindulged, overfed, overentertained Americans grown self-absorbed and apathetic." The prosperity of the good life, ironically, had made men flabby and weak.[16]

The sociologists of work and personality had set the stage for this analysis of growing masculine weakness. David Riesman, in *The Lonely Crowd,* had suggested that the shift toward bureaucracy, consumerism, and other-directedness had reduced male vitality. In an earlier age of entrepreneurial vigor and hardy self-reliance, he argued, work had dominated the male sensibility. But the postwar age of material abundance and white-collar labor brought a vast change. "The other-directed person's tremendous outpouring of energy is channeled into the ever expanding frontiers of consumption," wrote Riesman, "as the inner-directed person's energy was channeled relentlessly into production." So "today it is the 'softness' of men rather than the 'hardness' of material that calls on talent and opens new channels of social mobility." William Whyte, in *The Organization Man,* observed that with the decline of the Protestant work ethic and the rise of organizations "the upward path toward the rainbow of achievement leads smack through the conference room . . . [and] the committee way simply can't be equated with rugged individualism." Since the war, he continued, men "haven't been talking of self-reliance and adventure with quite the straight face of their elders." American males ensconced in postwar abundance, these critics contended, had become pale reflections of their vigorous ancestors, reduced to wielding the personality test rather than the railroad blueprint, the barbecue spatula rather than the hunting rifle.[17]

By the late 1950s, a popular outcry over the flabby American male reached a fever pitch. Images of men debilitated by suburban life and consumer comfort appeared everywhere. An article in *The New York Times* covering a conference on men and the family derided "dishwashing dads" and contained a sketch of a suburban male dutifully vacuuming the living room rug and furniture. *Look* suggested that many men had become sissified, noting that "the men's toiletry industry now does a $480 million business each year." *Cosmopolitan* saw a similar process at work, concluding that "the American male is becoming a peacock," and disdainfully noted a series of trends: "Beach jackets and tailored swimming trunks are available in burnt ochre.... Men's slacks are being made in peach and lemon." Sales of men's hairpieces and girdles had skyrocketed. Spas reported a burgeoning male clientele, while "reconstructed males are now spending a stupendous annual sum—$356,430,000—on things to make us look and smell nice: aftershave lotion, eau de cologne, razors and blades, shaving creams, talcum, and scented soap." It illustrated this dandified scene with several photographs: a man wearing a hairnet as he prepared for his custom haircut, mud pack, facial massage, manicure, and sunlamp treatment; a portly salesman awkwardly trying on a tie-up girdle over his suit; a businessman getting his pocket handkerchief sprayed with perfume.[18]

A fascinating sign of the male consumer softened by abundance came in one of the most interesting fads in 1950s America. As *Time* observed in a 1954 cover story titled "The Shoulder Trade"—the phrase referred to men who trudged out of hardware stores with boards balanced on their shoulders—a craze for do-it-yourself projects had swept through middle-class society. Millions of men flocked to improve their suburban homes with comfortable patios and customized garage shelving, elaborate landscaping and attractive fences, upgraded plumbing fixtures and redwood lawn furniture. They rehung doors, patched driveways, replaced shingles, and painted rec rooms. Nearly every suburban male in the postwar era, it seemed, had become an amateur carpenter, electrician, or mechanic and in so doing had created "a booming $6 billion-a-year business." While these do-it-yourselfers constituted a huge consumer market for new tools manufactured especially for them—electric saws and drills and sanders, lathes, paint supplies, chisels, hammers, wrenches, wheelbarrows, lawn tractors—they also sought to recapture vital functions from an earlier period. Happily covered in the sawdust of the basement workshop or the grease of the garage tool bench, the suburban dads and husbands took a stab at recapturing the masculine labors of their predecessors the sturdy entrepreneur, rugged farmer, and skilled craftsman. Here was a masculine yearning to do something real, productive, and authentic in an atmosphere otherwise dominated by consumption.[19]

For many observers, however, the corrosive effect of abundance on masculine vigor had an actual physical cost. Dr. Shane McCarthy, the director of the President's Council on Youth Fitness, emerged as an outspoken critic of physical decline among boys and young men. Dwight Eisenhower established this body in 1956 when John Kelly, a Philadelphia businessman and former Olympian, had come to him with information about the sorry state of physical fitness among American kids. Shortly thereafter, Kelly published an indignant article in *American* magazine titled "Are We Becoming a Nation of Weaklings?" For Kelly, a life of "modern conveniences" was destroying physical vigor, and boys were clearly the primary victims because it was assumed that girls would take on the role of mother and homemaker. McCarthy subsequently traveled the United States for the president delivering a similar analysis. Encouraging programs of physical fitness, he rooted the need in recent historical developments. Whereas rugged American men in the past had overcome a host of problems with muscular assertion, in a modern society of technology and material abundance "the tendency is to put first the aspects of ease and soft enjoyment." Jean Mayer, a public health official, voiced similar fears that consumer plenty had sapped American physical energies in a 1955 piece in *The New York Times Magazine*. He wrote, "It seems difficult to avoid the conclusion that our motorized, mechanized, 'effort-saver' civilization is rapidly making us as soft as our processed foods, our foam rubber mattresses, and our balloon tires."[20]

Declining male vigor had dire implications for national survival, many suggested. In a 1959 jeremiad in *The Saturday Evening Post*, Hanson Baldwin, the military editor at *The New York Times*, complained bitterly in an article titled "Our Fighting Men Have Gone Soft." He rattled off a list of statistics about problems among American military personnel—growing numbers of courts-martial and significant disciplinary actions, indifference or sullen attitudes among recruits, the high rate of collaboration among prisoners captured during the Korean War—and probed the reasons for this troubling trend. His conclusion was straightforward: the modern male "has been pampered," and consumer abundance was the clear culprit. "The automobile age has made us almost a helpless nation," he wrote. "We are vulnerable like all the rich and surfeited empires and kingdoms of the past to the slow corrosion of luxury, the attrition of ease." Military and governmental leaders, he added, well knew the conditions creating the sad physical state of many recruits. "Sedentarianism, push buttonitis, and indoorism have taken a heavy toll on fitness," Baldwin declared. Men have been "subtly victimized by an age of mechanization, standardization, urbanization, and materialism." Awash in abundance, the article argued, many modern men had simply become too soft to meet the physical challenges of military service.[21]

Once again, a Hollywood film sharpened the image of the modern male softened by prosperity. The brilliant comedy *The Seven Year Itch* (1955), directed by Billy Wilder, presented a satirical portrait of the domesticated middle-class male. Richard Sherman, the hapless protagonist played by Tom Ewell, is the head of advertising for a paperback book company who lives with his family in a comfortable Manhattan brownstone apartment. The plot of the film revolves around Richard's fantasy of seducing a beautiful blond neighbor, played by Marilyn Monroe, while his wife and son are on vacation. He proves to be hapless rather than suave when inviting her to his apartment, knocking her off a piano bench as they play "Chopsticks" together. After persuading her to go with him to a movie, Richard can only imagine his wife returning and shooting him with a revolver, so he abandons the seduction and flees the apartment in his stocking feet to catch the train and join his family. In *The Seven Year Itch*, the male protagonist's masculine urges are frustrated by his own ineptitude. A tamed Richard, like many middle-class men, embraces domesticity and abundance while abandoning virility and adventure.[22]

Fears of bureaucratic enervation and prosperous softness among modern men, however, often brought to the surface an additional element: gender resentment. In fact, the rhetoric of masculine crisis frequently expressed a growing sense of threat regarding this issue. An onslaught from aggressive women during the postwar era, many believed, was undermining the authority of American men, which in turn was driving significant numbers of them in the degenerate direction of homosexuality. In both cases, the result was the same: an emasculation that cut deeply into the fiber of American masculinity.

For many critics of the modern male condition, a postwar expansion of female authority lay at the heart of the contemporary crisis of masculinity. In nearly every area of life, the argument went, men were in full retreat before advancing legions of aggressive women. One saw among many American males, noted one commentator, "the widespread expression of resentment toward women in conversation, plays, novels, and films. Modern women are portrayed as castrating Delilahs busily leveling men's individuality and invading the strongholds of masculinity in work, play, sex, and the home." Such complaints about emasculation had become ubiquitous in American social commentary by the late 1950s.[23]

Dire warnings about female domination came from many directions. The journalist Richard Gehman, for instance, cast a jaundiced eye on growing female power in American social life and told readers of *Cosmopolitan* that in emotional terms "deep conflicts have developed between the sexes." Women were becoming more aggressive, while "the U.S. male seems to draw ever within himself. He is becoming more passive." Similarly, *Woman's Home Companion* warned its female readers that their tendency to manipulate their mates was wreaking emotional havoc. Too many women, it argued, pressed their husbands into a social mold. Even more damagingly, they wanted their man to be masculine but then worked to create "a simple, innocent, faithful, unsophisticated 'male-child.' The babying can take obvious forms—from calling him 'Baby' to acting like a proud mother when he comes home each evening, quizzing him on his day's work and giving him grades for achievement. It can take the form of adult toilet-training: of insisting that he wash his hands and hang up his towels and dispose of his razor blades at the same time, in the same way, in the same place."[24]

The *Look* series painted a particularly lurid picture of female domination of men. It argued that since the end of World War II, women had moved into a position of power in American life. "She discovered she didn't have to imitate men in order to rule," the magazine noted of the modern woman. "The feminine partner took charge and she did so as a woman." *Look* contended that women now dominated every stage of the male life cycle, beginning with hospital nurses who brought him into the world. This was followed by a mother's love that was extended or withheld to control his every boyhood move, a phalanx of female teachers who molded his education, girlfriends who pressured him to go steady and controlled the intensity of sexual experimentation, and wives who regulated not only sexual relations but a plethora of domestic decisions during manhood. "Scientists who study human behavior fear that the American male is now dominated by the American female," the magazine concluded starkly. "From the moment he is born, the American boy is ruled by women."[25]

Mounting complaints about female aggression focused on several trends. Many perceived a growing invasion of the workplace by women, a process that seemed to be driving men out of their traditional bastion as breadwinners. During World War II, millions of American women had moved into the workforce for the first time with men away serving in the armed forces, and in the postwar era aspirations for middle-class prosperity had reinforced this trend. Problems resulted. A woman working in the white-collar milieu, many feared, would create an unfair advantage if she was "not above using her attractiveness in a business battle." Others believed that men lost respect, both from themselves and from others, if they were outdistanced by female co-workers or by competitors. A more subtle difficulty involved male emotional confusion. As growing numbers of women left the home for jobs, which brought with them new responsibilities and privileges, many men grew uncertain about their own positions as breadwinners. According to Lawrence K. Frank, the noted mental health expert, modern men often found it difficult to accept the fact that women were out earning money and became "much more confused about what they should and should not do to fulfill their masculine roles . . . [and such a man] may find it difficult to develop any consistent design for living in which he can fulfill the masculine role as he understands it."[26]

Others pointed to a striking female ascendancy in the family as a source of male disarray. In an earlier period, men had wielded unquestioned authority as head of the household by dispensing punishment to children when needed, maintaining a benevolent dominion over their wives, and making ultimate decisions about the disposal of family economic resources. But in the suburban family of 1950s America, women were increasingly assuming many of these prerogatives. The typical husband, according to *Cosmopolitan,* now appeared "a henpecked, harassed male who is no longer boss of his home." This abdication of male authority could be seen in child rearing, where, according to the anthropologist Margaret Mead, "the mother's withholding of love has replaced the father's punishment" as the primary instrument of shaping children's behavior. Then there was housework, where women increasingly expected their husbands to shoulder a significant portion of household chores "that a man of a generation ago would have laughed at." This both weakened men and confused their sons, according to one observer, because "a boy growing up today has little chance to observe his father in strictly masculine pursuits." In the home, men had simply ceded much of their authority to women and become subordinate, a fact that children quickly realized. As Lawrence Frank observed of the modern American family, "The authoritarian husband-father is regarded either as ridiculous or tyrannical or simply out-of-date, often to his astonishment and angry bewilderment." At a 1957 meeting of the Child Study Association of America on "the man in the family," conferees pondered the contemporary male predicament in the family and reached a disquieting conclusion. "They find dad's current position hopelessly undefined," summarized a journalistic account. "How can a boy learn what it means to be a man, some are asking themselves worriedly, when mother and father in so many homes carry out identical tasks in relation to home and children?"[27]

Critics of female domination also found cause for concern in the consumer ethos of 1950s America. While men certainly enjoyed the fruits of American abundance, many commentators contended that it was women

who drove the process of accumulating consumer goods. *Fortune* magazine estimated that women controlled over 60 percent of all consumer pur-
chases, while a Gallup poll reported that the wife helped manage the
funds in 71 percent of American households. In *Fortune*'s judgment, in
many areas of household spending "the husband has completely surren-
dered the power of the purse." But it was more than mere numbers. It was
women, critics argued, who were the primary force behind the pursuit of
status and security in middle-class America. It was women "who sustain
the principle of keeping up with their neighbors," contended *Look* magazine. "Wives may say they want their husbands to ease up, but they still hold
out the carrot to lead their husbands up the hill to success—and toward
two cars in the garage." In the economy as in the workplace and the home,
the American woman had emerged triumphant as the man receded.[28]

Perhaps the most strident voice condemning female encroachment in
all its various forms came from Philip Wylie. This novelist, science fiction
writer, newspaper columnist, essayist, and social critic had first made a
splash in 1942 with *Generation of Vipers,* a scathing critique of American
life that became notorious for its denunciation of "momism." He pictured
the typical American mother as a cloying, manipulative shrew who brow-
beat her husband, sissified her sons, and reshaped American culture into
a sentimental, maudlin mess. Now, in a series of articles in the late 1950s,
he caustically denounced a more general, and growing, female domination
of men. In "The Abdicating Male" (1956), he condemned women's perva-
sive influence in the modern consumer economy, a trend that turned
browbeaten men into "merely earners, not spenders," who dutifully provided their wives with "three cars, a split-personality ranch house, mink,
and European trips and such, [while they] are obliged to steal from the
petty cash fund in their own offices for weeks to accumulate the price of
a trout rod." In 1958, Wylie followed up with "The Womanization of America," which broadly attacked the "taffeta tide" sweeping women into a
position of dominance in social clubs, entertainment, teaching, and the
arts. While modern men were out earning money, women had taken command of the home as well as the schools. Some men hoped they could
"regain a sense of masculinity they knew to be lost," contended Wylie, but
they were too weakened to do so. "Most American husbands are, or soon

become, flabby parodies of the physical male," he wrote. "Nearly all lack—even sneer at—those qualities of body and spirit wherein true masculinity has its being." A few years later, in "The Career Woman," Wylie announced that in this "age of cowed men and bullish women" females had pushed their way into the world of industry, commerce, and business enterprise. These "mink-bearing dragons of our time," Wylie asserted, had invaded offices in companies throughout the land and were threatening to take over. The career woman's pursuit of power, money, and abundance, he maintained, was working to "cripple manhood and masculinity on earth." As women were winning the battle to become "the primary sex," casualties were piling up in a "disgraced, tormented, castrated, and frustrated manhood."[29]

Wylie's images of emasculation became staples in the rhetoric of the masculinity crisis. In particular, two developments seemed to illustrate this process. First, commentators pointed to a reported surge in impotency among American males. The *Look* series contended that sexual dysfunction was an unfortunate masculine reaction to the threat of female domination, noting, "The decline in male sexual potency that doctors observe may be the man's most dangerous defense." Helen Mayer Hacker, an academic specialist in the family, added that impotence was a particularly urgent problem because of its importance to male identity. With men increasingly confused about their position and females increasingly demanding sexual satisfaction, pressure had mounted. "Virility used to be conceived as a unilateral expression of male sexuality, but is regarded today in terms of the ability to evoke a full sexual response on the part of the female," she wrote. "Men as the dominant group feel the strains of accommodating." Such difficulties, concluded *Cosmopolitan,* had created an epidemic of impotence. Experts, it reported, suggested that about 10 percent of American males under the age of fifty suffered from this problem, while another 15 percent struggled with related sexual difficulties. Sadly, "most middle-aged men are either consciously or unconsciously worried about their potency."[30]

Equally disturbing was the reported growth of homosexuality among American men. The mental health expert Lawrence K. Frank related that many expert observers believed that "male homosexuality is increasing." According to another analyst, this represented a desperate "flight from masculinity" in the current atmosphere of crisis and quoted experts who estimated that one in every thirteen American men between the ages of sixteen and fifty-five had been a full-fledged homosexual for at least three years during his adult life. For Philip Wylie, this was simply a reaction to female aggression as "thousands of men, who, faced with asexual Harpies and antisexual Circes, have, simply, given up even trying to be male and turned in shrieking dismay to homosexuality. These victims of the transcendent American She have tried, in effect, to beat their assailants by joining them." But others argued more broadly that it was the result of growing uncertainty about, and tensions within, the modern male role. Homosexuality could be seen as "one index of the burdens of masculinity," wrote one critic. Some individuals who struggled with feelings of inadequacy about their status as men "may become confused in their sexual identification, and feel that they must also change their sexual object."[31]

Ultimately, however, concern about a crisis of American masculinity came to rest on an overarching public issue in 1950s America: the Cold War. Fears about meeting the aggressive forces of international Communism with a weakened male population became the issue that drew together the various concerns about masculinity and bureaucracy, consumerism, and womanization. Social strains and male emotional devastation were bad enough. But in a larger sense, national survival was at stake.

Lurking in the background of every discussion concerning weakened American masculinity in the late 1950s was a concern about the American struggle with the forces of Communism around the globe. Implied on occasion, but usually addressed directly, this preoccupation supplied enormous import to the debate. The emergence of the Cold War in the late 1940s with its clash between the United States and its ideological allies, on the one hand, and the Soviet Union and Red China and their allies, on the other, had gradually permeated nearly all aspects of political, social, and cultural life to become the overarching issue of the era. By all accounts, there was a pressing need for strong, vigorous men to prosecute this conflict successfully. Thus, for many observers and critics, the growing specter of declining American masculinity promised dire consequences. It lent a special sense of urgency to the discussion.

Mounting questions about American men weakened by bureaucratic maneuvering, material affluence, and female domination flowed quickly and powerfully into concerns about stopping the tide of Communist expansion around the globe. With the stalemate of the Korean conflict still fresh in the national memory, and the Soviet premier Nikita Khrushchev's 1956 promise of "We will bury you!" still ringing fresh in American ears, questions about the American capacity to prevail lingered uncomfortably. As the *Look* series noted, great danger lay in the prospect that modern American males had become "too soft, too complacent and too home-oriented to meet the challenge of other dynamic nations like China and the Soviet Union."[32]

Max Eastman, a former leftist who had repented of socialist leanings by the 1950s, exhorted consumers of *Reader's Digest*, "Let's close the muscle gap!" Playing off the Cold War trope of the missile gap, which claimed that the Soviets had pulled ahead of the United States in nuclear missile capacity, he warned of a greater danger within. "The Soft American. The Flabby American," he wrote. "Such headlines are becoming more and more common." Sadly, men had become victims of "our modern sedentary life" with its material comforts and labor-saving devices. But America's Communist foes, still stuck in a cruder but physically demanding stage of society, were forced to cultivate a sterner, hardier approach to life. "It is an easy guess that the young people of the Soviet Union, which is still far behind mechanically, are ahead . . . in muscular fitness," declared Eastman. Thus the United States needed to embrace a program of manly physical development. "Let's start a crusade in pursuit of muscular health and attendant well-being, a crusade . . . toward our adequate leadership in the defense of the free world," he urged. "For the indubitable muscle gap between us and those who would bury us may well in the long run prove more disastrous than any alleged missile gap ever will be."[33]

Other commentators found similar cause for concern in contemplating weakened American masculinity and the Cold War. The United States had dominated the Summer Olympics for nearly half a century, noted one, yet the Soviet Union triumphed with the greatest number of total points in just the second time it competed in 1956. Moreover, journalists reported that of over six million young men called up for the military draft since 1948, more than 40 percent were turned down for physical deficiencies. Such anxieties caused Hanson Baldwin, a former naval officer and Pulitzer Prize–winning journalist for *The New York Times,* to publish in 1959 a critique with the pungent title "Our Fighting Men Have Gone Soft." American combat capabilities had been undermined, he argued, by a marked decline in masculine vigor. "What's happening to our fighting men? Is the morale, the will to fight, the *elan,* the spirit, the *esprit de corps,* the motivation, the guts of the armed services what it ought to be?" he asked rhetorically. Part of the problem lay in the entanglements of military bureaucracy and congressional meddling in military operations, but the biggest difficulty lay in modern social patterns. The modern male had been "pampered" by a life of ease and abundance, and many could no longer meet the physical and mental demands of military service, insisted Baldwin; "Military Man has changed because Civilian Man has changed." Now the Cold War was calling this situation to account. The comfortable affluence of American life, with its sheltering and softening of men, contrasted sharply with "the stark life of Russia and Red China, where hard work takes precedence over security. Can American man—after years of protective conditioning—vie with the barbarian who has lived by his wits, his initiative, his brawn? Will he retain the will to fight for his country?" For Baldwin, the answers to such questions were far from clear.[34]

An arresting portrait of the Cold War male in disarray came in one of the most popular American films of the late 1950s. In its own symbolic way, the movie presented an analysis of American masculinity in the postwar era as probing as those by David Riesman, William Whyte, and Arthur Schlesinger Jr. *North by Northwest* (1959), a clever thriller produced and directed by Alfred Hitchcock, explored modern manhood in crisis as its protagonist (played by Cary Grant) is thrown into a confusing cauldron of Cold War espionage and proves consistently inept before barely escaping with his life (and his love interest). The advertising poster for the movie clearly suggested male confusion and weakness, depicting Grant falling through space, all flailing arms and legs askew, unable to find firm footing and with a frightened look on his face as a woman stands to the side, gun in hand, having apparently just shot him.

North by Northwest's Roger Thornhill, a busy Madison Avenue advertising executive, is a typical white-collar organization man, even down to the gray-flannel suit that he wears throughout the film. When he becomes caught up in a case of mistaken identity and is thrust into a complex Cold War spy caper, Thornhill recoils from the struggle and flees cross-country. Told by the Central Intelligence Agency that national security is at stake, he replies angrily, "Maybe it's time you started losing a few cold wars." He wants no part of the anti-Communist struggle. As he maneuvers to survive in an atmosphere of confusion and turmoil, Thornhill meets a beautiful, blond young woman named Eve Kendall. With a first name signifying a female archetype, she proves to be an aggressive, shrewd double agent working for the CIA. Eve, not Thornhill, steps forward to act as a heroic cold warrior and defend her country's vital interests. In the dramatic climax of the film at Mount Rushmore, Thornhill glances upward and comments ruefully, "I don't like the way Teddy Roosevelt is looking at me." His choice is significant. TR, of course, had been a notable advocate of "the strenuous life" and manly assertion from the early twentieth century, and the juxtaposition of this symbol of vigorous masculinity with the desperate, floundering adman is striking. Even though Thornhill survives his ordeal, he stabilizes his life at the film's conclusion only by marrying Eve and fleeing to the comfort of marriage, the family, and his gray-flannel job. Like hosts of white-collar American men, he finds abundance and the domestic comforts to be far more fulfilling than dangerous Cold War confrontations.[35]

A more probing analysis of the Cold War and the troubled American male came in one of the most popular novels of the decade. *The Ugly American* (1958), by Eugene Burdick and William Lederer, presented an interwoven series of vignettes focused on Sarkhan, a fictional nation in Southeast Asia that has emerged as a battleground in the struggle between the United States and the Soviet Union. The book aims to show how and why America is losing ground to Communist expansion among poorer unaligned countries in the region. Perhaps the key element in this failing fight is the weakened state of American men. In instance after instance, the failure of American representatives to halt the inroads of hardened Communist insurrectionists stems from their bureaucratic mediocrity, addiction to consumer luxuries, soft bodies, and lack of willpower. Serialized in *The Saturday Evening Post* and selected by the Book of the Month Club, it spent a year and a half on the bestseller list and sold nearly five million copies.[36]

The Ugly American presented a gallery of American representatives that was far from flattering. The ambassador to Sarkhan, "Lucky Louis" Sears, is overweight, red of face, perspiring, and fond of hobnobbing with the country's elite, hosting cocktail parties for visiting dignitaries, providing glowing briefings to American congressmen, and releasing news stories that paint rosy, inflated assessments of American endeavors. Meanwhile, trouble festers in the countryside as peasants steadily flock to the Communist standard under the influence of hardened, skillfully trained Soviet agents. Joe Bing, chief of information for the State Department, is a loud, corpulent, brash glad-hander who is fond of big meals and comfortable circumstances. According to the disdainful appraisal of a local journalist, he drives "a big red convertible which he slews around corners and over sidewalks. And he's got exactly the kind of loud, silly laugh that every Asian is embarrassed to hear." Another functionary, after spending a few weeks in Sarkhan, writes home describing the high life prevalent in the American compound: "They all give parties and plenty of them; there's at least one cocktail party or dinner every night. It's easy to do, of course, because everyone has [hired] help." Not only abundance but a deskbound bureaucratic mind-set hamstring any attempts at manly effectiveness. "They sat in their freshly pressed clothes, ran their clean fingers over their smooth cheeks, and smiled knowingly at one another," the authors wrote of one official policy meeting. Women also represent another weakening influence. Female Foreign Service officers are not only attracted to the embassy high life but obsessed with finding husbands. They undermine male vigor and pose a threat to achievement.[37]

In contrast to these weak, flabby government officials, *The Ugly American* presented a small group of tough, vigorous, practical-minded individuals who hold out some hope for success in meeting the Communist threat in Sarkhan. Without fail, these men are physically fit, mentally flexible, self-sacrificing, and tough. They range from a rugged, athletic, highly educated Catholic priest who ministers to common people to an engineer full of innovative ideas about how to help Sarkhanese peasants improve their daily lives. "His fingernails were black with grease. His fingers bore the tiny nicks and scars of a lifetime of practical engineering. The palms of his hands were calloused," wrote the authors. "He was most proud and confident of his ugly strong hands . . . [and] still had the smell of the jungle about him." Colonel Hillandale, an expert in counterinsurgency, makes a special impact. Tall, lean, fun loving, and an enthusiastic harmonica player, he interacts with ordinary people and embraces the food and drink of Sarkhan. All of these figures make significant inroads because they flee the material comfort and bureaucracy of the embassy and go into the field, learn the language, immerse themselves in native culture, and prove tough enough to flourish in jungle villages. After interacting with such figures, no natives "in that area believed any more that all Americans were rich and bloated slobs."[38]

Perhaps the ultimate symbol of manly vigor in *The Ugly American* is Gilbert MacWhite. A State Department diplomat, he has grasped the weakness of both American policy and the men who promote it. With red hair, a body that is "hard and muscular," and a tough-minded sensibility, he learns the Sarkhanese language and reads everything available on the country's history and politics. Determined to "keep out of the cocktail circuit and away from the bureaucrats," he eventually puts his career on the line by urging an overhaul of American policy toward the country. Mac-White passionately tells his superiors that success in combating Communism in Sarkhan depends on the "men who have sacrificed and labored here. . . . They are tough and they are hard. . . . Superior people are attracted only by the challenge." Reliance on portly, glad-handing bureaucrats and flacks guarantees failure. "By setting our standards low and making our life soft, we have, quite automatically and unconsciously, assured ourselves of mediocre people," he insists, before concluding "Russians will win without firing a shot."[39]

Ultimately, the heroic men of *The Ugly American* fail. Unable to overcome a system fueled by institutionalized luxury and stodgy bureaucracy, they are pushed out of the picture. The State Department relieves MacWhite of his duties and replaces him with Joe Bing, while the others are marginalized as "crackpots." Colonel Hillandale falls out of favor when he punches an officious, incompetent deputy chief of the mission in the eye. Thus the novel concludes as a kind of morality play showing how a masculine fiber weakened by abundance and bureaucratic habits points toward failure in the fight against Communism.

Thus a raft of troubling issues engendered by the masculine crisis of the late 1950s finally converged in the public arena and raised serious concerns about the United States' survival in the Cold War. But key questions remained: Could weakened American males be revived? And if so, how? Once again, a leading American intellectual and political activist, having diagnosed the problem, stepped forward with a solution.

For Arthur Schlesinger Jr. and many of his contemporaries, the problems besetting modern men—bureaucratic torpor, debilitating material abundance, frayed identity—reflected the larger problems of American society in the 1950s. As early as 1949, in his book *The Vital Center,* he had identified troubling issues in public life with personal kinds of masculine weakness. Schlesinger complained that mainstream politics had grown "fat and complacent" and that only the "new virility" of liberal anti-Communism could overcome the "emasculated political energies" of both older, traditional ruling groups and their radical critics. He described the allure of Communism as a "womblike" impulse to find security, a collectivist urge to immerse oneself "in the broad maternal expanse of the masses." Later, as Schlesinger analyzed the problems and proclivities of the 1950s, this tendency to conflate the personal and the public, the sexual and the political, only increased. More than any other, one word came to describe his view of both modern masculinity and modern America: "impotence."[40]

The age of Eisenhower, Schlesinger argued, had pushed forward a pedestrian, restricted notion of America in the postwar world. The dominant mind-set, which combined a limited sense of government, an embrace of social conformity, and enthusiasm for a booming economy, advanced the idea that the pursuit of material abundance and personal security was the critical component for a rich, compelling life. In Schlesinger's words, ordinary middle-class Americans resembled nothing so much as a collection of "satisfied stockholders in a satisfied nation" as the United States became "a country drowning in its own passivity—passive because it had come to accept the theory of its own *impotence*." In this placid society of conformity and consumerism, he argued, many people were drawn to one of two extremes. "The vast majority were the 'silent generation,' the 'uncommitted generation,' the 'careful young men,' the 'men in grey flannel suits,'" wrote Schlesinger. "A small minority, rejecting this respectable world as absurd, defected from it and became beats and hipsters, 'rebels without a cause.' Pervading both groups was a profound sense of *impotence*—a feeling that the social order had to be taken as a whole or repudiated as a whole and was beyond the power of the individual to change." Yet each of these impulses "created only a partial man. There was need for a way of life, a way of autonomy between past and present, the organization man and the anarchist, the square and the beat." Trapped in this social swamp, men in particular felt hemmed in, powerless, impotent.[41]

But as a man of action as well as an intellectual, Schlesinger was eager to propose a cure for the malady that had weakened American men (and the larger society). Some observers, he noted, endorsed simplistic solutions. They proclaimed the need for males to pursue greater physical fitness or to reassert their authority in the face of female ambition. Schlesinger, however, endorsed a more sophisticated program. A revitalized sense of manhood, he argued, would not come from lifting weights or trying to restore an outdated masculine supremacy, which he derided as "the neurosis of an immature society." Instead, he proposed a three-part crusade for rejuvenation. He urged men to reject pressures toward conformity and togetherness and instead embrace a spirit of "individual spontaneity" that would invigorate their masculinity. He suggested that men also reach out to embrace "the liberating experience of art" and explore how music, painting, sculpture, poetry, and literature could help them recover "something more exacting and more personal, an intensified questing for identity." Most important, he endorsed the notion of a "virile political life" that rejected piety and platitudes in favor of a new, vigorous approach to public issues that was "definite and hard-hitting, respecting debate and dissent, seeking clarity and decision."[42]

Schlesinger's diagnosis of, and remedy for, the 1950s crisis of American masculinity proved to be more than merely an intellectual exercise. In fact, his manifesto in *Esquire* helped set the stage for a new public figure who was rising to ascendancy in national politics during the late 1950s. This charismatic young man, in many ways, embodied Schlesinger's reform ideals of vigorous individualism, cultural curiosity and sophistication, and especially a "virile political life." With a message attracting millions of followers and reams of publicity, he promised to overcome the crisis of masculinity in modern American life.

⟨ TWO ⟩

STYLE MAKES THE MAN: CANDIDATE
JOHN F. KENNEDY

n the crisis of masculinity that preoccupied so many in late 1950s America, a few beacons of hope pierced the gloominess. *Cosmopolitan,* in its 1957 special issue examining the conundrums of the modern American male, included a piece titled "The Fascinators." It presented brief sketches of thirty-five men who had been selected by women as particularly interesting, attractive, and compelling figures. They seemed to provide models for masculine regeneration. Near the front of the list appeared a youthful political figure with this description under his photograph: "The tall, sandy-haired Democratic Senator from Massachusetts defeated Henry Cabot Lodge Jr. in the race for the United States Senate by attending tea parties. Now thirty-nine and married to a pretty photographer, he is the author of a best-selling book, *Profiles in Courage,* and has been mentioned as the next Democratic Presidential candidate."[1]

This same senator also signaled masculine redemption with a high-profile public endorsement of *The Ugly American,* the popular novel that had raised such an alarm about weak, glad-handing American men and the dangerous implications for the Cold War. On January 23, 1959, he took out a full-page advertisement in *The New York Times,* along with several other prominent figures, to praise the book. It was, said the text, a compelling critique of "the Americans who go overseas for the various governmental agencies, their activities abroad, and the policies they are entrusted to carry out." The senator then sent a copy of the novel to every member of the Senate. A short time later, he wrote privately to the author Eugene Burdick, explaining that it had been "a pleasure for me to give a public endorsement of *The Ugly American,* which I also feel has begun to have some visible influence both in Congress and in Foggy Bottom [the State Department]." Subsequently, he gave speeches addressing "the economic gap" in under-developed countries and the need for "a volunteer corps" of young people who would personify the physical and personal virtues of the effective Americans praised in the novel. In the senator's words, "Many have been discouraged at the examples that we read of 'the ugly American.' And I think the United States is going to have to do much better in this area if we are going to defend freedom and peace in the 1960s."[2]

As these episodes made clear, at least one prominent American was meeting head-on the crisis of modern American masculinity. Senator John F. Kennedy, a youthful and confident political figure with an eye on the White House, seemed to embody everything many American men felt nervous about losing in the postwar era: physical vigor, decisive action, personal heroism, individual initiative, tough-mindedness, and abundant sex appeal. As he geared up to run for his party's presidential nomination in the mid-1950s, he relied upon the usual partisan boilerplate of the Democratic Party—condemning Republican reliance on the wealthy, up-holding the federal government's regulation of the economy and protec-tion of the less affluent, advocating the need for vigorous prosecution of the Cold War—but here he differed little from his Democratic opponents such as Hubert Humphrey, Stuart Symington, Lyndon Johnson, and Adlai Stevenson. What set JFK apart was his personification of vigorous, elegant, assertive manhood. An aura of confident masculinity permeated both his persona and his campaign.

Upon accepting the Democratic Party's nomination in the summer of 1960, Kennedy revealed the essence of this appeal. In ringing tones, he proclaimed that the time had come for a new generation of leadership— new men to cope with new problems and new opportunities:

All over the world, particularly in the newer nations, young men
are coming to power—men who are not bound by the traditions
of the past—men who are not blinded by old fears and hates and
rivalries—young men who can cast off the old slogans and delusions
and suspicions. . . .

[W]e stand today on the edge of a New Frontier—the frontier
of the 1960s. . . . I am asking each of you to be pioneers on that
New Frontier. . . . [C]ourage—not complacency—is our need
today—leadership, not salesmanship. And the only valid test of
leadership is the ability to lead, and lead vigorously.

All the touchstones of the Kennedy campaign—and image—were there:
youth, strength, toughness, decisiveness, courage, imagination, vigor. And
woven throughout was the bright thread of "young men" moving forward
to seize their historical moment.

These were more than rhetorical tropes. For JFK, the picture of vigorous
young men replacing a tired, unimaginative, tradition-bound generation of
older males held the key to his considerable political appeal. The candidate
John F. Kennedy's stylish rendering of regenerated masculinity promised to
resolve the cultural crisis of the late 1950s. It would make him a new kind of
political figure and promised to make him a new kind of president.

John F. Kennedy had first gained national attention with his election to the
House of Representatives in 1946, when he surprisingly surged to the
front of a crowded Democratic primary field in Massachusetts's Eleventh
Congressional District and then handily beat his Republican opponent in
the general election. The twenty-nine-year-old had sprung from the upper
echelons of the Irish Catholic community in Boston. He was the son of
Joseph P. Kennedy, a wealthy businessman and financier who had served
as chairman of the Securities and Exchange Commission and then U.S.
ambassador to England for President Franklin D. Roosevelt, while his
paternal grandfather was Patrick Joseph "P. J." Kennedy, a long-standing
political figure in the Irish communities on the east side of the city. On his

mother's side, he was the grandson of John "Honey Fitz" Fitzgerald, the popular, charming, and knavish former mayor of Boston. Jack Kennedy had graduated from Harvard University in 1940 and then served a stint in the navy in the Pacific theater during World War II. Returning home and deciding to enter public life, the young man ran a vigorous and innovative congressional campaign based on the vaguely inspiring slogan "The new generation offers a leader." His large family—he was the second oldest of nine children—blanketed the district with personal appearances, robust speeches, and gracious "tea parties" to welcome voters, while his father blanketed it with money. The youthful candidate won going away.

After three rather indifferent terms in Congress, Kennedy made a much bigger national splash in 1952 with another surprising electoral victory in Massachusetts. This time, in a race for the U.S. Senate, he defeated the highly favored incumbent, the Republican stalwart Henry Cabot Lodge Jr. Kennedy swept to victory by a margin of almost 70,000 votes, while the Republican presidential candidate, Dwight D. Eisenhower, was carrying the state by 200,000 votes over the Democrat Adlai Stevenson. Again, with the Kennedy clan fanning out to ring doorbells and host get-togethers throughout the state, the youthful candidate expounded upon his slogan, "Kennedy will do more for Massachusetts." Thrown off stride by his young opponent's enthusiastic campaign, Lodge never recovered as the Democrat swept to victory.[3]

In these initial electoral victories, Kennedy displayed a number of distinctive personal characteristics that would prove crucial to his success as a political figure. Some of them had been molded by his father. Hard-driving Joseph Kennedy instilled in his second son—the oldest, Joseph junior, had been killed during World War II—generous portions of energy, charm, ambition, and a certain ruthless determination to win. The father had risen from modest circumstances in Irish Catholic Boston to attain a Harvard education, earn a financial fortune as an investment banker, thrive as an influential studio mogul in Hollywood, and finally become an important, if controversial, figure in the Roosevelt administration. Joseph Kennedy was determined that his sons would climb even higher by entering public life, and he pushed Jack into national politics when the young man returned from the war. The son, although more reserved and introspective, had inherited no small portion of his father's drive, intelligence, and competitive spirit, and he was happy to comply.[4]

The large, vibrant, close-knit Kennedy family shaped other notable qualities in the young politician. Over the course of his boyhood and many summers spent at the family compound in Hyannis Port, Jack Kennedy had developed a fondness for physical activity and boisterous competition in contests with his three brothers and five sisters. Whether racing sailboats in the bay or engaging in softball games, the Kennedys played hard, and they played to win. Jack had carried that spirit to Harvard, where he competed as a swimmer and freshman football player, and then on into adult life, when sailing and family football games on the expansive lawn at Hyannis Port remained standard fare. As a family, the Kennedys radiated a sense that they were special—brighter, tougher, more energetic, more resilient, more physically attractive, and more successful than the average American. As Joseph Kennedy frequently proclaimed to his offspring, "We want winners around here, we don't want losers."[5]

The large brood of Kennedy children pushed and tested one another, jockeyed for position, and good-humoredly needled each other over clothes, speech, achievements, and failures. According to one family friend who observed this raucous interplay, "Nothing was sacred. It was like getting pecked by a flock of chickens." The Kennedy siblings competed relentlessly with a "ceaseless sense of urgency," according to one observer. "They never relax even when they are relaxing. After dinner they all play guessing games like Categories or Charades or Twenty Questions—you're doing mental somersaults all the time." But they stuck together fanatically, as in Jack's senatorial election when Rose and her children fanned out through Massachusetts and campaigned tirelessly. "Poor old Lodge never had a chance," reported a family friend. "The Kennedys were like a panzer division mowing down the state."[6]

The Kennedy clan believed fervently in one another and in their collective destiny to achieve great success. Two historians of the Kennedy family have described them as "a time-lapse photograph of the workings of the American dream." In fact, Rose Kennedy recalled that "Joe thought the children would never be married because they all enjoyed going out together so much. They were stimulated by each other's interests and plans, problems and ambitions." Charles Spalding, a childhood friend of Jack's, described the Kennedys as a clan that seemingly "existed outside the usual laws of nature; there was no other group so handsome, so engaged.... [E]ndless competition, people drawing each other out and pushing each other to greater lengths. It was as simple as this: the Kennedys had a feeling of being heightened and it rubbed off on the people who came into contact with them." As visitors to the family compound often noted, whenever inquiries were made about activities or appearances or achievements or states of mind, members of the Kennedy family invariably declared, "Terrific!" The word illuminated much about their perception of themselves and the arc of their lives. Jack Kennedy internalized this ethic of sparkling energy, intense competition, and high achievement. Like his family, he made it seem more exuberant than arrogant.[7]

Being a Kennedy, of course, also entailed a privileged upbringing, a fact that influenced the young politician's sensibility in several ways. Joseph Kennedy's great wealth had provided his son with an elite education at private prep schools and Harvard, European vacations, and introductions to many of the most important people in the world ranging from Pope Pius XII (the Kennedys attended his inauguration in Rome in 1939 and were granted a special audience with the new pontiff) to the influential *New York Times* columnist Arthur Krock, from the Hollywood actress Gloria Swanson to the king and prime minister of England. Ensconced in this privileged world, young Jack Kennedy not only moved easily within a network of high-profile figures but never had to worry about finances. Coming of age during the Great Depression, he lived in a world of servants, big houses, and frequent vacations. "I really did not learn about the depression until I read about it at Harvard," he would admit later. Kennedy took for granted a life of material ease and habitually displayed a cavalier attitude about money. "He never carries more than two or three dollars with him," explained *McCall's* magazine in 1957. "Often he goes off on a long trip with no cash at all, relying on whoever is around to pay for taxis and meals." Sometimes, this habit even extended to dates when he would take a young woman out to dinner and then find himself with no cash, necessitating a frantic phone call to friends for funds or a chagrined request that she pay.[8]

Although he was blessed with abundant intelligence, Kennedy's privileged background meant that he was never forced to develop it. He contented himself with mediocre grades throughout his schooling except when particular subjects, mostly history and biography and English, engaged his fancy and stimulated his talents. At Choate, a boarding school, he became notorious for his lack of mental discipline, intellectual indifference, and devil-may-care attitude. He graduated in the middle of his class. While at Harvard, Kennedy appeared bright and inquisitive to many of his professors but devoted minimal attention to his studies while spending most of his time winning a reputation as a ladies' man. He embodied the tradition of the privileged student largely content to receive "gentleman's Cs." Kennedy's elite upbringing also instilled an unshakable self-confidence along with an aristocratic sense of natural authority and noblesse oblige. He idolized the British nobility—among his very favorite books were *The Young Melbourne* and *Pilgrim's Way,* both salutary (and romanticized) treatments of the English patrician class—and he seems to have imbibed from them a spirit of carefree sophistication, public service, adventurous engagement with the world, libertinism, and social privilege. Thus Kennedy entered adulthood, and began his early political career, certain that he would make something of his life and sporting a casually elegant style that downplayed sentiment and elevated cool calculation. The young patrician simply assumed a personal trajectory of success.[9]

Kennedy's reputation as a war hero added a brighter sheen to his manly persona. In World War II, during his naval service in the Pacific, the young lieutenant had been involved in a famous incident involving PT-109, the craft he commanded. While stationed at night to intercept a Japanese convoy in the Solomon Islands, his boat was cut in half by a Japanese destroyer. Two of the crew members were killed immediately, and the other eleven were cast adrift. In succeeding days, Kennedy first helped bring the survivors to the floating hull, then led them on a five-hour swim to a small deserted island as he pulled along a wounded man by grasping his life-jacket ties in his teeth. He swam into the channel and remained for hours unsuccessfully trying to flag down any passing American boats. Finally, Kennedy and another man swam to an adjacent island, found a canoe and fresh water and some crackers, and made contact with some islanders who conveyed their whereabouts to a unit of New Zealanders. After a rescue, the young lieutenant was awarded the Navy and Marine Corps Medal for valor. Reporters for the AP and UPI quickly picked up this story and presented Kennedy to the public as a war hero. John Hersey, the famous war correspondent, did so even more with a long piece in *The New Yorker* titled "Survival" that was later condensed in *Reader's Digest*. In his early political campaigns, the young candidate took full advantage of the PT-109 incident, making the story part of his stump speech, while his father paid for 100,000 copies of the Hersey article to be distributed to voters. Thus at the outset of his public career, Kennedy was able to position himself as cool and courageous, abundantly endowed with "grace under pressure." He seemed the very picture of masculine heroism and prowess in an age when many feared such qualities were vanishing among modern men.[10]

At the same time, Jack Kennedy's long history of illness had fostered a certain fatalistic attitude about his own life. Although the American public, of course, would be carefully shielded from the facts of his health, the impact of these maladies helped to shape the personality that so many found attractive. Since childhood, Kennedy had suffered an onslaught of illnesses that regularly placed him in hospitals, clinics, and homestays with his life hanging in the balance a couple of times. Chronic stomach trouble, ulcers, spinal degeneration, and finally Addison's disease frequently laid him low for weeks at a time during adolescence and young manhood. In 1954, unrelenting pain prompted the young senator to undergo life-threatening back surgery, which he barely survived after enduring a serious infection and a coma that had brought a priest to his bedside to administer the last rites of the Catholic Church. This long struggle with illness molded in Kennedy an attitude of "you only live once" that was equal parts recklessness and stoicism. In college, while undergoing one of his periodic hospitalizations, he joked to a friend that he had peeked at his chart "and could see that they were mentally measuring me for a coffin." But behind the jokes, as one historian has observed, "was Jack's fear that he was slated for an early demise, making him almost manic about packing as much pleasure into his life as he could in the possibly short time remaining to him. His letters . . . are full of frenetic talk about partying and having sex." Kennedy once told George Smathers, a close friend, "You've got to live every day like it's your last day on earth. That's what I'm doing." Chuck Spalding, another boon companion, observed that Kennedy "always heard the footsteps. . . . Death was there. . . . [H]e tried to burn bright, he tried to wring as much out of things as he could." But the public only saw the manifestation of this impulse: a young man energetically embracing the possibilities of life.[11]

The crowning aspect of Kennedy's popular image—an overarching impression that helped knit together its various features—was biological in nature. The youthful senator was a very handsome man, perhaps the best-looking public figure in modern American history. In the age of graying, paunchy eminences such as Harry Truman and Dwight Eisenhower, Adlai Stevenson and John Foster Dulles, the young politician appeared on the national scene with the good looks of a movie star. At the same time, this physical attractiveness was understated and did not threaten men while setting many female pulses racing. With his boyish facial features, thick shock of auburn hair, ready grin, and athletic physique, Kennedy made an instant impression without saying a word. His close friend Lem Billings reported that Kennedy had met Marlene Dietrich during a stay in Los Angeles, and the famous actress declared that "he's one of the most fascinating and attractive young men she's ever met." A female journalist who knew the young man in the early 1950s reported that "he didn't have to lift a finger to attract women; they were drawn to him in battalions." Thus a handsome demeanor capped off the Massachusetts senator's vigorous, attractive masculinity in an age when many worried about the ascendancy of the plump, balding, deskbound, rapidly aging organization man.[12]

Kennedy's sparkling array of personal qualities quickly reaped dividends. Almost immediately after the 1952 election, journalists flocked to analyze and portray the handsome, vigorous young politician with the bright political future. One trend immediately appeared. This onslaught of publicity, this chorus of national acclaim, had virtually nothing to do with Kennedy's political positions or policies. Most attention focused on his personal image and attractive aura of vibrant, confident masculinity. While this rendering would persist, indeed intensify, throughout the later 1950s, its basic template appeared clearly in the very first magazine story that presented Kennedy to a national audience and helped launch his meteoric career.

On June 13, 1953, only a few months after his election, *The Saturday Evening Post* presented "The Senate's Gay Young Bachelor," a lengthy analysis of the young politician who was capturing the imagination of the national capital. Significantly, the article noted that John F. Kennedy's recent victory over Henry Cabot Lodge Jr. represented no great triumph of political policies or ideological principles because there was little separating the beliefs of the conservative Democratic candidate and the liberal Republican one. "There were no real issues splitting Kennedy and Lodge," it admitted, "and their voting records were not strikingly different." Instead, *The Saturday Evening Post* argued that the youthful Democrat had swamped his more experienced and more prominent Republican opponent because of his personal appeal. The magazine eagerly inventoried its characteristics.[13]

First of all, it noted, the young politician cut a young, manly, even seductive figure. "Kennedy appeared to be a walking fountain of youth. He is six feet tall with a lean, straight, hard physique and the innocently respectful face of an altar boy at High Mass," it said. "[He has] a trademark—a bumper crop of lightly combed brown hair that shoots over his right eyebrow and always makes him look as though he had just stepped out of the shower." It also underlined Kennedy's physical vigor, noting that he played touch football every weekend on the streets and playgrounds of his Georgetown residence. The lead photograph for the article showed him sailing on the Potomac River with a member of his staff, skillfully steering the small boat under full sail as it tipped at an angle and the wind tousled his hair.[14]

The Saturday Evening Post played up Kennedy's status as a war hero. It noted the PT-109 incident during World War II, explaining, "In August 1943, he earned the Purple Heart and the Navy and Marine Corps medal for his 'extremely heroic conduct' in a dramatic episode in the mid-Solomons." At the same time, the magazine took pains to describe the young senator as intellectually serious. "Kennedy not only reads books with hard covers—as many as six or eight a week—but he has written one," the author observed. His *Why England Slept* had been "lauded by critics for his perception and objectivity."[15]

One of Kennedy's defining traits, the article contended, was his determination to steer his own course in life and in politics. "He prides himself on his intellectual independence," it observed, as he often charted a "strictly lone-wolf course and held resolutely to it." In particular, Kennedy strenuously resisted all efforts "to tag him with an ideological label," especially those that described him as a liberal. "I'd be very happy to tell them I'm not a liberal at all," he declared. "I never joined the Americans for Democratic Action or the American Veterans Committee. I'm not comfortable with those people." Here, *The Saturday Evening Post* suggested to its readers, was a self-directed young man determined to remain unbound by the demands of any organization, including political ones.[16]

Finally, of course, the article made much of the young senator's vaunted sex appeal. "Many women have hopefully concluded that Kennedy needs looking after. In their opinion, he is, as a young millionaire Senator, just about the most eligible bachelor in the United States," it explained. "Kennedy lives up to that role only occasionally, when he drives his long convertible, hatless and with the car's top down, or accidentally gets photographed with a glamour girl in a nightclub." One photograph in the story showed him with Maria Attolico, the beautiful daughter of a former Italian ambassador to the United States, at a formal ball in New York City, while another depicted him surrounded by adoring, wide-eyed young women during a school visit in Massachusetts. This masculine attraction clearly translated into political appeal. During the recent senatorial campaign, *The Saturday Evening Post* noted, Kennedy was frequently "in danger of being mobbed by hundreds of smitten high-school or college girls." As several observers had commented, "During the campaign every woman who met Kennedy wanted either to mother him or marry him."[17]

Thus from the inception of his national political career as a member of the U.S. Senate, Kennedy created the outline of a compelling image. He represented a manly ideal, a symbol of male regeneration and confident assertion in an age, many feared, that was dominated by timid organization men and suburbanized drones. As the young senator began to plan his ascendancy to the presidency over the last half of the 1950s, this persona would be elaborated, enhanced, and polished, eventually becoming synonymous with the man himself.

The broadcast of Kennedy's image onto a national screen began only a few years after his election to the U.S. Senate. At the 1956 Democratic convention, he was chosen to narrate the party's campaign film, titled *The Pursuit of Happiness,* and also asked to give a nominating speech for the party's presidential candidate, Adlai Stevenson. Then, when the nominee threw open the vice presidential nomination to the convention rather than choosing a running mate himself, JFK launched a last-minute run for the prize that came very close to succeeding. He narrowly lost to Senator Estes Kefauver of Tennessee but gained much national publicity and a measure of additional respect from a gracious concession speech urging the unanimous approval of his rival after he had surged ahead. In the aftermath of the convention, as favorable commentary surrounded the youthful, glamorous, handsome young senator from Massachusetts, he began to consider a run for president the next time around.

That same year, Kennedy greatly enhanced his national profile with the publication of *Profiles in Courage,* a bestseller that won the Pulitzer Prize. The book had a curious genesis. Kennedy had begun outlining the project in 1954 during his lengthy convalescence from major back surgery. While bedridden, he took notes, sketched rough ideas, and suggested themes, while a galaxy of associates—James Landis of his father's staff, William R. Tansill of the Library of Congress, and the noted scholars Jules Davids, Allan Nevins, and James MacGregor Burns—gathered source material and helped shape the text in terms of organization and historical accuracy. His chief speechwriter, Ted Sorensen, provided much of the compelling writing style that characterized the narrative. As a Kennedy biographer has accurately concluded, the book "was more the work of a 'committee' than of any one person." Moreover, Joseph Kennedy, sensing a unique opportunity to promote his son's political aspirations, stepped in when the book came out. He poured considerable money into buying up thousands of copies to push it onto the bestseller list and then applied pressure through his close friend the columnist Arthur Krock to have it awarded the Pulitzer Prize. The Pulitzer Advisory Board did so after overturning the decision of the jurors, who had ranked five other biographies ahead of it. Despite such irregularities, the publicity and honors surrounding Kennedy's book showcased its author as a thoughtful and educated man, a war hero given to historical analysis and intellectual achievement as well as manly physical courage.[18]

Profiles in Courage opened a window on the youthful senator's values and worldview. It examined eight members of the U.S. Senate who, over the sweep of American history, had demonstrated a willingness to follow their own judgment against the tide of popular opposition. John Quincy Adams, Daniel Webster, Thomas Hart Benton, Sam Houston, Edmund G. Ross, Lucius Q. C. Lamar, George Norris, and Robert A. Taft, the book contended, had stood up to popular pressures or risked the wrath of constituents to take an unpopular course of action they deemed in the best interests of the country. In telling this tale, however, Kennedy's book also presented a thinly disguised lament about contemporary demands for conformity, mass values, and the organization man and praised the independent, tough-minded, manly individuals who went their own way despite such pressures. For those concerned about the constraints of bureaucracy, the shallowness of the other-directed personality, and the flabbiness of the suburban male in 1950s America, here stood a galaxy of inspiring counterexamples.

Profiles in Courage opened with a reference to the most notoriously manly figure in mid-twentieth-century America: "This is a book about that most admirable of human virtues—courage. 'Grace under pressure,' Ernest Hemingway defined it." Kennedy then bemoaned a "nation which has forgotten the quality of courage which in the past has been brought to public life" and decried the glad-handing impulses of the modern organization man. "Americans want to be liked—and Senators are no exception," he wrote. "We enjoy the comradeship and approval of our friends and colleagues.... We are anxious to get along." In a modern mass society increasingly shaped by "mass communications" and "public relations men," acts of courageous individualism had become ever harder but even more necessary. The "man of conscience," Kennedy argued, must examine the popular pressures facing him and "judge for himself which path to choose, which step will most help or hinder the ideals to which he is committed," while realizing that such a decision could put his career in peril. Even if it meant correcting or even ignoring popular sentiment, the courageous leader must "be able to take the hard and unpopular decisions necessary for our survival in the struggle with a powerful enemy."[19]

Profiles in Courage's vignettes offered case studies of how senators had stood up to the crowd in the American past. John Quincy Adams, for example, a man of irascible independence, had broken with his constituents and Federalist colleagues when they tried to block the advance of Jeffersonian democracy. Daniel Webster had risked his career to hold the Union together in 1850, while the rugged Thomas Hart Benton—"I never quarrel, sir. But sometimes I fight, sir; and whenever I fight, sir, a funeral follows, sir"—bravely battered Southerners in his own party to oppose the extension of slavery. Sam Houston, according to Kennedy, was a genuine man's man. This independent figure of "stoical courage and rugged individualism" had led Texas military forces to independence from Mexico but then broke with his colleagues and constituents when he opposed the state leaving the Union during the secession crisis years later.[20]

Kennedy concluded *Profiles in Courage* by evoking masculine fortitude in defiance of popular pressures to conform. All of these heroic senators, he contended, had believed self-respect was more important than popularity, ethics and integrity more compelling than public approval. Courage, in Kennedy's rendering, was ultimately a matter of manly determination. "A man does what he must—in spite of personal consequences, in spite of obstacles and dangers and pressures—and that is the basis of all human morality," he declared. "The stories of past courage can define that ingredient—they can teach, they can offer hope, they can provide inspiration. But they cannot supply courage itself. For this each man must look into his own soul." *Profiles in Courage* provided inspiration for those who sought to reassert manliness in the face of corrosive pressures in modern life.[21]

Throughout the late 1950s, developments seemed to elevate Kennedy ever nearer to this pantheon of heroic political leaders. A swelling volume of articles in national magazines and newspapers brought the young politician's name before the public as a rising national leader. A cover story in *Time* on November 24, 1958, posited Kennedy as the front-runner among the "Democratic Hopefuls" and pictured him front and center surrounded by other figures such as Hubert Humphrey, Stuart Symington, Lyndon Johnson, and Adlai Stevenson. He also appeared on the covers of *Newsweek, Life,* and *The Saturday Evening Post* while becoming the object of articles in serious journals of opinion such as *The New Republic, Harper's, The Progressive, The Atlantic,* men's magazines such as *Esquire,* and women's magazines such as *McCall's, Redbook,* and *Cosmopolitan.* Once again at the heart of these stories, regardless of the venue, lay favorable, even breathless descriptions of his personal appeal and vigorous masculine persona. "John Fitzgerald Kennedy is a young man who seems to have just about everything," declared a typical 1957 magazine piece. "He was a combat hero in World War II; he married a beautiful and talented girl; he was educated in the best schools; he has traveled widely. He has brains, ability, good looks, wealth, and the respect of those who know him. He also has great ambition and the ability to mobilize all his resources to get what he wants." Such analyses, as they streamed before the public, stressed several themes.[22]

Strikingly, most analyses of Kennedy's appeal barely mentioned his political positions or policy proposals, relegating them to afterthoughts. When noted at all, they were described vaguely. "A Moderate Democrat with a record of middle-of-the-road voting, he has won nods from Eisenhower Republicans," said one article. He evinced his own "peculiar brand of undoctrinaire liberalism," contended another. "Kennedy is basically a moderate liberal, but with many conservative leanings," said a third. The political reporter Richard Rovere simply admitted, "He is hoping to go to the Democratic Convention next year with a clearer political identity than he now has." Most accounts emphasized that the young politician had jettisoned ideological rigidity for pragmatism and a determination to chart his own course politically. As a story in *The Progressive* summarized, Kennedy "does not run with the liberal pack, the moderate pack, or any other. He stands pretty much by himself."[23]

Stories on this rising political star also stressed his detached, calculating sensibility, a quality that influenced both his personal style and his approach to public issues. A piece titled "The Cool Eye of John F. Kennedy" noted his "cool detachment" toward politics and politicians and suggested that "discrimination and taste and style" rated highly in his measure of them. It noted that even in congested, sweaty receptions with countless handshakes and inevitable indignities, "no one has ever seen him rattled." This unflappable style carried over into the arena of ideology and policy, where Kennedy's self-possession and intellect—"He reads far more than most senators and is more candid, informal, and disarmingly relaxed," said *Newsweek*—led him to approach issues with a calm detachment. In fact, one observer noted, Kennedy liked to take a hot issue, draw the emotion out of it, and calmly come up with a moderate reform. His aides called it "'de-passionating' an issue." This self-disciplined, unemotional sensibility seemed to elevate Kennedy above the push and pull of impulsive feelings. "He does not appear to have any great moral fervor," concluded a writer for *The Progressive*. "He looks like a young man who has carefully calculated what it takes to be a success in politics and is moving deliberately and intelligently along that road. He does not allow strong emotions to pull him off course."[24]

Evaluations of Kennedy typically underlined his tough-minded independence, a quality that clearly separated him from the plethora of glad-handing types in national politics. He was "singularly free of the posturing and phony piety to which even the more enlightened politicians succumb," one journalist wrote admiringly. "'No politician really likes to be a whore,' he has remarked drily, 'but I must say some are less reluctant about it than others.'" Kennedy made it clear that he sought that same quality of clear-eyed, sturdy judgment among those with whom he associated politically. As the editor of *Harper's* reported after an interview, the young senator had declared that a president must attract to his administration "men of stature, competence, and creative imagination within both parties—for it is the men, not merely the stated policies, that determine the effectiveness of American policy."[25]

Journalists treating Kennedy in the 1950s liked to portray him as an icon of vigorous physical fitness. In contrast to the flabby modern male softened by suburban comfort and enervated by plodding through the bureaucratic maze, the Massachusetts senator appeared the very picture of vitality. *Life* featured a photograph of him in shorts, a casual shirt, and sunglasses, barefoot, skipping stones on the ocean, with a caption reading, "Kennedy shows manly skill in Atlantic surf on private beach at family's summer home in Hyannis Port, on Cape Cod." *Newsweek,* in a 1958 cover story, described how an increasingly hectic life "has reduced Kennedy's gangling 6-foot frame from a lean 167 pounds to an even leaner 163 pounds." *Cosmopolitan* described how the junior senator from Massachusetts pursued golf, swimming, and junior varsity football while in college and could now often be found at a playground near his Georgetown home "in faded sweater and dungarees . . . spurring on a motley crew of adults and small fry in a game of touch football."[26]

Stories on Kennedy invariably trumpeted his wartime heroism as a revealing expression of the manly character that informed his approach to public life. The PT-109 incident became a lens through which the public could view the inner substance of this potential leader. His labors on this small craft had demonstrated enormous dedication, said one journal: it was "the most rugged type of service a man with a bad back could sustain, because of the continuous jouncing the boat took from the waves." Another observed that Kennedy was credited "with having saved three of his crew members, towing one of them three miles to shore," and noted his "war-incurred wounds." According to *Time,* he was "an authentic war hero" whose swimming skills "saved his life and those of his PT-boat mates." His courageous exploits in the South Pacific in 1943, noted many publications, had earned the young naval officer the Navy and Marine Corps Medal and demonstrated both physical courage and a genuine strength of character.[27]

Most write-ups on Kennedy after 1956 excitedly described his youthful, glamorous appearance as emblematic of a new generation of American men. Authors vied with one another in piling up adjectives, or constructing metaphors, to describe his mesmerizing personal appearance. "As slim and erect as a telephone pole, he seems taller than his six feet and lighter than his 160 pounds," wrote *McCall's.* "He has green eyes below his famous shock of reddish-brown hair." Kennedy had "the bright glow of youth," Richard Rovere wrote in *Esquire;* "the fact of youth not merely the appearance of youthfulness—is a large part of his charm."

"Boyishly handsome," "a boyish matinee idol," "a press agent's dream," "the clean-cut, smiling American boy, trustworthy, brave, reverent, boldly facing up to the challenges of the atomic age" were the kinds of phrases appearing in many accounts. This glamorously good-looking young political leader was "reaping a public reaction against tired old men." As one account put it, he appeared visually as "the antithesis of Senator Phogbound, the portly old fourflusher. . . . Kennedy is the new type increasingly elected to public office—young, physically vigorous, attractive, well-educated, shunning the old-time political vocabulary."[28]

Such breathless descriptions of Kennedy's youthful, handsome charm made for a natural transition to a topic that appeared inevitable: his abundant sex appeal. The young politician's vaunted attraction for women colored almost every portrait of him, and a 1953 article in *Cosmopolitan* set the standard. Titled "The Senator Women Elected," the story observed, "Few senators in U.S. history have been kissed, hugged, and generally mauled by their female constituents to the extent sustained by John F. Kennedy of Massachusetts. His devastating impact on women was one of the major factors, in the view of veteran political observers, in electing him to the Senate." It went on to describe him as "glamorous" and "very handsome" with an "incandescent personality," a man who "combines the somewhat disparate appeals of Walter Lippmann and Frank Sinatra. For he can talk like a pundit, while wearing a boyish grin and an air of wistful entreaty that enchants women of all ages." Women would patiently line up and wait three or four hours for the privilege of shaking hands with their idol, related the article, while the "more enterprising matrons would propel their daughters down the line, hoping their young charms would linger in his memory. . . . Kennedy was in occasional danger of being mobbed."[29]

As he geared up to run for the presidency, attention to Kennedy's appeal to women became ubiquitous in press accounts of his rising career. A 1957 cover story in *Time,* for example, opened with the story of a University of Minnesota coed who came to a Young Democrats convention with a message from her fifty-eight sorority sisters: "Every girl told me to give Senator Kennedy all her love and to tell him they would all vote for him." The article added, "Jack Kennedy has left panting politicians and swooning women across a large spread of the U.S." Even *The Progressive,* a serious journal of political ideas and ideological analysis, noted that he radiated "a high degree of sex appeal and 'sincerity.' Women are tempted to run their fingers through his hair."[30]

The fact of Kennedy's marriage added a curious and complicating element to his larger image of glamorous sex appeal. On September 12, 1953, at age thirty-six, he had taken an important step in his personal life by marrying Jacqueline Bouvier in Newport, Rhode Island. Beautiful and accomplished, she came from an impeccable aristocratic background of old money, yet she had worked in Washington, D.C., as a journalist and photographer. In many ways, Jackie projected a glamorous image to match that of her new husband. When he met her, according to a woman's magazine, Bouvier was twenty "with a lithe, long-legged figure, thick, shining brown hair falling like a curtain near one of her enormous brown eyes, and a face with beautiful bone structure." She was "one of the prettiest girls in Washington." Their wedding in Newport was a high-society event and perhaps the "celebrity marriage of the decade." It also rounded out Kennedy's image as he shifted from being the most eligible bachelor in the national capital to settling down to the status of respectable family man, an achievement holding a powerful appeal in 1950s America. A 1958 cover in *Life* captured this new wrinkle with its photograph of an ideal American family: a smiling Jack sitting next to a radiant Jackie and proudly holding his infant daughter, Caroline. A photograph in the inside story showed the proud father peering into a bassinet as his daughter grinned up at him. The caption read, "Four-month-old Caroline Kennedy gives father a bashful smile. 'I'm not home much,' says Jack, 'but when I am she seems to like me.'"[31]

But, of course, the backstory remained. Kennedy had a legendary sexual appetite that stretched back to his first arrival in Washington, D.C., in 1946, when a steady stream of young women flowed through his town house in Georgetown. From his father he had derived a penchant for blatant, omnivorous womanizing. Joseph Kennedy, without bothering to hide it, had kept the actress Gloria Swanson as a famous mistress for several years while operating as a business tycoon in Hollywood and in later years conducted a much-publicized affair with Clare Boothe Luce. Throughout his adult life, the ambassador indulged in countless casual couplings and sexual conquests with dozens of women all over the United States and Europe. His sons could not help but internalize what appeared as a normal pattern of male behavior in the Kennedy household.[32]

Jack, blessed with good looks, great wealth, a casually elegant style, and a bright political future, radiated a magnetic attraction for women, and he soon began to exceed his father in female conquests. As a young congressman, he had dozens of trysts, and his fellow congressman Tip O'Neill later recounted that "he had more fancy young girls flying in from all over the country than anyone could count." A female acquaintance related that he went through women at a fast clip and had no interest in anything beyond sex. "The young girls—the secretaries and the airline hostesses—they were safe grounds. They were not going to make intellectual or strong demands on him which he wasn't ready to fulfill." Gloria Emerson, who would go on to a distinguished career as a journalist and writer, met Kennedy in the 1950s, and they began an affair. "He was such a stunning figure," she recalled. "He didn't care if a woman said 'yes' or a woman said 'no.' There would be another one."[33]

Kennedy's marriage did little to alter this pattern of sexual behavior. As nearly everyone in Washington either knew or suspected, this leopard had not changed his spots upon taking the vows of matrimony. His womanizing continued nearly unabated as he slept with numerous women and his new wife struggled to accommodate to the situation. Lem Billings, a close friend of the young senator's, observed that Jackie was not "prepared for the humiliation she would suffer when she found herself stranded at parties while Jack would suddenly disappear with some pretty young girl." Another friend of Kennedy's added, "After the first year they were together, Jackie was wandering around looking like the survivor of an airplane crash." Only occasionally did she give a glimpse of her discontent. "Sometimes, when he is at home, he is so wrapped up in his work that I might as well be in Alaska," she told *Redbook* in 1957. The magazine added another tidbit, telling readers that "Jack was not with her when she had the miscarriage [of her first pregnancy]. . . . He was aboard a yacht somewhere in the Mediterranean."[34]

Most of the time, however, Kennedy was able to use his reputation as a ladies' man to enhance his public image as a vigorous, masculine figure.

Somehow, he succeeded in having it both ways: he appealed to the public, on the one hand, as a respectable married man with a beautiful wife and family and, on the other, more indirectly but equally powerfully, as a good-looking, charming young man whose sexual appeal could not be fully restrained. In other words, Kennedy's marriage supported a wholesome image without damaging his powerful female allure, creating a two-sided coin that was central to the currency of his public appeal. The handsome young leader whom women adored strode across the public landscape as a walking antidote to the emasculated, drooping organization man whose biggest expression of manliness was a weekend golf game or using his new power tools to build shelves in the rec room.

Thus Kennedy prepared his run for the White House as a symbol of revitalized American masculinity. In the years leading up to the 1960 election, he had positioned himself as the candidate of manliness, engaging in a self-conscious cultural maneuver that revealed the candidate's instinctive grasp of the American state of mind. As the presidential campaign unfolded, this image would be sharpened and projected throughout the country.

The presidential election of 1960 offered a curious contrast. In many ways, John F. Kennedy and Richard M. Nixon differed little in their policy proposals and ideological orientations: a young, moderate Democratic cold warrior versus a young, moderate Republican cold warrior. The columnist Eric Sevareid, in fact, complained that the candidates represented a dearth of political ideas and passions. "The 'managerial revolution' has come to politics and Nixon and Kennedy are its first Processed Politicians," he wrote. "They are junior executives, trained in the home office with an unerring eye to the main chance."[35]

Nevertheless, the candidates differed mightily in terms of style and personal appeal. While the Republican seemed to embody the much-lamented crisis of modern manhood, the Democrat promised a liberating escape from it. While the Republican specialized in paeans to the spirit of Dwight Eisenhower, the elderly national grandfather from the glory days of World War II, the Democrat stressed his connection to a new generation of vigorous young men ready to seize direction of American society. While the Republican reflected the conformist spirit of the modern organization man, the Democrat embodied the individualist spirit of the maverick male eager to throw off the heavy hand of tradition. This contrast of cultural styles, and images, emerged clearly as the contest unfolded.

On January 1, 1960—he would officially announce his candidacy for president the next day—Kennedy delivered a speech, titled "Are We Up to the Task?," that highlighted his masculine mystique. "As a nation we have gone soft—physically, mentally, spiritually soft," he declared. "With a tough test facing us for a generation or more, we seem to be losing our will to sacrifice and endure. . . . The slow corrosion of luxury, the slow erosion of our courage—is beginning to show." Whereas earlier, hardier Americans had displayed initiative and fortitude, now "we have cars to drive and buttons to push and TV to watch—and precooked meals and prefab houses. We stick to the orthodox, to the easy way, and the organization man." In Kennedy's view, modern Americans must decide where to stand: "Among the weak or the tough-minded? Among the lovers of comfort or the lovers of liberty?"[36]

Over the next year, Kennedy would offer the New Frontier as a rousing metaphor for his tough-minded, individualist, pioneering ethos that would define men and attract women. It was, he liked to tell audiences, a period "when the world is changing rapidly. The old era is ending. The old ways will not do. All over the world a new generation of leadership is emerging, new men to cope with new problems and new opportunities. These younger men who are coming to power are . . . men of vigor and imagination who can cast off the old slogans and delusions and suspicions." With his oft-repeated promise to "get the country moving again," the candidate insisted that the sedentary, supine spirit threatening to undermine modern masculinity—and the nation as well—could be overcome with a bracing jolt of energy. This approach included a trio of components, which he outlined repeatedly throughout the 1960 campaign.[37]

First of all, as Kennedy campaigned for the presidency, he insisted repeatedly that a tougher, more assertive stance in international affairs was necessary to overcome the sloth, decay, and defeatism that seemed to have spread at home during the Eisenhower era. Presenting himself to voters as a vigorous, forceful cold warrior, he vowed to overcome the malaise and drift encouraged by his elderly predecessor. "I would like to tell you facts that any American would like to hear. I would like to be able to say to you categorically and proudly that the United States is first in the world militarily, economically, scientifically, and educationally, and will be in the future," he declared. But such comments would be "the siren call of false content" because, in fact, American influence and prestige had slipped around the globe. Communist power was growing at a faster clip than American, Kennedy insisted, and for proof he pointed to the recent ascendancy of Fidel Castro and his Communist regime in Cuba, only ninety miles from the Florida coast, and to America's military unpreparedness as reflected in a growing "missile gap" with regard to the Soviet Union and nuclear capability. Kennedy offered a vigorous remedy. "I believe that there can only be one possible defense policy for the United States. It can be expressed in a word. That word is 'first.' I do not mean first, *but*. I do not mean first, *when*. I do not mean first, *if*. I mean first, *period*. I mean first in military power across the board," he told an audience in Michigan.[38]

Kennedy presented himself as a strong, tough-minded leader who would bring the United States back to dominance and cast his opponent as a blusterer who tried to substitute rhetoric for decisive action. Nixon, accused Kennedy, tried to hoodwink American voters with "soothing words that our prestige has never been higher and that of the Communists never lower," but such language "cannot hide the basic facts that American strength in relation to that of the Sino-Soviet bloc relatively has been slipping, and Communism has been steadily advancing." He mocked Nixon for praising his own recent verbal confrontation with the Soviet premier at an exhibition in Moscow. "Talk is cheap, words are not enough, waving our fingers under Khrushchev's face does not increase the strength of the United States," Kennedy insisted. Instead, the situation demanded an increase in American military power on all fronts: conventional weapons, nuclear weapons, delivery systems with missiles and submarines, a modernization of training and tactics. While Nixon was content with threatening rhetoric, Kennedy contended, he was ready with manly determination and firepower. As he assured a Florida audience, "I have never believed in retreating under any kind of fire."[39]

Second, Kennedy promised to overcome America's masculine degeneration and social sloth by sidestepping bureaucracy. Throughout the 1960 campaign, Kennedy offered himself as an alternative to the modern bureaucratic paper shuffler grown flabby and weak from avoiding responsibility and action. Such figures, he suggested, had taken possession of national policy during the Eisenhower era and created a stultifying atmosphere. Kennedy delighted in characterizing his opponent as all too representative of the "organization man" who took refuge in restraints and committees. Nixon, he liked to say, was little more than a glorified bureaucrat whose "grand strategy is to create a series of committees, conferences, councils, and goodwill tours" when facing any pressing issue. "But to win the peace—to prevent another war—and it will not be a war of words—we need more than words, harsh or soft, more than committees, conferences, and goodwill trips," countered Kennedy. "We need a stronger America." The times demanded a leader, not a facilitator. They demanded an individual willing to make hard decisions, not an organizational mediator striving to reach consensus. In Kennedy's words, the pressures of the Cold War demanded "a man capable of acting as Commander in Chief, not merely a bookkeeper who feels that his work is done when the numbers on the balance sheet come even." Kennedy employed a telling metaphor that suggested both his opponent's fidelity to organizational restraint and his reliance on Eisenhower's geriatric influence. "We have all seen these circus elephants complete with tusks, ivory in their head, and thick skins who move around the circus ring and grab the tail of the elephant ahead of them," Kennedy said. "Dick Nixon grabbed that tail in 1952 and 1956, but this year he faces the American people alone." [40]

Third, Kennedy worked hard during the 1960 presidential campaign to present himself as a cure for the consumer softness that had infected American society, as well as American men, and was now threatening its health. Two months before formally declaring his candidacy, the Massachusetts senator appeared at the annual Al Smith dinner in New York and emphasized this theme. In praising the former Democratic Party nominee, Kennedy argued that Smith's "battle against sloth and drift and decay" in the 1920s provided a lesson for the present. Now, once again, "life in our time is gay and careless, prosperous and contented. People come and go, more concerned with the good life than with the good society. . . . The slow corrosion of luxury—the slow erosion of our courage—are already beginning to show." But the future would demand more of America, argued Kennedy, and if the United States hoped to prevail, its people must transcend material pursuits and embrace "a greater discipline, sacrifice, and vitality than our country has ever known. . . . The secret of freedom is a brave and happy heart."[41]

Over the following year, Kennedy returned again and again to this need to rise above the ease and self-satisfaction encouraged by consumer abundance. "We assume that the Good Life we have been enjoying here at home is somehow the same as building the Good Society here at home and abroad," he proclaimed on January 1, 1960. "We have allowed a soft sentimentalism to form the atmosphere we breathe." A few months later, in a campaign speech in Detroit, he explained his vision of an America defined not by "easy promises of a soft life—but an America that is on the move, that is shoring up its weaknesses, facing up to its challenges, living up to its name and its traditions." Nixon's famous kitchen debate—the much-publicized 1959 verbal joust between the vice president and Nikita Khrushchev in Moscow, where the latter proclaimed the coming victory of Communism and the former insisted that America's consumer abundance would guarantee the triumph of capitalism—became a special target of Kennedy's manly critique of ease and softness. The Republican, suggested the Democrat, in fact had displayed a weak and feminized sensibility in this encounter. "Mr. Nixon may be very experienced in kitchen debates," he quipped. "So are a great many other married men I know." He scorned Nixon's argument, claiming that the vice president ignored American military decline while offering a limp riposte to Khrushchev: "'You may be ahead of us in rockets, but we are ahead of you in color television.'" Kennedy's retort was disdainful: "I will take my television black and white." On the eve of the election, Kennedy summarized his position. "I do not promise an easy life in the sixties," he declared. "We will call for increased concern and effort on the part of every American. . . . Events demand it. Facts demand it. The realities of our danger demand it. And we have no choice but to respond or decline. . . . [I]f we revive the American spirit that conquered old frontiers, then we will cross the New Frontier to realize the unparalleled opportunities for freedom that lie ahead."[42]

Unfolding his grand vision of the New Frontier, Kennedy appeared before Americans as a figure of regenerated masculine spirit—courageous and assertive, vigorous and decisive, and determined to face up to the challenges of a changing world. Giving added import to this manly message was the glamorous image of the candidate himself. Kennedy, personally, stepped forward as the solution to political problems of the age and the general spirit of malaise that many saw gripping the country and its male population. Some observers grasped this fact. *Time,* in noting the Democratic candidate's stress on the decline threatening America, observed, "Kennedy's panacea for these problems is simple: himself. Elect me, he says, and I will start the U.S. moving forward again. . . . His politics are essentially to be for Kennedy, with complete faith that Kennedy will be good for whatever cause he chooses to lead." The same magazine, in another article, noted that much of the young senator's appeal "lay in the force of his own youthful and confident personality, which seemed to promise freshness and vigor." Despite a political program that was often vague, Kennedy generated great appeal "with strength of personality."[43]

This projection of Kennedy's "personal" appeal relied especially on his vibrant image as a handsome "movie star" candidate, a charismatic leading man, a youthful but battle-tested hero. During the 1960 campaign, the candidate clearly emerged as a figure whose magnetic attraction went far beyond political positions and public policies. His appeal reflected the modern, media-driven public fascination with the looks and personality, the charisma and private life, the entertainment cachet and "personal touch" of the celebrity. As Richard Schickel has brilliantly argued in *Intimate Strangers: The Culture of Celebrity in America,* the modern culture of celebrity has created the "illusion of intimacy" between the viewer and the star that makes the former think that he really knows the latter. In modern celebrity culture, fame itself has become the key dynamic—what Daniel Boorstin described as the doings of those "well-known for their well-knownness"—and Kennedy took full advantage. Joseph Kennedy understood this cultural dynamic, telling reporters in the late 1950s, "Jack is the greatest attraction in the country. I'll tell you how to sell more copies of a book. Put his picture on the cover. Why is it that when his picture is on the cover of *Life* or *Redbook* they sell a record number of copies? You advertise the fact that he will be at dinner and you will break all records for attendance. He can draw more people to a fund-raising dinner than Cary Grant or Jimmy Stewart."[44]

Kennedy was well aware of the power of celebrity in modern life, and he cultivated its qualities. As a young man, he had spent some time in Hollywood and rubbed shoulders with movie stars such as Gary Cooper, Spencer Tracy, and Clark Gable. According to his friend Charles Spalding, who accompanied him, "Charisma wasn't a catchword yet, but Jack was very interested in that binding magnetism these screen personalities had. What exactly was *it*? How did you go about acquiring it? Did it have an impact on your private life? How did you make it work for you? He couldn't let the subject go." According to Spalding, "We'd spend hours talking about it." By the time of his run for the presidency, Kennedy had added to this awareness an acute appreciation of the new medium of television and its enormous power to enhance celebrity. A few weeks before officially launching his presidential bid, he wrote an article for *TV Guide* titled "A Force That Has Changed the Political Scene." Television, Kennedy argued, had emerged as a "revolutionary" force in modern politics because of its power to reach millions of people instantaneously. "Honesty, vigor, compassion, intelligence—the presence or lack of these and other qualities make up what is called the candidate's image," and television also allowed the ordinary citizen to size it up. He added, "My own conviction is that these images or impressions are likely to be uncannily correct." Moreover, the senator understood that the medium tended to favor "youth," a quality that was "definitely an asset in creating a television image people like and (most difficult of all) remember."[45]

Indeed, as the 1960 campaign developed, Kennedy's celebrity power went on full display as he traversed the United States. "When Kennedy appears on the platform or stage, the air is filled with a high-pitched squealing" that forced reporters to cover their ears, noted *Newsweek*. In reporting on one of the senator's feverish campaign swings through Pennsylvania, *Time* noted that hundreds of thousands of spectators turned out "screaming, tossing food and gifts into Kennedy's open car, waving flags." It quoted a grizzled state politician who muttered, "These people look to this fellow like a Messiah—there's never been anything like this in the history of Pennsylvania, including Roosevelt." Added the magazine, "What Kennedy said made no difference: he could have recited the Boy Scout oath and brought forth ovations." Indeed, Kennedy utilized his youth and telegenic good looks in 1960 to launch the first "modern presidential campaign," as one observer has termed it, an effort that relied on the media—not just television, but newspapers and magazines and movies—to project an image of manly sophistication and glamour. "Image" was not the whole story in 1960, this historian has written, "but because of image, as it was played that year, American elections would never be quite the same again. Growing directly out of this election would be the manufactured candidate, someone who could look good for the cameras."[46]

While Kennedy utilized his image of celebrity appeal and manly vigor, Richard Nixon, according to many observers, seemed to personify the modern masculine degeneration that the glamorous, confident Massachusetts senator promised to rectify. In news accounts, Nixon was frequently described as weak, vacillating, nervous, indecisive, and physically unattractive. William Costello, for instance, in a piece examining Nixon in *The New Republic* titled "Candidate in Search of an Identity," argued that the Republican was a man of "singular plasticity" for whom "no soil is alien, no posture is inconsistent. As a result, he has failed to distinguish between personality and character, between form and substance, between illusion and reality." Nixon, without a hard core of self and desperately seeking to adapt to circumstances, demands, and events, lacked authenticity. He was an organization man whose automatic response was to address issues with "the machinery of committees and conferences" and advocate solutions rooted in "the systematic proliferation of bureaucracy." Rather than a figure of manly determination and conviction, he stood "revealed as a man without a spiritual home . . . devoid of genuine moral commitment to either liberalism or conservatism but trying to feel at home wherever the tides of circumstance happened to lodge him." Many of the fears about the plight of the modern man—"Nixon's stature has been shrinking," noted the article—seemed to gather in the figure of the Republican candidate.[47]

Kennedy's campaign image of cool, tough, manly decisiveness found its greatest moment of triumph over Nixonian impotence in the 1960 presidential debates. Held in late September and early October, these events created a stir not only because of their novelty but because they seemed to embody the deeper cultural symbolism of the campaign. To be sure, political issues provided the stuff of these exchanges. But as *The New York Times* noted, "To what extent substantive points of debate affect a huge viewing audience like tonight's is a moot point. . . . [A]ll were intensely interested in the battle of 'images.'" The first debate, held on September 26, particularly cemented a mental picture of the two candidates in the popular mind. Kennedy appeared as the elegantly cool, naturally confident, effortlessly sophisticated, courageous symbol of manly regeneration, while Nixon came off as the shifty, sweating, weak symbol of masculine decline, the organization man wilting when pulled from behind his desk and thrust into the bright lights.[48]

Many media descriptions of that first debate focused on the contrast of two men reacting quite differently to a challenging situation. One displayed grace under pressure, and one did not. In many newspapers and magazines, Nixon was portrayed as the personification of male weakness: "faceless, ill-at-ease"; "strangely nervous, perspiring profusely, so badly made up . . . that under the baleful glare of floodlights he looked ill as well as ill at ease"; "tense, almost frightened, at turns glowering and, occasionally, haggard-looking to the point of sickness. . . . [H]e half-slouched, his 'Lazy Shave' powder faintly streaked with sweat, his eyes exaggerated hollows of blackness, his jaw, jowls, and face drooping with strain"; "clearly nervous, pacing up and down and mopping his brow." As one voter told a magazine reporter, "Why did Nixon look so scared if he's the only one tough enough to face Krushy?" His opponent offered a manly contrast with a confident, articulate, and vigorous performance. In the words of *Time,* "Kennedy was alert, aggressive and cool," while another publication described him as "calm and nerveless in appearance." As *Newsweek* summed up, the youthful senator "showed the nation that he was quite a man under fire." And many voters responded viscerally to these two opposing images.[49]

While Kennedy's bravura performance in the first presidential debate embedded his manly image among the electorate, his notorious attraction for women helped round it out during the 1960 campaign. The Democrat's sex appeal clearly emerged as a key factor in the race. References to the erotic charge emanating from the handsome young senator became ubiquitous in the many press stories on his candidacy. Murray Kempton, the legendary New York journalist, for example, described a Kennedy swing through Ohio as similar to how "Don Giovanni used to treat Seville. His progress, as ever, was an epic in the history of the sexual instinct of the American female." He described how the charismatic candidate would wave often "at a quietly pretty girl and the hand says that, if he did not have miles to go and promises to keep, he would like to walk with her where the mad river meets the still water." A journalist for *The Saturday Evening Post* described how "Kennedy's good looks and personality exercise a magnetism on the womenfolks. . . . We could see this attraction every day along the campaign trail as the gals, old and young, jumped up and down, smiled ecstatically, or uttered piercing shrieks. . . . One woman burst into tears and I asked her why she was crying: 'Because—because he's so beautiful!' "[50]

The female "jumpers" at rallies became a special hallmark of Kennedy's extraordinary physical attraction. Theodore White described how the handsome young candidate generated a powerful sexual energy among women—his language was packed with double entendres—who "would bounce, jounce, and jump as the cavalcade passed, squealing 'I seen him, I seen him.' Gradually, over the days their jumping seemed to grow more rhythmic, giving a jack-in-the-box effect of ups and down in a thoroughly sexy oscillation." *Newsweek* reported similar reactions among women as they greeted the Democrat's motorcade. "As Kennedy's car passes by, the women lining the parade route begin jumping up and down. Age makes no difference—the jumpers may be young schoolgirls, mothers with infants, middle-aged matrons, and even prim old ladies," noted a dispatch. There was also an abundance of "clutchers"—women who crossed their arms and hugged themselves, screaming, "He looked at me! He looked at me!"—and "runners," women, sometimes holding infants, who broke through police lines to get near the candidate and try to kiss him. *Time* described another female variation at a Kennedy rally in New York: "In Manhattan, a dazed girl stood in the torrent of humanity that swirled around a black convertible. 'She touched him!' shrieked her companion. 'Quick, Mary, let me touch your hand, and then Sally can touch mine, and then . . .'" The candidate's powerful aura of sexual power was palpable.[51]

Kennedy's private behavior, which lived up to his much-whispered-about reputation for female conquest, corroborated this public image. Throughout the presidential campaign in the spring and fall of 1960, the candidate indulged in numerous sexual dalliances while traveling the country. These included Pamela Turnure and Janet DesRosiers, staff members who accompanied him on the road; Judith Campbell, a beautiful young woman who became his mistress; several famous Hollywood actresses, including Marilyn Monroe and Angie Dickinson; and, more casually, many stewardesses, campaign workers, and models. The national press was complicit in abetting Kennedy's flagrant philandering. A genteel standard of reporting kept this activity from the public view, but as George Reedy, a UP reporter who later became an aide to Lyndon Johnson, admitted much later, "We knew. We all knew." Many other journalists confessed similarly. Maxine Cheshire, a longtime reporter for *The Washington Post*, frankly addressed the situation in her memoirs over fifteen years later. "Contemporary readers must feel that the Washington press corps was guilty of covering up JFK's extramarital affairs; we were," she confessed. "Even if we had written about his girl friends, our editors would never have published the information. That doesn't mean we weren't cognizant of what was going on." She went on to list several firsthand observations of JFK's philandering. A number of other leading Washington journalists—they included Robert Novak, Haynes Johnson, Hugh Sidey, James Kilpatrick, David Brinkley, Robert Donovan, Rowland Evans, Mary McGrory, Nick Kotz, Marianne Means, Bruce Morton, and Tom Wicker—later admitted to Kennedy biographers that they were well aware of his rampant womanizing. While they never wrote about it directly, this knowledge of his private behavior clearly influenced their accounts of his "public" appeal to American women.[52]

Thus JFK, throughout long months of campaigning in 1960, symbolized a new kind of national leadership that promised relief from the
festering crisis of masculinity that many commentators had warned about.
His virile male image—projected both directly and indirectly onto a screen
of national consciousness—became a crucial part of his successful run for
the White House and a key to his electoral appeal. And nothing made
this clearer than a small book on the two presidential candidates from the
very man who had sounded the alarm about the crisis of American manhood several years earlier.

Once again, Arthur Schlesinger Jr., in *Kennedy or Nixon: Does It Make
Any Difference?*, stepped forward to summarize the vibrant, compelling
masculinity of JFK's candidacy. This booklet, published during the fall of
1960, examined the two candidates and concluded that the Republican
personified the problem of the modern American male while the Democrat personified its solution. Nixon, Schlesinger argued, was "the 'other-
directed' man in politics" who sought merely "to be in harmony with the
crowd. . . . He lacks a solid sense of his own identity. . . . He remains a
strangely hollow man." For the Harvard historian, the Republican embodied the characteristics of the modern American male in crisis: bureaucratic timidity, suburban conformity, frayed identity, frantic search for
manly expression.[53]

John F. Kennedy, by contrast, offered an inspiring model for masculine
regeneration. He was pragmatic and tough-minded, Schlesinger contended, combining an "authentic war heroism" with a fondness for "the
company of intellectuals with perfect confidence in his capacity to hold his
own." He displayed genuine "taste" (defined as respect for "dignity—for
one's own dignity, and for the dignity of others") that promised to elevate
the discourse of public life. The young senator distrusted bureaucracy, dis-
dained consumer comfort, and disliked other-directedness. He embraced
an older tradition, "one whose values and purposes are implanted within
and whose fulfillment comes from the effort to realize these internal goals."
While his opponent was given to outbursts of emotion and histrionics,
Kennedy was calm and strong. In Schlesinger's words, "His is the world,
not of the sob story, nor of the high-school debater, but of serious men
trying to find serious solutions to serious problems."[54]

Thus John F. Kennedy personified an image of cool, vigorous masculine leadership in the 1960 presidential campaign. But he did not own it exclusively. Allied with the young Massachusetts senator and his quest for the White House was a collection of dynamic public figures in other areas—entertainment, literature, popular culture, journalism, space exploration, the military—who contributed to this new ethos. The Kennedy Circle, as it might be called, reinforced the candidate's masculine mystique in myriad and important ways. And none was more important than one of the most popular singers and actors of the age. A man who had joined with a number of high-profile Hollywood friends to offer a new definition of male "cool" that took the country by storm in the late 1950s and early 1960s, he became a huge supporter of the Kennedy campaign. He also emerged as an important architect of its crusade for masculine revitalization.

THREE

HOLLYWOOD COOL:
FRANK SINATRA AND THE JACK PACK

On January 19, 1961, the evening before his inauguration, President-elect John F. Kennedy took the stage at a huge Washington, D.C., gala to praise the man who had brought together a dazzling array of entertainers for the show. An audience of nearly ten thousand had gathered at the National Guard Armory to enjoy the performances of figures such as Gene Kelly, Nat King Cole, Bette Davis, Harry Belafonte, Sidney Poitier, Milton Berle, Fredric March, Anthony Quinn, Ethel Merman, and Ella Fitzgerald. The gala, a party fund-raiser as well as a celebration of Kennedy's election victory, raised several million dollars to help pay off the candidate's campaign debts. Now, standing at the microphone, the president-elect declared, "We're all indebted to a great friend—Frank Sinatra. You cannot imagine the work he has done to make this show a success. Long before he could sing, he used to poll a Democratic precinct back in New Jersey. That precinct has grown to cover the country, and long after he has ceased to sing he's going to be standing up and speaking for the Democratic Party. I thank him on behalf of all of us tonight."

Indeed, Sinatra had organized the entire show and, rumor had it, personally bought out tickets at several Broadway theaters so their star performers could be released to perform at the national capital. Now, during the festivities, he sat with the Kennedys in their box and then took the stage to sing "You Make Me Feel So Young" and "That Old Black Magic," the latter of which featured reworked lyrics: "That old Jack magic had them in its spell / That old Jack magic that he weaves so well." JFK's words of appreciation publicly acknowledged what everyone already knew: Sinatra's yeoman effort to bring Hollywood glamour to the campaign had done much to promote his election to the presidency.[1]

Indeed, by 1960 Sinatra occupied an important position in the Kennedy Circle of cultural figures along with his wildly popular Rat Pack, a cadre of close friends from the entertainment world whose shows and movies had attracted enormous attention. Including the comic and crooner Dean Martin, the singer and dancer Sammy Davis Jr., the actor Peter Lawford, and the comedian Joey Bishop, the group had become wildly popular through a series of shows at the Sands hotel in Las Vegas over the previous two years. Their hip, urbane style, musical brilliance, and comedic camaraderie defined masculine "cool" for a new generation at the dawn of the Swinging Sixties. With their tuxedos and loosened ties, onstage glasses of whiskey, casually elegant cigarettes, swinging music, and irreverent humor, the Rat Pack generated an aura of sophistication and sexual appeal with their banter about "broads," suggestive double entendres, and slangy sexual references to "ring-a-ding-dings." Sinatra's notorious reputation as a Lothario completed the image as he and his pals were constantly surrounded by a bevy of Hollywood actresses, aspiring starlets, and showgirls at lengthy after-show parties.[2]

The Rat Pack's cultural style supported a key feature of the Kennedy crusade for the White House. Like the young senator from Massachusetts who headed it, they promised a regenerated style of masculine cool that would save American males from the ravages of bureaucracy, consumer softness, and emasculation. Joining forces seemed a natural move as Kennedy and these Hollywood entertainers found much in common in the early stages of the campaign. The impact of the alliance was felt almost immediately.

Frank Sinatra's rise to superstardom had followed a serpentine path over the previous two decades. Born into modest circumstances in Hoboken,

New Jersey, in 1915, as the only child of Italian immigrants, the youth had become involved with a local gang, engaged in petty crime, and was expelled from high school for rowdy behavior and never graduated. Since hearing Bing Crosby sing at the age of sixteen, however, Sinatra had been entranced by big band music and the role of the male vocalist. He began singing professionally in the mid-1930s, performing at neighborhood saloons both as a solo act and with several local groups, winning a talent contest, and making a number of demo recordings. In 1939, Sinatra gained his first major break when the bandleader Harry James signed him to a contract. Later that year, Tommy Dorsey, leader of perhaps the hottest big band in America, persuaded the young singer to join his group, and his ascendancy to fame began. Over the next few years, Sinatra became the most popular male singer in the country, rising to the top of the polls in music magazines such as *Billboard* and *Down Beat*. Released from his Dorsey contract, he became a solo artist and began to attract rapturous attention from young female "bobby-soxers" throughout the 1940s. Screaming "Frankieee" and swooning by the thousands in a riotous atmosphere at his live shows, they made Sinatra into a major national celebrity.[3]

Sinatra had developed an intimate, smooth vocal style that reached the listener on a personal level. Crucial to his technique was a new technological advancement, the condenser microphone, which allowed the vocalist to sing more expressively, even softly, while still reaching an audience. With his warm, resonant baritone, young Sinatra adopted a free-flowing, gliding approach that sustained notes with a kind of romantic élan while embracing the rhythmic swing of dance music. The young vocalist also added subtle sensual elements to his singing—passages of breathy tenderness, controlled extensions and contractions of phrases, flashes of emotional vulnerability—that triggered an erotic reaction among his audience, particularly females. This distinctive vocal style became a crucial element in Sinatra's emergence as a heartthrob sensation.[4]

In the 1950s, Sinatra's career fluctuated wildly. When his bobby-soxer appeal faded at the start of the new decade, Columbia Records dropped him from the label in 1952. Although despondent, a determined Sinatra reinvented himself as a movie star by securing the role of a victimized Italian American soldier, Angelo Maggio, in the World War II drama *From*

Here to Eternity (1953). Sinatra's gritty, powerful performance won an Academy Award for Best Supporting Actor, and he went on to successful roles in many other films. As *The New York Times* noted in an admiring article titled "Rise, Fall, and Rise of Sinatra," the entertainer nicknamed "The Voice . . . is now more securely on top than ever—as The Actor."[5]

Sinatra also transformed himself into a serious, mature jazz singer. Jettisoning his earlier persona of boy crooner, he joined forces with the arranger Nelson Riddle and made a string of groundbreaking recordings for Capitol Records such as *In the Wee Small Hours* (1955), *Songs for Swingin' Lovers!* (1956), *Come Fly with Me* (1958), and *Only the Lonely* (1958). On these albums, Sinatra forged the mature vocal style for which he became legendary: a masculine, dynamic approach that could be swaggering at one moment, bruised and emotionally exposed at another; an impeccable, innovative legato phrasing that made every song a story and brilliantly conveyed emotions ranging from tenderness to toughness, regret to euphoria; a masterful sense of phrasing that highlighted certain words and phrases to convey the story at work in a song; and a swinging rhythmic sense that perfected what Riddle called the "heartbeat rhythm," a steady, driving beat slightly slower than most swing tunes and meant to emulate "the pulse rate of the human heart after a brisk walk." For millions of Americans who now flocked to buy his records, Sinatra simply became "The Voice." In concert with his status as a movie star, this had made him into a huge celebrity and powerful figure in Hollywood by the late 1950s. "With charm and sharp edges and a snake-slick gift of song," wrote *Time* in a cover story, "he has dazzled and slashed and coiled his way through a career unparalleled in extravagance by any other entertainer of his generation."[6]

Several personal qualities contributed to the growing Sinatra legend. His explosive temper, moodiness, and egomania triggered a penchant for brawling that regularly enveloped him in controversy. He slugged the journalist Lee Mortimer when the latter called him a "dago" at a nightclub. The singer smacked the Hollywood press agent Jim Byron when he insulted Judy Garland, whom he was accompanying to a restaurant. He (and his bodyguards) punched photographers, hotel clerks, and private citizens when they invaded his privacy or acted disrespectfully. As Sinatra once told Walter Winchell, the influential columnist, after an incident of fighting, "The creep was bothering me. When someone bothers me, I belt him." He elaborated in an interview with *Redbook* magazine: "I don't go looking for trouble, but I'll be damned if I'm going to duck it." His reputation became so bad that Don Rickles, the comedian whose act was based on good-natured insults, once called out to Sinatra in the audience, "Come on, Frank, be yourself—hit somebody." The singer's reputed Mafia connections—he was photographed with mob bosses such as Lucky Luciano and Sam Giancana—added a slight whiff of danger to this penchant for fighting.[7]

At the other emotional extreme, an extravagant, sometimes impulsive generosity also became a Sinatra hallmark. He sent flowers to singers, actors, and comedians he barely knew when they were ill in the hospital or to their wives when they were giving birth. When he heard that a manicurist at a Hollywood studio where he was working was going on vacation, he bought her an expensive luggage set and had her initials engraved on the bags. He paid the funeral expenses for older entertainers who had fallen on hard times, gave gold-plated cigarette lighters to members of his band, served as godfather for dozens of children, and chartered planes for his friends to attend shows. As one of his Hollywood pals declared of Sinatra's generosity, "He makes us all look like bums."[8]

A powerful sex appeal rounded out the Sinatra mystique. His tremendous allure for women had first surfaced during the bobby-soxer hysteria of the 1940s. This romantic, erotic charge had a way of spreading its warmth and compounding its impact. As a 1946 profile in *The New Yorker* noted, "Why is Sinatra better than Don Juan? Because Don Juan only made women want to sleep with him, while Sinatra's singing makes everybody want to sleep with everybody." In the 1950s, his erotic magnetism had evolved into a more mature, romantic image. Women loved Sinatra's unique combination of compassion and toughness, vibrant masculinity and unguarded emotions, a quality that radiated from all his work. As Deborah Kerr, who worked with him in *From Here to Eternity,* told *Woman's Home Companion,* "There's a curiously tender and vulnerable quality about Frank. That is what touches the audience—and it wants to touch back." This male sex symbol of the era, noted one publication, "casually ambles into the phantasies of females young and old, dances on the ceilings near their beds, bids them come fly with him down to Acapulco Bay. And if the real Sinatra were to make the offer, a goodly number would hop at the opportunity." The singer liked to joke that most baby boomers had been conceived with his romantic album *In the Wee Small Hours* playing in the background.[9]

The entertainer's well-publicized private life enhanced this public persona. Sinatra was a notorious ladies' man who conducted numerous affairs with well-known actresses such as Lana Turner, Marilyn Monroe, Anita Ekberg, Judy Garland, Lauren Bacall, and Angie Dickinson and had countless trysts with a host of models, waitresses, showgirls, and prostitutes. He successfully wooed the most beautiful movie star of the age, Ava Gardner, in 1951, and their volatile marriage became the stuff of breathless headlines, as did their divorce six years later. As George Jacobs, his valet from 1953 to 1968, recounted, the singer and actor had a voracious sexual appetite. He "always needed a girl, and she didn't have to be famous," wrote Jacobs. "First, he'd go for his leading lady. If she wasn't free, he'd try some famous ex. . . . Then he'd work his way down the food chain, starting with the starlets, then the hookers." Sinatra put it more succinctly to *Playboy* in 1958: "I love broads." Many women responded to the entertainer's powerful allure. A female friend in his Hollywood circle described it as a mysterious "animal magnetism," noting that when he entered a room and said "Hiya, doll" to a woman, she immediately wanted to go to bed with him. This sexual attraction became a key part of the Sinatra image.[10]

The force that welded together all of the elements, both personal and public, to create the Sinatra image was a potent masculinity. Pervading everything about this small, slender man who was not particularly handsome was a male bravado, a cool macho power and charisma that often left people awestruck. Even critics of the entertainer's love life, Anita Ekberg told a magazine in 1959, were motivated by jealousy of his virile power: "The men object because Frank is doing all the things they wish they could do. As for the women, I suspect the ones who vilify him would change their minds if Sinatra called and asked for a date." But it was the entertainer's personality, not an imposing physique or good looks, that lay at the heart of his masculine appeal. In the 1940s, it had been defined by a boyish insouciance, ready smile, and understated cockiness that made him a male idol. In the 1950s, he projected a more weathered, jaunty image of a mature man-about-town with his fedora perched at a cocky tilt, loosened collar and tie, and jacket slung casually over one shoulder, someone who had survived everything the world could throw at him and had lessons to impart. He was ferociously independent, telling a *Time* reporter in 1955, "I'm going to do as I please. I don't need anybody in the world. I did it all myself." The Sinatra image of the intense, independent, virile, yet vulnerable male who was determined to live life on his own terms became iconic. As a journalist concluded in the December 1957 issue of *Metronome,* a popular music magazine, "Frank Sinatra is the most complete, the most fantastic symbol of American maleness yet discovered."[11]

Many of Sinatra's movies reinforced this potent masculine image of swinging bachelorhood and hip urban sophistication, of the tough guy with a heart of gold who held a magnetic attraction for women. *The Tender Trap* (1955), for example, features his character, Charlie Reader, as a Broadway theatrical agent who is a swinging playboy bachelor. His fashionable apartment, stylish clothing, and cavalier treatment of the steady stream of attractive young women who come through his door became a trademark. The plot revolves around Charlie's confrontation with matrimony as he maneuvers amid his many girlfriends while harboring a growing attraction to Julie Gillis, a talented yet innocent singer and dancer determined to get married and have children, played by Debbie Reynolds. After a number of emotional complications, Julie finally captures Charlie in the "tender trap" of love and matrimony, a conventional ending that happens only after Sinatra's character enjoys many years of swinging bachelor bliss.

Pal Joey (1957) further burnished Sinatra's masculine image. The film, a Rodgers and Hart musical, revolves around Joey Evans, a singer and entertainer who becomes the headliner at San Francisco's Barbary Coast Club. He revels in a sexually liberated life with a cadre of showgirls and female customers before becoming involved with a pair of attractive women: Linda English, a young and naïve showgirl at the club, and Vera Simpson (Rita Hayworth), an older ex-stripper who is now a wealthy widow and San Francisco socialite. This playboy from the wrong side of the tracks— uneducated, wisecracking, supremely confident—maneuvers between Linda and Vera, toying with the former and repressing his genuine feelings for her while romancing the latter to persuade her to finance the opening of his own club, Chez Joey. Ultimately, Vera tires of his ploys and rescinds her financial support, shutting down the opening of Chez Joey. As a bitter Joey departs San Francisco to start over, Linda chases after him to proclaim her love. Joey initially resists but then agrees that they can be together, once again nodding to the prevailing cultural standards of the era, and they walk into the sunset framed by the Golden Gate Bridge. Despite this sentimental conclusion, Sinatra emerged from the film with his charm and male appeal intact.[12]

In 1960, with the start of a new decade, however, this masculine icon reached a peak of popularity as he embarked on a new venture in his entertainment career. Sinatra began a series of highly publicized appearances with a group of fellow entertainers who captured the American imagination with their irreverent repartee, singing and dancing, and casually elegant male style. The Rat Pack, as they were quickly termed in the press, became the hottest entertainers in the country in a series of legendary Las Vegas shows that accompanied their filming of a movie set in the same city. Their nightly performances combined bravado, machismo, a swinging, partying lifestyle, a glamorous send-up of "square" social norms, and an aura of sexual power and conquest. Sinatra's Rat Pack came to embody the very definition of male "cool" at the dawn of a new, post-Eisenhower era.

Originally, the name had been applied to Humphrey Bogart and a cadre of moviemaking friends (including Sinatra) who had formed the Holmby Hills Rat Pack to enjoy manly pursuits of drinking, gambling, witty conversation, and club hopping. Following Bogart's death, Sinatra formed his own version of the Rat Pack with several entertainers he had grown close to over the years: the singer Dean Martin, the singer and dancer Sammy Davis Jr., the actor Peter Lawford, and the comic Joey Bishop. Although a number of auxiliary members would spring up over the years, this quintet of Hollywood figures formed the primary group. It was a diverse, sparkling collection of talent.

Dean Martin had come from a working-class background in Ohio. First singing with local bands, he slowly worked his way up through the vocal ranks like a number of other Italian American crooners such as

Perry Como and Tony Bennett. Martin had an attractive personality and nonchalant sense of humor, and while performing in New York in 1946, he struck gold. He met the comedian Jerry Lewis, and they joined forces. The handsome crooner played straight man with a perfect sense of timing, while the manic Jewish comic ran amok displaying a vast array of out-landish physical gags and rubber-faced expressions. Over the next decade, Martin and Lewis became the biggest act in American show business. After they split in 1956, Martin went on to record a number of popular albums and took several minor roles in the movies. He crossed paths with Sinatra on several occasions as fellow recording artists on Capitol Rec-ords, and the two soon began palling around. They appeared together on several television specials, and Sinatra occasionally joined Martin on-stage during his shows, to the great delight of the audiences.[13]

Sammy Davis Jr., a prodigiously talented singer and dancer, had dazzled audiences in African American clubs and theaters—the famous "chitlin' circuit"—since he had first appeared onstage as a child prodigy at the age of three. The offspring of a marriage between two vaudeville dancers, he grew up dancing with his father as part of the Will Mastin Trio. Davis displayed great physical fluidity and grace along with a soaring tenor voice that was featured on several albums. By the 1950s, he had recorded title tracks for several Hollywood movies, starred in a Broadway play, and reg-ularly appeared at Las Vegas nightclubs. Davis had met Sinatra in 1941, after which the Italian American singer took him under his wing and nurtured his career. Sinatra often had him as an opening act and packed Davis's shows with his show business friends whenever he appeared in Los Angeles. When Davis had a horrible automobile crash in 1954 and suffered the loss of his left eye, Sinatra helped him recuperate and encour-aged him to resume performing. (This recuperation period saw Davis's unusual conversion to Judaism.) Within a few years, he had branched out as an actor. By 1960, this small, physically graceful, and highly energetic man, like Sinatra and Martin, had emerged as one of the brightest, most multitalented stars in Hollywood.[14]

Peter Lawford, an Englishman, came to the Rat Pack from a stellar act-ing career in Hollywood. Tall, handsome, debonair, and possessed of impeccable manners and some dancing talent, he had found his way into films as a contract actor with MGM in the 1940s. In the following decade, the urbane, elegant Lawford settled into a series of supporting film roles and occasional television appearances. A legendary swain, he was romantically linked to a series of Hollywood actresses such as Lana Turner, Rita Hayworth, Anne Baxter, Judy Garland, and June Allyson. He also became friends with Sinatra in the late 1950s and along with his wife, Patricia Kennedy Lawford, sister of Senator John F. Kennedy, he became a regular visitor to Sinatra's Palm Springs home.[15]

Joey Bishop, "the Hub of the Big Wheel" for the Rat Pack, as Sinatra once described him, had been raised in South Philadelphia as the youngest child of Jewish immigrant parents. As a comic, he climbed through the entertainment ranks working the borscht belt circuit in the Catskills and small East Coast nightclubs. He was often billed as "the Frown Prince of Comedy" for the deadpan, even morose quality of his comedic stage persona. In 1952, Bishop met Sinatra in New York, the two hit it off, and Bishop opened for the singer whenever he played large venues around New York. Appearing as an average guy casting a doleful eye on the world and its myriad impositions, he had a knack for breaking up his famous friend, once replying to Sinatra's question about the crowd as he prepared to go on, "Great for *me*. I don't know how they'll be for *you*." By the mid-1950s, he was making regular television appearances and taking small movie roles, as in the cinematic adaption of Norman Mailer's famous war novel, *The Naked and the Dead* ("I played both parts," he deadpanned).[16]

The Rat Pack came together in 1959, when Sinatra and Davis showed up at Martin's show at the Sands hotel in Las Vegas and joined him onstage and performed a couple of numbers together. The audience went wild. Within a few weeks, Bishop and Lawford started joining them, and a more official grouping began. This launched the famous "Summit" shows—playfully named after the gatherings of world leaders taking place in this period—at the Sands in early 1960. With hundreds of patrons crowding into the room (and thousands more clamoring for tickets) and dozens of Hollywood stars flying in to be part of the scene, these appearances soon attracted massive press attention.

The shows were largely improvised, although certain gags and songs were placed at regular intervals to create a loose structure for the proceedings.

The evening began with a Joey Bishop introduction of Dean Martin: "And now, direct from the bar . . ." Martin sauntered onstage with a large tumbler of liquor, soaked up the ovation, and then stage-whispered to the band leader, "How did all these people get in my room?" He then began a song but worked it for laughs with silly lyrics such as "the gentleman is a tramp" while tickling the audience with a knowing look of feigned unawareness that said, "We all know the showbiz game is just a lark." Then Sinatra replaced him onstage to do a couple of serious songs—always fast and swinging—and Davis followed with a favorite tune and a display of his incredible tap-dancing skills. Davis and Lawford then joined forces for a soft-shoe dance routine.

At this point, all five Rat Packers convened, and the high jinks began. They wheeled a bar cart onstage and poured large glasses of whiskey (or what looked like whiskey) to imbibe as they joked, bantered, and hazed one another and wandered the stage in various combinations. A genial pandemonium ensued. Sinatra performed a couple of hits from his popular albums, for instance, while the others heckled him from the sidelines. Martin would be in mid-song when Lawford and Bishop strolled across the stage behind him clad in tuxedo jackets and boxer shorts with their pants folded neatly across their arms waiter-style. Davis introduced one of his tunes, and Sinatra marched onstage beating a bass drum lettered "Eat at Puccini" (his restaurant) as the band struck up the martial music from the movie *Bridge on the River Kwai.*

The Rat Pack shows projected an image of irreverent, sophisticated urbanity that was the very definition of modern "cool." Each participant, with his tuxedo tie loosened, cradling a liquor glass and languidly waving a cigarette while cracking one-liners, contributed to the atmosphere. Martin displayed an amiable, ostensibly booze-addled take on the world that reveled in irony and bemused detachment. Davis appeared as the earnestly striving entertainer, hip to the latest trends, often bending over to slap his knees at the least witticism, who almost desperately utilized every ounce of his massive talent to win the approval of his audience. Lawford personified the elegant movie-star sex symbol with his sophisticated English accent, winning smile, and matinee-idol good looks. Bishop came across as the world-weary cynic whose wisecracks illuminated the absurd aspects of life. Sinatra, of course, was the kingpin, the centerpiece, "The Leader" as the others called him, who personified the coolness of the ensemble with his stylish singing, irreverent comments, and powerful personal charisma. His allure for women also figured prominently. As one of his gang always yelled from the wings when he swung into the Cole Porter classic "What Is This Thing Called Love?," "If *you* don't know, we're all dead!"

In fact, Sinatra's abundant sex appeal reflected an essential element in the Rat Pack shows. These sophisticated, attractive male Hollywood entertainers generated a sexual charge that suggested the dawning of a new cultural era. Their virile, worldly presence radiated an erotic attraction, while their stage banter featured a special slang that was often sexual in connotation. The Rat Pack's knowing references to "ring-a-ding-dings," "clydes," "charlies," "broads," and "chicky-babies" created an atmosphere that tantalized the audience with visions of sensual adventure. This public image was reinforced by the Rat Pack's well-publicized sexual shenanigans in Las Vegas as the group consorted into the early hours of the morning after nearly every performance with a revolving cast of beautiful actresses, showgirls, and newfound female friends. Bishop only highlighted the atmosphere when he mocked his own inability to keep up. Because he was working with four big stars, he confessed to the audience, he had been denied a dressing room and was forced to dress with the chorus girls "on the honor system." "They're very nice girls, though," he said. "I just spoke to one and she said 'no.'"

The Rat Pack shows also emphasized racial and ethnic themes. The group was decidedly eclectic in its social makeup—two Italian Americans, an African American (who had converted to Judaism), a Jew, and an immigrant Englishman—with not one traditional American WASP among them. Not only was it daring in itself to have an interracial act in 1961, but the Rat Pack mocked a host of restrictive attitudes about minorities and immigrants that still persisted in traditional American society. They joked about prevailing racial, ethnic, and religious stereotypes, often playing off the very ones that dogged each member's own social type. Bishop often took the lead here by skewering Italian and Jewish images. "Frank and Dean are going to come out and tell you about some of the *good* work the Mafia is doing," he quipped. When the two Italians had playfully derided him about some shortcoming, he feigned anger and warned them to watch out for retribution because "I got my own group, the Matzia." He regularly cracked up the Copa Room audience during a lull in the show by looking into the distance and saying wistfully, "Sometime I want to work in a room where there's a Jewish orchestra and Spanish people are dancing."

Much of the Rat Pack's repartee focused on racial prejudice, aiming to ridicule it, and racial tension, aiming to defuse it. Sinatra had long advocated racial equality, even making a short film, *The House I Live In* (1945), that denounced racial and ethnic prejudice and condemning bigotry as a "disease" in a 1958 article titled "The Way I Look at Race" in *Ebony*. But now Davis became the central figure in the Rat Pack's maneuvers. When Lawford appeared onstage near the beginning of the show and suggested they do a tap dance number, Davis asked, "Do you realize I happen to be one of the greatest Jewish Mau Mau dancers?" When Lawford replied indignantly, "I'm not prejudiced," Davis answered, "I know your kind. You'll dance with me but you won't go to school with me." Bishop commented on "The Clan," another nickname the press had given the group. "Clan, clan, clan! I'm sick and tired of hearing things about the clan. Just because a few of us guys get together once a week with sheets over our head . . . ," he joked. Then Davis, straight-faced, asked innocently, "Would I belong to an organization known as the clan?" At some point during the shows, Martin always walked onstage carrying the smallish Davis in his arms and announced pompously, "I would like to present this special award from the NAACP," causing Davis to declare indignantly, "Put me down!" Davis saved the best line for himself, telling the audience, "I'm colored, Jewish, and Puerto Rican. When I move into a neighborhood, I wipe it out."[17]

With the genial mayhem, glamorous imagery, and irreverent social commentary of their famous Las Vegas shows, the Rat Pack launched a swinging assault on "square" America—the conforming, suburban, staid middle-class culture of the Eisenhower years. Sinatra and company strode forward as cultural pioneers of the Swinging Sixties with an agenda of sexual revolution and casual disdain for the norms of middle-class family life. As one magazine put it, the Rat Pack was "supremely free of the rules and almost never earthbound." Entertaining and partying, swinging and cracking wise, embracing recreational sex and liberated views on race, the group made it clear that their goal was not family solidarity or bureaucratic advancement or suburban comfort but sophisticated enjoyment and female conquest. Martin, for instance, habitually told the audience in a poke at the "personality" model of success, "On your way out, please buy a copy of my latest book, *The Power of Positive Drinking*." As a contemporary observer of the Rat Pack scene noted, Sinatra and his gang represented "a kind of jaunty and irreverent good humor that has vanished from American life . . . what many of us, sodden with the Eisenhower conformity that weighed us down for those eight dreary and unthinking years, wish our government itself had been saying all during this time."[18]

As they launched cool's assault on square—erecting what one observer described as "the billboard for the zeitgeist of a swinging new age"—the Rat Pack projected an assertive, stylish, cool masculinity. They exuded a new male ideal that departed sharply from the standard suburban male of 1950s America and presented an antidote to the fears of multiplying, and stultifying, organization men, suburban dads, and emasculated males. The five entertainers displayed "talent, charm, romance and a devil-may-care nonconformity . . . a wild iconoclasm that millions envy secretly or even unconsciously—which makes them, in the public eye, the innest in-group in the world," as one magazine described them. Clearly, the Rat Pack understood and relished this prominence. Bishop often began a show at the Sands by walking to the microphone and adopting a sincere, just-between-us tone. "There's a tendency on a night like this to be a little nervous," he confided to the audience. "Please don't be."[19]

Ocean's Eleven, the movie being filmed during the daytime hours prior to the Summit shows, provided a cinematic vehicle for the Rat Pack's strong male sensibility. The plot involves a group of ex-commandos from World War II, led by Sinatra's Danny Ocean, who plan an elaborate heist to rob five Las Vegas casinos on New Year's Eve and walk away with millions of dollars. Their complex plan works like clockwork as they disrupt power to the casinos, hold up the cashiers in the confusion, and sneak the money out in trash cans.

The movie radiated Rat Pack cool. The characters played by Sinatra, Martin, and Lawford are bachelor playboys who effortlessly attract women, strolling through the film joking and drinking, gliding out of close scrapes, and facing their task with bravado and confidence and a devil-may-care sophistication. The Rat Pack connection is underlined in the final scene of the film when Ocean's gang walks down the street outside the Sands hotel and passes beneath the large neon sign advertising a show by Sinatra, Martin, Davis, Lawford, and Bishop.

Ocean's Eleven also highlights a powerful masculinity among this band of brothers, one that had been forged in World War II but frustrated by the materialistic, conformist social milieu of postwar society. The heist gives the ex-soldiers an opportunity to revive their masculine vigor. The successful heist, in Ocean's words, is "a military operation, executed by trained men."[20]

Overall, *Ocean's Eleven* offers a wonderful cultural expression of early 1960s masculine revival. It tells the tale of a regenerated, war-forged masculinity triumphing over a money-fixated, emasculating system that has muffled such a spirit. But as would be true with the historical fate of this male crusade, the film's darkly humorous surprise ending casts this victory into the shadows of irony. Trying to sneak their take of several million dollars out of Las Vegas in the casket of a colleague who has died from a heart attack during the robbery, Ocean's group is double-crossed by fate when the widow unexpectedly cremates her husband's body (and all the money along with it). Despite this twist, Sinatra and his gang strode out of this film as larger-than-life symbols of the vigorous, stylish modern male who was determined to beat the system.

Perhaps the biggest boost to the Rat Pack's brand of vigorous masculinity, however, came from the group's association with a serious public figure. A young senator in pursuit of the American presidency became enamored of their legendary Las Vegas shows, and a growing friendship soon moved Sinatra and his friends from the arena of entertainment onto a much larger stage. The Rat Pack's iconic cultural style began transforming American political life at the dawn of a new decade.

Frank Sinatra came from a strong Democratic background—his mother had been a party ward heeler in New Jersey and his family reverent supporters of FDR—and after becoming a star, he served as a strong liberal figure in Hollywood and campaigned for Harry Truman and Adlai Stevenson. He attended the 1956 Democratic convention to sing the national anthem and then remained to observe the political maneuvering when Stevenson threw open the vice presidential nomination and Kennedy almost won with a last-minute surge. Sinatra saw the youthful, charismatic politician as a future star in the party. Most likely, the senator and the singer became personally acquainted in 1958 at the Santa Monica home of Kennedy's brother-in-law Peter Lawford, where they both attended parties. JFK, for his part, had nourished a strong interest in Hollywood since his father's days as a studio mogul, and he remained fascinated by its glittering social life. For these two powerful and ambitious men, a connection seemed almost inevitable. By November 1959, their friendship had grown to the point that Kennedy extended a political trip in Southern California and stayed two nights at Sinatra's Palm Springs estate.[21]

The entertainer and the politician shared a certain commonality of experience as glamorous public figures. In 1946, when he entered the political arena, Kennedy's tremendous attraction for women as a candidate had often been compared to the singer's bobby-soxer appeal, which was in full bloom at the time. "We'd go to the junior colleges, women's colleges and he'd come in there like Frank Sinatra in the early days. They would scream and holler and touch him. . . . I mean, these girls were just crazy about him," said Kennedy's good friend Paul "Red" Fay. When Kennedy spoke at East Boston High School, the girls swooned, and many of them screamed, "Sinatra!" His campaign manager, noting that female enthusiasm was at a high pitch, described how "the girls sort of saw a Sinatra of politics." In the 1960 election, upon observing Kennedy's swoon-inducing effect on a large group of female supporters, a reporter for *The Boston Globe* declared, "It's like watching a crowd of Frank Sinatra fans."[22]

A practical connection between the two men emerged when Peter Lawford became part of Sinatra's Rat Pack. The English actor had married Jack's sister Pat in April 1954, and he soon ushered Kennedy into the Rat Pack circle. Sinatra jokingly called him the "Brother-in-Lawford," and the actor made light of the attraction between the two stars: "Let's just say that the Kennedys are interested in the lively arts, and that Sinatra is the liveliest art of all." But as the Kennedy-Sinatra friendship developed, it became apparent that each man saw a deep appeal in the world of the other. And each wanted to taste it.[23]

For Kennedy, Sinatra represented the glittering social world of Hollywood with its movie stars, sophisticated social mores, and erotic charge. The senator, since his adolescence, had visited the movie capital and enjoyed the company he found there. The creativity of moviemakers intrigued him—Kennedy was a movie buff and saw films frequently from young adulthood through his tenure in the White House—and beautiful actresses attracted him even more. Sinatra, as perhaps the most powerful figure in Hollywood by 1960, provided access to that world, and Kennedy leaped at the chance. Not only did the entertainer introduce him to the most prominent movie stars and entertainers of the age, but he provided numerous stories about their private lives and peccadilloes. As Kenneth O'Donnell, an aide and close friend of Kennedy's, explained, "His fondness for Frank Sinatra, which perplexed a lot of people, was simply based on the fact that Sinatra told him a lot of inside gossip about celebrities and their romances in Hollywood." The singer's legendary appeal to women, of course, cemented his fascination for the politician, who marveled at Sinatra's success as a Lothario. As one woman, who had affairs with both men, later confessed, Kennedy had a favorite topic he always raised "on the telephone and in person. He would say, 'Who's Frank seeing now?' or 'I heard Frank is seeing so-and-so and isn't she married?' . . . What was Frank doing? Was it true that he was seeing Janet Leigh?"[24]

For Sinatra, the world of John F. Kennedy represented social respectability, political power, and genuine public influence. For the intensely ambitious entertainer who had fought his way to fame from the wrong side of the tracks, such qualities were immensely attractive. They defined a new world to conquer. In the late 1950s, Joseph Kennedy had played to these aspirations when he visited Southern California during the formative stage of the campaign and urged Sinatra to back his son for the presidency. According to an inside observer in the Sinatra camp, the crafty old man suggested to the singer that "the road to power would be his road to respect, and that road was the road to the White House in 1960. He dangled ambassador to Italy, he threw out the idea of senator from Nevada." Sinatra took the bait hard. Helping Kennedy succeed would provide a kind of legitimacy that even Hollywood could never bestow. "JFK conveyed a weight and solidity suggestive of Harvard, summers on the Cape, lazy days surrounded and protected by a vivacious family. All that the bright, garish Rat Pack lifestyle—a blue-collar fantasy of what it meant to be rich— eminently lacked," declared a historian of Hollywood's politics. "Kennedy's favor gave Sinatra respectability—a reason to be admired, not just feared, by his peers."[25]

In fact, Sinatra might have eased Lawford into the Rat Pack for a cynical reason. In private, the singer often denigrated the affable, dissolute actor as "cheap, weak, sneak, and freak," according to a Sinatra friend. But then Joseph Kennedy began painting a rosy future for a Kennedy-Sinatra alliance, and Pat Kennedy, Lawford's wife, who had a crush on Sinatra for many years, persuaded Gary and Rocky Cooper to invite them and the singer to a party in 1958. The possibility of a friendship "opened Mr. S's eyes to the even more exciting prospect of John Kennedy." When the Lawfords had a daughter in 1958 they named her Victoria Francis, honoring both JFK's recent Senate reelection victory and the first name of their favorite singer. Around the same time, Sinatra cast Lawford in his new movie, and the two became partners in a new restaurant, Puccini. Thus the inclusion of "the Brother-in-Lawford" in the Rat Pack, when everyone recognized him as the weak link, was probably less about genuine friendship and more about establishing a dependable connection to Kennedy.[26]

But the bond between Kennedy and Sinatra's Rat Pack also had a broader social dimension that transcended personal considerations. Like these multiethnic entertainers, the parvenu politician was an outsider seeking to break into the existing power structure. For the Rat Pack, it meant the triumph of Italian, Jewish, and African American ethnic and racial minorities as they climbed the social ladder to success, the ultimate assimilation of urban immigrants as they took the modern show business world by storm. In the words of one observer, "This was something completely different, stars at the pinnacle of American entertainment who acted as if style and class and success were not at all incompatible with ethnic identification, whose act in fact proclaimed that they were truly American *because* they were Italian, or black, or Jewish." For Kennedy, the aspiring Irish American Catholic from Boston, a similar impulse meant ending the stranglehold of a WASP sensibility on American political culture. In this act of social rebellion and second-generation upward mobility, Kennedy and the Rat Pack shared a deep commonality of purpose.[27]

In more potent cultural terms, Kennedy's vibrant masculinity closely matched that of the Rat Pack. A kindred spirit of sophisticated male vigor pulled them together as they sought to loosen the postwar constraints on men imposed by bureaucracy, suburbia, and family. The youthful senator, with his glamorous image and sex appeal, cool elegance and war-hero past, seemed anything but a white-collar organization man. This coincided perfectly with the members of the Rat Pack, who embodied a male fantasy described by one critic as "a life without rules, without the constraints of fidelity, monogamy, sobriety, and the dreary obligation to show up for a job every morning. For Sinatra and his cronies, life seemed a canvas with no borders." These vigorous, virile men from the worlds of politics and show business wanted to have it all, not only public success, but private carnal fulfillment, a life "lived more fully than anyone else in their time. To a remarkable degree for a politician in the public eye, Kennedy shared the Rat Pack life of parties and beautiful women." Kennedy was everything the Rat Pack envisioned themselves to be, and vice versa.[28]

Thus the stage was set for the public announcement of the Kennedy–Rat Pack alliance: the senator's attendance at the entertainers' Summit show on February 7, 1960. JFK was on a western campaign swing during the presidential primary season, and he stopped by Las Vegas for a few days to enjoy the scene. When he appeared at the Copa Room at the Sands and sat at a table near the stage, Sinatra stopped the proceedings and introduced him as the "next President of the United States," and the crowd rose to its feet applauding. Martin brought down the house when he sauntered up to Sinatra and loudly whispered, "What did you say his name was?" Kennedy also visited the set of *Ocean's Eleven* to observe the filming and from his suite in the Sands joined in the post-Summit revelries that went into the early morning hours. The young senator, in other words, became part of the aura radiating from the Rat Pack's glamorous endeavors. The following year, Richard Gehman, in his popular 1961 book on Sinatra and the Clan, listed "John F. Kennedy, President," as an official "Rat Pack Affiliate."[29]

In part, Kennedy's Las Vegas visit with the Rat Pack was political. The senator, according to Sammy Davis, sat up late with the entertainers one evening and talked about the campaign and his quest for the presidency. They agreed that they would try to rally the show business community to his side, and Sinatra would take the lead role. "Frank's plan was twofold. First, we would root around and get all the pals to do benefits to raise money for the senator. Second, we would try to get the support of all the major stars for Kennedy rallies. Kennedy was excited and grateful for this support," said Davis. Ultimately, Davis was unsure if the Rat Pack's support was crucial to their candidate's election, "but during those nights of animated conversation back in Las Vegas we *thought* we could make a big difference. We got caught up completely in the Kennedy optimism, and it was an exciting time for all of us, especially Frank. It was very much Sinatra's baby, and he played it to the hilt." In part, the Kennedy visit to Las Vegas was financial. During one evening when the candidate had joined the Rat Pack for drinks in their rooms, Lawford whispered to Davis, "If you want to see what a million dollars in cash looks like, go into the next room; there's a brown leather satchel in the closet. It's a gift from the hotel owners for Jack's campaign."[30]

But Kennedy's visit to Las Vegas also involved more earthy desires. In this hotbed of masculine sexual energy, Kennedy joined Sinatra and his pals in another aspiration: the pursuit and enjoyment of attractive females, and lots of them. The parties-and-women scene at the Summit appealed greatly to the young senator with the notorious sex appeal (and appetite), and with his womanizing impulses at full throttle he propelled himself headlong into the sexual high jinks surrounding the Rat Pack. In Las Vegas, and then later at Lawford's Santa Monica beachfront home and other hangouts of the Rat Pack, Sinatra introduced Kennedy to several prominent actresses, including Marilyn Monroe and Angie Dickinson, with whom he would have intermittent liaisons over the next few years. Along with Lawford, Sinatra also supplied the candidate with numerous less famous but equally willing partners. When JFK was partying with the Rat Pack after their Summit show, Davis later recalled, "I was also told there were four wild girls scheduled to entertain him . . . and I got out of there. Some things you don't want to know." Within a short time, the FBI was investigating the sexual shenanigans of Kennedy, Sinatra, and Lawford: "indiscreet parties" in Palm Springs, late-night orgies in Las Vegas where "show girls from all over town were running in and out of the Senator's suite," assignations in New York City with "mulatto prostitutes," and dalliances with a "high-priced call girl" and an "airline hostess." As an FBI investigator reported, a worried JFK campaign manager confided that "there are certain sex activities by Kennedy that he hopes never are publicized."[31]

In Las Vegas, Sinatra also made a connection that initially bound him to Kennedy more tightly but would ultimately have far-reaching, corrosive consequences. The singer introduced Judith Campbell, a beautiful, dark-haired former Sinatra mistress—in terms of looks, she was often compared to Elizabeth Taylor—to the presidential candidate, and the two soon struck up a sexual relationship that lasted through the campaign and most of his presidency. Kennedy, she noted, "had sex appeal. And he knew it." As an intimate of both powerful men, she had an up-close view of their bond. Sinatra, she noted, seemed drawn by Kennedy's status as a public figure with legitimate political power and position. During a dinner with Peter and Pat Lawford, she observed, "Frank was all ears as Pat analyzed Jack's chances in the coming primaries. He seemed so subdued and respectful. . . . 'Jack's a great guy [he said]. And don't forget, he's my friend. I know how to help my friends.'" For his part, Kennedy was fascinated by Sinatra's Hollywood lifestyle and enormous attraction for women, and he pumped Campbell for information about the singer's latest female conquests. Kennedy loved gossip about Sinatra, and Hollywood in general, and would often say, "I don't want the phony stuff. I want the real inside dope." The candidate also was intrigued by the singer's charismatic and volatile personality. "He thought Frank's temperament was a riot," Campbell reported. "He was amused at the havoc Frank could cause and at the way people around him would cower in fear."[32]

Thus Kennedy's friendship with Sinatra and his friends took shape around common qualities of glamour, sexual power, and potent masculinity at the outset of a new decade. With the aura of Hollywood surrounding him, Kennedy sharpened an image as he strode onto the public stage: the political leader as a virile, handsome leading man with abundant sex appeal. And as the presidential campaign unfolded throughout 1960, that powerful masculine image would be further enhanced as the Rat Pack leaped fully into the electoral fray.

Fate seems to have preordained that the 1960 Democratic convention would be held in Los Angeles, the home of the movies. As the party faithful gathered there in early July to nominate a presidential candidate, a Hollywood atmosphere prevailed. The *New York Times* noted, "There was a patina of glamour provided by the presence of notorious faces, which politicians normally see only on the covers of movie magazines." On July 10, the night before the nominating session, Sinatra helped set the tone by organizing an expensive dinner for Hollywood donors at the Beverly Hilton hotel. A galaxy of stars appeared among the twenty-eight hundred attendees: not only the Rat Pack, but Judy Garland, Milton Berle, Joe E. Lewis, George Jessel, Angie Dickinson, Mort Sahl, Janet Leigh, Tony Curtis, and many others. "There were so many people there they needed two ballrooms to put on the show," Davis recounted. "We all entertained in both rooms. Frank did his piece, then me." Sinatra and Garland sat on the dais with Kennedy, Lyndon Johnson, Adlai Stevenson, Stuart Symington, and Eleanor Roosevelt.[33]

When the convention opened on July 11, 1960, the Rat Pack, joined by other movie stars such as Janet Leigh, Tony Curtis, Edward G. Robinson, Nat King Cole, Lee Marvin, Hope Lange, and Shirley MacLaine, sang the national anthem. Sinatra and his buddies were in the thick of things as they talked up delegates and schmoozed with party officials. "We all called Kennedy Jack, and the whole thing was very pally, more like a star-studded party than a convention," Davis recalled. Then, on July 12, Sinatra watched the convention's nominating night on television with Joe and Bobby Kennedy, Peter Lawford, and various members of the candidate's entourage at the Marion Davies mansion in Beverly Hills, which the Kennedy patriarch had rented for the duration. When Kennedy's nomination was finally secured, an exuberant Sinatra slapped Lawford on the back. "We're on our way to the White House, buddy boy!" he proclaimed. "*We're on our way to the White House!*"[34]

Meanwhile, privately, Kennedy reveled in his Rat Pack cachet during his stay in Los Angeles for the convention. He spent much of an evening partying at Lawford's Santa Monica home with Hollywood stars. After he took Janet Leigh for a spin on the dance floor, the dazzled actress enthused, "Imagine a possible president dancing with just a girl like me." Typically, Kennedy also indulged in a number of sexual trysts. Judith Campbell, who lived in Los Angeles, noted that on the night of July 11 the senator requested her to come to his hotel room and then tried to set up a ménage à trois with another young woman in attendance. Campbell angrily rejected the scheme and fled. Kennedy also dallied with a pliant Marilyn Monroe. During dinner with Lawford on July 12, the actress related, with a wink and a nod, that she and Kennedy had spent time together earlier in the afternoon and that the senator had been "very democratic" and "very penetrating" in his performance.[35]

Following the convention, the Rat Pack—now christened the Jack Pack—joined the Kennedy campaign. Sinatra, particularly, threw himself into various efforts throughout the late summer and the fall. According to Kennedy's aide Thomas M. Rees, Sinatra turned up regularly at strategy sessions of Kennedy and his team held at Lawford's oceanfront house. In early September, the singer appeared at a fund-raiser and campaign rally for two thousand women held at the home of the actress Janet Leigh and her husband, the actor Tony Curtis. Sinatra was so overwhelmed by female admirers that he gave two performances, each time singing three songs to the adoring crowd. As he told a reporter in attendance, he "hoped to be very active in the Kennedy campaign." And indeed, he was. Over the next several weeks, he appeared jointly with Eleanor Roosevelt in a radio appeal for the senator. He lent the campaign his private airplane and persuaded stars such as Ella Fitzgerald, Milton Berle, Bobby Darin, Nat King Cole, Steve Allen, and Jayne Meadows to appear at campaign events. Sinatra hosted a special concert for Kennedy in Hawaii with Lawford, and then in late October he attended a huge rally of over forty thousand Kennedy supporters in New Jersey. Typically, Sinatra did not speak at these rallies but enlivened them by singing "High Hopes," the lyrics of which the songwriter Sammy Cahn had reworked for the Kennedy campaign:

K-E-double-N-E-D-Y, Jack's the nation's favorite guy.
Everyone wants to back Jack, Jack is on the right track.
And he's got HIGH HOPES, he's got HIGH HOPES,
He's got high-apple-pie-in-the-sky hopes.[36]

Sinatra also helped with fund-raising for the Kennedy campaign. He helped establish a crucial conduit for Hollywood money, raising many thousands of dollars by tapping his friends and associates in the show business world. Milt Ebbins, talent manager and liaison between Hollywood and JFK's people, described how Sinatra would use his influence on the financial front: "Frank snapped his fingers and people fell into line. He'd get on the phone to somebody and before you knew it he'd be saying, 'Gotcha down for ten thousand' and that would be the end of it. Frank was fantastic." Even more, Sinatra lavishly contributed his own money to the Democratic Party and the Kennedy campaign. "When you did an event with Sinatra," said Joseph R. Cerrell, the executive director of the California Democratic Party, "let me tell you what that meant. I'm telling you he got the other performers, he got the orchestra, he paid the orchestra. He paid the limos. It was rare that you got bills. . . . [When he lent his private plane] I mean, we didn't pay the gas, much less the food, much less the crew." This barrage of activity seemed to energize Sinatra. "During the Kennedy campaign, I had never seen Mr. S happier," said his valet and friend, George Jacobs. "Now he had a purpose, a higher purpose, than Hollywood stardom. 'We're gonna take this mother, George,' he'd say constantly."[37]

The rest of the Rat Pack also chipped in. Martin, whose cynicism about politics made him an infrequent campaigner, nonetheless claimed that Kennedy planned to appoint him "Secretary of Liquor." Davis, who joined the effort more enthusiastically, made appearances in some twenty large cities and often joked that he also nurtured cabinet ambitions in the new administration. "I'm hoping for Jerusalem, but I'll be lucky if I get Kenya," he quipped. Lawford appeared at a number of campaign rallies, usually in the company of Sinatra, and made brief, humorous plugs for his brother-in-law. But he made his greatest contribution by drawing upon his movie experience to advise Kennedy before the first televised debate with Nixon. "Don't be afraid of the camera," he told JFK. "Look directly into it, as though it were a friend across the dinner table. You'll be making contact with millions of people at the same moment, but each one will feel as though you were talking only to him."[38]

In many ways, however, the alliance between Kennedy and Sinatra's Rat Pack forged only the first link in a much bigger and stronger chain: an emerging linkage between the political world and the entertainment world in modern America. The youthful, vigorous young senator with the movie-star looks captured the imagination of much of Hollywood in the 1960 election. Many actors and entertainers saw Kennedy as a kindred spirit—stylish, sophisticated, attractive, a celebrity—and they responded enthusiastically. They sensed that the candidate was interested in the Hollywood scene and valued the show business world. As the entertainer Steve Allen observed, "There was sort of an easy social connection between the Kennedys and show business, the Hollywood community, that I had never sensed before. There was something about Jack Kennedy . . . youthfulness . . . idealism . . . personal charm . . . hip and easy to talk to. . . . [He] just seemed like one of the gang."[39]

All in all, as one historian of entertainment and politics has put it, "Kennedy fit Hollywood's image of what a president should be. For most of Hollywood, he was a figure of inspiring grace and style. . . . Kennedy imbued politics with a shimmer and a glamour it lacked for Hollywood since Franklin D. Roosevelt. . . . More than any president before or since, Kennedy testified to the irresistible attraction between power and glamour." Thus it caused little surprise when many Hollywood stars joined the Rat Pack to help the Kennedy campaign. Henry Fonda and Harry Belafonte appeared in television commercials; Ella Fitzgerald, Gene Kelly, and Milton Berle recorded radio ads; a stable of stars and their wives attended events in California; and Jeff Chandler, Janet Leigh, and Melvyn Douglas appeared at events on the East Coast. One incident illustrated the new bond between Washington and Hollywood. At a banquet hosted by reporters in the national capital after the election, the new president took his place on the dais, smiled broadly, and said, "Hello, Angie." The prominent diplomat Angier Biddle Duke, chief of protocol in the State Department, stood up and extended his right hand. But Kennedy, unseeing, brushed right by him to warmly greet Angie Dickinson, the beautiful actress who had starred with the Rat Pack in *Ocean's Eleven*.[40]

After Kennedy's victory over the Republican Richard Nixon in the November election, plans for his inauguration began, and they had a distinct Hollywood flavor. In fact, the inaugural festivities in January 1961 would mark the high point of Sinatra and the Rat Pack's influence with Kennedy. Sinatra, assisted by Lawford, had been chosen to organize a gala scheduled for the evening before the inaugural. He came through spectacularly, persuading over twenty top-tier Hollywood entertainers to fly in from Los Angeles and New York to put on a show. The troupe was entertained the night before the gala at a dinner dance organized by JFK's brother-in-law and sister Stephen and Jean Smith at their Georgetown home. The performance itself, held at Washington's National Guard Armory on January 19, showcased the new politics-entertainment alliance with John F. Kennedy and Frank Sinatra filling the starring roles.[41]

The three-hour preinaugural gala, even though held in a snowstorm that paralyzed much of the capital, went off beautifully. The famous radio dramatist Norman Corwin and several prominent screenwriters wrote much of the script; Nelson Riddle conducted the orchestra; Sinatra planned the sequence and content of appearances to perfection; and the performers rehearsed dutifully until the early hours of the morning the day before to hone the show. Joey Bishop began things with a laugh, looking up at the president-elect in his box and saying, "I told you you'd get a good seat. And you were so worried." Bette Davis entered and announced what would be the larger theme of the evening: "The world of entertainment—show-biz, if you please—has become the Sixth Estate, just as Hawaii became the 50th state." The actor Fredric March intoned a kind of prayer asking God to "give us zest for new frontiers, and the faith to say unto mountains, whether made of granite or red tape: remove!" Ethel Merman offered a boisterous rendition of "Everything's Coming Up Roses," while Laurence Olivier recited what was described as a "florid tribute" to JFK of his own composition; Gene Kelly performed a song-and-dance version of the Irish favorite "The Hat Me Dear Old Father Wore"; the comedians Milton Berle and Bill Dana did a routine together; Harry Belafonte sang "John Henry"; Jimmy

Durante delivered a poignant version of "September Song"; the singers Mahalia Jackson, Nat King Cole, and Ella Fitzgerald performed numbers; and Sinatra himself took the stage for a swinging rendition of "You Make Me Feel So Young." All in all, some two dozen entertainers performed, and the evening's climax came with "Ode to the Inauguration," an amalgam of popular songs with special parody lyrics written by Jimmy Van Heusen and Sammy Cahn, Sinatra's favorite composers, that lightheartedly recounted JFK's rise to the presidency. The show ended with Sinatra's performance of "High Hopes." At 1:30 A.M., Sinatra introduced Kennedy, who spoke extemporaneously about his pride in the Democratic Party and asserted, "The happy relationship between the arts and politics which has characterized our long history I think reached culmination tonight." He concluded by offering his heartfelt thanks to Sinatra for his yeoman effort in putting the program together.[42]

Sinatra, primed to make an impression with his new respectability, had proudly assumed a key position in the proceedings. He met the Kennedys at the door when they arrived, escorted Jackie Kennedy to the presidential box, and then sat with the First Couple for much of the show. He took the stage to participate in a comedy routine and then to sing two songs. Sinatra had taken great pains with his clothing for the inauguration and emerged as a "sartorial star," as one newspaper put it. The fashion designer Don Loper had made him several outfits, including a white-tie suit, dinner clothes, an inverness cape, and an ebony walking stick with silver crook and for the ceremony itself a swallowtail coat, striped trousers, double-breasted weskit, black calfskin oxfords, and black pearl stickpin. "Everything I've made for Frank is elegantly tailored and terribly chic," said Loper. "To me he is one of the most elegant men in the world."[43]

The next evening, after the inaugural ceremony, Sinatra made a final, indelible imprint on Hollywood regarding his status with the new president and his administration. He held a private party for the gala entertainers in an upstairs banquet room at the Statler Hilton hotel, also the site of one of the inaugural balls. Kennedy had told Sinatra he would drop by to personally thank the stars for their appearance at the gala, but it started to get quite late and he had not appeared. Finally, there was activity at the door as several Secret Service agents entered the room followed by

Kennedy, who graciously went from table to table and personally greeted the performers and conversed easily with them. According to one attendee, Sinatra sat there "beaming like the Cheshire cat."[44]

While Sinatra was basking in his triumph at the inaugural festivities, Sammy Davis Jr. suffered a much sadder fate. He had been deeply upset after being booed by some southern delegates at the Democratic convention. Now, after making plans to wed May Britt, a beautiful white actress, he had been asked to stay away from the inauguration to avoid alienating southern congressmen and hindering the start-up of the new administration. Politics had prompted Kennedy to this decision and, as Evelyn Lincoln put it, "He very much hopes you will understand." Davis agreed, but he was devastated.[45]

During the first year of the Kennedy administration, Sinatra enjoyed access to the new president and basked in the warmth of his privileged position. The singer took out an ad in *Variety* that reprinted Kennedy's praise of him at the preinaugural gala, and for years afterward he would endlessly play his tape of the event for friends who visited his home. According to a Sinatra friend, "Frank would stand by the mantel and play it over and over, and we had to sit there for hours on end listening to every word." Kennedy would occasionally call Sinatra in Los Angeles, and the singer would pick up the phone and say casually, "Hiya, Prez," and then proudly report the gist of the conversation to his associates after hanging up. Sometimes, he would even tell friends that Kennedy had called but he was too busy to talk. The singer came to the White House for a visit in September 1961, talking with the president in the Oval Office before taking a tour of the family's quarters upstairs. He then flew on Kennedy's private plane, the *Caroline,* to the family compound in Hyannis Port for a weekend of sailing on the family yacht, *Honey Fitz.* In November 1961, when the president visited Los Angeles for a $100-a-plate fund-raiser at the Hollywood Palladium, Sinatra sat at the head table next to him.[46]

Peter Lawford, of course, continued to provide a crucial conduit between JFK and Sinatra's Hollywood world. The Lawford beach house in Santa Monica became, essentially, the western White House for the president during his administration. While he officially stayed at the Beverly Hilton hotel during his visits to Los Angeles, he spent most of his time at the Lawfords', where the presidential flag would fly over the property and the landing and departure of the presidential helicopter would scatter sand into the neighbors' swimming pools. Peter Lawford, of course, continued the Rat Pack tradition by throwing parties attended by movie stars and, in greater numbers, for later in the evening, attractive starlets, models, and occasionally hookers. These bacchanals became legendary. Jeanne Martin, Dean's wife, described them as "a nasty business—they were just too gleeful about it, not discreet at all. . . . The things that went on in that beach house were mind-boggling." Peter Dye, a next-door neighbor, declared, "It was La Dolce Vita over there. It was like a goddamn whorehouse. And Jack Kennedy hustled my wife. He wanted her to go to Hawaii with him. It was the most disgusting thing I've ever seen." Lawford summed up the situation rather crassly many years later: "I was Frank's pimp and Frank was Jack's. It sounds terrible now, but then it was really a lot of fun."[47]

Thus Sinatra was riding high in the saddle as friend and cultural associate of the glamorous, youthful young president. But sooner than anyone expected, Sammy Davis's fate befell the king of Hollywood as the Kennedy administration began to marginalize him. There were several problems. Jackie Kennedy loathed Sinatra and did not want him at the White House, and the president was reluctant to cross her directly by inviting him. Sinatra also proved to be rather clumsy politically. During the 1960 campaign, he had blundered by announcing his plans to make a film, *The Execution of Private Slovik,* and to hire the blacklisted writer Albert Maltz to do the screenplay. The resulting uproar caused Joseph Kennedy to call Sinatra and angrily explain that the controversy was harming the candidacy of his son. He demanded that Sinatra fire Maltz, and the singer reluctantly did so. Then, when cruising on the *Honey Fitz* with the Kennedy family in September 1961, Sinatra offended Bobby Kennedy, who had been rather leery of the entertainer from the beginning. The entertainer stood up and said, "I want to offer a toast to the man who made the greatest contribution to this campaign of anybody I know." Everyone raised a glass, expecting him to salute the attorney general, who had worked tirelessly as the manager of his brother's campaign. Instead, Sinatra toasted Bart Lytton, a big California contributor, as a nervous laugh came from the guests.[48]

Conservative public opinion also bridled at the Rat Pack influence on the new administration. Not long after the election, *Time* magazine disparaged the new president's Hollywood friends and noted that "some of his biggest headaches may well come from an ardently pro-Kennedy Hollywood clique that is known variously as The Rat Pack or The Clan and peopled by such as actor-singer Frank Sinatra and Kennedy's own brother-in-law, British-born Peter ('Pee-tah') Lawford." The *Los Angeles Times* reported, "Now that the Kennedy clan has taken over the White House, there are those who fear occupancy of another clan. This is the Hollywood clan also known as the Rat Pack, which features Frank Sinatra as the big cheese." Sinatra, it said, had followed a "riotous, rocky road from Hoboken to Hollywood" and had gained an unsavory reputation as "a bourbon-guzzling lover of beautiful women—a swinger par excellence." The Hearst writer Ruth Montgomery wrote a column claiming that Sinatra and his friends had behaved arrogantly at the Democratic convention and expressed her concern that "the Rat Pack may be making a nest for itself in the White House." After Sinatra's visit to Hyannis Port, *U.S. News & World Report* huffed that JFK had come under fire for his association with "the Hollywood set." It quoted a disgruntled Cape Cod neighbor from near Hyannis Port after a Sinatra visit: "It's about time President Kennedy does something about those people."[49]

Ultimately, however, it was Sinatra's ties to the Mafia that proved to be his undoing with Kennedy and his administration. By the fall of 1961, as Robert Kennedy, the attorney general, was pursuing a crusade against the mob and its influence, rumors and reports began to circulate about the singer's friendship with Mafia kingpins such as Sam Giancana, Johnny Roselli, Carlos Marcello, Johnny Formosa, and Santo Trafficante. The FBI, through extensive wiretaps, had uncovered various contacts between these Mafia figures and Sinatra. The mobsters had pressured Sinatra to use his friendship with the president to curtail the attorney general's prosecution of Mafia activities. But the singer could not deliver; in fact, his attempts to do so only caused Bobby Kennedy to view him with increasing suspicion. The final straw was when wiretaps uncovered a host of phone calls between Sam Giancana and Judith Campbell, who had become his mistress, and then, more shockingly, many phone calls between Campbell and the White

House, where, of course, Campbell had been visiting as the president's mistress. On February 27, 1962, J. Edgar Hoover, director of the FBI, submitted a report to Robert Kennedy detailing these connections, and then on March 22 he had a private lunch with JFK to discuss the tangled web connecting the president, Sinatra, Giancana, and Campbell. No report of that lunch conversation is available, but it is not difficult to imagine the trepidation felt by the president over the possibility of such news going public.[50]

Kennedy took swift action to limit the damage and protect himself from catastrophe. He cut off contact with Campbell immediately and instructed Peter Lawford to call Sinatra and cancel the president's forthcoming stay at the entertainer's Palm Springs home. He made it clear that while Bobby Kennedy was investigating Sam Giancana, it would be impossible for the president to stay in a residence where the gangster had visited and slept on several occasions. When Sinatra heard this news, he exploded in anger. He had put up a gold plaque outside a bedroom in his home saying, "John F. Kennedy Slept Here"; he had framed notes from the president decorating the walls of his home; for JFK's visit, he had constructed a concrete heliport, built several cottages to house the Secret Service, and installed a communications center with twenty-five available phone lines. Now furious and out of control, the singer went on a rampage and smashed telephones, pulled out phone lines, and took a sledgehammer to the heliport. Then Sinatra turned on his own house, and according to his valet "the whole compound was a sea of glass shards" as the singer smashed every Kennedy photograph in sight and then kicked in the door of the Kennedy bedroom. A few days later, when JFK flew to California, gave his speech, and spent the weekend at the Palm Springs home of Bing Crosby, a Republican, the snub was complete. Sinatra turned his fury on Peter Lawford, an easy target, cut him out of two upcoming Rat Pack movies, and never appeared with him onstage again. As shock and anger turned into sullen resentment, Sinatra accepted his banishment from the Kennedy Circle as the new president sought more respectable masculine associates befitting the dignity of his office.[51]

Dean Martin, it appeared, had been right after all in his cynical take on the political world. Sinatra had believed that the male camaraderie he shared with the president would overcome all obstacles and resolve all issues. But he misread both his man and the hardball nature of national politics. As one observer has argued, Sinatra "knew Kennedy the bon vivant, Kennedy the libertine; that John Kennedy might have winked at an illicit relationship with a mobster. But Sinatra's shock at his exile suggests he didn't understand John Kennedy the politician, who could move coldly and ruthlessly to protect his vital interests."[52]

Nonetheless, despite the unhappy ending to their friendship, Frank Sinatra and the Rat Pack had served as key cultural allies for Jack Kennedy in the 1960 campaign. The aspiring president and his talented Hollywood friends—"the swinging minstrels of Camelot," as one observer termed them—personified a new model of vigorous masculine "cool" that subverted the staid values of the 1950s and promised to overcome the rampant fears of male degeneration caused by its bureaucratic, consumerist, emasculating ethos. As an honorary member of the Rat Pack, Kennedy had successfully translated its glamorous, sophisticated, masculine style into a political idiom as he sought, and assumed, the leadership of the most powerful nation on earth.[53]

FOUR

EXISTENTIAL TOUGH GUY:
NORMAN MAILER

I n late summer 1960, the adviser Arthur Schlesinger Jr. arrived at the Kennedy compound in Hyannis Port for a day of political consultation and socializing. After maneuvering through the crowds of tourists, knots of Democratic Party functionaries, and police cordons that surrounded the property, he and his wife made their way into the house as JFK, who was shaking a few hands outside, waved them in. When he entered the shaded living room, Schlesinger reported, "My eyes were still dazzled from the sun on the terrace, so I did not at first make out the figure sitting patiently in the shadows. It was Norman Mailer." The famous novelist and essayist, it turned out, was writing a major piece on Kennedy for *Esquire,* and the candidate had agreed to an interview. JFK came in shortly and told Mailer that he admired his writing, and the two disappeared for a lengthy chat. They would hold a second session the following day. These encounters marked the beginning of the prominent writer's obsession with the Massachusetts senator.[1]

Two months later, Mailer published "Superman Comes to the Supermart," an account of Kennedy's appearance at the Democratic convention in Los Angeles and a lengthy analysis of the man and his candidacy. It proved to be one of the most influential pieces to appear during the 1960 presidential election. But Mailer's Kennedy was less a politician than a cultural icon. The writer lauded him as a new kind of public figure in American life, a transformational leader who had appeared as an existential hero, a tough, sexually assertive masculine presence who promised to rescue the country from the swamp of timid conformity and enervating "squareness" that it had fallen into during the Eisenhower years. Kennedy, the article argued, represented revitalization. He promised to be "a hero central to his time, a man whose personality might suggest contradictions and mysteries which could reach into the alienated circuits of the underground, because only a hero can capture the secret imagination of a people, and so be good for the vitality of his nation."[2]

Mailer's enthusiastic endorsement meant a great deal to the Democrat's campaign. It boosted JFK's standing among the young, hip readers. Given Mailer's elevated, if controversial, standing in the literary and intellectual community, it also signaled that Kennedy had been endorsed by the intellectual class. It was the campaign's most dramatic sign that the young candidate had emerged as the darling of the intelligentsia, a cadre overwhelmingly concerned with the stultifying effect of conformity, mass society, and consumer materialism in postwar America. Mailer's definition of this malady and his firm stamp of approval on Kennedy's embodiment of a cultural cure mirrored the worldview of most thinkers, writers, and opinion shapers as they approached the presidential election. As Schlesinger noted, "Superman Comes to the Supermart" had captured something essential—regarding both the electorate and the candidate—in the 1960 contest. Kennedy's campaign, he wrote, transcended policy debates by offering "hope for spontaneity in a country drowning in its own passivity. . . . This was what Norman Mailer caught at Los Angeles in 1960— Kennedy's existential quality, the sense that he was in some way beyond conventional politics, that he could touch emotions and hopes thwarted by the bland and mechanized society."[3]

Even more broadly, this journalistic blessing validated Kennedy's standing as a symbol of male vigor. Since World War II, Mailer had emerged as the most prominent representative of the "virility school" of American literature—here he followed in the wake of figures such as Ernest Hemingway,

Jack London, James T. Farrell, and John Dos Passos—and established a reputation as a literary tough guy and outlandish advocate of masculine assertion. His outspoken criticism of growing female influence in American society prefaced his calls for men to recapture a sense of vital, vigorous manhood. Mailer believed Kennedy could lead the way. As he wrote in *Esquire,* this vigorous, highly intelligent, war-tempered young man "had the eyes of a mountaineer . . . the remote and private air of a man who has traversed some lonely terrain of experience, of loss and gain, of nearness to death, which leaves him isolated from the mass of others."[4]

Norman Mailer, through the "Superman" article, and then later in a number of other pieces about JFK after his election, emerged as a key figure in the Kennedy Circle. As much as anyone, he shaped a public appreciation of Kennedy as a symbol of masculine regeneration. His *Esquire* article, perhaps more than any other single journalistic piece written during the election, helped establish JFK's image in the popular imagination as a vibrant, virile, transformational leader who could overcome male malaise and reshape American public life in the process.

Mailer came to John F. Kennedy in 1960 on the arc of a meteoric career as an American literary figure. Born into a middle-class family of Jewish immigrants in 1923, he had grown up in Brooklyn, where he excelled at school. In 1939, Mailer entered Harvard as a sixteen-year-old freshman and soon gravitated to literature following encounters with the novels of John Steinbeck, James T. Farrell, John Dos Passos, Thomas Wolfe, and Ernest Hemingway. Mailer threw himself into writing and had one of his short stories, "The Greatest Thing in the World," chosen by *Story* magazine in 1941 as the best undergraduate submission in a national contest and awarded publication. After graduating in 1943, he entered the army the following year with hopes of finding inspiration "to write the Great American Novel." As part of General Douglas MacArthur's expedition to recapture the Philippines, he saw action in the Pacific theater and rose to the rank of sergeant by the time of his discharge in May 1946.[5]

After demobilization, Mailer began feverishly writing his first novel. It was a war tale based on his own experiences in the Pacific as well as combat stories he had heard from more seasoned comrades. Published as *The Naked and the Dead* in the spring of 1948, the novel follows the life of a platoon of soldiers on a fictional island in the Philippines during the late war. Composed of individuals from various sections, ethnicities, and classes of American society, the unit is sent to scout the rear of the Japanese forces, an assignment that reveals essential impulses and values among the soldiers and their officers. *The Naked and the Dead* offered an unvarnished view of modern war that underlined both the obscenity, brutality, tedium, and primal urges accompanying it and the bureaucratic and technological growth encouraged by it. The abundant use of profanity led him to invent a new word—"fug"—to replace the forbidden four-letter expletive that infantrymen used compulsively as a verb, noun, adjective, and adverb. Liberally sprinkled throughout the dialogue, it conveyed the profane essence of army language without running afoul of the censors. The novel treats war as a test of manhood where life-and-death situations enhance or crush certain qualities among the young males in the unit. While the book implies an antiwar message with its portrayal of the brutalizing destruction of modern armed conflict, Mailer also betrayed an attraction to war as authentic experience, a heightened arena for action where superficiality and pretension are banished and life is reduced to its most elemental features. Through threatening death, war intensified the very experience of life.[6]

The Naked and the Dead immediately became a tremendous popular and critical success. It shot to the top of the bestseller list, remaining at number one for several months, and sold some 200,000 copies in its first year of release. More important for Mailer's literary reputation, the critics praised the book almost unanimously. While pointing out the flaws endemic in the work of a very young writer—derivative organization, some stereotyped characters, stretches of overwrought writing—most reviewers applauded the novel's raw emotional power and truthfulness, its realism, and its compelling style. Several critics judged *The Naked and the Dead* to be among the best war novels ever written and portrayed its youthful author as one of the most promising writers of his generation. "Undoubtedly the most ambitious novel to be written about the recent conflict, it is also the most ruthlessly honest," claimed *The New York Times Book Review*. The resulting fame, adulation, and money not only created a lofty reputation for the twenty-five-year-old in the world of letters but made him a celebrity in postwar America. The acclaim transformed the author's life in overwhelming and disorienting ways. "Suddenly if I went into a room, I was the center of the room," Mailer recounted. "Regardless of how I carried myself, everything I did was taken seriously, and critically."[7]

Mailer's subsequent novels suffered a harsher fate. *Barbary Shore* (1951) reflected Mailer's dabbling in radical politics. It focuses on a young writer's attempts to escape the ideological pressures of the Cold War and forge a genuine, humane, revolutionary socialism. Unlike its predecessor, this polemical, rather ponderous novel earned almost unanimously harsh reviews. Mailer followed with *The Deer Park* (1955), which explored sexual repression as a key manifestation of totalitarian power in postwar America. Set in Hollywood—Mailer had dawdled there for several months in the late 1940s as an aspiring screenwriter after the success of his first novel—it follows a series of actors, directors, and movie executives as they embrace sexual experimentation and the search for pleasure as the central endeavor of life. In Mailer's hands, sex becomes a way of gaining knowledge, even if it leads to confusion and despair. *The Deer Park* earned very mixed reviews, prompting complaints that it made sex dull even as its author struck many as a tremendous, if underdeveloped, literary talent. As the notable critic Malcolm Cowley wrote, "The book leaves us with the feeling that Norman Mailer, though not a finished novelist, is one of the two or three most talented writers of his generation."[8]

At mid-decade, after absorbing a critical mauling for *The Barbary Shore* and a lukewarm reception of *The Deer Park*, Mailer walked away from fiction. He embraced journalism, but in a strikingly new fashion. He eschewed the traditional journalistic goal of objectivity and fact gathering, instead embracing a full-blown subjectivity that often placed the writer, namely himself, at the heart of the story. Mailer also employed a highly literary style that moved capriciously among topics, burrowed into the underlying social or cultural strata of a topic, adopted philosophical or artistic or moral perspectives in a provocative manner, explored character proclivities or flaws of his dramatis personae, and speculated wildly about his subject's significance for the larger landscape of American life. Mailer, in other words, began to adapt fictional techniques to the writing of non-fiction, a technique that would later be adopted by figures such as Tom Wolfe, Gay Talese, and Joan Didion. This fresh approach, and new role, suited Mailer. As a high-flying, free-form, unfettered man of letters in postwar America, Mailer began to burnish his reputation less as a novelist than as a critical commentator on modern life. In 1955, along with two friends, he helped found *The Village Voice* and made it a mouthpiece for criticism of mainstream American life. In subsequent years, he not only wrote a weekly column in that periodical but began publishing a growing number of essays and social commentaries in journals of opinion and magazines that reached a broad audience.[9]

In his work from the end of World War II up through the late 1950s, both fiction and nonfiction, Mailer developed a notable literary style. It was marked by an intense subjectivity, a penchant for self-revelation, a mystical streak, and a stark naturalism punctuated with passionate out-bursts of romanticism. In the words of one critic, his writing displayed "formidable sinuosities and cascades of metaphor . . . [and] mirror-happy convolutions of shape-shifting prose." Mailer also stomped through polite discussions of American life in the garb of a cultural malcontent, offering scathing criticisms of prevailing middle-class values of conformity, bu-reaucracy, and materialism while bombarding the bastions of political power with accusations of authoritarianism. To enhance his public effect, Mailer also created a larger-than-life literary persona and then strove mightily to live up to it. He became noted for a combative personal style characterized by outbursts of egotism, unrepentant machismo, and a pugna-cious antipathy to other critics and writers. Bristling with a tremendous self-regard and eagerly courting controversy, Mailer established a reputa-tion as the enfant terrible of modern American writing by late in the decade.[10]

All of these elements of the Mailer persona—the literary lion, the celebrity, the provocateur—came together in a landmark work at the end of the decade: *Advertisements for Myself* (1959). The book grandly announced its goal in the introduction: "I am imprisoned with a perception which will settle for nothing less than making a revolution in the consciousness of our time." What followed was a collection of stories, essays, journalistic pieces, novel fragments, polemics, critiques of other writers, poetry, political pieces, and autobiographical reflections. Mailer explored widely and deeply the zeitgeist of Eisenhower's America and diagnosed a rebellion brewing against it. Time and time again, he juxtaposed his own psychic state with that of America itself in a game of critical ping-pong. "An author's personality can help or hurt the attention readers give to his books, and it is sometimes fatal to one's talent not to have a public with a clear recognition of one's side," he wrote of this self-promotion. "The way to save your work and reach more readers is to advertise yourself." Mailer proved more than equal to the task.[11]

Advertisements for Myself underlined a trio of broad, intertwined themes that had come to preoccupy Mailer by the late 1950s. First, it explored the threat posed by a growing totalitarianism in both the United States and the Soviet Union. Referring to the two superpowers as "the Colossi," he denounced the spirit of authoritarian power, the production of armaments, and a "regimentation of thought" that had emerged in the two Cold War opponents. While the Soviet Union was dominated by a dictatorship, the United States had fallen under the sway of monopoly capitalism and a powerful constellation of "management and labor executives, the military and the government hierarchy, the Church and mass-communication media." In such a world, Mailer contended, there was little to choose from between the totalitarian impulses of both combatants.[12]

Second, Mailer believed modern America had been overwhelmed by a "national conformity which smothered creativity," and he vowed to cut through "the smog of apathy, gluttony, dim hatred, glum joy, and the general victory of all that is smug, security-ridden and mindless in the American mind." He railed against cultural standards for mental health, "togetherness" of the family, and "citadels of Protestantism" that enforced work discipline and repressed bodily impulses. Modern America, Mailer insisted, was preoccupied with "science, factology, and committee rather than with sex, birth, heat flesh, creation, the sweet and the funky."[13]

Third, *Advertisements for Myself* turned time and again to the difficulty of achieving genuine manhood in postwar society. One had to constantly prove one's masculinity, Mailer insisted, a task that was illustrated in his literary struggle with Ernest Hemingway. For Mailer, this famously virile writer had demonstrated that in the modern literary world, as in the larger culture, "every time you meet a new man, the battle is on . . . [and] it is inevitable that a bad fall come to the strong-willed man who is not strong enough to reach his own peak." The older writer, speaking powerfully and simply and courageously, had "achieved a considerable part of his dream— which was to be more man than most." He embellished *Advertisements for Myself* with reflections on modern masculinity, asserting, for example, that the United States "could stand a man for president, since for all too many years our lives have been guided by men who were essentially women." He added, "I think President Eisenhower is a bit of a woman." As a writer, he vowed to uphold a masculine standard in the broader society: "A good novelist can do without everything but the remnant of his balls."[14]

In fact, Mailer often turned to himself to illustrate the contemporary struggle for manhood. He described the fluctuations in his literary career in terms of masculine struggle. After the unexpected success of *The Naked and the Dead,* he spent years "trying to gobble up the experiences of a victorious man when I was still no man at all." Then the failure of *Barbary Shore* and his struggle to complete and publish *The Deer Park* produced a dawning awareness that "the life of my talent depended on fighting a little more, and looking for help a little less." Mailer concluded that "being a man is the continuing battle of one's life, and one loses a bit of manhood with every stale compromise to the authority of any power in which one does not believe."[15]

Over the next few years, Mailer grew increasingly outspoken in his jeremiad about the decline of American manhood. He complained that as women were fleeing the confines of the home, they became "more selfish, more greedy, less romantic, less warm, more lusty, and also filled with hate." Men had collaborated in female domination as, obsessed with climbing the ladder of corporate success, they increasingly married with an eye toward "who will be less good for them in the home and more good for them in the world." The mass media and advertising also were complicit in this process, as in ads showing burly males admiring the newest model washing machine. Here, he claimed, was an attempt to "draw the fangs of male resentment."[16]

Thus genuine manhood had become an increasingly elusive goal in postwar America. "Masculinity is not something one is born with, but something one gains," Mailer proclaimed. "And one gains it by winning small battles with honor." But the cultural deck was stacked against men. Emasculating women and the allure of consumer comfort had combined to create "a certain built-in tendency to destroy masculinity in American men . . . to destroy virility slowly and steadily." Modern men were like green soldiers first sent into combat who quickly realized "the world is much worse than they've been prepared for" and, traumatized, "lost a lot of their virility in these first early skirmishes." For Mailer, men needed to be "harder and tougher" to better survive the battle of life.[17]

Mailer's concern with totalitarianism, conformity, and the corrosion of masculinity was encapsulated in the centerpiece of *Advertisements for Myself*: "The White Negro: Superficial Reflections on the Hipster." This controversial and influential essay offered a scathing critique of the debilitating malaise created by the prospect of death by atomic destruction in the international arena and "slow death by conformity" on the domestic scene. In this stifling atmosphere, a stark alternative faced individuals seeking a humane, meaningful life. "One is Hip or one is Square," argued Mailer; "one is a rebel or one conforms, one is a frontiersman in the Wild West of American nightlife, or else a Square cell, trapped in the totalitarian tissues of American society, doomed willy-nilly to conform if one is to succeed."[18]

For this outspoken writer, redemption lay in the alienated figure of the hipster, the existential tough guy, the "psychic outlaw," who rejected social expectations, sought pleasure and mocked guilt, and pursued "the liberation of the self from the Super-Ego of society." This rebellious figure against the togetherness of postwar American life first drew inspiration from the "Negro" experience in America, Mailer contended. Black Americans, he argued, were imbued with intense sensuality and sexual prowess, while at the same time they suffered intense alienation from the society that consistently sought to humiliate them. The African American had survived by "relinquishing the pleasures of the mind for the more obligatory pleasures of the body" and by inventing jazz, a musical form that gave voice to "his rage and the infinite variations of joy, lust, languor, growl, cramp, pinch, scream and despair of his orgasm." The hipster rebel, Mailer contended, "had absorbed the existential synapses of the Negro, and for practical purposes could be considered a white Negro."[19]

Mailer's hipster had emerged by the late 1950s in the vanguard of rebellion against the strictures of postwar America. He rejected the suburban home and the bureaucracy of the gray-flannel suit, instead moving "to divorce oneself from society, to exist without roots, to set out on that uncharted journey with the rebellious imperatives of the self." This "American existentialist," as Mailer liked to call him, worshipped at the shrine of sexuality and threw himself into the "search for an orgasm more apocalyptic than the one which preceded it. Orgasm is his therapy." In fact, he embraced "the senses of his body, that trapped, mutilated, and nonetheless megalomaniacal God who is It, who is energy, life, sex, force." The rebel even displayed a tinge of the "psychopath" who instinctively rejected authority and appeared as "a rebel without a cause, an agitator without a slogan, a revolutionary without a program," acting "to open the limits of the possible for oneself, for oneself alone, because that is one's need." The hipster came forward as an "American existentialist" because "the heart of hip is its emphasis upon courage at the moment of crisis."[20]

Mailer, outfitted as an existential tough guy, shaped his own trademark hipster agenda. Sexual machismo and experimentation—"In his search for a sexual life which will suit his orgiastic needs, the hipster willy-nilly attacks conventional sexual morality," he had declared in *Advertisements*—became a prominent feature of Mailer's private life as he launched a course of conduct that would eventually produce six marriages and numerous affairs by the end of his controversial life. He had divorced his first wife, Bea, and taken up with Adele Morales, an aggressive young woman of Spanish-Peruvian descent, whom he would marry in 1954. Their relationship became noted for both its volatility and its sexual high jinks. "We had a lot of orgies. Mostly with women because Adele was very attracted to other women," Mailer told his biographer. "I was having two women and that gave me a feeling of great superiority. I'd feel, 'Oh well, these other literary lights, they had their social superiority but I had my sexual superiority' and that was what was feeding me."[21]

Mailer reveled in a cult of experience. Gorging himself at a smorgasbord of Dionysian urges by the mid-1950s, he confessed in *Advertisements for Myself,* "There may have been too many fights for me, too much sex, liquor, marijuana, benzedrine and seconal, much too much ridiculous and brain-blasting rage." Convinced that manhood resulted from the lonely male's struggle with the world, Mailer punctuated his life with regular bouts of fisticuffs and brawling. "I've been hit on the head with a hammer, and had my left eye gouged in a street fight, and of course I'm proud of this," he bragged. He became a connoisseur of boxing, both as a reporter and as an amateur participant, and savored "the way the blood rolls down the guy's mouth onto his shoulder . . . the cigar smoke . . . the spit on the floor . . . the body odor." For Mailer, such primal, bodily endeavors were "real," a way to be genuinely alive amid the choking conformity of postwar American society.[22]

Mailer, disturbingly, went further. He began to romanticize violence as a meaningful, manly existential exercise, making outrageous rationalizations for acts that were, in fact, horrendous crimes. While rape horrified the square, he asserted, the hipster knew that "the act of rape is a part of life too, and that even in the most brutal and unforgivable rape, there is artistry or the lack of it, real desire or cold compulsion." While a hoodlum's beating of a store owner appalled the square, the hipster knew "courage of a sort is necessary, for one murders not only a weak fifty-year-old man, but an institution as well." Rape and murder, in other words, could be justified as an assault on the system and a fulfillment of the demands of the self. For Mailer at his most unattractive, these barbaric acts of violence were "acts of violence as the catharsis which prepares growth."[23]

Advertisements for Myself, with its unusual format and radical declarations, befuddled many of the critics. Many praised it as the expression of a forceful, vibrant literary voice with immense talent and insight. But an equal number found the book disturbing. They complained about the author's unflagging narcissism where everything was "always and relentlessly, about Norman Mailer." As Gore Vidal gibed in the *Nation,* "Mailer is forever shouting at us that he is about to tell us something we must know or has just told us something revelatory and we failed to hear him, or that he will, God grant his poor abused brain and body just one more chance, get through to us so that we will *know.*" Others noted the irony of the author's excoriating middle-class Americans for their shallow pursuit of advancement when he so obviously, and frantically, sought distinction and approval. In the words of one critic, "Mailer has rarely written a line without asking himself: what will They think of it? how many will They buy? where will They place me?" Some challenged Mailer's entire notion of the hipster, asking, "Do living specimens bearing the psychopathic grandeur with which Mailer invests them, actually walk the streets of our cities?" Finally, a number of observers chided him for playacting at revolution from the safe confines of the writer's study, noting that "Mailer mistakes the life of action with the life of acting out." But whether you loved or loathed Mailer, the consensus seemed to be, he was someone who must be heeded.[24]

From atop his newly elevated perch as a major commentator on American culture, Mailer spied fresh opportunities at the dawn of a new decade. In 1960, his hipster pursuit of genuine experience, manly endeavor, and sexual gratification—his "existential" worldview, to use one of his favorite words—became the lens through which he turned to examine the presidential race. In particular, the candidacy of a young senator in the Democratic Party promised the possibility of revival and redemption. The 1960 presidential election, Mailer decided, provided a means for replacing the national grandfather with the existential hipster, the conformities of mass society with the spontaneous vitality of the authentic individual, and the cloying sentiment of a feminizing culture with the tough calculations of a regenerated masculinity. With typical brashness, he leaped into the fray.

One evening in the spring of 1960, Mailer was at a jazz club on the Lower East Side in New York with his wife, Adele, and another couple. They were joined at the table by Clay Felker, the editor of *Esquire*, and during the ensuing conversation Felker offhandedly asked the novelist if he would be interested in writing something about politics for the magazine. Perhaps, Mailer replied, but he didn't know much about political writing. So Felker suggested something concrete: the upcoming Democratic National Convention in Los Angeles. Mailer agreed, and Felker was delighted. The arrangement "fitted the way we were thinking at *Esquire* at the time," he wrote later; "namely, to compensate for our long lead-time by leaning on a writer's style and unique point of view."[25]

Arriving at the convention, Mailer worried that he did not know the political world and its processes and personalities. So Felker, who had many contacts from his days as a political reporter for *Life*, agreed to show him around and make introductions. Mailer groused that the only type of political writing with which he was familiar was Marx, but with typical bravado he overcame his misgivings and threw himself into the proceedings. He had lunch with Arthur Schlesinger Jr. and exchanged views; he attended parties and receptions; he had long discussions with Hollywood political activists such as Shelley Winters; he got into a lengthy debate with the public intellectual Max Lerner, whom he castigated as an "old-fashioned liberal."[26]

Throughout, Mailer played the role of the confident outsider determined to shake up the political establishment. In Lerner's words, "What he was talking about was a fresh voice, a new vision. His demeanor was that of an initiate, but a brash initiate, as though in his own mind he was in L.A. to take us all on." True to his persona, Mailer dominated every gathering of which he was a part. "Wherever he was, he was at the center of the group," recalled Martin Peretz, the political writer and future publisher of *The New Republic*. "He was coming on. He was pugilizing. The physical movements were those of a boxer, and the words were sharp jabs." Finally, near the end of the convention, the writer told Felker, "I think I know how I'm going to do it." He had decided to focus on Kennedy as a new kind of figure in American public life, a politician whose import transcended politics.[27]

After departing Los Angeles, Mailer stumbled upon a fortuitous opportunity. Pierre Salinger, Kennedy's press liaison, had learned about the writer's forthcoming article and arranged for him to meet and interview the candidate at Hyannis Port. "Jack Kennedy was very aware of the power of magazines. *Esquire* didn't have the mass circulation of *Life* but it had great impact on opinion leaders, and Kennedy was aware of our interest," reported Felker. So Mailer drove to the Kennedy family compound for a brief talk and then returned the next day for a lengthier meeting—the second time driving nearly a hundred miles per hour, according to his wife, because he was upset that he did not have a clean summer shirt to wear with his suit. When they arrived, they met first Jackie Kennedy, who chatted a bit before leaving on a sailing jaunt, and then Jack, who took them on a brief tour of the house.[28]

All parties were a bit apprehensive about the interviews. Kennedy and his people were curious about Mailer but a little skittish, in Schlesinger's words, because "Norman is totally unpredictable and they had no idea what he was likely to say." For all of his usual bluster, Mailer was also nervous and on his best behavior, very soft-spoken and courteous. Kennedy immediately disarmed the writer with a clever comment. As they sat down, Mailer noted, JFK said that he had enjoyed the novelist's books and commented, "I've read *The Deer Park* and the others." Mailer was enormously pleased, noting that it was the first time in memory that a new acquaintance had not said, "I've read *The Naked and the Dead* and the others," but instead chose the book the author saw as his neglected masterpiece. Kennedy, in fact, although a great reader, was not a fan of fiction, and it is highly doubtful that he had read any of Mailer's books. Instead, the candidate had been briefed by Salinger, who had learned from a contact that Mailer's favorite among his books was *The Deer Park*. Kennedy used the same ploy of praising an obscure favorite with other writers, Schlesinger observed, to successfully cultivate their favor.[29]

Mailer, once the interview started, tried to regain the upper hand by tossing out a couple of outrageous items to get Kennedy's reaction and knock him off stride. First, the writer noted that *The Village Voice* had recently conducted a poll on its readers' preferences in the upcoming election, and one respondent had said, "Well, as between Kennedy and Nixon, Kennedy is a zero and Nixon is a minus, so I'll vote for Kennedy." JFK, taken aback, protested, "I really don't think of myself as a zero, and I'm sure Richard Nixon doesn't think of himself as a minus." Then Mailer cheekily claimed that he had seen an ad picturing a surly, shadow-bearded Nixon with a caption reading, "Would you buy a used car from this man?" and then beneath it an elaboration: "If you bought the car from Jack Kennedy, you would trust him and after you bought the car, he'd drop by to see how it was working, and he'd seduce your wife." A nonplussed Kennedy replied, "I really don't know what that means." According to Mailer, "It was one of the few times he had ever been rattled, I think."[30]

The following day the sparring for dominance continued. Kennedy tried to corner Mailer by suggesting that he was an effete intellectual, asking, "What kind of car do you drive? Let me guess—it's a Volkswagen, right?" Mailer replied smugly, "No, it's a Triumph TR-3," and concluded, "Now I had him twice." JFK pulled ahead in the manly struggle, however, when, in Mailer's words, "I made the mistake of inviting my wife. The moment I did, he knew more about me than I knew about him, which is this poor fellow has got to bring his wife along to impress her." Kennedy regained his equilibrium and dominance. "So the second interview was all his," Mailer admitted. "He controlled it. He was very skillful; he was charming; he was perfect."[31]

Mailer was won over by Kennedy, both at the convention and in the interview, and his approval of the youthful candidate became obvious as he composed his essay in the early fall of 1960. "I wanted to affect the election; I wanted to advance my career; I wanted to advance Kennedy's career," he confessed. "It's the first piece I wrote in my life which was written with deliberate political intention; I wanted to get a man elected." At the same time, while excited by Kennedy's potential to be a new kind of political leader, Mailer harbored reservations about his own enthusiasm. "I hoped I wasn't blowing smoke," he admitted. "I was worried that it was superficial and propagandistic, that I was phony, that I was making too much of JFK's personality and too little of the objective political strengths." Mailer realized that in so strongly endorsing Kennedy, he had shifted from a radical position to a liberal one and was uncertain "whether I was reversing my field in fear or on an honorable tack."[32]

When Mailer's "Superman Comes to the Supermart" appeared in *Esquire*, it gave a significant boost to JFK's campaign. It was an unusual piece of political journalism. Eschewing the usual factual descriptions of political alliances and fights, maneuvers and speeches, deal making and debates, Mailer approached the Democratic convention in the manner of a novelist, trying to capture the feel of the atmosphere, the personalities of the contestants, and the deeper impulses at work amid the electioneering.

Uninterested in taking an objective stance, he described them from the inside in highly impressionistic language. Instead of genuflecting before the venerable democratic processes of American politics, he offered a darker, almost comic rendering of the gathering as a cultural carnival. The delegates, he wrote, were "not the noblest sons and daughters of the Republic" but mostly small-time operatives from around the country rewarded for their service to the local political organization—"lawyers, judges, ward heelers, *mafiosos,* Southern goons and grandees, grand old ladies, trade unionists, and finks." The convention hall, he wrote, had the fetid smell of "carnival wine, the pepper of a bullfight, the rag, drag, and panoply of a jousting tourney, all swallowed and regurgitated by senses into the fouler cud of a death gas one must rid oneself of—a cigar-smoking, stale-aired, slack-jawed, butt-littered, foul, bleak, hard-working, bureaucratic death gas of language and faces." The Democratic Party piled into the venue like "a crazy, half-rich family, loaded with poor cousins . . . it's the Snopes family married to Henry James, with the labor unions thrown in like a Yankee dollar."[33]

Mailer saw Los Angeles, the setting for the convention, as a perfect symbol of America's conformist, suburban society in the 1950s. In his words, "The spirit of the supermarket, that homogeneous extension of stainless surfaces and psychoanalyzed people, packaged commodities and ranch homes, interchangeable, geographically unrecognizable, that essence of the new postwar SuperAmerica, is found nowhere so perfectly as Los Angeles's ubiquitous acres. . . . [It is] a kingdom of stucco, a playground for mass men." It was a city of barbarisms and billboards where energy lay in "the screamers of neon lighting, the shouting farm-utensil colors of the gas stations and the monster drug stores, the swing of the sports cars, hot rods, convertibles."[34]

Against this backdrop, Mailer presented the key political actors as characters in a novel. Adlai Stevenson projected the luminous "sweet happiness of an adolescent who had just been given his first major kiss. And so he glowed, and one was reminded of Chaplin." Eleanor Roosevelt was "fine, precise, hand-worked like ivory . . . now satisfying the last passion of them all, which was to become physically attractive, for she was better-looking than she had ever been." The party boss Jim Farley was "huge.

Cold as a bishop." Stuart Symington betrayed "disappointment eating at his good looks so that he came off hard-faced, mean, and yet slack." New York's mayor, Robert Wagner, had the "blank, pomaded, slightly worried look of the first barber in a good barbershop." Lyndon Johnson, the wily Texas senator, had "compromised too many contradictions and now the contradictions were in his face: when he smiled, the corners of his mouth squeezed gloom; when he was pious, his eyes twinkled irony; when he spoke in a righteous tone, he looked corrupt."[35]

But the charismatic protagonist of the tale, of course, was John F. Kennedy, Mailer's "Superman," whose appearance at the Democratic convention swept all before it. Significantly, Mailer said nothing about JFK's political positions or policy proposals as a presidential aspirant, instead painting him as a cultural figure who had emerged as the harbinger of a new era in American life. The critic saw the youthful senator as a different kind of potential president: an existential hero, a hipster, a revitalized male. In shaping this image, the author grafted "the white Negro" of his famous essay onto the man who emerged as the Democratic candidate for the highest office in the land in the 1960 election and made him into the leader of a cultural insurgency to save the country. Mailer's Kennedy displayed several striking dimensions.

Most important was his glamour and style. Mailer described Kennedy when he initially appeared at the convention hall in a motorcade: "He had the deep orange-brown suntan of a ski instructor and when he smiled at the crowd his teeth were amazingly white and clearly visible at a distance of fifty yards." The handsome young senator broke from his security detail and strolled into the crowd that had gathered to greet him, smiling and shaking hands, and after a time he made his way to the hall entrance "surrounded by a mob, and one expected any moment to see him lifted on its shoulders like a matador being carried back to the city after a triumph in the plaza." Later, Mailer would explain that this incident was an epiphany, where he first realized that Kennedy had somehow bridged a chasm between widely dispersed groups in postwar America. Standing on an outdoor balcony of the Biltmore Hotel and looking down on the scene below, the writer saw "a crowd of gays on the other side of Pershing Park, all applauding, going crazy, while the convention itself was filled with the whole corrupt trade-union Mafia Democratic machine." Somehow these two worlds had come together around the youthful Democratic candidate, said Mailer, and "at that moment it was almost as if I saw it like a great painting."[36]

In fact, Mailer argued, Kennedy had created a new type in American public life: the politician as movie star, the charismatic and attractive leader who had successfully fused the imagery of the silver screen with hard-nosed electoral success. He described JFK's appearance as a stock scene lifted right out of the movies where the matinee idol comes to the palace to claim the princess or the handsome football hero strides across campus to successfully garner a date with the dean's beautiful daughter. Kennedy, Mailer insisted, would be approved by the electorate as "a great box-office actor." But Kennedy's movie star image also stemmed from his internal features. Mailer sensed a certain detached, elusive quality in the young candidate and concluded that it was the self-awareness of an actor who had been cast as a candidate and maintained a certain distance between himself and his role. Moreover, JFK displayed an ability to subtly change the shadings of his appearance—he "had a dozen faces. . . . [T]he quality was reminiscent of someone like Brando, whose expression rarely changes, but whose appearance seems to shift from one appearance into another as the minutes go by." Because of Kennedy's persona, Mailer predicted, "America's politics would now be also America's favorite movie."[37]

Mailer sculpted Kennedy as a figure of genuine cultural redemption. He argued that the Democratic nominee promised to be an existential hero, a hipster leader who would save America from the suffocating effects of bland conformity, bureaucratic malaise, and authoritarian restriction. Postwar America, the author maintained, had moved along "two rivers, one visible, the other underground." On the surface ran a massive, placid waterway of middle-class homogenization devoted to family life, organized religion, an increasingly authoritarian government, anti-Communism, and a manipulative mass media where men were "as interchangeable as commodities." President Dwight Eisenhower stood as a symbol of this dominant culture. His "incredible dullness" had ushered in the triumph of corporate values in the power structure, while in general society a "tasteless, sexless, odorless sanctity in architecture, manners, modes, styles has been the result. Eisenhower embodied half the needs of the nation, the needs of the timid, the petrified, the sanctimonious, and the sluggish."[38]

At the same time, deep beneath the gray landscape of American conformity flowed a subterranean stream of powerful, untapped emotional energy and visceral desires, a panoply of "orgiastic vistas." Bubbling in the underground, Mailer contended, were "untapped, ferocious, lonely and romantic desires, that concentration of ecstasy and violence which is the dream life of the nation." This represented a vital American myth that "each of us was born to be free, to wander, to have adventure and to grow on the waves of the violent, the perfumed, and the unexpected." If Eisenhower's America represented a small-town vision of the good life that was cautious, rooted, and narrow, the underground America represented the spirit of the city, which is "dynamic, orgiastic, unsettling, explosive, and accelerating to the psyche."[39]

This widening divergence between America's official society and its underground, Mailer asserted, had created a yearning for a new kind of political leader. "It was a hero America needed, a hero central to his time, a man whose personality might suggest contradictions and mysteries which could reach into the alienated circuits of the underground, because only a hero can capture the secret imagination of a people," he wrote. Such a hero would not simply advocate politics as usual with threadbare assertions that congressional bills and government programs could cure a crisis of the national spirit. Mailer's hero would be a man "who reveals the character of the country to itself."[40]

John F. Kennedy fit the bill. He was "the hipster as presidential candidate," in Mailer's phrase, who promised to tap into America's underground energy and revitalize its life. A man who had stared death in the face, during both the PT-109 incident during World War II and his life-threatening back surgery in the 1950s, he had triumphed with a keener awareness of the vitality of life. A man impatient with the bromides of the past and the security of the safe path, he dared to declare that youthful rather than elderly wisdom was better fitted to direct the nation's fortunes. With such a man in office, Mailer argued, "the myth of the nation would again be engaged," and America would find the courage to "take an existential turn, to walk into the nightmare, to face into that terrible logic of history which demanded that the country and its people must become more extraordinary and more adventurous, or else perish." As Mailer elaborated years later, "I knew if he became President, it would be an existential event; he would touch depths in American life which were uncharted. . . . America's tortured psychotic search for security would finally be torn loose from the feverish ghosts of its old generals, its MacArthurs and Eisenhowers."[41]

Mailer's existential hero also emerged as the embodiment of masculine virility in American public life, the leader of a crusade for male regeneration. "Superman Comes to the Supermart" was filled with subtle allusions and sly images that constantly implied the candidate's sexual allure and physical prowess. Kennedy, Mailer noted, would be "not only the youngest President ever to be chosen by voters, he would be the most conventionally attractive young man ever to sit in the White House." Mailer utilized the adjective "orgiastic" to describe the hipster discontent the candidate had corralled. His images of Kennedy were drenched in sex appeal: the ski instructor, the matador, the movie star. JFK "was hard, he was young, he was In," and he carried himself with "the poise of a fine boxer, quick with his hands, neat in his timing," Mailer wrote. Ancillary images underlined the appeal of Kennedy's virility. When describing the coteries of young women demonstrating for the various candidates on the convention floor in Los Angeles, the author noted that "the Kennedy ladies were the handsomest; healthy, attractive, tough, a little spoiled—they looked like the kind of girls who had gotten all the dances in high school and worked for a year as an airline hostess." The citizen who feared creative change and opted for the security of Nixon, wrote Mailer, acted "the way a middle-class man past adventure holds on to the stale bread of his marriage."[42]

Ultimately, Mailer contended that in preparing to elect Kennedy, America stood poised for a huge swing away from the smothering, bureaucratic, family-obsessed blandness of the 1950s. Such a decision would signal that "the country had recovered its imagination, its pioneer lust for the unexpected and incalculable." The choice was clear in the 1960 election, he insisted: one could vote for drama or stability, adventure or monotony, expression or conformity, even "for glamour or for ugliness." One could choose a candidate devoted to the idea of the mass man who would keep

American vitality buried in the underground or a candidate who was one of America's "ablest men, its most efficient, its most conquistadorial . . . one of its more mysterious men . . . handsome as a prince in the unstated aristocracy of the American dream." John F. Kennedy, the best hope for America's regeneration, was "the image in the mirror of its unconscious . . . a son to lead them who was heir apparent to the psychic loins."[43]

"Superman Comes to the Supermart" created a stir. Mailer, with characteristic bombast and self-regard, believed that the piece won the 1960 election for Kennedy. He claimed it had warned Democrats about the possibility of their candidate losing at the last minute and inspired them to keep working hard right up to the moment of the election. More important, it had shaped an image of Kennedy that attracted countless voters to his side. The essay "added the one ingredient Kennedy had not been able to find for the stew—it made him seem exciting, it made the election appear important. Around New York there was a turn in sentiment, one could feel it; Kennedy now had glamour," wrote the controversial author. "I had created an archetype of Jack Kennedy in the public mind which might or might not be true, but which would induce people to vote for him, and so would tend to move him into the direction I had created." He had been successful in "bending reality like a field of space to curve the time I wished to create," Mailer concluded. "This piece had more effect than any other single work of mine."[44]

Esquire's editor, Clay Felker, was delighted with what he saw as a seminal piece. He believed that Mailer had ascended to a new level of understanding about politics, going beyond the mechanics of party maneuvering and policy formulation to grasp the larger meaning of the candidate. The writer understood that elections were "about how politics touch people, their deepest aspirations and fears and hopes, and that's what Mailer articulated more brilliantly than any other writer at the time." It "articulated an appeal to young Americans, and *Esquire* had an audience of young Americans," Felker contended. "We were a new generation—here was a new political figure for whom Mailer more than made the case."[45]

Kennedy reacted favorably, if a bit uncertainly, to Mailer's *Esquire* article. An aide, Richard Goodwin, showed him the piece and, after Kennedy read it, asked him what he thought. Kennedy replied enigmatically, "It really runs on, doesn't it?" But Arthur Schlesinger Jr. recalled that JFK expressed his pleasure when the article came out, although it was leavened with skepticism. When advisers kidded him about Mailer's portrayal of an "existential hero," the candidate confessed that "he wasn't quite sure what an existential hero might be, and whether he actually qualified." Jacqueline Kennedy deeply admired Mailer's piece and sent him a four-page handwritten letter of appreciation on October 24, 1960. "My breath was taken away by your article in *Esquire*," she wrote. "I never dreamed that American politics can be written about that way. Why don't more people have the imagination to do so—then more people like you & Jack would be in them."[46]

"Superman Comes to the Supermart" resonated widely. While it is impossible to quantify, or even calculate, the practical effect of a journalistic piece in terms of influencing opinion or votes, it was evident that Mailer's essay elicited widespread discussion. In particular, many journalists, political commentators, and opinion shapers were struck by the essay. "When it came out, it went through journalism like a wave. Something changed," observed Pete Hamill, a young writer for the *New York Post*. "Everybody in the business, guys my age, were talking about it. Norman took political journalism beyond what the best guys—Mencken, Teddy White, Richard Rovere—had done. Rather than just a political sense, there was a moral sense that came out of the piece."[47]

With his influential *Esquire* essay, Norman Mailer thus emerged as a key figure in the Kennedy Circle during the 1960 election. "Superman Comes to the Supermart" painted a striking, memorable portrait of JFK as a virile cultural figure who could revive the drooping fortunes of American men and regenerate the larger society in the process. His image of Kennedy became a persuasive one precisely because it gathered together so many strands of opinion and feeling—those emanating from the candidate himself, from his association with Frank Sinatra and the Rat Pack, from effusive journalistic accounts—and gave them a dramatic literary form.

At the same time, however, Mailer outsmarted himself. In his eagerness to portray Kennedy as a hipster leader and existential hero, he overlooked the many ways in which the young senator was nothing of the kind. The misgivings he expressed about "blowing smoke," in fact, gradually kindled into flames as events unfolded. History, Mailer discovered ruefully, rarely conforms to the strategies and tropes of the novelist.

Within a short time, Mailer's connection to the new president and his administration began to fray. It started in late November 1960, only a couple of weeks after JFK's election, when the macho hipster writer stabbed his wife, Adele, at a party in New York and nearly killed her. She had been baiting him throughout the evening—for years, verbal and physical confrontations had generated excitement in their volatile relationship—when a belligerent Mailer, sporting a bloody nose from a fight and extremely drunk, grabbed a penknife and stuck it in her back and then her chest, coming perilously close to the heart. She was rushed to the hospital and underwent surgery. Mailer, after wandering the streets in a daze before returning to their apartment, was arrested and incarcerated in Bellevue Hospital for two weeks of psychiatric evaluation. Adele refused to sign a complaint against her husband, several hearings took place, and Mailer eventually pleaded guilty to third-degree assault, and he escaped with a legal slap on the wrist: a suspended sentence and probation. This infamous incident sullied his reputation and illustrated the dangerous possibilities embedded in an irresponsible creed of physical adventure and violence.[48]

This personal crisis portended a public crisis as Mailer, almost immediately, suffered misgivings about the young president he had done so much to elect. Despite the writer's grandiose claims about "bending reality" to his will, it became clear, first, that JFK was no hipster and, second, that his masculine virility fed, rather than undermined, his politics of Cold War liberalism. Mailer had fooled himself on several counts, it became apparent, and he reacted with customary intellectual bluster and rolling torrents of verbiage. In a number of essays, open letters, and miscellaneous pieces written in the early 1960s and published in venues such as *Dissent*, *Esquire*, *The Realist*, *Commentary*, and *The Village Voice*—they were then collected in *The Presidential Papers* (1963)—Mailer chastised Kennedy for failing to live up to his expectations.

Almost wistfully, the novelist recounted his contention in "Superman

Comes to the Supermart" that JFK's emergence had marked a new opportunity for revamping American life. A postwar America "of tasteless,
toneless authority" dominated by corporate executives, public relations
men, media executives, mass entertainers, and government agencies such as
the FBI had prevailed. But Kennedy had offered new possibilities by recall-
ing the country to "its existential beginnings, its frontier psychology, where
the future is unknown and one discovers the truth of the present by accepting the risks of the present." During the election, Kennedy had appeared
as a brave, complicated, intelligent figure who inspired the compelling
thought that "a young man with a young attractive wife might soon become
President. It offered possibilities and vistas; it brought a touch of life to the
monotonies of politics, those monotonies so profoundly entrenched into
the hinges and mortar of the Eisenhower administration."[49]

But the result, Mailer now insisted, fell far short of the expectation.
Kennedy, once elected, showed too little of the hipster existential hero and
too much of the conventional politician. Outraged by the debacle of the
Bay of Pigs in April 1961, when an American-backed invasion of Cuba
was crushed by Fidel Castro's forces, Mailer published an open, highly
personal letter to the president. His influential 1960 essay, he reminded JFK,
had "ventured the notion that you gave promise of becoming the first
major American hero in more than a decade. I also upheld the private
hope . . . that you were Hip, that your sense of history was subtle because it
extracted as much from flesh as fact." But now this enormous mistake had
cast all into doubt by escalating the Cold War to a point where "we have
driven Cuba inch by inch to alliance with the Soviets, as deliberately and
insanely as a man setting out to cuckold himself."[50]

Feeling burned, the writer acerbically detailed the president's shortcomings over the next two years. Kennedy as president, Mailer argued,
demonstrated intellectual shallowness and a lack of imagination in his
approach to leadership. In the face of nuclear holocaust abroad and a deadening conformity at home, his "mind seems never to have been seduced
by a new idea. He is the embodiment of the American void, that great
yawning empty American mind which cannot bear any question which
takes longer than ten seconds to answer." The president, said Mailer, took
in predigested information from his advisers, embraced tired political

solutions to broader cultural problems, and suffered from the malady of "intellectual malnutrition." Focusing on statistics, budgets, and bureaucratic policy, Kennedy could not approach "the center of the problem, which is that life in America becomes more economically prosperous and psychically impoverished each year. The real life of America is not being enriched." The president, in Mailer's scathing words, "embodies nothing, he personifies nothing. . . . We have a President who is brave but politically neuter, adept at obtaining power and a miser at spending it, an intellectual with a mind like a newspaper's yearbook, and a blank somewhat stricken expression about the eyes."[51]

Moreover, JFK reinforced the totalitarian drift of American life by favoring the corporate and bureaucratic forces in modern America. "You've cut the shape of your plan for history and it smells," accused Mailer. "It smells rich and smug and scared of the power of the worst, dullest, and most oppressive men of our land. You will use brains but fear minds, seek for experts and eschew spirit." Kennedy's anti-Communist policies only reinforced the choke hold of the existing power structure by encouraging a mindless patriotism and supporting a corrupt capitalism. The president continued to shape "an America run by committees. . . . [This attitude] has helped to hold back the emergence of an America more alive and more fantastic."[52]

Overall, Mailer complained, Kennedy failed to be sufficiently existential in his politics. "No President can save America from a descent into totalitarianism without shifting the mind of the American politician to existential styles of political thought," he declared. This meant nurturing, not suppressing, the "strong ineradicable strain in human nature . . . and find[ing] an art into which it can grow." This meant using "your popularity to be difficult and intellectually dangerous. There is more to greatness than liberal legislation." This meant going beyond the Peace Corps and establishing an "Adventurer's Corps" that would provide young men a place for discovering emotional mettle and physical bravery.[53]

Mailer's existential critique of Kennedy, in one sense, revealed that he misunderstood the basic nature of politics. As one critic observed, the outspoken writer asked of politics "what it cannot give. . . . [P]olitical procedures and truth are not the procedures and truth of art. A president is not supposed to 'enrich the real life of his people,' he is supposed to protect and preserve it, enrichment being precisely the function of the author." Garry Wills, writing in the *National Review,* offered a withering put-down of Mailer's unique combination of pretension and confusion on this point. Convinced that his essay had elected Kennedy in 1960, Mailer, in Wills's words, had foolishly believed he would become "something of a Cultural Minister, who would redo the White House in Early Neanderthal and set up a Department for Improving the Orgasm." At the same time, however, despite his delusions Mailer surpassed many observers in grasping something fundamentally new about Kennedy and public life in the early 1960s: cultural imagery, particularly that associated with personality and celebrity, had moved center stage in the American political process.[54]

Thus Mailer stood on firmer ground when he contended that President Kennedy met one key standard for a new kind of political leader: he personified sexuality and style. The postwar generation of American writers had struggled to incite a sexual revolution, the writer argued, agreeing that "sex is good, sex has to be defended, sex has to be fought for, sex has to be liberated." Sex was the essence of modern reform, because it was an authentic expression of the animalistic impulses in humans against the falsities of bureaucratic conformity. "The orgasm is anathema to the liberal mind because it is the inescapable existential moment," Mailer declared. Kennedy had provided a boost of energy for this crusade. His assertive masculinity had worked "to keep America up. Virility is the unspoken salesman in American political programs today." Kennedy had prompted a loosening of sexual restraints and an acceptance of sexual expression that helped break the stranglehold of staid traditionalism. Think of going to a party given by Eisenhower as opposed to a party thrown by Kennedy, Mailer urged. Was there any doubt as to which party would provide a better time? While you would worry about being proper at Eisenhower's home, the thought of a Kennedy party meant "having a dance with Jackie. Things liven up." Even if JFK failed to navigate the country on a course away from traditional authority, Mailer contended, Americans at least had been "granted by the cavalier style of his personal life and the wistfulness of his appreciation for the arts the possible beginnings of a resistance to American totalitarianism."[55]

Thus Mailer, despite his disappointment on some fronts, never quite abandoned his belief in Kennedy's positive impact. To the end of his life, he looked back on "Superman Comes to the Supermart" as largely correct in its assessment of the youthful president as an important agent of change in American culture. Kennedy had "changed the style of America: he opened it up," he asserted in 1968. "Something racy came back into American life. The country was saltier; it swung more." Even forty years after the 1960 election, Mailer contended that JFK had personified an existential prescription for America's ills: "the instinctive life . . . a return more to the pagan, to the sense of oneself who lived in the field of the senses." For the writer, Kennedy's stylish masculine figure at least pointed America away from its desiccating addiction to security, conformity, success, and family togetherness. In his words, JFK "meant that our national life had become a little like an adventure movie. That was exciting."[56]

Mailer's ultimate ambivalence about Kennedy—backing away from the notion of the president as a transformational hipster while maintaining a broad belief in his cultural impact—was probably inevitable. After all, in the choice of an existential hero who could lead America from the morass of repression and authoritarianism, there had always been only one legitimate candidate who appealed to the controversial author: himself. As he had admitted in the very first sentence of *Advertisements for Myself,* "I've been running for President in my own mind for the past ten years." In this private election with a voting constituency of one, Mailer always triumphed. But it was Kennedy, of course, perhaps to the writer's unconscious chagrin, who actually won the popular affection and approval the author so craved.[57]

Norman Mailer made a vital contribution to JFK's electoral victory in 1960 and brightened the cultural glow that enveloped the new national leader. In an arresting passage from "Superman Comes to the Supermart," he observed that the existential hero should "kill well (if always with honor), love well and love many, be cool, be daring, be dashing, be wild, be wily, be resourceful, be a brave gun." While written as a description of Kennedy, the masculine ideal of the piece, these words applied even more aptly to another celebrated figure in American popular culture in the late

1950s and early 1960s. The exploits of a fictional British secret agent, as presented in several popular novels and then in several high-grossing movies, had gained a vast public audience. They also gained an enthusiastic fan in JFK. The image of this urbane, alluring masculine character soon became indelibly connected to Kennedy's own portrait of vigorous manhood.

FIVE

SECRET AGENT MEN:
IAN FLEMING AND JAMES BOND

At midday on March 13, 1960, the British author Ian Fleming was visiting Washington, D.C., and driving through Georgetown with a longtime friend, Marion "Oatsie" Leiter. As they headed for lunch, Leiter spotted a young couple walking down the sidewalk and immediately stopped the car. "You must meet them," she said. "They're great fans of yours." As they came together, Leiter introduced Jack and Jackie Kennedy. The young man immediately widened his eyes and inquired, "Not *the* Ian Fleming?" and then quickly invited him to dinner that evening at their home. In such fashion, the author of the popular James Bond novels made the acquaintance of Senator John F. Kennedy, then in the middle of his primary battles to gain the Democratic Party's nomination for the presidency, and the candidate met the creator of one of his favorite series of books.[1]

An interesting group gathered at Kennedy's home that evening. It included, in addition to the hosts and Fleming and Leiter, the influential newspaper columnist Stewart Alsop, the painter William Walton, and the CIA official John Bross. The director of the CIA, Allen Dulles, was supposed to attend the dinner but was detained by business at the last moment and asked Bross to report to him on the events of the evening. Kennedy, an enthusiastic Bond fan, quizzed Fleming about the British secret agent he had created, and as the meal progressed, the talk turned to espionage. JFK asked Fleming for his views on how to topple the Fidel Castro regime in Cuba. The group, knowing the author's vaunted imagination, expected a creative answer, and they were not disappointed. Fleming argued that instead of obsessively denouncing the Communist dictator and inflating him into a world figure, the United States should give him "the Bond treatment" and undermine his revolution with deceit and "ridicule." Cubans cared mostly about three things, Fleming argued—money, religion, and sex—and the strategy should focus there. He suggested that American planes fly over Havana scattering money along with leaflets declaring, "Compliments of the United States," a move that would throw the Cuban economy into disarray. Fleming recommended employing technology to project a giant cross in the sky, inducing the population to look constantly skyward and be reminded of godly power. Finally, he suggested distributing pamphlets on the island nation claiming that beards were a natural receptacle for radioactivity created by atomic testing and that this toxic substance induced impotence, a maneuver that would force Castro and his bearded revolutionaries into the humiliation of shaving. The dinner party laughed good-naturedly as they pondered the writer's outlandish schemes.[2]

Bross promptly reported Fleming's ideas to Dulles, expecting his chief to dismiss them immediately. But to his surprise, the CIA director thought they had great potential and tried to reach Fleming by phone for further discussion the next day. According to Leiter, whom he phoned, Dulles "was desperate to find Ian." But the author had already left Washington to return to London. What Bross did not know was that Dulles and Fleming had struck up a personal friendship a short time before and that Dulles shared Kennedy's love of the Bond novels. Moreover, the CIA had already begun developing schemes with a similar technological and psychological thrust to use against Castro.[3]

The American fascination with James Bond, however, was not restricted to the Democratic nominee for president and the head of the CIA. Fleming had published seven novels featuring the fictional British secret agent from 1953 to 1960, and they became bestsellers. By the time of Fleming's death in 1964, and the publication of more Bond novels, readers had purchased an astonishing thirty million total copies, and that number would soar to seventy-nine million copies by the end of the decade. Meanwhile, the production and release of several James Bond movies attracted tens of millions of additional fans. The novels and the movies offered many attractions to an American audience: the excitement and suspense of the espionage world, elite social settings of glamour and sophistication, a charge of erotic energy from numerous sexual encounters, and a Cold War triumph of a heroic protagonist over villainous opponents. But Fleming's tales, above all, projected a notable masculine appeal. James Bond, much like the Rat Pack, Norman Mailer, and Kennedy himself, is a tough-minded, attractive, sophisticated male presence who promises new vistas of experience for plodding organization men and weary suburban dads. For women, the dashing, sexy secret agent promises a more sensual kind of satisfaction. As one reviewer noted of a Fleming novel, "James Bond is what every man would like to be, and what every woman would like between her sheets." In either case, the prospect was exhilarating.[4]

JFK, both during his run-up to the presidency in the late 1950s and after taking office, cultivated a strong association with the daring, sophisticated British secret agent and his creator that became part of his public image. Thus his eager personal encounter with Ian Fleming during the 1960 campaign not only revealed his personal interest in the figure of James Bond but suggested the larger American attraction to an urbane, virile, manly image at the dawn of a new decade. The association of the young American leader with one of the most compelling characters in postwar popular culture told much about the underlying masculine appeal of Kennedy's campaign.

Ian Fleming came from a rather privileged social background. Born in London on May 28, 1908, to a wealthy merchant family—his father served in Parliament as a Tory MP—he was educated at a series of exclusive preparatory schools. Following a desultory year at the Royal Military College at Sandhurst, Fleming decided against a military career and departed for the Continent to attend the University of Geneva and Munich University, where he learned French, German, and some Russian. He then became a journalist for Reuters News Agency in 1931 and covered news stories in Europe. After tiring of reporting, he tried his hand at banking and stock-broking, but his sense of privileged nonchalance kept him from taking the business world very seriously. He confessed to having "great fun, but I could never figure out what a sixty-fourth of a point was."[5]

In 1939, Fleming entered upon a trajectory of success when, with England on the cusp of war, he was invited to become the personal assis-tant to Rear Admiral John Godfrey, director of intelligence for the Royal Navy, and was awarded the rank of lieutenant in the Royal Naval Reserve. He would eventually rise to become a commander. When hostilities broke out, the young Englishman worked in the famous Room 39 in Whitehall and excelled as a manager and draftsman, a "skilled fixer and vigorous showman," in the words of a colleague. He exhibited a certain flair and bravado along with a studied competence as he served as the primary liai-son for Godfrey with many branches of the British military on espionage matters. He also helped set up British commando units and participated in secret operations in France, North Africa, and Spain to combat the German conquest.[6]

But Fleming's most important role during the war came when Britain established intelligence sharing with the United States. He served with a group that worked with the American William "Wild Bill" Donovan, a former war hero, diplomat, and lawyer who was a friend of President Franklin Roosevelt's, to set up the intelligence service that later became the Central Intelligence Agency in 1947. When the young British officer returned home, an appreciative Donovan presented him with a gift: a .38 Colt revolver inscribed with "For Special Services." It would be one of Fleming's prized possessions. The young officer attended several Churchill-Roosevelt wartime conferences and was sent to the Far East to analyze the intelligence structure for the newly created British Pacific Fleet.[7]

With the end of World War II in 1945, Commander Fleming returned to civilian life. It was not an easy transition. During the war, he had found intelligence work enormously fulfilling and had shaped a romantic and glamorous persona. He was frequently seen in the company of important people and seemed to know everyone who was important in the govern-ment or the military as he scurried from meeting to meeting during the day and attended numerous social functions in the evening. Fleming's in-the-know style projected an aura that was equal parts inside information and self-confidence, imparting a sense to others that they were confronting an important man of the world. Wide-ranging and clever in conversation, he came across as "urbane and irreverent, invulnerable and unconcerned," in the words of one observer.[8] Invariably, Fleming appeared stylish and sophisticated. Tall in stature, with classic English features, swept-back hair, and an aristocratic bearing, he had an expressive face that projected a heavy-lidded sensuality as he looked out languidly on the world from behind a cloud of smoke emitted by his custom-made, hand-rolled Morland cigarettes blended from three choice varieties of Turkish tobacco. Vain and a bit of a prima donna, Fleming dressed with a casual elegance and cultivated an image as a connoisseur of food and drink with a special fondness for martinis, champagne, and caviar. As a young man, he grew fond of gambling on baccarat at casinos in the French resort towns of Le Touquet and Deauville and spent much time with a loose group of comrades from London clubs who gathered regularly for lighthearted games of bridge and golf and drinking. An interviewer once described Fleming as "suave, amused, sardonic . . . and one versed in these matters could place Fleming instantly—as Eton and Sandhurst, inherited money, government service, world travel, social assurance."[9]

But Fleming also embraced a standard of personal toughness that stressed physical bravery and endurance. As a student at Eton, he had been an extraordinary track athlete and later became a wild, reckless skier who craved the excitement of dangerous downhill runs. During the war, Fleming had joined with other British and American men in a boot camp for espionage and intelligence personnel, where he pushed himself relentlessly and excelled at underwater demolition, small arms fire, and judo. According to the director of the facility, "He was one of the best pupils the school ever had." In later life, Fleming took plunges into ice-cold lakes, embarked upon grueling long-distance ski runs, and mounted exhausting mountain-climbing forays. Years later, while living in Jamaica, he enjoyed hunting barracuda and sharks with a speargun.[10]

Fleming spent much of his life engaged in a constant search for stimulation and excitement, possibly to ward off the melancholy that lurked

behind his facade of sophisticated nonchalance. He grew easily bored—
with people, social situations, the normal round of life—and restlessly
sought novel experiences. Fleming liked to embellish life, and even as a
young man he displayed a vivid sense of fantasy. "Ian was always contriv-
ing situations and then making life fit into them," recalled a friend of the
young man's. Fleming traveled to nearly every corner of the globe and developed a special affection for exotic locales far removed from staid
English society. During the war, he fell in love with Jamaica during a trip
to the Caribbean and purchased a picturesque plot of land on the north
shore with cliffs, a hidden beach, and much surrounding wilderness. He
built a modest but gracious house, named the small estate Goldeneye, and
spent many months there every year. Almost desperate to avoid inactivity,
the Englishman developed a love of fast, expensive cars and cultivated
hobbies ranging from golf to bird-watching to rare book collecting. His
wife declared, "His aim as long as I knew him was to avoid the dull, the
humdrum, the everyday demands of life that afflict ordinary people."[11]

One of Fleming's most striking characteristics, however, was his notorious reputation as a womanizer. The elegant Englishman had a long string
of seductions, dalliances, and affairs throughout his life and seemed able
to attract countless female companions with little effort. "He was irresistible to women, and he was the only man I have ever known who was," reported a close friend from the 1930s. Fleming had a voracious sexual
appetite and few scruples about fulfilling it. He had an extensive collection of French pornography, for example, which he would casually show
to females he was trying to seduce. After marrying Anne Rothermere in
1952 at the age of forty-four and ending his bachelorhood—they had conducted a lengthy affair while she was married to someone else—Fleming's
philandering past occasionally caught up with him. Anne wrote him a bemused note while visiting New York: "It is astonishing that I cannot be in
any capital in the world for more than a day without meeting some woman
with whom you have had carnal relations." Over the last few years of his
life, the writer nurtured a long-term affair with a Jamaican neighbor,
Blanche Blackwell.[12]

Fleming's numerous sexual encounters were noteworthy for a special
quality: they were almost entirely physical. He evinced a callous attitude

about women that sent him from one to another for sexual gratification with little sense of obligation or emotional attachment. "Women were all a bit of a joke for Ian, a treat to enjoy but not to make any sort of fuss about afterward," explained a female acquaintance. Fleming, in his notebooks, explained his attitude. "Men want a woman whom they can turn on and off like a light switch," he wrote. "Women have their uses for the relief of tension." Men, he suggested at another point, were for friendship and exchanging ideas, while females were for physical gratification: "Some women respond to the whip, some to the kiss. Most of them like a mixture of both, but none of them answer to the mind alone, to the intellectual demand, unless they are man dressed as woman." As a friend noted, Fleming "explained to me that women were not worth that much emotion."[13]

After spinning his wheels for a time following World War II, Fleming accepted an offer to manage the foreign news service for a chain of national and provincial newspapers, which included *The Sunday Times*. From his office in London, he directed overseas coverage for the chain, appointed correspondents in the field, and circulated their articles. He also cultivated his own writing. Fleming had a lifelong interest in literature, reading literary journals, magazines of opinion, and novels such as Thomas Mann's *Magic Mountain,* from which he memorized passages to recite at social gatherings. In the late 1930s, Fleming had been drawn to the fictional thrillers of Geoffrey Household, author of books such as *The Third Hour* (1937) and *Rogue Male* (1939), and in this period he even tried to start a weekly magazine modeled on *The New Yorker.* Following World War II, Fleming established friendships with a number of literary figures, including Noël Coward, the poet and novelist William Plomer, the novelist Paul Gallico, and the poet Dame Edith Sitwell.[14]

Gradually, Fleming began to focus on an idea that had been germinating for quite some time in the back of his mind: writing a thriller set in the world of international espionage. During the war, Fleming had casually mentioned to his friend and fellow intelligence office Robert Harling that he was "going to write the spy story to end all spy stories." His work in intelligence for the Royal Navy provided impetus for the idea, of course, as did his own personal predilections for fantasy, adventure, excitement, sex, and global travel. Now, in the early 1950s, engaged to Anne

Rothermere—she was already pregnant with their first child—the philanderer who was leery of marriage grew nervous about providing adequate financial support for his wife and child. He decided to act on his long-simmering idea for a book.[15]

So in mid-January 1952, while at Goldeneye, Fleming took his usual morning swim in the ocean, ate breakfast, and then sat down at his roll-top desk in the living room and began to type. As would be his custom, he had made no preparations or outlines but simply started writing on his aged portable typewriter. For the next seven weeks, every morning from about nine to noon, he worked on the manuscript and completed about two thousand words a day, writing quickly with little revision to maintain the pace of the story. He went back later to edit, adding details and sharpening episodes. His espionage thriller told the tale of a British secret agent whose name he pulled from a famous ornithological reference book, James Bond's *Birds of the West Indies,* a work he often utilized on his bird-watching jaunts. Fleming folded into the story all the elements of his life, both actual and fantasy: dangerous intelligence maneuvers and Cold War clashes, physical adventures and deadly encounters, sophisticated social life on the Continent and sexual entanglements.[16]

Casino Royale (1953) tells the story of the British Secret Service's mission against Le Chiffre, a Soviet agent and leader of a Communist-controlled trade union in France. This powerful, unscrupulous figure is using his union's funds to gamble at Royale, a French coastal town noted for its casinos. The Secret Service comes up with a simple plan: bankrupt him at the baccarat table, after which the Soviets would be forced to kill him to avoid the severe political fallout. M., the head of the agency, chooses James Bond, agent 007, noted for his espionage skills, toughness, and gambling acumen, to take the lead in this venture. The subsequent story involves bomb explosions, high-stakes baccarat games, and kidnappings. The British agent also becomes involved with a beautiful female colleague who turns out to be a double agent.

Casino Royale had all of the elements for which the James Bond novels would become famous in the English-speaking world over the next decade. It presented a Cold War story with serious political stakes as the British Secret Service, aided by the American Central Intelligence Agency, fought

Communist subversion in Europe. But rather than unfolding a dry story of ideological maneuver, Fleming offered an exciting tale full of adventure and close scrapes, intrigue and danger, suspense and violence. *Casino Royale* also featured a favorite Fleming touch: a socially sophisticated setting where the protagonist could display his excellent taste in clothing, food and drink, manners, and automobiles while interacting with other denizens of an elite social stratum. The novel is set in the elegant gambling milieu of a French seaside town on the channel, filled with fancy hotels and exclusive restaurants. There "was something splendid about the Negresco baroque of the Casino Royale, a strong whiff of Victorian elegance and luxury," Fleming wrote. The British agent has his special automobile shipped across the channel, a four-and-a-half-liter Bentley with a supercharger by Amherst Villiers. He nurtures a deep knowledge of French cuisine and wine and has even created his own martini: "Three measures of Gordon's, one of vodka, half a measure of Kina Lillet. Shake it very well until it's ice-cold, then add a large thin slice of lemon." Bond's glamorous world radiates a seductive attraction.[17] *Casino Royale* introduced another signature trait of the James Bond series: a strong dose of sexuality. The secret agent, with his good looks, cosmopolitan tastes, and virile persona, presents an irresistible allure to women. Vesper Lynd, the attractive double agent, was the first "Bond girl," as the female characters in Fleming's novels came to be known. With dark hair and deep blue eyes, a light suntan, minimal makeup, and a curvaceous figure, Vesper makes a stunning appearance when she meets Bond to accompany him to the baccarat tables. "Her dress was of black velvet, simple and yet with a touch of splendour that only half a dozen couturiers in the world can achieve," wrote Fleming. "There was a thin necklace of diamonds at her throat and a diamond clip in the low vee which just exposed the jutting swell of her breasts."[18]

The secret agent, while enticed by Vesper, makes it clear that he views women almost exclusively in sexual terms. When first told that she will serve as his "Number Two" on the Le Chiffre mission, he grouses, "Women were for recreation. On a job, they got in the way and fogged things up with sex and hurt feelings and all the emotional baggage they carried around." Then later, when she falls for a crudely forged note and is kidnapped, Bond grows completely exasperated: "These blithering women who thought they could do a man's work. Why the hell couldn't they stay at home and mind their pots and pans and stick to their frocks and gossip and leave men's work to the men." His eventual involvement means little beyond sexual gratification. Bond loathes the inevitable pattern of an extensive affair—"sentiment, the touch of the hand, the kiss, the passionate kiss, the feel of the body, the climax in the bed, then more bed, then less bed, then the boredom, the tears, and the final bitterness"—and is determined to avoid it.[19]

Ultimately, the key element in *Casino Royale* is James Bond himself, one of the most memorable figures in modern popular fiction. Fleming's inspiration had come from a number of influences. In interviews, he claimed that Bond had been modeled on intelligence operatives and commandos he had met during World War II, particularly British and American agents he had seen working together. The author also contended that Bond was partly "autobiographical," in that he gave the character many of his own personal predilections for fast cars, beautiful women, fine cuisine, and cigarettes of "a Balkan and Turkish mixture made for him by Morlands of Grosvenor Street." But the notion of Bond as Fleming's alter ego was more a product of Fleming's rich fantasies about thrilling spy work in the international arena than his actual intelligence experiences during the war, which mainly involved bureaucratic management in London.[20]

The character who habitually introduces himself as "Bond, James Bond" offers a compelling array of features. Fully versed in the savvy of international espionage, sophisticated and daring, resilient and brave, and effortlessly attractive to women, he strode out of Fleming's novels as a figure of self-possessed, manly independence whom the author once described as "an amalgam of romantic tough guys." With gray-blue eyes and an ironic manner, he carries a .25 Beretta automatic with a skeleton grip in a chamois leather holster beneath his left armpit. He has earned his stripes in the Secret Service by undertaking the most dangerous missions and performing deadly tasks. "It's not difficult to get a Double O number if you're prepared to kill people," Bond explains coldly. "That's all the meaning it has. It's nothing to be particularly proud of." He embraces man-to-man contests and does not shrink from physical pain. When Le Chiffre captures and brutally tortures him, Bond sees it as a "supreme test of will." As a doctor later tells him, "It is remarkable you are alive and I congratulate you. Few men could have supported what you have been through." While a man of action, Bond also is a thoughtful figure who can question the Cold War and his own role in conducting it. After surviving his torture and witnessing SMERSH's killing of Le Chiffre, he reflects, "This country-right-or-wrong business is getting a little out-of-date. . . . History is moving pretty quickly these days and the heroes and villains keep on changing parts." If Le Chiffre were to stand in front of him, he claims, "I wouldn't hesitate to kill him, but out of personal revenge and not, I'm afraid, for some high moral reason or for the sake of my country."[21]

The success of *Casino Royale* led to a contract for two more James Bond novels, which sold even better, and then spawned a whole series of volumes that appeared throughout the 1950s with escalating popularity. Over the next decade, Fleming would write and publish a Bond book once a year: *Live and Let Die* (1954), *Moonraker* (1955), *Diamonds Are Forever* (1956), *From Russia with Love* (1957), *Dr. No* (1958), *Goldfinger* (1959), *For Your Eyes Only* (1960), *Thunderball* (1961), *On Her Majesty's Secret Service* (1963), and *You Only Live Twice* (1964). As they took popular culture by storm and gained millions of readers, the series embroidered many of the traits first established by *Casino Royale*. The books feature deadly clashes with Cold War villains, most with connections to Soviet-controlled organizations such as SMERSH and SPECTRE. This gigantic contest between Communism and criminality, on the one side, and democracy and security, on the other, has global stakes of the highest magnitude. The Bond novels also vie with one another in presenting exotic locales and glamorous social milieus, be they the beaches and the crystal-line waters of Jamaica, the exclusive clubs of London, the diamond-smuggling centers of Sierra Leone and Las Vegas, the elite horse-racing country near Saratoga, New York, or the ski slopes of Switzerland. In all of these tales, glamour and extravagance compete to attract the reader's attention.

In these various stories of international intrigue, Bond's refined tastes and effortless embrace of the high life form an important aspect of his image. The British agent, with cosmopolitan self-assurance, always appears impeccably attired and ready to order the best food and drinks, drive the most powerful and sportiest cars, and enjoy the most sophisticated material accoutrements of life. As Bond travels about the world, he dines on cold langouste in France, *tagliatelle verdi* in Italy, stone crabs and melted butter in the United States, and beluga caviar wherever he can get it; he demonstrates his skills on the mountain slopes by cutting the difficult Sprung-Christiana figure on skies outfitted with Attenhofer Flex forward releases and Marker lateral releases; he dresses with elegant restraint, favoring single-breasted dark blue suits, single-breasted dinner jackets with silk shirts and satin ties, casual trousers and Sea Island cotton shirts, and dog-toothed suits for country outings or golf; and he drives a battleship-gray Aston Martin DB III tricked out with numerous special devices. Always a stylish figure with exquisite taste who is neither a pretentious aristocrat nor a boorish bourgeois, Bond reflected the aspirations of a broad, postwar middle class who envisioned the good life in terms of material abundance.[22]

A string of attractive, available young women offer indelible markers of the James Bond novel, ranging from Solitaire in *Live and Let Die*, the disgruntled girlfriend of Mr. Big; to Tiffany Case in *Diamonds Are Forever*, the tough but lonely member of the diamond-smuggling gang; to Gala Brand, the beautiful undercover agent working as a personal assistant to the dastardly Sir Hugo Drax in *Moonraker*; to Domino Vitali, the mistress of a SPECTRE leader in *Thunderball*. Unfailingly beautiful, youthful, and sexually experienced, these females willingly, and often enthusiastically, succumb to the charms of the British secret agent. The Bond girls often have suggestive names, such as Mary Goodnight in *The Man with the Golden Gun*, Honey Rider in *Dr. No*, and, most outrageously, Pussy Galore in *Goldfinger*. At the same time, many of them also have independent jobs and careers, often in intelligence or law enforcement and occasionally as criminals in their own right. Their sexual connection to Bond displays a certain spirit of female independence and erotic adventurism that contrasted sharply with the housewife model of American middle-class life.

Bond's considerable sex appeal became an important part of his popular legend. Fleming's novels were filled with tributes to the secret agent's virility. "I hoped I would one day kiss a man like that," Solitaire confesses after her first intimate encounter with Bond. "And when I first saw you, I knew it would be you." While they are in bed after their first sexual encounter, Bond comments to the notorious lesbian Pussy Galore, "They told me you only liked women." She replies, "I never met a man before." Indeed, the secret agent's power over women helped define his appeal as a solution to a broader crisis of masculinity. For Bond, this is partly a case of combating a modern confusion of sexual identity. Bond notes at one point, "As a result of fifty years of emancipation, feminine qualities were dying out or being transferred to the males. Pansies of both sexes were everywhere, not yet completely homosexual, but confused, not knowing what they were. . . . He was sorry for them, but he had no time for them."[23]

In fact, Bond's intense masculinity glues the elements of the novels together. For a society harboring endemic fears of male decline, his manly, assertive, sophisticated presence offered a bracing antidote. The secret agent, far from being trapped in suburban family life and bureaucracy, moves about in elite social circles eating gourmet meals and drinking martinis, driving expensive sports cars, and dressing with understated elegance. He effortlessly beds a bevy of beautiful women, displays great courage and intelligence in escaping from close scrapes, and defeats powerful enemies of Western democracy. Bound neither by family nor by institutions, he personifies masculine individual action in an age of social conformity and restriction. For the buccaneering secret agent, individual determination and deeds, not rules and regulations, bring success in the treacherous world of international espionage. He believes that the determined, capable individual agent, not the fuddy-duddy intelligence service bureaucrat ensconced in "a snug nest of papers," can best defend British society and values.[24]

Fleming's James Bond novels elicited a mixed critical reception. Some denounced the books as nasty concoctions of "sex, snobbery, and sadism," sniffed at their vulgar "cult of luxury," and bemoaned their "total lack of any ethical frame of reference." Others praised their colorful descriptions, suspenseful plots, and exciting chains of action. As the *Los Angeles Times* claimed, "The espionage novel has been brought up to date by a superb practitioner of that nearly lost art." *Time* even compared Fleming favorably to Raymond Chandler, while the *New York Herald Tribune* praised his "quite marvelous adroitness in all the elements of narrative."[25]

With the public, the Bond books suffered no such ambiguity. By 1958, they had sold 105,000 copies; 237,000 in 1959; 323,000 in 1960; and 670,000 in 1961. With the appearance of the first two James Bond movies from Hollywood in the early 1960s that garnered millions of new fans, sales skyrocketed to over 1.3 million copies in 1962 and over 4.46 million copies in 1963. Sales would peak in 1965 at nearly 6.8 million copies. Fleming's books displayed such a huge appeal that eventually they produced a popular craze.[26]

By 1960, James Bond had entered into modern culture as a striking figure of manly, sophisticated heroism fighting against evil in the world. Part potboiling thriller and part travelogue, part portrait of stylish living and part catalog of consumer abundance, part tough-guy adventure and part heroic quest, part political morality tale and part titillating story of sex and seduction, the tales of 007 and his global fight against Communism and gangsterism struck a resounding chord with the public. As Kingsley Amis, the famous British writer, noted of the growing legions of Bond fans, "We don't want to have Bond to dinner or go golfing with Bond or talk to Bond. We want to be Bond." Fleming's stories of international espionage, he continued, worked "to entertain the reader by showing him glimpses of a semi-fantasy world he might like to inhabit, but dare not. In addition, however, he is also the more likely to admire Bond as one who not only inhabits such a world by choice, but survives the worst it can do to him and comes out on top."[27]

Bond's supercharged masculine image thus appealed to a vast and growing audience by the late 1950s. It also attracted a young American political leader who was shaping his own image of masculine vigor with an eye trained on the White House. The secret agent and the presidential candidate, it turned out, had much in common.

Throughout 1955, Jack Kennedy spent many weeks in New York hospitals dealing with surgery and various treatments for his chronic back problems, followed by extensive stints of recovery in Florida, Hyannis Port, and Newport, Rhode Island. In all these places, he surrounded himself with books that lay stacked on the bed and adjoining night tables. Among the volumes was *Casino Royale,* Ian Fleming's first James Bond novel. Opinions differ as to who first gave it to him, with some claiming that it was Jacqueline Kennedy and others pointing to a family friend, Marion "Oatsie" Leiter. But in either event, the result was the same: the young senator became a keen James Bond fan. As his wife noted, JFK read voraciously in history and biography but rarely touched fiction except for "three Ian Fleming books. . . . You know, he liked Ian Fleming." His closest aide and speechwriter, Ted Sorensen, concurred. "Novels and mysteries were relatively rare in his reading," Sorensen observed, "but for relief from the rigors of his office he sometimes turned to the fantastic escapades and escapes of Ian Fleming's delightfully exaggerated British Secret Agent, James Bond."[28]

Kennedy's attraction to these novels had been foreshadowed by an adolescent fondness for an earlier British writer, John Buchan, whom one critic has described as "the father of the modern spy thriller." In books such as *The Thirty-Nine Steps, Greenmantle,* and *Mr. Standfast,* his heroic central character, Richard Hannay, uncovers and quashes perfidious conspiracies while embodying a manly ethic of "grit and pluck and hardihood," as one observed described it. A patriot of great physical courage and mental fortitude, Hannay battles sinister, vaguely authoritarian spy rings that threaten to undermine modern liberal institutions. Written in the second and third decades of the twentieth century, the stories offer cliff-hanging episodes that take Hannay from deadly danger to ultimate triumph. Jack Kennedy, along with his younger brother Bobby, devoured these tales of secret agent derring-do during adolescence.[29]

In 1940, the year of his death, Buchan's autobiography, *Pilgrim's Way,* was published, and John F. Kennedy read it eagerly. Less a memoir than a series of character sketches of famous men he had known and admired (they included Rudyard Kipling, Aldous Huxley, H. G. Wells, and Arthur Balfour), the volume defined its dramatis personae as models of masculine fortitude. Buchan described the slightly built T. E. Lawrence, for example, as a man with a "bodily toughness and endurance far beyond anything I have ever met. . . . I could have followed Lawrence over the edge of the world." Raymond Asquith, the brilliant, debonair, and brave son of the English prime minister who was tragically killed in World War I, received high praise as a young man of "cool and grace," "brilliance," and "easy stateliness" who was "curiously self-possessed and urbane." Buchan also lamented that modern society, with its mechanization and bureaucracy and consumerism, was growing soft. In such a world, life was becoming "largely a quest for amusement. . . . In such a bag man's paradise, where life would be rationalized and padded with every material comfort, there would be little satisfaction for the immortal part of man."[30]

Pilgrim's Way had a profound effect on young Jack Kennedy, and it became a lifelong favorite. One of JFK's navy buddies during World War II recalled the young lieutenant talking at length about the book as they traveled on a troopship in the Pacific. Jacqueline Bouvier remembered that shortly after she had begun dating the young congressman, he gave her a copy of *Pilgrim's Way* as a way of explaining his deepest values and aspirations. For John F. Kennedy, John Buchan's gallery of adventurous spies and heroic historical figures plowed the ground for his appreciation of Ian Fleming's later stories of international espionage and manly vigor.[31]

James Bond also generated a natural appeal for Kennedy on more personal grounds. They shared a number of traits and parallels in their lives that drew JFK to the fictional spy. Both the politician and the secret agent came from prosperous families—Bond's father was an executive with the Vickers armaments firm on the European continent—and had been sent to boarding schools, where they were on their own from a young age. Both attended exclusive prep schools, the American at Choate and the Englishman at Eton. They threw themselves into sports, with Kennedy competing at swimming and football and Bond at boxing and judo. Both developed a certain sense of self-possessed, competitive independence at an early age and enjoyed a cosmopolitan upbringing, with young JFK traveling extensively in Europe, meeting heads of state and the pope while young Bond lived on the Continent until age eleven and achieved a command of both French and German.[32]

Bond and Kennedy had been navy officers in World War II before rising to prominent positions in government service. The senator, of course, had commanded a PT boat in the Pacific before returning home to become a member of Congress, while Bond had gained the rank of commander in the Royal Navy, been awarded the Order of St. Michael and St. George, and served in the Special Operations Executive, a covert British military organization. Both men emerged from wartime service with an admiration for individual initiative and a distaste for bureaucratic restriction. James Bond, the maverick secret agent who never worked easily as a member of a team, was described by his MI6 chief as a man with "an impetuous streak in his nature, a streak of the foolhardy that brought him in conflict with higher authority." He found a kindred spirit in the young American navy lieutenant who complained about the inept, unqualified military brass he observed in the Pacific theater leading "this heaving, puffing war machine of ours."[33]

In their personal lives, the fictional character and the American politician shared a style that reflected superb taste, effortless sophistication, and cool, understated elegance. Kennedy became noted for his well-dressed, urbane presence as he sailed off the coast at Hyannis Port, mingled with movie stars in Hollywood, and moved easily among Las Vegas casinos and entertainers. Bond became renowned for a cosmopolitan image of impeccable clothes, fine food and wine, and presence at elite social clubs, ski slopes, and golf courses. Their worldly, irreverent social style was also shared by the Rat Pack, who strolled through American popular culture clad in tuxedos, whiskey tumblers in hand, cracking wise and charming everyone in sight as the hip minstrels of a new age. It was no accident that Dean Martin would star in the Matt Helm film series later in the 1960s, playing the character of a James Bond look-alike.

Kennedy and Bond exhibited a common ethos of manly courage that lay close to their sense of identity. Kennedy had demonstrated great bravery after the sinking of the PT-109 and then stressed this trait in his Hemingwayesque *Profiles in Courage*. Bond's espionage work in World War II led to a postwar career in the British Secret Service, where he became notable for "outstanding bravery and distinction." The secret agent fought to the death with one of Mr. Big's henchmen in *Live and Let Die*, battled a villain in a terrifying railroad chase in *Diamonds Are Forever*, and grappled with Auric Goldfinger and the thuggish Oddjob aboard a hijacked jetliner in *Goldfinger*. As Fleming observed, Bond was probably Kennedy's "favorite action character" because the secret agent's "patriotic derring-do was in keeping with the President's own concept of endurance and courage and grace under pressure."[34]

Finally, of course, Kennedy and Bond shared a powerful attraction to beautiful women and promiscuous sex. The two men became noteworthy for legendary libidos—explicitly for the spy, more indirectly for the politician—that formed a key part of their public attraction. While Kennedy spent time with an array of glamorous actresses, attractive showgirls, and female staffers in Washington, D.C., Bond dazzled readers with his seduction of an assortment of gorgeous women—fellow spies and villains' mistresses, innocent victims and skeptical lesbians—around the globe. In *From Russia with Love,* the female character is so enamored of Bond's photograph that she considers defecting to the West with a top secret cipher machine. Much the same dynamic seemed to drive many female voters regarding Kennedy as they entered the voting booth, and many male voters who sought emulation. But it was not just an enjoyment of numerous sexual encounters that marked Kennedy and Bond; it was the casualness of them. Both men saw women as little more than playthings to be enjoyed for physical pleasure and then discarded. This image of the sexual conquistador created a compelling alternative to the stodgy organization man and meek, compliant suburban father in mid-1950s America.

But the connection between Kennedy and Bond was more than personal and stylistic. They also held a common ideological position: a brand of fervent, if understated, Cold War romanticism. Firmly anti-Communist and anti-Soviet, it stressed the effectiveness of the daring, manly maverick over the hidebound organization man in fighting enemies of the free world. Kennedy, endorsing the antibureaucratic critique of *The Ugly American,* argued for an approach to combating Communism based on individual initiative and programmatic flexibility. Bond, chafing against the bureaucratic restrictions of the British Secret Service, similarly reacted to various threats emanating from SMERSH and SPECTRE with a personal set of skills and spirit of daring well adapted to the demands of the struggle.

In both cases, their attitudes valued the unconventional over the predictable, the insights of the individual over the consensus of the organization.

It is significant that Allen Dulles, director of the CIA, developed a friendship with John F. Kennedy in the 1950s that included a common fascination with James Bond. This legendary chief of American intelligence operations had first met JFK in 1955 when he was visiting a close friend in Palm Beach, Florida, and paid a social call to Joseph Kennedy, former ambassador to England, at his residence down the beach. He saw the junior senator from Massachusetts lying on the sofa, convalescing from a serious back injury. JFK and Dulles ended up talking for nearly two hours about international issues. The CIA chief noted that the young senator was fascinated by foreign affairs and "obviously wanted to learn . . . he was very respectful . . . he was trying to find out what the facts were." They struck up a friendship, and, according to the director, "We had many, many talks together. . . . I thought he had a very keen appreciation of foreign problems." During Kennedy's presidential run, Dulles briefed the candidate for two hours on a variety of Cold War issues.[35]

The two men soon discovered another common thread: a fascination with Ian Fleming's James Bond novels. Jackie Kennedy first gave Dulles a copy of *From Russia with Love* in 1957, saying, "Here is a book *you* should have, Mr. Director." Dulles was fascinated by the story and would go on to read the other Bond tales. In the process, he learned that JFK also loved Fleming's books, so he began sending copies of them to the Kennedys as they appeared, and, according to Dulles, "We often talked about James Bond." The director, like Kennedy, admired "the Bond characteristics like courage, resourcefulness, and ingenuity" and was intrigued by the special gadgets that he used to baffle his opponents. In fact, he commented to colleagues, "I would be glad to hire several James Bonds." Although he never said so publicly, he undoubtedly appreciated Bond's sexual adventures because the charming Dulles was a notorious Casanova who had dozens of affairs ranging from Mary Bancroft to Clare Boothe Luce to Queen Frederica of Greece. Yet he realized that many of the British agent's adventures and actions were far-fetched. "I fear that James Bond in real life would have had a thick dossier in the Kremlin after his first exploit and would not have survived his second," admitted Dulles.[36]

Dulles developed a friendship with Ian Fleming. Their paths had crossed indirectly during the war when Fleming recommended the appointment of a man of "absolute discretion, sobriety, devotion to duty, languages, and wide experience" to oversee intelligence gathering in New York, and William Donovan chose Dulles for the job. Then Dulles met Fleming in 1959 at a London dinner, and they hit it off immediately during several hours of conversation. "Fleming was a brilliant and witty talker, with ideas on everything," said the director. "Before we were through, we had pretty well torn orthodox intelligence to pieces." They talked about technological innovation and the future of espionage, agreeing about "new tools that would have to be invented for the new era." Dulles explained that after that night "I kept in constant touch with him—and he kindly kept sending me his books," many of which contained inscriptions such as this: "To Allen, who has been a strong arm for so long. Ian Fleming." In return, Dulles sent Fleming an early draft of his memoir, *The Craft of Intelligence*.[37]

Thus the stage was set by the early 1960s for public recognition of the Kennedy-Bond association. A few weeks after JFK's inauguration, a national magazine publicized the new president's fascination with the British secret agent. It would be one of the most talked-about incidents in the early days of the New Frontier.

On March 17, 1961, *Life* ran an article on the intellectual habits of the urbane, youthful, Harvard-educated young man who had occupied the White House a few weeks earlier. Titled "The President's Voracious Reading Habits," it detailed his keen appetite for "magazines, newspapers, books, government reports, technical papers, and just about anything else" in terms of reading material he encountered during his busy work schedule. Hugh Sidey, presidential correspondent for *Life* and *Time*, explained that John Kennedy read very rapidly, about twelve hundred words a minute, and that he began his day by perusing five newspapers every morning and then devouring over a dozen magazines when they appeared every week. He also searched for the work of columnists he particularly admired, such as Walter Lippmann and Joseph Alsop. The new president loved books, particularly works of history, biography, and public policy that he read in bed in the late evening or took with him on trips. It listed ten of his favorite volumes, including David Cecil's *Melbourne,* John Buchan's *Pilgrim's Way,* Samuel Flagg Bemis's *John Quincy Adams,* Allan Nevins's *Emergence of Lincoln,* and Winston Churchill's *Marlborough.* But the list also contained one atypical choice standing among these stalwart volumes: *From Russia with Love.* As the article explained, the new American leader had "a weakness for detective stories, particularly those of British author Ian Fleming and his fictitious undercover man, James Bond."[38]

This disclosure provided not only a glimpse into JFK's intellectual worldview but also a view of his public persona. His love of books about great political leaders as well as thrillers featuring a daring secret agent reinforced an image of a virile, manly, youthful man of courage who combined intellect with a yen for action. In a more practical vein, Kennedy's public endorsement also sent sales for the James Bond novels skyrocketing. Henry Brandon, correspondent for *The Sunday Times* who knew all the parties concerned, told Fleming later in 1961 that "the entire Kennedy family is crazy about James Bond." He reported that the president was fascinated by Fleming's flamboyant powers of imagination, often asking "how such an intelligent, mature, urbane sort of man could have such an element of odd imagining in his makeup."[39]

In the wake of this massive surge of publicity from Kennedy's endorsement of James Bond, Fleming expressed his gratitude. "I've always sent copies of them [the new Bond novels] direct and personally to him before they're published over here," he told an interviewer. He added, "I think the president likes my books because he enjoys the combination of physical violence, effort, and winning in the end—like his PT-boat experiences." Fleming also established ties with Robert Kennedy. "I am delighted to take this opportunity to thank Kennedys everywhere for the electric effect their commendation has had on my sales in America," he wrote gratefully to Bobby. The attorney general responded, "As you know, you have many Kennedy fans. We all can hardly wait for your next contribution to our leisure hours." In turn, Fleming offered encouragement to Bobby in his crusade against organized crime: "Over here we are all watching with fascination your gallant attempts to harass American gangsterdom. If James

Bond can be any help to you, please let me know and I will have a word with M."[40]

In the aftermath of the *Life* piece, the American public encountered myriad associations of the glamorous young president with the daring, sophisticated British secret agent. Promotional materials for the Bond novels displayed a picture of the White House with a single light shining upstairs and accompanying text: "You can bet he's reading one of those Ian Fleming thrillers." A cartoon in *The New Yorker* showed two policemen standing outside the White House as someone burned the midnight oil in a room, with a caption reading, "Then again, it may merely be the new Ian Fleming." United Artists, in its marketing campaign for the first James Bond film, actually pursued the idea (it never materialized) of arranging a visit by Ian Fleming to Cape Canaveral and having him introduce Sean Connery to President Kennedy and his family. As Vincent Canby, critic for *The New York Times*, recognized, the Bond novels and films "characterize[d] a number of aspects of the Kennedy Administration with its reputation for glamour, wit and sophistication, and its real-life drama and melodrama. Indeed, the President himself could be seen as a kind of Bond figure, and the 1962 Cuban missile crisis as a real-life Bond situation."[41]

Meanwhile, the release of the first two James Bond movies, *Dr. No* and *From Russia with Love*, took this popular phenomenon up another notch and illustrated even more graphically how James Bond shared Kennedy's intense masculine appeal. The producers Harry Saltzman and Albert R. "Cubby" Broccoli purchased the film rights for the Bond books and established a partnership to do a series of films. They signed up the action-film director Terence Young and after a lengthy search to find an actor to play the pivotal role of James Bond—candidates included Cary Grant, David Niven, and Roger Moore—chose a relative unknown, the young Scottish actor Sean Connery. After a deal with United Artists, in 1962 they launched one of the most successful, multidecade series in the history of the movies. The popular James Bond films brought the dashing, sexy image of the British secret agent before enormous audiences while inflating a ballooning readership for the novels. The appeal of Bond and Fleming soared into the popular culture stratosphere and blossomed into an expression of the New Frontier's spirit in the early 1960s.[42]

Dr. No tells the story of the secret agent's struggle to eliminate a villainous recluse—half-Chinese and half-German—who is working to sabotage American rocket launches at Cape Canaveral. On his private island fortress near Jamaica, Dr. Julius No has constructed a fearsome technological center that can emit rays to interrupt the American rocket program. Bond is able to infiltrate Dr. No's operation with the help of a friendly CIA agent and in the process meets a beautiful island girl. After several close scrapes, the two triumph by killing Dr. No and destroying his base as they make their escape. Connery, as reviewers noted, played Bond "with a winning mixture of urbanity and masculinity." The voluptuous Ursula Andress, with her memorable emergence from the sea wearing a bikini and a sheathed knife, became the prototype of the seductive "Bond girl."[43]

Kennedy arranged a screening of *Dr. No* at the White House shortly after its release. Public recognition of the JFK–Bond link appeared quickly, because *Time* began its review of the movie by noting the near certainty that the president of the United States would soon view the film and then "emerge into a world where his job seems relatively tame, for he will have seen *Doctor No,* the first attempt to approximate on film the cosmic bravery, stupefying virility, six-acre brain, and deathproof nonchalance of secret agent James Bond—the President's favorite fictional hero." The film, which premiered in London in October 1962 and then in the United States seven months later, also drew attention for another reason. Its theme of thwarting a villainous plot involving rockets in the Caribbean, along with the film's release date, offered an eerie reflection of the recent trauma of the Cuban missile crisis.[44]

The second Bond film, *From Russia with Love,* was released in the fall of 1963. It depicts Bond grappling with SPECTRE, an organization filled with ex-Soviet agents, over a top secret coding device. This group tries to eliminate the British agent using a beautiful Soviet agent, posing as a defector, who seduces Bond with the promise of a sophisticated cipher machine coveted by MI6. Then she genuinely falls for the handsome agent, and the pair flee from SPECTRE through the mysterious labyrinth of

Istanbul, Gypsy encampments in the Turkish countryside, and the *Orient Express* as it speeds toward Paris. After tricking, evading, and killing his adversaries, the British agent successfully escapes with his love interest. Bond's masculine image appears full-blown. "The blubbery arms of the soft life had Bond round the neck and they were slowly strangling him," Fleming had written of the agent's furlough at the tale's outset. "He was a man of war and when, for a long period, there was no war, his spirit went into a decline." In the movie, *Newsweek* noted, one saw a "battle between loner Bond, operating only with his wits and his license to kill, and SPECTRE, the organized calculated embodiment of evil." Regarding his combination of courage and sexuality, *Variety* added, "Every man in the theatre will identify himself as the cool James Bond and every woman will spend a blissful couple of hours imagining herself the blond seductress leading him to his doom." As with the first Bond film, Kennedy made special arrangements to show it at the White House on October 23, 1963, and according to his good friend Ben Bradlee the president "seemed to enjoy the cool and the sex and the brutality."[45]

Allen Dulles played an important role in reinforcing the cultural alliance of President Kennedy's administration and the secret agent James Bond. Addressing the American Booksellers Association, he declared that the CIA could use half a dozen or so James Bonds, which prompted Fleming to begin referring to Dulles as "Agent 008" in the British press. The director attended public screenings of Bond films as they appeared. Dulles even published an article in *Life* magazine explaining his own and the president's mutual admiration for the British author and his famous protagonist. "I liked Ian Fleming's books. Until John F. Kennedy—then Senator Kennedy—took him up, I think my friends felt I was a bit soft-headed in my interest in Fleming and my praise of James Bond," he wrote. "But when I found myself in such august company—together with a few million other addicts not so august—my hobby was then tolerated."[46]

With the president of the United States and the director of the CIA serving as de facto publicity agents, it was not surprising that Fleming began writing tributes to both in new Bond novels as they appeared in the early 1960s. In *The Spy Who Loved Me,* a character declared, "We need some more Jack Kennedys. It's all these old people about. They ought to hand the world over to younger people who haven't got the idea of war stuck in their subconscious." In *The Man with the Golden Gun*, Fleming described how Bond pours himself a glass of bourbon, "pull[s] a chair up to the window, put[s] a low table beside it, [takes] *Profiles in Courage* out of his suitcase," and reads it. In the same novel, Bond recuperates from a clash with a villain by "sitting in his chair, a towel around his waist, reading Allen Dulles' *The Craft of Intelligence*." Fleming also praised the CIA director privately, writing to the *New York Times* journalist Arthur Krock that Dulles's "organization and staff have always cooperated so willingly with James Bond."[47]

In the real world of public policy, Kennedy's affinity for James Bond–style operations seemed to have influenced his attraction to the CIA's program of covert operations. While it would be foolish to believe that JFK, a shrewd, calculating, and thoroughly realistic political leader, relied on a James Bond fantasy to determine his views on the conduct of foreign affairs, evidence suggests that the Fleming novels he loved helped shape his perceptions. The new president, for example, quickly became noted for his frustration with the fuddy-duddy bureaucracies of the State Department and the FBI and his preference for the freewheeling, buccaneering style of Allen Dulles's agency. Skeptical of Eisenhower's policy of massive retaliation and eager to use American power in new, unorthodox ways, the president was "a young and vigorous cold warrior, willing to rethink traditional arguments and reexamine traditional positions in an effort to stop the spread of communism," a leading historian of the CIA has noted. For a new administration presenting itself as primed for combating Communism in innovative ways, "the CIA—and its professional President's men—was an obvious place to get things done." Allen Dulles and his associates eagerly promoted this affinity from the earliest days of the New Frontier.[48]

Not long after Kennedy's election, the CIA hosted an exclusive dinner at Washington's Alibi Club with some of its top people and about a dozen top appointees in the new government. Dulles held forth on his agency's vigor, power, and skill in meeting the demands of a dangerous world, while other top CIA men told exciting stories of the agency's exploits and spread a message of its efficiency, capability, and innovative tactics. As William Colby, one of Dulles's lieutenants in this era, noted, the agency was full of "derring-do boys who parachuted behind enemy lines, the cream of the academic and social aristocracy . . . matching fire with fire in an endless round of thrilling adventures like those of the scenarios in James Bond films." As a historian of the CIA has noted, there were "plenty of hints from Allen Dulles that he was master to a whole crew of Agents 007, [and] the public wanted to believe this myth." So did the new president and many of his advisers.[49]

Kennedy's love affair with the CIA blossomed. McGeorge Bundy reported that shortly after taking office, the new president declared, "I don't care what it is, but if I need some material fast, CIA is the place I have to go. The State Department takes four or five days to answer a simple yes or no." Charles Bartlett, a journalist and friend, reported that JFK told him that while the State Department often delayed, consulted, and dithered, the CIA focused on getting quick, effective results. The president's dismissal of the State Department revealed more than a touch of macho sexuality because, he noted, "They're not queer at State, but . . . Well, they're sort of like Adlai." The president's disparaging sexual reference, of course, was to Adlai Stevenson, a Democrat often dismissed by the New Frontiersmen as an effete, effeminate egghead.[50]

The CIA eagerly presented itself as an organization filled with real-life James Bonds. Foremost among them was Richard Bissell, chief of covert operations, a tall, handsome figure educated at Groton and Yale and a principal architect of the Marshall Plan. A brilliant, tough-minded technocrat with an instinct for dispassionate analysis, an impatience with bureaucracy, and a hunger for innovative action in fighting Communism, he immediately appealed to Kennedy. Bissell had met with the candidate several times during the election, and now he set an appropriate tone of sardonic, sophisticated confidence with just a touch of self-deprecation at the CIA's get-acquainted dinner for the New Frontiersmen in early 1961. When asked to introduce himself, he quipped, "I'm your man-eating shark." Bissell told Kennedy off the record that he agreed with his philosophy, and JFK, when asked whom he trusted in the American intelligence community, replied immediately, "Richard Bissell." According to Bissell, Kennedy, soon after his inauguration, asked him to develop the "Executive Action Capability" program for a small group of handpicked American agents that mirrored the license-to-kill "00" agents in the Fleming novels. "Bond is what the public wanted to believe," Bissell noted. "One could argue that President Kennedy wanted to adopt the style of the novels into the working operations of the agency."[51]

Other CIA operatives played variations on the Bond theme. Tracy Barnes, a high-ranking officer in covert operations and an Ivy League graduate who combined social grace with a certain ruthlessness, loved the Fleming books and passed out copies of them to his family at holidays. "We thought of Daddy as James Bond," said his daughter, Jane. "A man of elegance who knew his martinis." Desmond FitzGerald, who specialized in Far East operations, cut a particularly dashing figure—a handsome Ivy Leaguer with charming manners and a debonair sensibility who claimed that his idea of perfection was "a Harvard Ph.D. who can handle himself in a bar fight." A skilled operative, he was at home in the wilds of Quemoy, the mountains of Laos, the social scene in Georgetown, or the Virginia countryside. Perhaps the CIA's most curious secret agent model was presented to Kennedy by Richard Helms, another high-ranking CIA officer in the early 1960s. Knowing the president's love of the Ian Fleming novels, Helms declared, "They want James Bond? We'll give them Bill Harvey." The comment dripped irony. While William Harvey shared Bond's love of guns, martinis, and daring action, the similarities ended there. Short, stout, alcoholic, and paranoid, Harvey carried two guns at all times because, he claimed, of all the secrets he knew. Nonetheless, because of his skill in covert operations, Bissell appointed him to head the Executive Action Capability program requested by Kennedy. When Harvey met the president in the Oval Office, JFK was somewhat taken aback by the squat, plump agent with bulging eyes (from a thyroid condition) and a frog-like voice. "So you're our James Bond?" he asked with obvious skepticism.[52]

Kennedy's love affair with the CIA influenced his endorsement of its clandestine campaign to unseat the Cuban leader, Fidel Castro. In the aftermath of the Bay of Pigs disaster, where an invasion of American-backed Cuban dissidents was crushed by Castro's forces, the chagrined president asked plaintively, "'Why couldn't this have happened to James Bond?" Yet Kennedy turned to the CIA for more covert action. The agency created Operation Mongoose, which developed an array of initiatives: psychological warfare, plots to assassinate the Communist dictator with poisoned cigars and exploding seashells, ploys to sabotage power plants and ruin crops, and guerrilla counterinsurgency. The spirit of Fleming's secret agent novels permeated this program endorsed by the new administration. Bobby Kennedy, like his brother, subsequently grew frustrated by slow progress in unseating Castro and impatiently asked Harvey, "Why can't you get things cooking like James Bond?" JFK, after screening *Dr. No*, joked, "I wish I had had James Bond on my staff." But he seems to have meant it.[53]

The Russians did their part to cement the association of James Bond with Kennedy's style of anti-Communism. In its usual ham-fisted manner, *Pravda*, the official Soviet newspaper, published a rant against James Bond, Ian Fleming, and President Kennedy that was reported in the American press. It denounced the author for creating "a nightmarish world where laws are written at the point of a gun, where coercion and rape are considered valour and murder is a funny trick." James Bond was a protector of the interests of the propertied classes, "a sort of white archangel, destroying the impure races." Even worse, *Pravda* continued, President Kennedy "declared that Fleming's books were his bedside reading" and endorsed Bond for "furthering the shameful aims of the Western Capitalists." Another Soviet newspaper, *Izvestiya*, claimed that the British author was Allen Dulles's best friend, and the CIA director consistently used "methods recommended by Fleming in his books."[54]

Perhaps the clinching case for JFK's identification with James Bond, however, came in a lark that revealed more than it meant to: the young president's own "James Bond novel." According to his close friend, Charles Spalding, the president called him occasionally with updates about a "James Bond 007 thriller novel he said he was writing about how Lyndon Johnson was trying to take over his presidency." One call reported how the vice president had captured him just as he was about to enter the White House swimming pool, then sealed off the facility and made it a center of operations. Another time, Kennedy said, "Now listen to this, Charlie—you're going to love it. Lyndon has tied up Mrs. Lincoln and Kenny O'Donnell in a White House closet and he's got a plane ready to take them away." In Spalding's words, "I don't know if he ever put any of it down on paper, but he sure had a lot of fun with it."[55]

In another version of this project, during a cruise on the family yacht in Hyannis Port, JFK persuaded his family and friends to act in a "pseudo James Bond movie" that was filmed by Robert Knudsen, a White House photographer. According to Knudsen, Jackie persuaded Secret Service agents to drive to the front of the house, jump out, and run toward the house looking frantic after Kennedy came off the yacht and walked up the pier and shots appeared to ring out. The president clutched his chest, fell flat, and red liquid spilled from his mouth (probably tomato juice) as the others stepped over his prone body. Kennedy did not realize, however, that two reporters were tailing the presidential party in a speedboat. They witnessed at least part of the high jinks and reported them the following day. While JFK was furious and his press secretary, Pierre Salinger, chastised "peeping Tom reporters," this escapade provided another glimpse of the president's James Bond fixation.[56]

Thus the suave, sexy, and immensely popular secret agent became an important contributor to JFK's model of masculine appeal. The president and the fictional hero shared an ethos of manly courage and physical bravery. They shared a casually elegant style: Kennedy with his tailored suits, chic White House parties, and "beautiful people" friends and Bond with his tuxedos, high-stakes gambling, and dry vodka martinis that were shaken, not stirred. They shared an ideological commitment to individualist, romantic anti-Communism that saw them face down dangerous ideological foes in life-and-death situations.

Finally, of course, Kennedy and Bond shared a reputation for successfully wooing beautiful women. JFK's reputation as a Lothario mirrored the sexual conquests of the British secret agent, just as it dovetailed with Sinatra's notorious skills as a Don Juan, the legendary Rat Pack parties in Las Vegas packed with willing starlets, and Mailer's outspoken agenda of machismo and erotic adventure. These exploits reflected the powerful strain of male sexuality that colored the New Frontier, with its insistence that physical pleasure, more than marriage and family, was the object of relationships with females. The epitome of this impulse, however, lay in another figure in the Kennedy Circle. A pioneering figure in the sexual revolution that had begun sweeping through postwar American society with great force by the mid-1950s, he established a template for a compelling new code of sexual behavior and social style. It soon encompassed JFK and many of his male associates.

SIX

A PHILOSOPHY FOR PLAYBOYS:
HUGH HEFNER

In January 1961, Hugh Hefner, owner and editor of *Playboy* magazine, flew to Washington, D.C., to attend the inauguration of John F. Kennedy. Sammy Davis Jr., a Rat Pack member and close friend, had arranged for the tickets. Hefner rented a town house in Georgetown for several days and secured a limousine, and now he and his party—his girlfriend Joyce Nizzari, *Playboy*'s associate editor Victor Lownes and his girlfriend, Lynne Rash, and the Chicago Urban League official Finis Henderson and his wife—flew into the national capital to enjoy the festivities. They began with the huge gala put together by Frank Sinatra the night before the ceremony, where the crowd thrilled to the performances of an array of Hollywood and Broadway stars along with the president-elect and his wife. The following day, after the inauguration ceremony, the Hefner party, with the men in formal evening wear and the women in elegant ball gowns, attended the inaugural ball held at the National Guard Armory.[1]

A few days later, Hefner flew to New York with the Rat Pack to attend a special benefit held at Carnegie Hall in honor of Martin Luther King Jr. In addition to Frank Sinatra, Dean Martin, Sammy Davis Jr., Peter Lawford, and Joey Bishop, a long list of entertainers performed at the tribute: Tony Bennett, Count Basie and his band, Sidney Poitier, Harry

Belafonte, Carmen McRae, and George Kirby. In such fashion, the magazine editor moved about easily within the Kennedy Circle, publicly supporting the dynamic young political figure who ascended to the presidency, giving money to his campaign, and contributing to the air of vigorous masculinity that surrounded his effort. The youthful new president "has many friends in show business," noted Hefner a short time later in his scrapbook diary. "It promises to be a swinging administration."[2]

Hugh Hefner, of course, had achieved fame, and no small amount of notoriety, as a pioneering figure in the sexual revolution that had gathered momentum in the postwar period. With the founding of *Playboy* in late 1953, he had become America's leading advocate of sexual pleasure and the good life of material consumption, a message that resonated powerfully for a large (and growing) audience among young urban males. Restless with the restraints of traditional morality and the expectations of suburban family life, and dubious about the growing influence of women in American society, Hefner had become one of the loudest voices proclaiming the crisis of American masculinity in the 1950s. Along with its large cadre of readers, which Hefner styled the "Upbeat Generation," *Playboy* embraced an ethic of unrestrained bachelorhood that combined sexual freedom, fashionable clothing, fine liquor, hip apartments, fast sports cars, and the latest hi-fi stereo equipment. The magazine, with its "Playmate of the Month" pictorials and journalistic jabs at the strictures of conformity and family obligation, promised to revive American masculinity for a new era.

John F. Kennedy was a kindred playboy spirit. While he never officially endorsed Hefner or his magazine—for a political candidate, no matter how daring, to publicly approve of a publication depicting nudity and endorsing extramarital sex in the late 1950s would have been political suicide—JFK's image of sophisticated, assertive masculinity comported smoothly with the *Playboy* agenda. In fact, Hefner made his magazine into a national forum for the Kennedy Circle: the music of Frank Sinatra and the escapades of the Rat Pack, the writings and reportage of Norman Mailer, the fiction of Ian Fleming and the image of James Bond. In the realm of popular culture, Hugh Hefner's determination to rescue American males from the torpor of the suburban age with a promise of self-fulfillment, both sexually and materially, expressed the same kind of impulses that threw JFK forward into public prominence.

Hefner, a great fan of Kennedy's, contributed to his 1960 campaign and supported his political and cultural endeavors. He also responded to the personal appeal and sexual adventurism of the charismatic young candidate, whom he described as "a handsome swinger." "He was one of us," Hefner declared, a new kind of public leader that he and his readership could embrace. Kennedy would become, simply, an embodiment of the *Playboy* male ideal in the White House.[3]

Earlier and more keenly than just about anyone, Hugh Hefner had sensed—indeed, he had experienced—a growing crisis of masculine identity in postwar America. After returning from military service in World War II, the young Chicago native, like millions of other young men mustered out of the armed services, spent several frustrating years spinning his wheels as he tried to find his way in life. After a stint earning a degree in journalism in 1949 at the University of Illinois, he cycled through a series of low-level jobs in advertising and magazine work. Marrying a girl he knew from high school, Hefner also traveled down the typical postwar path of domesticity and family with the arrival of a first child in 1952 and a second in 1955. On all fronts, he grew intensely dissatisfied. "I'm going around in psychological circles," he wrote of his jobs. "There's no kick in the work, no feeling of accomplishment." Marriage and family seemed equally stultifying because, in his words, "all this togetherness seemed meaningless. I went through the motions, but my heart wasn't in it." Hefner complained bitterly about the social conformity that forced Americans to be "security-conscious, committee-conscious, afraid to be different from anybody else, afraid to express a different opinion." He had grown profoundly unhappy with his own male identity, feeling hemmed in by the feminine trap of marriage and family on one side, stymied by the social ideal of the organization man on the other.[4]

In 1953, the young Chicagoan determined to smash through these conventions and activated a long-simmering idea. On a card table in his Chicago apartment, he began to piece together the elements of a new mag azine he decided to call *Playboy*. His formula was simple but brilliantly audacious: combine a yearning for sexual freedom with an intense desire for material affluence, both of which had grown steadily since the end of the war. Moreover, he would aim the magazine at young men like himself who were both frustrated by social constraints and ambitious to gain the good life. *Playboy* would seek to redefine masculinity for a new age by promoting a model of cool, affluent, and virile bachelorhood while condemning the stultifying influences of bureaucracy, suburban family life, and overweening female influence. *Playboy*'s critique quickly attracted a large readership.

In the very first issues, *Playboy* established a foundation for its social criticism. A jaunty introduction in the inaugural number in December 1953 announced a new kind of magazine for a new kind of male reader. "If you're a man between the ages of 18 and 80, *Playboy* is meant for you. . . . We want to make clear from the very start, we aren't a 'family magazine,'" it declared. "If you're somebody's sister, wife, or mother-in-law and picked us up by mistake, please pass us along to the man in your life and get back to your *Ladies Home Companion*. . . . We like our apartment. We enjoy mixing up cocktails and an hors d'oeuvre or two, putting a little mood music on the phonograph, and inviting in a female acquaintance for a quiet discussion on Picasso, Nietzsche, jazz, sex." *Playboy* promised sophisticated amusement for men eager to step outside the realm of women, family, and suburban togetherness. It would be, in Hefner's memorable phrase, "a pleasure-primer styled to the masculine taste."[5]

Articles in the magazine followed this template. The first issue contained Burt Zollo's "Miss Gold-Digger of 1953," a piece denouncing modern women for trapping men into marriage and then, when the relationship failed, socking them for 50 percent of their income in a sympathetic court system. Another piece warned against growing female power, declaring, "Take a good look at the sorry, regimented husbands trudging down every woman-dominated street in this woman-dominated land." For *Playboy*, female ascendancy and subsequent male decline were the social problems of the age. In "The Sorry Plight of the Human Male," Shepherd Mead humorously examined the shorter life span and poor health of overworked men—"this tatterdemalion band of human males going bravely on, its hair thinning, its whiskers growing, its paunches expanding, its arches falling"—and tutored them on how to defend themselves. It began with learning to handle your mother and female grade-school teachers, because "really fine maleness should begin early." In "The Handling of Women in Business," the same author joked that the emergence of women in the business world had caused "untold confusion and mental anguish." These new female executives "were able to draw upon their own crafty, feline powers" and "the male in business must learn to cope—or perish." Usually appearing in the guise of "The Siren" or "The Battle Axe," the "woman executive must not be allowed to spring up—and once having sprung up, must be suppressed as quickly as possible." While Mead made light of the male predicament in postwar America, the subtext made clear that it was really not a laughing matter.[6]

Playboy articles frequently attacked the female-and-family domination of modern American society. "Dear Ann and Abby: Move Over for the Masculine Point of View," for example, excoriated the preponderance of the woman's perspective in newspaper advice columns and urged "the point of view of the masculine free spirit." In "A Vote for Polygamy," a tongue-in-cheek Jay Smith argued that monogamy was a rather recent experiment in sex relations that ignored males' biological nature and was being "laughingly rejected by Mohammadens, Buddhists, and residents of Southern California." "I Only Want a Sweetheart, Not a Buddy" lamented the decline of the feminine woman and the rise of the "outdoor girl" and the "intellectual chum." "Love, Death, and the Hubby Image" argued that the idea of romantic love was a masculine creation, while women seemed to view matrimony "purely in terms of acquiring stuff and glomming onto a male provider."[7]

Playboy provided a forum for Philip Wylie's intemperate screeds on modern male-female relations. Overflowing with colorful language and provocative formulations, scathing articles such as "The Abdicating Male" claimed that women had captured "more than 80% of America's buying," a trend mercilessly manipulated by Madison Avenue and accepted by stifled men. In "The Womanization of America," he decried the flood of feminine influence in social clubs, teaching, entertainment, and the arts.

In "The Career Woman," he took aim at the "perfumed pirates," "girl guillotiners," and "she-tycoons" who were invading business and the professions, women who were determined to "compete with and, if necessary, cripple manhood and masculinity on earth." *Playboy* supported Wylie, asserting that "women are being masculinized even faster than the country is being womanized. Or is it, perhaps, that men are being effeminized?"[8]

Hefner assumed a central role in the crusade against the overweening influence of women and family in American society. In public pronouncements and interviews, he contended that modern men must demonstrate "initiative and derring-do . . . instead of settling for job security, conformity, togetherness, anonymity, and slow death." When a reporter asked if he would want his sister to marry a *Playboy* editor, Hefner shot back, "I don't want my editors marrying anyone and getting a lot of foolish notions in their heads about togetherness, family, home, and all that jazz." Postwar society pressured men to marry early, and he offered himself as an example: "I had never really been out on my own, never really been free, which is maybe a part of why this independent, free spirit thing is as important to me as it is."[9]

Hefner developed a full-blown critique of the contemporary masculinity crisis. Growing female authority had created a "submergence of the male" and a "female oriented society," he contended, and women's influence in magazines, movies, and television produced a "castrated, female view of life." In a radio program, Hefner vented his resentment. "We have a female-dominated and oriented society, with the roles of man and woman so similar that it is now quite difficult for a woman to discover exactly what her real identity is, or a man, either," he complained. "We've wound up with an almost asexual society, with women competing with men instead of complementing them."[10]

But how could this social crisis of masculinity, so consistently denounced by *Playboy* throughout the 1950s, be resolved? For Hefner and his magazine, one solution lay in sexual liberation. The magazine launched a full-blown attack on the notion that sex was either sacred or sinful and rejected the traditional moral position that it should be strictly relegated to marriage. *Playboy* promoted the simple idea that sex was for human pleasure. It depicted seduction, particularly male seduction of females, as neither improper nor immoral but a social ritual full of romance, excitement, and anticipation. Insisting that "nice girls enjoy sex, too," *Playboy* filled its pages with images of compliant females eager to embrace a new ethos of sexual freedom and glorifications of male virility and assertion, sexual conquest and fulfillment. As Hefner told one interviewer, "It is the normal, healthy, heterosexual thing for men to be interested in the full, well-rounded female." *Playboy* clearly met that interest.[11]

Throughout the 1950s, Hefner's magazine promoted the enjoyment of sex. "Don't Hate Yourself in the Morning" reassured male readers that "many women are beginning to adopt the sexual attitude of bachelors, in that they want physical pleasure without having to pay for it by signing up for a lifetime." It presented pictorials such as "The Girls of Hollywood," which offered intimate glimpses of some fifteen women while describing how "the sun-kissed strip of California coast known as Hollywood draws unto itself the most beautiful girls in the world." Regular features such as "The Ribald Classic," a series of short, humorous tales of seduction and romance, and the risqué "Party Jokes" page sought to replace sexual solemnity with laughs. Most famously, of course, *Playboy* presented its celebrated "Playmate of the Month," affirming the dictum that a picture is worth a thousand words. Beginning with the famous nude pose of Marilyn Monroe against a lush background of red velvet in its first issue, the magazine presented a monthly feature with several revealing photographs of an attractive young woman surrounding a nude foldout centerfold in full color. It quickly became *Playboy*'s signature item. Moreover, Hefner insisted that the Playmates be not professional models but fresh, wholesome "girls next door" from the byways of ordinary American life. The enormous popularity of the Playmate centerfold prompted the comedian Mort Sahl to quip that a whole generation of American men came of age believing that young women had a staple in their midsection.[12]

In addition to vigorously promoting sexual liberation, *Playboy* advocated an ethos of material abundance as a pathway to male regeneration. The magazine became an influential shaper of the consumer revolution sweeping through the postwar economy of the United States. Hefner's magazine served as a guidebook on informed consumption for young urban males with good jobs, and its ideal became the cool, well-outfitted, sophisticated, upwardly mobile bachelor. The *Playboy* reader could be, in its words, "a sharp-minded young business executive, a worker in the arts, a university professor, an architect or engineer. He can be many things, providing he possesses a certain point of view. He must see life not as a vale of tears, but as a happy time . . . he must be a man of taste, a man sensitive to pleasure, a man who—without acquiring the stigma of the voluptuary or the dilettante—can live life to the hilt."[13]

In a wide array of articles, advice pieces, and pictorials, *Playboy* instructed its readers on how to enjoy consumer prosperity, worldly success, and upward mobility. "The Well-Clad Undergrad" counseled readers on the male fashion trends, while pieces on food mentored young men on ordering in good restaurants or preparing elegant meals at home. "The Compleat Sports Car Stable" surveyed the fastest, most stylish automobiles on the road, and "The Stereo Scene" offered pointers on the latest developments in hi-fi equipment. The popular "Playboy's Penthouse Apartment" presented "a bachelor haven of virile good looks, a place styled for a man of taste and sophistication. This is his place, to fit his moods, suit his needs, reflect his personality." It took readers on a tour of this ultimate bachelor pad, dispensing descriptions and advice concerning sleek Scandinavian-style furniture, a state-of-the-art kitchen with dishwasher and glass-domed oven, a spacious living room with fireplace and elaborate stereo system, and a master bedroom suite with bedside controls to operate lights, drapes, and music. As Hefner explained, "*Playboy* redefined what it meant to be a man. It offered a much more sophisticated idea of manliness, someone who was urban, who was at home in the kitchen as well as the bedroom."[14]

With his magazine surging in popularity, Hefner became a celebrity. He garnered national media attention, emerged as a social commentator whose views increasingly demanded attention, and made numerous public appearances as an outspoken advocate of *Playboy*-style masculinity. By the mid-1950s, he had appeared in *Time* and *Newsweek* and on *The Mike Wallace Interview* television show. A cartoon in a 1957 *New Yorker* showed a sultan surrounded by dozens of beautiful harem girls as he sat reading a copy of *Playboy,* while *The Nation* described Hefner's publication as "the recent phenomenon of the sophistication business." *Playboy* showcased its leader in a feature article, describing him as "the man responsible for the pulse, the personality, the very existence of this magazine." As part of this flood of publicity, he suffered attacks from traditional moralists, cultural conservatives, and religious groups that sometimes took the form of legal attempts to censor *Playboy* or hinder its distribution. Nonetheless, by the end of the decade the editor and publisher had become a force to be reckoned with in American cultural life.[15]

With his influence growing, Hefner insisted that his social ideology promised the revival of both American males and American society. The "Upbeat Generation," as he called it—this term played off the much-publicized Beat Generation, the scruffy and disillusioned dropouts represented by writers such as Jack Kerouac—promised to reform and revitalize, not reject, mainstream America. They embraced "the play and pleasure aspects of life along with the work . . . turning life into a celebration that incorporated capitalism." They believed, as Hefner told a radio station, that "life can be an awful lot of fun, if you work hard and play hard, too."[16]

Hefner and *Playboy*'s message had strong political overtones. The publisher was an avowed centrist in his politics, vacillating between President Dwight Eisenhower and Governor Adlai Stevenson before swinging to the latter's support because of the Illinois governor's powerful intellect and home-state affiliation. Nevertheless, as late as 1960, in personal letters, he claimed that if *Playboy* were a political magazine, "it would probably be Republican in almost all its national views. I know that I am." More important than political affiliation, however, was Hefner's endorsement of certain ideological principles. He championed postwar American capitalism without reservation. A self-made man, he believed in entrepreneurship, arguing that in this system "the best ideas and the best people rise to the top, or at least have a chance to compete. And everyone benefits from that on every kind of level." The explosive growth of a consumer economy after World War II also earned his admiration because it provided a material foundation for the good life, a goal much proclaimed in *Playboy.* Hefner was broadly progressive in his politics. He supported the welfare state and government regulation of the economy, arguing that some controls were necessary for fair competition and that "complete laissez-faire capitalism wouldn't give us free enterprise any more than anarchy would give us political freedom." He strongly supported the civil rights movement and black equality in American society. Finally, Hefner took a strong libertarian stand in defense of individual freedom and expression. An opponent of censorship by the government, church, or social traditions, he insisted that "individual freedom in terms of sexual behavior was of a piece with individual freedom in the free enterprise system." Although staunchly anti-Communist, he raised the banner of free speech in protesting the spread of McCarthyism with its witch-hunting impulse. After a *Playboy* reader complained about *Playboy*'s willingness to publish articles by leftist writers, he replied, "This country is big enough, strong enough, and right enough to give free expression to the ideas of every man among us without fear of being hurt."[17]

As Hugh Hefner and his magazine reached the end of the 1950s, his attack on the postwar crisis of masculinity brought impressive results. *Playboy*'s readership soared. After one year of publication in 1954, its circulation stood at 185,000; the following year it exploded to 500,000 and to 1 million by the end of 1959. This spectacular growth was reflected in lavish media attention and the publisher's growing celebrity status. In fact, the popularity of the *Playboy* message carried Hefner into new territory around 1960. At the personal level, he overhauled his life. More broadly, he maneuvered to give his magazine—with its laceration of family togetherness, social conformity, sexual repression, and female influence and its promotion of an invigorated, virile, sophisticated masculine ideal—a new kind of political purchase. As Hefner told a radio interviewer near the outset of a new decade, a new realization had dawned that "the country had stood still for almost twenty years. . . . But with the new generation, there [now] seemed to be an unwillingness to accept a lot of these old taboos, old traditions, old concepts."[18]

Feeding the excitement was the presidential campaign of the young, dynamic senator who had emerged as the candidate of the Democratic Party. His calls to "get the country moving again" sounded remarkably similar to the sentiments of the youthful Chicago magazine publisher. Not surprisingly, Hefner became attracted to this political crusade, seeing it as a reflection of *Playboy*'s own values and proclivities. It would be a nearly seamless fit.

In late 1959 and early 1960, Hugh Hefner changed his life forever. Reinventing himself, he left behind any vestiges of the middle-class domesticity, social conformity, and bureaucratic humdrum so characteristic of the postwar United States. Hefner became "Mr. Playboy" and a high-profile figure in American life. Divorcing his wife in 1959 and leaving his two children in her care, he began to live the fantasy of the good life that he had been publicizing in his magazine. Hefner became the swinging young bachelor about town, haunting the nightlife of Chicago with a string of beautiful young Playmates on his arm, purchasing a Mercedes-Benz 300SL sports car, and hosting big parties that attracted the beautiful people from around the United States. Mr. Playboy solidified his new image with several moves that enhanced both the *Playboy* brand and his personal image.

In December 1959, Hefner purchased a large property at 1340 North State Parkway, located on the famous Gold Coast on Chicago's Near North Side, and created the Playboy Mansion. He remodeled the four-story, brick-and-limestone structure—it was the size of a small hotel—into an enormous bachelor pad, refurbishing its large ballroom and adding an indoor swimming pool and an enormous bedroom suite, complete with revolving round bed outfitted with controls for lighting, videotapes, music, and television. Such gadgetry, he noted, "helped give it a James Bond mystique." Major parties at the mansion soon became an almost weekly event as a long parade of celebrity entertainers, sports stars, and public figures began streaming through the front door that was emblazoned with a brass plaque reading, "Si Non Oscillas, Noli Tintinnare" (translation: "If You Don't Swing, Don't Ring"). Publicity on Hefner and his amazing home exploded, with stories appearing in the *Chicago Tribune, The Saturday Evening Post,* and *Time.*[19]

Around the same time, Hefner developed and starred in *Playboy's Penthouse,* a hip television show that stressed the glamour and sophistication of his life. It featured a format based on a cocktail party held in a chic bachelor apartment and opened with Hefner driving his Mercedes convertible around Chicago at night, after which he opened the front door of an apartment and announced, "Good evening. I'm Hugh Hefner. Welcome to the party." The show had musical guests such as Nat King Cole and Ella Fitzgerald, comedians such as Lenny Bruce and Bob Newhart, a wide variety of authors and artists, and, of course, numerous Playmates. The latest fashions, witty repartee, elegantly dangling cigarettes, and clinking martini glasses embellished the proceedings. *Playboy's Penthouse* brought Hefner's growing celebrity and lifestyle into living rooms throughout the United States. As a promotional piece in *TV Guide* proclaimed breathlessly, "Handsome, suave, urbane—he's the envy of every man, the idol of every woman!"[20]

In February 1960, Hefner opened the first Playboy Club in Chicago and soon began franchising clubs in cities around the country. In his words, they aimed to "project the plush and romantic mood of the magazine into a private club of good fellows interested in a better, more pleasurable life." Victor Lownes, associate editor at *Playboy,* put it more succinctly: "The idea was to bring the magazine to life." Signing up thousands of eager members nationwide, the Playboy Clubs offered a menu of fine food and drink, sophisticated entertainment, pretty girls, and liberated sexuality. With bars and lounges, spacious dining areas, and large rooms for comedy and music shows, the clubs created an ambience shaped by wood-paneled walls, rich colors, and leather furniture. Most famously, of course, they featured Playboy Bunnies, attractive young waitresses and hostesses outfitted in a one-piece satin garment replete with bunny ears, fluffy bunny tail, and bow tie and cuffs. The clubs, in other words, gave patrons a taste of the *Playboy* fantasy.[21]

Hefner's reinvention of himself coincided with the start of a new decade. "I had been in rehearsal for it in the 1950s," he explained. "Everything seemed to come to a focal point around 1960." That same year, of course, saw the emergence of John F. Kennedy as a new, stylish, intensely masculine candidate for president. Officially, *Playboy* maintained a distant, rather denigrating view of the political campaign. The Chicago Playboy Club promoted the satirical candidacy of the comic Irwin Corey, which featured a parade in downtown Chicago, complete with balloons, bunting, and signs reading, "Throw the Rascal In" and "Corey will run for any party . . .

and he'll bring his own bottle!" Such high jinks aside, the publisher realized that *Playboy* needed to proceed carefully in political matters. An endorsement by the controversial magazine could create a backlash among a great many traditionalists or alienate a significant portion of its own readership who might favor another candidate. The magazine tycoon needed to tread carefully over the political terrain.[22]

Nevertheless, Hefner came to see the 1960 election as a crucial event for the Upbeat Generation of sophisticated, invigorated young men who had followed *Playboy*'s clarion call. He sensed that his crusade for masculine regeneration needed to engage the political process. Thus *Playboy* in 1959 published a significant piece on the election that managed to express its political sensibility while avoiding the pitfalls of specific endorsements. "Cult of the Aged Leader" offered a critique of elderly figures who dominated modern American political life. "Why does the United States, a country that traditionally prizes youth, idealizes it, insists on it in top jobs, now find itself with superannuated leadership in the most critical areas of national life? . . . [T]he ages of men running the government are at an all-time high." It excoriated the national government for filling its positions, from President Eisenhower on down, with septuagenarians (even octogenarians) who were out of touch with the modern world. The article insisted that nearly all "the real giants of American history have been young men" and quoted Robert Kennedy, chief counsel to a Senate subcommittee and close adviser to his brother in that same body. "We have come to put such tremendous *over*-emphasis upon the need for age and maturity in our leaders that young men nowadays just don't have much chance at all to leap into the top jobs, even when they are far more capable than their elders," he complained. The presidency—the job was "a killer," and it "requires a person of superior stamina is a well-known fact"—was especially worrying in terms of an elderly occupant. While strict retirement rules could not be applied, *Playboy* urged voters to do the next best thing: "exercise the ballot with an increased awareness of the age factor," and go for younger candidates. This article came as close to backing John F. Kennedy, a famously youthful candidate, as possible without actually saying so. As Hefner noted proudly a few weeks after JFK's election, the *Playboy* article "seems to have been remarkably prophetic."[23]

More directly, Hefner and *Playboy* became a national forum for the Kennedy Circle. Throughout the late 1950s and early 1960s, the publisher and his magazine consistently provided a platform and publicity for the entertainers, writers, and public figures who joined JFK in shaping a new model of male vigor and virility. *Playboy* idealized Frank Sinatra as a strong masculine figure, favorably reviewing the singer's albums as the epitome of popular music excellence. In a long 1958 article titled "The Word on Frank Sinatra," it described the entertainer as "the most complete, the most fantastic symbol of American maleness yet discovered." It described how his inimitable voice—"bittersweet, magical, lean, insinuating, nudging, shrugging (yes, this man can shrug his voice)—weaves itself into the day-and-nightdreams of America's womankind." This larger-than-life personality with his maverick ways, fierce independence, and reputation as "the number one love god of our time" earned *Playboy*'s admiration.[24]

In fact, Hefner became a personal friend of Sinatra's. They met in Chicago in the mid-1950s, and the *Playboy* publisher, who as a youth had idolized the singer and adored his albums, was thrilled. The popular crooner had "supplied the words and music to our dreams and yearnings," Hefner explained, because "Sinatra really *was* the voice of our time." After appearing at the Chicago Urban League's Jazz Festival in 1960, Sinatra and the Rat Pack adjourned to the Playboy Mansion and partied with Hefner into the early hours of the morning. But there was a certain tension in the relationship. Sinatra, proud of his reputation as a Lothario, saw Hefner as something of an interloper and tried to steal away a couple of the publisher's girlfriends, Joyce Nizzari and Joni Mattis. Then, when he visited the Playboy Mansion, the singer acted badly at a couple of points, losing his temper and throwing a tray with a sandwich against the wall when it didn't please him. Hefner reacted mildly, simply noting that *Playboy* "was perceived as the personification of what a lot of guys wanted to be. Sinatra was one of those guys."[25]

Sammy Davis Jr. became a much closer friend to Hefner. The singer and dancer frequently performed at the Chez Paree, a Chicago nightclub across the alley from the *Playboy* offices, and he began to drop in for frequent visits. Davis secured tickets to the Kennedy inauguration for Hefner and then invited him to his own wedding and bachelor party. Davis not only liked and admired Hefner but appreciated the publisher's strong support for the civil rights movement. He appeared on *Playboy's Penthouse* in an hour-long special that kicked off its second season in September 1960, where he joked with Hefner and his guests, gave official approval to the March Playmate centerfold after going over it with a mock-critical eye, did several impersonations, and then swung through a couple of song-and-dance numbers that left the crowd enthralled.[26]

Not surprisingly, given Hefner's ties to Sinatra and Davis, *Playboy* held up the Rat Pack as a modern male ideal. In a June 1960 article titled "Meeting at the Summit," the magazine proclaimed them "the innest in-group in the world" with "talent, charm, romance, and a devil-may-care nonconformity that gives them immense popular appeal." Every night at the Sands hotel was like New Year's Eve, *Playboy* told its readers, where high-flying, irreverent entertainers, exemplars of modern masculinity, operated "supremely free of the rules and almost never earthbound." This "very special gang of Hollywood rebels" personified the kind of pleasure-seeking sophistication that *Playboy* had been championing since its inception. The Kennedy connection was evident. The *Playboy* article noted that the senator attended a Rat Pack performance and was given a standing ovation after being introduced to the large crowd. The joke at the time, Hefner recounted, was that Kennedy wanted to be Sinatra, and Sinatra wanted to be Kennedy: "The connection for Sinatra was power, and for Kennedy it was the ladies."[27]

Playboy also became a key outlet for Norman Mailer and his macho literary sensibility. The prestigious writer participated in two of its roundtables, "The Playboy Panel: The Womanization of America" and "The Playboy Panel: Sex and Censorship in Literature and the Arts," where he roundly criticized the growth of female influence, and the degeneration of male vigor, in modern America. Mailer contended that there was a connection between the productive demands of modern American capitalism and the repression of sexuality, which he described in a telling metaphor: "The authority in this country is like one vast, frozen, nervous, petrified mother who's trying to keep her favorite son—this utterly mad hoodlum—under control and she's getting more and more frantic as the years go by because she doesn't understand her son." The provocative writer joined William F. Buckley Jr. to write about "the role of the right wing in America today" and then served as the subject for a lengthy *Playboy* Interview. Mailer's version of assertive, virile masculinity, in other words, fit smoothly with the larger *Playboy* agenda.[28]

Hefner established a personal connection with Mailer. They met when the writer was a guest at a *Playboy* party while on assignment from *Esquire* covering the Sonny Liston–Floyd Patterson heavyweight boxing championship fight in Chicago. The Playboy Mansion, he wrote, provided "a timeless, spaceless sensation. . . . One was in an ocean liner which traveled at the bottom of the sea, or on a spaceship wandering down the galaxy along a night whose duration was a year." As for Hefner, he "had a quality not unlike Jay Gatsby." Mailer was fascinated by the publisher and the scene at his mansion, finding it a source of inspiration for his personal masculine quest. "I began in the plot-ridden, romantic dungeons of my mind, all subterranean rhythms stirred by the beat of this party, to see myself as some sort of center about which all that had been lost must now rally," he wrote.[29]

Hefner and his magazine also developed a deep connection to Ian Fleming and his James Bond novels. The affiliation seemed natural. "Bond was living the *Playboy* lifestyle," Hefner explained. "The first [Bond] novel was written just as the magazine was first published. The food and the drink and the clothes and the girls, first and foremost, fit the magazine's agenda. The 'Bond girls' were almost synonymous with Playmates." In March 1960, the magazine noted that Fleming—"tall, charming, Continental-suited, profoundly British, profoundly sophisticated"—had dropped by the Playboy Building in Chicago to visit the magazine's offices. He and Hefner chatted and exchanged compliments, with the author handing over a copy of a new Bond novel and the publisher suggesting that Fleming consider the Playboy Mansion and Playboy Club as the setting for his next book. As Hefner noted, "Fleming was a fan [of the magazine], and I was a fan of Bond. There was a strong connection between Bond and *Playboy*."[30]

Playboy, in fact, became the first American publication to serialize the British author's work, beginning in the spring of 1960, and it would eventually present a short story and three Bond novels in such a format. The magazine told readers that "President Kennedy and other Fleming fans" would be gratified by another serving of "sophisticated suspense . . . being compounded of damsels (both distressing and distressed), chilling chases, ingenious escapes, extravagant gambling scenes, epicurean episodes of wining and dining and, of course, a monstrously diabolical plot that threatens the free world." *Playboy* also presented several pictorials on "the Bond Girls" and made both Fleming and Sean Connery the subjects of extensive *Playboy* Interviews.[31]

Fleming appreciated the public association with *Playboy* and played it to the hilt. In a letter published in the magazine, he noted of his famous fictional character, "I'm sure James Bond, if he were an actual person, would be a registered reader of *Playboy*." He also posted a warm personal letter to Hefner, expressing his enthusiasm for *Playboy* and promising to try to visit Chicago and "see if I can't find some way of involving James Bond in your splendid affairs." The Bond movies also made *Playboy* connections. In *Diamonds Are Forever,* when the secret agent's wallet is opened in an attempt to clarify a mistaken identity, his London Playboy Club card is ostentatiously displayed. *On Her Majesty's Secret Service* showed Bond avidly reading *Playboy* while waiting in a lawyer's office. The image of James Bond "bears remarkable resemblance to the image Hefner carefully manufactured across the issues of *Playboy*," one observer concluded. "Both exist as coterminous symptoms of the cultural ideal of manliness . . . at the height of the Cold War." Fleming simply quipped that his books, much like Hefner's magazine, aimed at a target "somewhere between the solar plexus and the upper thigh."[32]

As a keystone for his masculine edifice, however, Hefner went beyond Frank Sinatra and the Rat Pack, Norman Mailer, and Ian Fleming and James Bond. He turned to John F. Kennedy himself. Personally, the *Playboy* publisher responded enthusiastically to the senator's candidacy and supported him in the 1960 election as a youthful, vigorous, liberated presidential candidate who promised to end the dominance of an older, stuffier, repressed male ideal in American public life. He clearly saw Jack Kennedy as a manifestation of *Playboy*'s masculine ideology in the world of public affairs. Hefner, a lifelong fan of the movies, described Kennedy as a kind of handsome, virile Hollywood leading man who burst into society to change its worst features. Combining political idealism with sex appeal, JFK reflected "a Frank Capra view of society that I strongly supported. He was, to me, a 'Mr. Smith Goes to Washington' candidate. But JFK's strong masculine aura appeared even more impressive."[33]

But it was more than politics. More broadly, Hefner viewed Kennedy as an antidote to the stifling atmosphere of 1950s America and the harbinger of a new, liberated age. "It was easy to identify with him. His politics were similar to mine, and he represented youth, vigor, a new beginning," said the publisher, "just as for many of us the 1960s represented a new beginning after the conservatism that existed after the war." The age of Eisenhower, the aging national grandfather with his social and political conservatism, represented for Hefner everything that *Playboy* was trying to subvert: conformity, togetherness, bureaucratic rigidity. Kennedy represented an overturning of traditional social values that had become oppressively dominant in modern America with its reverence for suburban life, family togetherness, and bureaucratic tedium. He was headed in the same direction as *Playboy* and its readers. As Hefner put it, "Kennedy fit with where we were all going, and he represented a new beginning, a younger generation."[34]

Crucial to Hefner's reading, of course, was JFK's powerful ethos of sexuality that combined erotic appeal, manliness, and sexual conquest. "*Playboy* had redefined what it meant to be a single man. Kennedy, although he was married, was part of that," the publisher contended. Hefner was well aware of the young senator's legendary sexual reputation and strongly endorsed it. Because of his friendship with Davis and Sinatra and the Rat Pack, he knew of JFK's womanizing on his visits to Las Vegas and Los Angeles. It was "an open secret," he explained. "There was no question about it. . . . There was an awareness of it, and he got a pass on it." But this only enhanced Kennedy's attractive image in contrast to the graying, paunchy traditionalism of Truman and Eisenhower. Kennedy "was the only president in my memory that had any sex appeal," the *Playboy* publisher declared. "It was not like who was number two; there was no number two!" Kennedy's marriage and children presented only a minor obstruction. "Although he was married, he seemed very modern. He was married, but he wasn't," Hefner noted. The image of virile, adventurous masculinity simply swept all before it. "He was a sexy president, and he was thought of in that way," concluded the publisher. "He had personal karma and sex appeal that was appealing on both the personal and political fronts."[35]

Thus Jack Kennedy symbolized *Playboy*'s attempt to "redefine what it meant to be a man—not outdoorsy male bonding, but urban, cool, sophisticated, eager for romance and sex. JFK was part of that," Hefner declared of this new paradigm. "Kennedy fit it, Bond fit it, Sinatra and the Rat Pack fit it." For the publisher of *Playboy*, Kennedy's election in November 1960, much like his own reinvention that same year, symbolized the start of a new age at the beginning of a new decade.[36]

With Kennedy's election in November 1960, a delighted Hugh Hefner believed that modern America had reached a turning point in its history. The young president's proclamation of the New Frontier suggested to the publisher that his young, energetic, male readership had come to power, that the sexual revolution had moved into the mainstream, and that a new era had begun in the nation's public life. In fact, this heady transformation became a central topic in a lengthy, rather unexpected exposition that began to appear in the pages of *Playboy*. The man who had forged his controversial reputation by popularizing nude pinups and flinging brickbats at middle-class respectability turned serious and tried to erect a foundation of ideas for his edifice of pleasure seeking. The result was "The Playboy Philosophy," a lengthy series of essays that began to unfold in the early 1960s.

Originally intended as a fairly brief statement of two or three parts, the project quickly swelled beyond all proportion. It became an obsession with Hefner, appearing in twenty-five installments before slowly grinding to a halt in 1966. Holed up in the Playboy Mansion, the author pored over dozens of files filled with research material and often stayed up for days on end writing and rewriting endless drafts of his thoughts on an array of social, cultural, legal, and sexual issues facing American society. He envisioned the Playboy Philosophy as a definitive statement of his magazine's guiding principles, and he stressed familiar themes: the liberated individual's need to enjoy sexual freedom, material abundance, economic opportunity, and leisure fulfillment. On the negative side, Hefner reiterated the evils of censorship and overweening religious morality. The result was an enthusiastic, if rather pedestrian and grinding, recycling of ideas common to modern liberal humanism wherein the good of the individual usually trumped social conformity, worldly affairs were more important than a religious afterlife, and restrictive traditions or institutions should be loosened or dismantled. The Hefner credo was part John Stuart Mill, part Ayn Rand, and part Alfred Kinsey.[37]

Amid this barrage of rhetoric appeared a serious attempt to define a sea change that Hefner perceived in American culture in the early 1960s, one in which both *Playboy* and John F. Kennedy played an important role. The evolution of the United States in the twentieth century, he asserted, had brought the country to the cusp of a great transformation in its values and commitments. Its implications were profound. "The first 30 years of the 20th Century were characterized by our unbounded faith in ourselves, both individually and as a nation," Hefner claimed. "It was a time of confidence . . . when most men believed they could lift themselves by their own bootstraps. . . . These were the years of the Uncommon Man—when uncommon ambition and deeds were the rule rather than the exception." With the stock market crash and the Great Depression of the 1930s, however, survival rather than the dreams of "Mr. Average Man" became the currency of the age. Then with the demands of World War II, and then the international threat of Communism, Americans muffled their individuality in order to defeat dangerous enemies. In Hefner's formulation, "Conformity was the safest road; to be outstanding or outspoken was to be exposed; to be invisible was to be secure."[38]

But discontent with tradition and conformity had become pronounced by the end of the 1950s In Hefner's words, "A new generation was coming of age that seemed unwilling to accept the current shibboleths, chains, traditions, and taboos." Some of these dissenters were nihilistic dropouts, the so-called Beat Generation, but many more were part of Hefner's cherished "Upbeat Generation," who were searching for "new answers and new opportunities in a spirit that was positive in the extreme." This youthful group evinced a "certain enthusiasm, a restless dissatisfaction with the status quo, a yearning to know more and experience more . . . put this youthful vigor and attitude to work as a national dream." The Upbeat Generation was determined to enjoy life by combining hard work and hard play because the man "who spends all his time in leisure activity never knows the intense satisfaction that is to be had through real accomplishment; but the man who knows nothing but his work is equally incomplete."[39]

Thus the dawn of the 1960s, for Hefner, marked the resurgence of the "Uncommon Man" and a youthful energy in the nation. He foresaw "an American renaissance—a period of growth and prosperity unequalled in the past." The signs were everywhere in science, art, music, entertainment, the civil rights movement, and the sexual revolution.[40]

Leading the change was a new generation of men, each "filled with purpose and . . . [who] thinks on a scale that often frightens his elders," Hefner wrote. "The daring young idea man is finally starting to lay the Organization Man to rest." This new male type believed that "the good life, the whole life, encompasses all of these—and all of them satisfy and spur a man to do more, see more, know more, experience more, accomplish more."[41]

Perhaps the most compelling voice proclaiming an American renaissance, and the most powerful figure in Hefner's cherished Upbeat Generation, emanated from the White House. John F. Kennedy's election to the presidency and his projection of a vigorous, assertive, individualist masculinity represented the profound shift in cultural sensibility that the *Playboy* publisher sensed so keenly. Hefner quietly praised JFK in "The Playboy Philosophy," making clear the affinity between the president and *Playboy*'s social and cultural agenda. He voiced his approval of JFK's initiatives and praised his eloquent denunciation of censorship: "The lock on the door of the legislature, the parliament, or the assembly hall, by order of the King, the Commissar, or the Fuhrer, has historically been followed or preceded by a lock on the door of the printer's, or the publisher's, or the book seller's." He endorsed the president's political sensibility of vigor and regeneration, his navigation between "extremist groups of the right or left," and his attempts at a "strengthening of democracy and the free enterprise system."[42]

A few months after JFK began his administration, "The Kennedys: Taste Makers in the White House" appeared in *Show Business Illustrated*, a short-lived companion publication to *Playboy* launched by Hefner in

1961. This article explored the important cultural transformation prompted by Kennedy. The parade of authors, poets, painters, architects, musicians, and scientists attending the inauguration and illuminating events in the Kennedy White House, it argued, "bolstered the morale of those who looked with despair on the White House as a cultural graveyard and its incumbents as cultural deadheads." While the Eisenhowers had preferred Lawrence Welk's music and television westerns, the new administration hosted luminaries in numerous creative fields and proposed a national cultural center. The president made clear that he "does recognize the value of excellence, truth, and beauty in a society which has more and more leisure to give to the arts. . . . He sees government as one of the means that can help create an encouraging artistic atmosphere." John and Jacqueline Kennedy regularly listened to music, with the First Lady preferring the works of Ravel, Schumann, Debussy, and various nineteenth-century composers, while the president's tastes ran to musicals such as *Oklahoma!* and *South Pacific.* They attended plays such as *The Best Man*, by Jackie's distant relative Gore Vidal, and *Critic's Choice,* starring Henry Fonda, and had strong connections to Hollywood and the entertainment world. But Kennedy was no snobbish cultural elitist. "The President is, above all else, a politician, a student of the art of getting and using power. This is his job and his passion," noted the article. For him, the arts were "natural tributaries to the main stream of his life, and no more." For JFK, a friend said, "the esthetics of the cut of his suit are as important as the esthetics of a canvas by Renoir." Here, in a nutshell, was a near-perfect description of the *Playboy* masculine ideal, and Kennedy fulfilled the requirements.[43]

Hefner made a direct connection with the Kennedy family in the early 1960s when he met JFK's father in Chicago. Joseph Kennedy called the publisher out of the blue and, after having problems getting through to him, quipped, "You're more difficult to reach than the president, and I know what I'm talking about there." The elder Kennedy had business interests in Chicago and, being an admirer of *Playboy,* decided to contact Hefner for an introduction. The publisher, along with a couple of associates, took him to dinner at the Drake Hotel and then to the Playboy Club, where they watched a young comedy team do a satirical routine on President Kennedy. As the party spent several hours being entertained and sharing views on politics and business, the older man, a notorious womanizer, particularly enjoyed the array of beautiful Bunnies swirling about. While the social encounter was pleasant, one aspect of Joseph Kennedy's conduct struck Hefner as odd. "I was impressed by the fact that he had a son who was president, and a son who was attorney general, and what he talked about for most of the dinner was Joe junior, the older son who was supposed to be the president and who had died."[44]

But it was JFK who most intrigued Hefner as a paragon of *Playboy* manhood. The magazine's ideal male, of course, displayed considerable sexual power, and the publisher rightly believed that Kennedy far exceeded the standard. Like Hefner himself, the president's legendary sex appeal was clearly a powerful element in his popular fascination. "The joke at the time was that Kennedy would do for sex what Eisenhower had done for golf," Hefner noted. "He was one of us." In fact, the entire Kennedy image of glamour, physical beauty, and desire ran so parallel to Hefner's magazine that satirists eagerly made the connection. A 1962 cartoon in *Los Angeles* magazine, for example, depicted JFK sitting in his famous rocking chair in the Oval Office. Holding up a *Playboy* sideways and gazing upward at the extended centerfold, he exclaimed rather disconcertedly, "Jackie, come here please!"[45]

Another factor linked the publisher and the politician. In 1953, as he was struggling to launch his fledgling magazine, Hefner had stumbled across photographs that would create a lifelong obsession. They portrayed Hollywood's hottest new sexpot, Marilyn Monroe, a few years earlier as she posed nude against a red-velvet backdrop, and Hefner used them to create his first Playmate. Monroe provided a vital attraction that helped get *Playboy* off the ground, and the grateful publisher never forgot. He would memorialize her in the magazine over three decades later as "a celestial enigma with which every incandescent blonde has been (usually unfavorably) compared." Eventually, he would even buy a burial plot next to Monroe's in a Los Angeles cemetery so they would rest near each other for eternity. A few years later, during his campaign for the presidency and then during his administration, JFK connected with Monroe in a more earthy fashion when she became one of his mistresses. Meeting in Hollywood and New York on several occasions for liaisons, the president and the blond-bombshell actress came together in a conjoining of the nation's leading sex symbols.[46]

For Hugh Hefner, and many other acolytes of the sexual revolution in postwar America, JFK was simply "the Playboy President." This political leader's sophisticated image of erotic adventure, masculine vigor, and casual, elegant consumption mirrored almost perfectly the ideal propounded by *Playboy*. It reflected a new generation of males eager to seize the reins of American life—its social aspirations, cultural values, and political processes—and steer it into a new age of masculine regeneration. The publisher, gathering others in the Kennedy Circle such as Frank Sinatra and the Rat Pack, Ian Fleming and James Bond, and Norman Mailer, had shaped a nourishing context in which JFK's masculine mystique flourished. Hefner helped define him as a national solution to the 1950s crisis of masculinity, and much of the electorate responded positively, even fervently.[47]

As the new president prepared to occupy the White House after his electoral victory, only two questions remained: Would John F. Kennedy's brand of virile, cool, tough-minded, sophisticated manhood survive the actual assumption of power, and if so, what form would it take in these new circumstances? The answers appeared quickly.

SEVEN

VIGOR AND VIRILITY:
PRESIDENT JOHN F. KENNEDY

I n early January 1961, it became clear that Americans had elected a new kind of president and entered a new stage of the nation's history. The inauguration of John F. Kennedy was unlike any seen in the recent past, perhaps ever. Most notable was the atmosphere of glamour and style. The preinaugural gala organized by Frank Sinatra had applied a glittering Hollywood sheen to the festivities that was simply unimaginable in the staid atmosphere of Truman and Eisenhower. Then the following day's ceremony at the Capitol had a guest list that included not only popular entertainers but a long parade of artistic and literary luminaries, including John Steinbeck, Carl Sandburg, Paul Tillich, Ernest Hemingway, Robert Lowell, and Mark Rothko. It also featured Diana Vreeland, editor of *Vogue* and influential empress of female fashion, who Jackie Kennedy instructed should be given the greatest VIP treatment. Five elegant inaugural balls were held that evening, with the handsome young president and his lovely First Lady in attendance.

The Kennedy inauguration also reverberated with a conspicuous youthful energy. The outgoing president, Dwight D. Eisenhower, was the oldest holder of that office in American history, at age seventy, while his successor was the youngest, at age forty-three. The contrast was striking, and a subtext for much commentary focused on the imagery of the weary, retiring old man giving way to the vigorous, virile young man. As an aging Ike departed the White House for the last time, sat at the rostrum for the swearing in of the new chief executive, and then left Washington, D.C., his successor swept into office on a surge of vibrant enthusiasm. *Time,* in its coverage of the Kennedy inaugural, highlighted the charge of social energy that pulsed through the capital with the dawn of a new, youthful administration. "Swirling with Kennedys, Washington society turned itself inside out in its most glittering display in years. Dinner dances, luncheons, buffets, receptions, cocktail parties—they flashed on and off like the lights on an electronic computer," it reported. "No event could be considered a success without the appearance of at least one Kennedy—and, since there were more than enough Kennedys around, there were few failures on that account." *Life* magazine highlighted the generational shift in leadership: "A New Hand, a New Voice, a New Verve." The inaugural ceremonies, it explained, displayed not only the usual pomp and circumstance but the exhilarating spirit of "the Kennedy challenge" that clearly marked a point where "the country passed into the charge of a new generation."[1]

The inaugural atmosphere of hip sophistication and youthful energy reflected above all, however, the power of JFK's masculine mystique. The aura of tough, youthful, male vitality that had permeated his election campaign carried over into the confident, eloquent cadences of his inaugural address. "Let the word go forth from this time and place, to friend and foe alike, that the torch has been passed to a new generation of Americans," the young leader declared confidently. "In the long history of the world, only a few generations have been granted the role of defending freedom in its hour of maximum danger. I do not shrink from this responsibility—I welcome it." Upon hearing these stirring words, even Speaker of the House Sam Rayburn, a savvy and battle-hardened veteran of national politics for several decades, was moved to remark, "He's a man of destiny."[2]

This powerful aura of youthful male revitalization, in fact, seemed to permeate the American atmosphere in the early 1960s. Eighteen months after Kennedy's inauguration, *Life* addressed this striking sea change in a special issue titled "The Take-Over Generation." It argued that "a new breed of American" man—there were only two women profiled out of two dozen—"thinks on a scale that often scares his elders" and was "at this moment in history starting to take over our destiny." The new president was the leader in this youthful crusade, but following hard behind him was a cadre of young, energetic innovators in business, science, education, technology, and the arts as well as public life. Even in corporate America, the power of ideas was challenging the imperative of the organization. As *Life* concluded, the new decade had pushed forward a large group of "extraordinary young people now poised for take-over."[3]

Thus Kennedy's assumption of the presidency and his much-publicized launch of the New Frontier symbolized more than a political program. They penetrated deeply and broadly into American life, promising to reinvigorate it with an injection of the new leader's compelling brand of masculine vigor: individualist, action oriented, youthful, sophisticated, vigorous, and full of sex appeal. JFK, as he assumed office at the start of a new decade, seemed to personify a triumphant resolution of the crisis of masculinity that had beset 1950s America. As his administration took shape over the following months, it promoted this revitalizing agenda on several fronts.

The first chief executive born in the twentieth century, a confident JFK prepared to lead the country into a new era. "Toughened by the grueling campaign, triumphant in a breathlessly close struggle, the nation's new leader . . . started on the job with vigor," reported one magazine. "Kennedy, for good or ill, is the first leader of a wholly new age, and now has his chance to voice and establish America's role in it. No greater chance could come to a man." He quickly established a memorable watchword for his administration—"vigor," or "vigah," as it sounded in his unique northeastern accent. Recurring in a host of presidential pronouncements, the word embodied the vibrant, assertive masculinity of the New Frontier and its dynamic young leader. Its influence soon became apparent in his appointments.[4]

Upon taking office, Kennedy quickly staffed his administration with exemplars of the youthful male standard that he had represented in his campaign. The ideal New Frontiersman came from a common mold: a brilliant student and successful athlete, a junior officer in World War II often decorated for bravery, an innovator in government or academia or business with a bent for action, and above all a young man with an aura of male authority and prowess. Highly intelligent and physically energetic, JFK's lieutenants had often attended top schools where, as one magazine explained, "they tended to excel, to win the prizes and scholarships and invitations to honor societies, and often to distinguish themselves as well in athletics." *Newsweek* observed that the Kennedy cabinet, with an average age of forty-seven, was a group of "forceful men" who would not be easily dominated. Only a strong president could ride herd over them, and "that is precisely what Jack Kennedy means to be."[5]

The New Frontiersmen displayed several notable characteristics. First, they had an evident practical orientation. Kennedy favored young men who were tough-minded pragmatists rather than ideologues, analysts who saw issues facing the United States as discrete, practical problems with solutions that would come from examining data and evidence, not theorists who were determined to fit circumstances into predetermined paradigms. The political journalist Joseph Kraft noted that the new president's appointees "put all matters on a pragmatic, case-by-case basis," an approach that encouraged practical advances rather than "the systematic elaboration of coherent programs expressing easily identified public policies." According to another analyst, the New Frontiersmen were marked by "reasoned conviction" rather than ideological belief, a new breed of men who were "skilled, ambitious, resourceful, hard-working, extremely effective— and temperamentally calculating rather than fervent."[6]

The typical New Frontiersman also had a yen for action rather than contemplation. The new president set the standard, declaring that unlike Dwight Eisenhower, who preferred to remain at a distance until his underlings had narrowed options for him to consider, he wanted to be "in the thick of things." His staff and cabinet, Kennedy made clear to all, would be structured in a manner to keep him there. Moreover, Kennedy's appointees were expected to display "toughness." According to one of the new president's talent hunters, toughness "wraps up a lot of things that Jack likes and wants to have in the people around him. Guts, nerve, stamina, staying power. Having ideas and being ready to defend them. Having the kind of determination that makes you finish something once you've made up your mind. It's the iron in your soul." This quality was part mental forcefulness and part physical effort. "The strenuous life is being promoted with a vigor not seen since Teddy Roosevelt," noted *Look* magazine. "Be lean, muscular, walk with a bounce. . . . If you are near a mountain, climb it." Yet Kennedy's ideal leavened physical vigor with intellectual ambition and cultural style. "Buy a few modern paintings for home and office use. . . . For literary acceptance, you might consult the list of favorite books read by Cabinet members. . . . Egghead words like 'apocalyptic' and 'sententious' may be used in everyday speech," noted one tongue-in-cheek journalistic guide for aspiring New Frontiersmen. "If caught in a crossfire of argument about some Kennedy policy, hedge by murmuring, 'Well, the President undeniably has blind spots, but you must admit he has style.'"[7]

The epitome of Kennedy's New Frontiersman was the new secretary of defense, Robert McNamara. The dynamic young ex-head of Ford Motor Company was featured on the cover of *Newsweek* a few weeks after the election under the heading "Picking the Very Best." His impressive array of achievements and imposing personal presence made him a man to reckon with in the heady days of the new Kennedy administration. Famous for his "tightly disciplined personality . . . confident, secure, independent," he also displayed the valued trait of political pragmatism and independence. "The Democrats think I'm a Republican, and the Republicans think I'm a Democrat," he told one journalist. "I've contributed to both, and I don't get benefit from either. I consider myself an independent." This forty-four-year-old dynamo exemplified everything that the new Kennedy administration wanted to project to the public.[8]

McNamara had been a Phi Beta Kappa at the University of California while also taking summer jobs as an ordinary seaman and traveling to Panama, Hawaii, and the Orient. After he won a scholarship to Harvard Business School, an impressive academic performance led to an instructorship. During World War II, he worked for the U.S. Army Air Forces and utilized his management skills and expertise in statistical control to keep track of planes, parts, and people and rose to the rank of lieutenant colonel. After being mustered out of the armed forces at the war's conclusion, he and a few other "stat control" officers sold themselves as a management team to Ford Motor Company. They became known as the "whiz kids," and by November 1960 McNamara had risen to become president of the company. He had served only a month in that position when his brilliant reputation prompted JFK to tap him for the Department of Defense.[9]

McNamara made for a natural fit with the youthful, vigorous male energy of the Kennedy administration. A tough-minded realist in love with figures and data, he had a relentless, driven personality and a reputation for getting things done. Disdaining corporate gamesmanship and bureaucratic glad-handing, McNamara became known for his reliance on "the systematic gathering of hard facts and logical analysis, avoiding emotion and instinct." He approached key decisions by demanding that possible solutions "be reduced in every instance to a detailed, quantitative range of alternatives—with facts and figures for each option open to him." During his years at Ford, McNamara had stayed aloof from many aspects of corporate life and even criticized its encouragement of conformity and obsession with profit seeking. In 1955, he had created controversy by stating in a college commencement speech, "More and more, I believe, idealistic and progressive young people will seek and find in industry not just a road to personal enrichment, but a more direct and effective means of public service." Taking over the Defense Department in early 1961, he managed it with "such cool detachment and decisiveness that some of the military brass, privately, called him the 'human IBM machine.'"[10]

At the same time, McNamara was a genuine intellectual. He avoided the cocktail circuit, spending much downtime reading tomes such as *The Western Mind in Transition* and *The Phenomenon of Man*. He claimed that his favorite book was Camus's *Rebel*. Journalists described him as a "modern version of the Renaissance man" whose conversation ranged comfortably "from modern abstract art (which he understands and enjoys) to existentialism (which he studies but rejects). He is enthusiastic about the music of Brahms, Beethoven, and Bartok." Instead of living in a tony suburban area of Detroit like most high-ranking auto executives, McNamara resided in Ann Arbor, where he enjoyed the companionship of University of Michigan professors, participated in book discussion groups, and attended the opera with his wife. But he was also an avid sportsman who escaped from work to go skiing, camping, and mountain climbing. While in Washington, D.C., he exercised by regularly playing squash and, in fact, was pictured in shorts, shirtless, and sweating in *Sports Illustrated* during a heated match with the secretary of agriculture, Orville Freeman.[11]

While McNamara was a committed family man who had a close relationship with his wife, two daughters, and son, he radiated a subtle masculine charm that women found irresistible. "Why is it," Bobby Kennedy once remarked, "that they all call him 'the computer' and yet he's the one all my sisters want to sit next to at dinner?" Jackie Kennedy, while lightheartedly discussing the most attractive men in the New Frontier with her husband and another couple, opined that "the first was obviously Bob McNamara. 'Men can't understand his sex appeal,' Jackie said.'" When the two men looked surprised, she laughed and teased, "Look at them. They look just like dogs that have had a plate of food grabbed from under their nose."[12]

Kennedy's administration was filled with a battery of youthful, dynamic, athletic, independent New Frontiersmen cut from the same mold. Secretary of the Interior Stewart Udall, for example, was a forty-year-old Arizonan who had served in World War II as a gunner on B-24 bombers in Europe and received an Air Medal with three Oak Leaf Clusters. Later at the University of Arizona, he played on the basketball team and graduated from law school. Udall served three terms in Congress, married and became the father of six children, and pursued hobbies of hiking, mountain climbing, fishing, and camping. A magazine piece offered a description of the new secretary that read like a checklist of traits for the ideal Kennedy official: "a rugged ex-athlete," "goes about his tasks with time's-a-wasting briskness," "agrees with the serviceable cliché that 'politics is the art of the possible' but he has a muscular notion of what is possible," and a combination of "combativeness, tenacity, idealism, and tough practicality." In a new Washington atmosphere of energy and enthusiasm, it concluded, "the young man from Arizona has stood up to stake his claim."[13]

Byron "Whizzer" White stood as another exemplar of the masculine ethos of the New Frontier. Appointed deputy attorney general, the forty-three-year-old attorney had attended the University of Colorado, where he served as student body president and starred as an all-American halfback for the football team. He won a Rhodes Scholarship to Oxford, after which he returned to play in the National Football League and led it in rushing yards for two years. In the navy during World War II, he served as an intelligence officer and won two Bronze Stars. At the conclusion of hostilities, he entered Yale Law School and graduated magna cum laude in 1946. After practicing law in Denver for fifteen years, he headed the 1960 Kennedy campaign in Colorado and then came to Washington with the new administration. Known for his sharp mind, modest demeanor, and calm pragmatism, White would be appointed to the Supreme Court in 1962 and, in Kennedy's words, was "the ideal New Frontier judge."[14]

But at the head of such young, vigorous figures stood Kennedy himself, the alpha male in the new administration. Suspicious of bureaucratic entanglements and restraints, he was determined to remain in control and assert his personal authority over the government more directly. During the search for figures to fill the cabinet, the new president made it clear that he was disturbed by "what has seemed to him to be a dangerous flabbiness of Executive control these past few years." Eisenhower's cabinet, JFK believed, had accumulated too much executive power because their leader had stayed in the background and only made the most important decisions after options had been prepared, even predigested for him. The new chief executive assembled a "bright, brisk, tough cabinet," but he insisted on being a strong, assertive leader. He embraced the Wilsonian injunction: "The President is at liberty both in law and conscience to be as big a man as he can." Kennedy wanted his appointees, in the words of one journalist, "to meet the needs of a President with abundant stores of restless energy, with a great capacity for assimilating detail, and with a taste for tackling issues before the rough edges are planed away in coordination. 'When things are very quiet and beautifully organized,' he once said, 'I think it's time to be concerned.'" The Kennedy model was not a hierarchical pyramid but "a wheel figuring a network of bilateral relations between the President and his aides." Another observer compared it to a basketball team: "Everyone is on the move all the time. Nobody has a very clearly defined position. The President may throw the ball in any direction and he expects it to be kept bouncing." Regardless of the analogy, JFK stood at the center of all activity and was determined to overcome "the monumental inertia of the bureaucracy."[15]

The New Frontier's spirit of masculine vitality influenced one of Kennedy's pet projects: a crusade for physical fitness in American life. The
steady increase of soft, flabby men as the result of modern consumer comfort, sedentary bureaucratic work, and feminized family endeavors had
been a central fear in the broader crisis of masculinity in 1950s America.
During the campaign, JFK had stood as a symbol of male regeneration,
and now he meant to actualize this impulse. Thus the new national leader
surrounded himself with active, athletic young men who pursued strenuous physical activity, an ethos that began with "Jack's (we Kennedys play
for keeps) football games" on the lawn at Hyannis Port. Stories on the New
Frontier stressed the athletic prowess of its denizens, noting that many of
Kennedy's subalterns had been college football players while others pursued the outdoor life of hunting, fishing, camping, and hiking.[16]

The president-elect quickly codified the New Frontier's principles of
physical vigor. He wrote an article titled "The Soft American" for *Sports
Illustrated* that laid out the problem of modern masculine decline and suggested a solution. Ancient Greece and nineteenth-century Great Britain
exemplified the traditional Western belief that a sound body as well as a
sound mind among citizens formed the basis of a nation's vitality. But in
modern America, "a decline in the physical strength and ability of young
Americans" was becoming apparent. Tests and studies revealed that
American youth were lagging behind their counterparts in other parts of
the world with regard to muscular strength, flexibility, and physical fitness.
The harsh facts, Kennedy argued, revealed the appearance of "increasingly
large numbers of young Americans who are neglecting their bodies—
whose physical fitness is not what it should be—who are getting soft. And
such softness on the part of individual citizens can help to strip and destroy the vitality of a nation." The age of abundance, he argued, ironically
worked to "destroy vigor and muscle tone" as hard labor was being engi-
neered out of work life. Kennedy warned that in the Soviet Union the
United States faced a hardy and implacable adversary and the successful
defense of liberty would demand a strength that came only from "a lifetime of participation in sports and interest in physical activity. . . . Only if
our citizens are physically fit will they be fully capable of such effort." It

was time, the new leader concluded, to move forward with "a national program to improve the fitness of all Americans."[17]

In a special addendum, *Sports Illustrated* admiringly surveyed the new president's own physical activities. "Jack Kennedy practices the fitness that he preaches," it proclaimed, and publicized his endeavors in swimming, sailing, golfing, and touch football. It showed him walking on the beach at Hyannis Port and quoted his reflection: "I played here as a boy and relax here as a man." It portrayed him single-handedly sailing his twenty-five-foot sloop, *Victura,* around the bay outside his home and noted its Latin meaning: "About to conquer." It described him as a "savage contestant" in the many sports contests held among "the members of his large, vigorous, and fiercely competitive family." It concluded with the observation that JFK's swimming skills and "hardiness of body and toughness of spirit developed through rough-and-tumble games" had saved his life, and those of many of his crewmen, during the PT-109 disaster in the Pacific during World War II.[18]

After assuming the presidency, Kennedy quickly established the President's Council on Physical Fitness to kick-start a national program of physical exercise and revitalization. He appointed Charles B. "Bud" Wilkinson, noted football coach at the University of Oklahoma, to head it. While this body had no power to mandate national standards, it launched a campaign to actively promote physical exercise in schools and homes. With the cooperation of several educational and medical organizations, it designed a series of exercises and activities that were outlined in a long pamphlet titled *Official U.S. Physical Fitness Program* (the cover featured a photograph of, and a quotation from, President Kennedy). Over 200,000 of the booklets were distributed at no cost to schools, and another 40,000 were sold. As Wilkinson explained, "The majority of our youngsters are just not as physically capable as the average youngster in foreign countries." In particular, he noted, Russian youth "are far, far ahead of us."[19]

Kennedy supported the President's Council on Physical Fitness in a series of public statements. He authored an article in *Good Housekeeping* that discussed the problem of "our unfit youth" and published a supportive piece in *Sports Illustrated* titled "The Vigor We Need." JFK particularly aroused public interest with his advocacy of the "fifty-mile hike." Discovering that Teddy Roosevelt had challenged members of the Marine Corps to finish a fifty-mile hike in twenty-four hours, Kennedy now did the same to see if "the strength and stamina of the modern Marine is at least the equivalent to that of his antecedents." When news of the president's challenge leaked out, a national craze erupted as ordinary citizens rushed to perform the feat. New Frontiersmen such as Robert F. Kennedy successfully walked the fifty miles, but the rotund press secretary, Pierre Salinger, to the amusement of the press corps, successfully avoided the full regimen, walking only six and a half miles and quipping, "I may be plucky, but I'm not stupid."[20]

But the New Frontier model of male regeneration also involved cultural sophistication. After all, James Bond and Frank Sinatra, Norman Mailer and Hugh Hefner, had demonstrated that modern manliness demanded appreciation of the finer things in life as well as physical prowess. With the assistance of his wife, Jacqueline, JFK made the White House a public stage for displaying the best in arts and letters and music. Again, the contrast with Eisenhower was vividly drawn. The White House no longer featured Fred Waring and the Pennsylvanians, Ike's favorite musical group, or hosted stilted parties where guests grew bored and went home early. Instead, the Kennedy style swept into Washington on a tidal wave of hip sophistication.

The inaugural, where the poet Robert Frost had proclaimed the "next Augustan age," the dawning of "a golden age of poetry and power of which this noonday's the beginning hour," set the tone. Kennedy's guest list of over fifty prominent writers, composers, and painters reinforced this impression. Leonard Bernstein conducted the National Symphony Orchestra in performing a special fanfare he had written for the occasion, before a choir joined it in a rendition of the "Hallelujah Chorus." The writer Archibald MacLeish wrote to the new president shortly after the festivities and expressed a typical reaction among American intellectuals: "It left me proud and hopeful to be an American—something I have not felt for almost twenty years."[21]

Within a few weeks, the cultural atmosphere of Washington, D.C., seemed almost magically transformed. "Inspired by the New Frontier spirit, Washington is striving to erase a long-held notion—that, compared to other world capitals, it's a cultural hick town where there's nothing to do at night. The White House has set a new tone in making it an agreeable and fashionable civic duty to encourage the arts," noted *Look* magazine. With a new emphasis on ballet, concerts, poetry, painting, and acting, the American capital was in the full throes of a "big, new culture kick." Crawling with movie stars and celebrity artists and cultured New Frontiersmen, *Esquire* claimed, "Washington has become Glamor City." The *Washington Post* detailed an array of arts projects promoted by the new administration— the restoration of the White House interior with period furniture and decor, the acquisition and display of two Cézanne paintings in the Green Room, performances by several renowned classical musicians, the flood of "eggheads" into government positions, special dinners for major literary and artistic figures, the appointment of a cultural adviser to the president—and concluded that "culture is breaking out all over" in the American capital.[22]

JFK nurtured this impression with a series of high-profile gatherings for creative figures. In November 1961, he hosted a special performance by the famed Spanish cellist Pablo Casals, who had long refused to perform in countries that recognized the government of Francisco Franco. In his introduction of Casals, Kennedy said, "We believe that an artist, in order to be true to himself and his work, must be a free man." A few months later, the White House hosted a reception and dinner for Nobel laureates that also included a large number of writers and critics such as Lionel Trilling, James Baldwin, and William Styron. JFK welcomed the distinguished guests by commenting upon "the most extraordinary collection of talent, of human knowledge, that has ever been gathered together at the White House, with the possible exception of when Thomas Jefferson dined alone." A short time later, a White House reception honored the French minister of culture, André Malraux, a prominent novelist and art critic and one of Jacqueline Kennedy's favorites, and JFK noted in his toast that "creativity is the hardest work there is." He also joked that the White House "was becoming a sort of eating place for artists. But, they never ask us out." Malraux, at this occasion, agreed to send the famous painting the *Mona Lisa* from the Louvre to the United States for a special exhibition. Yet another special dinner honored the famous Russian composer Igor Stravinsky.[23]

A striking aspect of this glittering new cultural scene at the White House was its unique combination of elegance and informality. The typical Kennedy dinner party was vastly different from an Eisenhower one. At events hosted by the elderly president in the 1950s, guests could not smoke, there were no drinks served before dinner, a very stiff guest line had people shuffling along in a rote manner, protocol reigned in seating people at a giant horseshoe-shaped table where no one could really talk, the food was bad, and the wine was worse. Neither Dwight nor Mamie Eisenhower was a convivial host, and they seemed as uncomfortable as most of the guests. But at the Kennedy dinner for Pablo Casals, Bernstein explained, there were "many little tables seating about ten people apiece, fires roaring in all the fireplaces, and the tables are laid out in three adjacent rooms so that it's almost like having dinner with friends. The food is marvelous, the wines are delicious, there are cigarettes on the table, people are laughing out loud, telling stories, jokes, enjoying themselves, glad to be there."[24]

The glamour and sophistication of the Kennedy White House, however, involved more than just a lighter touch, ashtrays, and better food and drink. It represented a shift in social class values and taste. The Trumans and Eisenhowers, of course, had been middle-class midwesterners whose backgrounds smacked of staid bourgeois values. The new administration, in contrast, was rooted in the Boston–New York–Washington corridor where social and cultural elites poured forth from a privileged milieu—Ivy League universities, Manhattan apartments, prestigious legal and financial firms, Georgetown town houses, posh vacation communities in Newport, Cape Cod, and the Hamptons—to replace Washington's shabby, middle-class lack of taste with upper-class refinement. The New Frontier, in other words, ensconced the beautiful people in the national capital. Diana Trilling, noted writer and wife of the legendary cultural critic Lionel Trilling, illuminated this upper-class refinement when she reported Jackie Kennedy's description of the new White House social agenda. The First Lady explained to a circle of guests that she and her husband used to come to the White House during the Eisenhower administration and it "was just unbearable. There would be Mamie in one chair and Ike in another. . . . Everybody stood and there was nothing to drink, and we made up our minds, when we came to the White House, that nobody was ever going to be as bored as that. We do try to make it a good party." The journalist George Plimpton similarly described how Kennedy popularized an upper-class "water" tradition: yachting, cabanas at the beach, waterskiing at Hyannis Port, glamorous parties where uninhibited New Frontiersmen jumped fully clothed into swimming pools (rumor had it that Pierre Salinger once took the leap smoking a cigar and surfaced with it still lit). As Schlesinger reported, the Kennedy's social style represented "a dream of civilization and beauty" and "a suggestion that America was not to be trapped forever in the bourgeois ideal."[25]

Kennedy's image of cultural sophistication and glamour certainly dazzled a popular audience. Yet the new president's relationship with the genuine world of ideas was more complicated. JFK, in a general sense, welcomed intellectuals onto center stage in American life, and there was no doubt about his commitment to this goal. In a 1963 speech at Amherst College to honor Robert Frost, who had died earlier in the year, he contended that men who wielded power as political leaders led the nation to greatness. But intellectuals and artists played an indispensable role. "When power leads man toward arrogance, poetry reminds him of his limitations," Kennedy observed. "When power narrows the area of man's concern, poetry reminds him of the richness and diversity of existence. When power corrupts, poetry cleanses." Many intellectuals deeply appreciated the new tone and atmosphere, with Thornton Wilder claiming that the administration had established "a whole new world of surprised self-respect" among those involved with the arts.[26]

At the same time, however, the intellectualism of the New Frontier clearly involved style more than substance. The First Lady, with her knowledge of French and serious study of literature, art, and music as a young woman, first in college and then in Paris, was an authentic disciple of the arts with a profound appreciation of artistic achievement. But the new president, while proud of his wife's sophisticated tastes and eager to exploit them to foster a public image, was neither a highly cultured man nor a genuine intellectual, despite attempts to position him as such. While an omnivorous reader of history and political biography, he eschewed literature almost completely. As for painting, he preferred seascapes with naval ships and landscapes of the American West and found nonrepresentational art completely baffling. In terms of music, he liked Broadway show tunes and Irish ballads and fidgeted at concerts that featured Mozart or Beethoven. He had never heard of Igor Stravinsky and did not know what instrument Pablo Casals played. When asked about her husband's musical tastes, Jackie Kennedy quipped that his favorite piece was "Hail to the Chief." At White House performances of classical music, the president tended to applaud at the end of a movement rather than at the conclusion of the entire piece. To remedy such embarrassing gaffes, he had Letitia Baldrige, the White House social secretary, cue him by opening a door in his line of sight about two inches as the entire piece was about to end.[27]

To his credit, however, JFK never claimed anything other than great respect for literature, art, and music. As Bernstein noted, the young leader did not try to fake knowledge but simply expressed appreciation and awareness of artistic endeavor. Several conversations with Kennedy, he reported, revealed "the reverence he had for thought itself or for the functions of the human mind in whatever form, whether as pure thinking or political thinking or creative functions of any sort, including art and literature." He displayed "love of knowledge and this great reverence for the artistic act which made him terribly curious." Bernstein especially appreciated that JFK "never pretended to understand music or know anything about it; he never apologized for not knowing about it. . . . There was never any of that attitude—self-excusing or apologetic. On the other hand, he never put his foot into it; he never pretended to know anything he didn't know."[28]

Other intellectuals, perhaps less exhilarated about being drawn into the Kennedy orbit, were skeptical about the intellectual depth of the new leader and his administration. While they appreciated the emphasis on literature and poetry, painting and architecture, dance and opera, in the New Frontier, they sensed superficiality. The journalist Joseph Kraft, writing on "Kennedy and the Intellectuals," for *Harper's,* suggested that the image of cultural sophistication was misplaced. Kennedy and the New Frontier, he argued, for all of the refined window dressing, favored not traditional intellectual endeavor but the specialized, managerial, technocratic expertise "of the trained intellectual bureaucrat."[29]

Some took a harsher position, insisting that the president had little grasp of big ideas in philosophy, literature, art, or even political theory but merely sought to cultivate an intellectual image. Alfred Kazin, the noted literary critic, made this argument in a controversial article in *The American Scholar*. He dismissed the notion of JFK as a real historian and offered a stinging assessment of the president's famous book: "*Profiles in Courage* always reminds me of those little anecdotes from the lives of the great men that are found in *Reader's Digest,* Sunday supplements, and the journal of the American Legion." For all of his intellectual aspirations, Kazin continued, Kennedy's cool, pragmatic intelligence actually combined an agile assimilation of fact with an air of knowing sophistication and a managerial reliance on the research of others. It was an intellectual style that "modern Americans have learned to admire in journalism, in business, in conversation, and on television quiz shows . . . [and in] the big universities and scientific 'research and development.'" It was a shallow notion of the intellectual, one propounded by politicians and "professional communicators" in the age of mass media, and Kennedy excelled in broadcasting a "cultivation of the highbrow world as an executive taste and Presidential style." (JFK, who had invited Kazin for a luncheon discussion after learning about his plans to write the essay, was irked by the result. "We wined him and dined him and talked about Hemingway and Dreiser," he complained to Arthur Schlesinger, "and then he went away and wrote that piece." This reaction, of course, unintentionally supported Kazin's point.)[30]

Perhaps the shrewdest observer of Kennedy's intellect was Isaiah Berlin, the Oxford professor of political theory and intellectual history, who had lengthy talks with the president on several occasions. The youthful leader initially struck him as being the most attentive listener he had ever encountered other than Lenin. JFK was interested in Berlin's knowledge of Russian culture and traditions and paid such close, intense attention to his comments that the Englishman suspected he would "exhaust people by listening to them." Berlin also concluded that Kennedy did not have a sophisticated historical sense but embraced the "great man" theory of history. When he mentioned Churchill, Stalin, Napoleon, Lenin, and other world leaders, Berlin observed, "his eyes shone with a particular glitter, and it was quite clear that he thought in terms of great men and what they were able to do, and not at all of impersonal forces." Kennedy clearly imagined the Cold War in this fashion, where he "was a duelist, with Khrushchev at the other end. There was a tremendous world duel being carried on by these two gigantic figures."[31]

Berlin was also struck by JFK's qualities of mind. The famous intellectual had expected an amiable, charming Irish American politician, but instead he encountered a man who gave off "an air of luminous intelligence and extreme rationality" who "glowed with a kind of electric energy." Berlin immediately sensed that Kennedy was a natural, charismatic leader who inspired those around him and directed his own life in a highly conscious and willful way. He seemed to have little interest in abstract or theoretical ideas but only the practical world where those ideas must be applied. He had a concentrated intellect that sought to bring around every conversation, every answer, every concept, every book, to focus on the issue at hand with great diligence. "The idea was to act. To act! Always act," noted Berlin. "Never relax. Always act. Strive for something. Try for something." Finally, Berlin concluded that Kennedy was preoccupied with ushering in a new age and wanted to surround himself with "people who gave him the impression of understanding the new techniques and the new situations brought about in the sixties. He had a tremendous sense of *soyos de notre temps:* we ought to be men of our time." To that end, Berlin believed, JFK had self-consciously gathered around him an elite group of young men "with a great deal of energy and ambition. . . . Kennedy wanted to be not only stimulated but to march at the head of a small, dedicated band of men with a passion and shining eyes." The young leader, Berlin observed, "liked vitality; and I think anybody who was dim, no matter how virtuous, how wise, how valuable . . . was no good to him. Somehow I'm sure he felt the sheen of life, the light of life, went out in their presence."[32]

What Berlin sensed intuitively, and accurately, was Kennedy's powerful union of intelligence and masculine energy. The vaunted cultural sophistication and intellectual energy of the New Frontier was, ultimately, a component in the young leader's larger agenda of masculine regeneration. While deferring to his wife about knowledge of artistic creativity, President Kennedy believed that treasuring art and respecting intellect served to broaden masculine horizons. In other words, he personified one of Arthur Schlesinger's revitalizing remedies for the beleaguered modern male in his famous 1958 *Esquire* article: embracing the arts. "Very little can so refresh our vision and develop our values as the liberating experience of art," Schlesinger had written. "Thoughtful exposure to music, to painting, to poetry, to the beauties of nature, can do much to restore the inwardness, and thereby the identity, of man." By adopting this posture of "thoughtful exposure to" (as opposed to searching engagement with) and clearly identifying himself with the best in painting, music, and literature, the youthful leader in the White House, indeed, became the embodiment of the vibrant, cosmopolitan, modern male.[33]

In the popular imagination, the president's masculine mystique also became visible, literally, in his garb. A shift in fashion on the New Frontier first became noticeable, of course, on the feminine front when Mamie Eisenhower's dowdy spit curls and frilly dresses disappeared and a new, beautiful First Lady appeared on Kennedy's arm in an array of elegant designer gowns, pillbox hats, and stylish coiffures. But such imagery soon enveloped JFK himself. During the late 1940s and the 1950s, Harry Truman and Dwight Eisenhower had reflected a sober sartorial tradition with their dull, conventional, rather stuffy wardrobes of double-breasted suits, wide ties, and fedoras that reached back to the 1930s. It was lightened only occasionally by Truman's garish Hawaiian shirts and Ike's eccentric golf outfits of baggy pleated pants, sweater vests, and baseball caps. Now JFK quickly revamped the fashion image of the presidency.

Kennedy set a new presidential standard of cool male elegance. Early in his administration, he created a stir by refusing to wear a hat, believing the traditional fedora to be an old-fashioned hindrance that masked his thick shock of auburn hair, one of his most attractive physical assets. Under Jackie's influence in the mid-1950s, he had jettisoned the boxy three-button or double-breasted suit in favor of a sleeker two-button model and eschewed button-down shirts for those with a short, straight collar and restrained ties of narrower width. Both his suits and his shirts were carefully tailored to flatter his youthful, athletic physique. In more casual settings, Kennedy displayed a tousled elegance—crewnecks or polo shirts, chinos, loafers sans socks, sunglasses often perched atop his head, smiling at the world from a sailboat or open convertible—that enhanced an image of understated grace and confident, masculine style.[34]

Upon moving into the White House, the new president, somewhat shockingly for a modern American leader, emerged as a style setter. In March 1962, *Gentlemen's Quarterly* put the president on its cover along with an article titled "New Fashion Frontier: In the American Manner." It observed that because of his "good taste," "athletic build," and "commanding appearance" Kennedy exerted "a salutary influence on the dress habits of American men." Other magazines agreed. "John F. Kennedy may turn out to be the most suitable President the nation has ever had, or at least the best-suited," claimed *Life* magazine. It noted that he paid close attention to his own attire and favored a "modern conservative" style of understated elegance. He owned about twenty suits, all in grays and blues but never browns, which were custom made by the New York tailor Sam Harris. *Esquire* offered fulsome praise in "The Well Appointed Wardrobe of President John F. Kennedy." It described JFK as "the first fashion-setting President since the nineteenth century" and asserted that he had mastered the "art of good dress," which, paradoxically, was "to know how to wear clothes so that they call no attention to themselves yet suggest an immaculate taste." Through such efforts, Kennedy brought the sartorial elegance of Frank Sinatra and James Bond onto the national political stage and created a new kind of image for the modern male public leader.[35]

The new president's vibrant masculinity also reached a broad public audience through the cinema. A few months after Kennedy took office, Warner Bros. Studio launched a movie project based on the PT-109 incident during World War II, where Kennedy's vessel had been rammed and sunk by a Japanese destroyer in the Solomon Islands. While two of the dozen crew members drowned, the young navy lieutenant led the rest to safety while bravely swimming for miles among several islands. The incident, with an emphasis on Kennedy's selfless heroism, had been heavily marketed during all of his political campaigns, but when he assumed the presidency, a flurry of activity guaranteed an even larger role for it. The inauguration parade featured a large float from the state of Massachusetts with a life-size re-creation of the PT-109. Then a journalist, with the cooperation of Kennedy and the White House, published *PT 109: John F. Kennedy in World War II,* a bestselling book that was serialized in *The Saturday Evening Post.* The Revell company brought out a plastic model kit of the boat for children, and emblazoned on the box was "Commanded by LTJG John F. Kennedy." The popular singer Jimmy Dean released a single titled "PT 109," with such lyrics as "In '43 they put to sea, thirteen men and Kennedy. Aboard the PT 109, to fight the brazen enemy."[36]

But the movie promised the greatest dividends for JFK's masculine image. It was shepherded into production by Jack Warner, who had been lobbied by Joseph Kennedy, and Warner Bros. envisioned an epic, blockbuster World War II film that might compete with Twentieth Century Fox's *Longest Day*. Filming began on an island near Key West, Florida, in the spring of 1962, and the White House played a key role in developing the film. The press secretary, Pierre Salinger, and George Stevens Jr., the director of the Motion Picture Service of the United States Information Agency, coordinated the administration's input into the film while JFK himself had a veto power over certain elements. He insisted on getting a first-rate director, suggested several changes in the early script, and viewed the screen tests of several young actors considered for the role of Lieutenant Kennedy. After viewing the hit film *Splendor in the Grass* (1961), Jackie Kennedy pushed for Warren Beatty, but he turned the role down flat. (After a contentious discussion with the politically radical young actor, the producer reported that the only way Beatty would take the role was if "Kennedy is a pacifist and won't go to the South Pacific [to serve in the military].") The president eventually chose Cliff Robertson to play him as a young wartime hero.[37]

The shooting of *PT 109* received extensive coverage in *Life, Look, Newsweek,* and *The Saturday Evening Post*. These popular magazines, in articles such as "The Man JFK Picked to Play His Wartime Role" and "President Kennedy Casts a Movie," greatly boosted publicity for the project, and for the president. Released in the summer of 1963, the film did not achieve blockbuster status but was moderately successful before the assassination caused it to be pulled prematurely. The film offered some good action scenes and a compelling narrative, but it was weak on drama and character development. Lieutenant Kennedy appears from the outset as a resolute, heroic leader rather than a young man who develops those qualities under the pressures of armed conflict. As Bosley Crowther noted in *The New York Times,* the protagonist comes across as a "pious and pompous bloke who stands up straight, looks at you squarely, and spouts patriotic platitudes" as if ready to say at any moment, "I have to get back to become the President of the United States." President Kennedy, however, liked the film very much. He viewed it twice at the White House, in February and May 1963, before its premiere at the Beverly Hills Hilton in June. He voiced his approval to several associates and at a White House luncheon told Jack Warner it was "a fine job." But regardless of its quality or box office success, *PT 109* served as a vehicle for conveying Kennedy's heroic masculine image to the public. The president had made sure of that.[38]

After becoming president, Kennedy elevated his stature as a vigorous symbol of modern masculinity. In public pronouncements, appointments, cultural events, and books and movies, the youthful leader of the New Frontier projected an image of male vigor that promised to overcome the crisis of purpose and conduct besetting men in 1950s America. But for all of its impact on American culture and values, Kennedy's pragmatic, assertive, cool, masculine style also penetrated matters of policy on both the foreign and the domestic fronts. Its influence appeared in many of the signature undertakings of the young leader's New Frontier.

Kennedy's carefully cultivated masculine mystique—particularly its emphasis on practical, nonideological problem solving and antibureaucratic individualism—quickly became a powerful influence on the political deliberations and sensibility of the New Frontier. The bright young men in the new administration evinced a "tough-minded realism," to use one of their favorite phrases, to shape a number of initiatives and positions. A glimpse of this cool, unsentimental pragmatism could be seen in JFK's position on civil rights, for example. While sympathetic to the postwar struggle against segregation in the South led by Martin Luther King Jr., Kennedy had never shared a deep moral commitment to equal rights for African Americans. He had voted against the 1957 Civil Rights Act, for example, and carefully calibrated his stance in subsequent years to avoid alienating southern Democrats. Now, as president, he put forward a few modest initiatives, dragged his feet on desegregating federal housing, appointed segregationist judges in the South, dawdled over sending civil rights legislation to Congress, and moved behind the scenes to tamp down the Freedom Rides in the South. Eventually, the force of events, such as the enormous controversy over desegregating the University of Mississippi, compelled Kennedy to take action. But it was not until June 1963 that the president presented an integrationist Civil Rights Bill to Congress, and then he opposed a proposed march on Washington to support it. Clearly, a pragmatic JFK saw civil rights primarily as a political problem to be solved.[39]

Kennedy's vigorous masculine sensibility helped form his attack on Appalachian poverty. During the 1960 primary in West Virginia, he saw close-up the depressed standard of living in much of the Appalachian region, and many of his speeches addressed the need to remedy it. He approached the problem, however, in terms of the degeneration of a hardy, courageous race of pioneers who had been stripped of the manly virtues in the modern era. West Virginians, JFK argued, were "a proud and independent people" who had fought bravely in every conflict from World War I to Korea. "Yes, when there were battles to be fought, when men were needed, when bravery and patriotism and strength were in demand, the nation turned to West Virginia," he argued. But in recent decades economic decline had destroyed jobs, closed off opportunity, and pushed those staunch masculine figures into hard times. JFK proposed a combination of defense contracts, food assistance, economic development, education funding, and job training from his administration as the road to recovery. "'Give me men to match my mountains,' says an old children's song. West Virginia already has the men to match her mountains—men of vigor and fortitude and determination—men who have contributed to America's strength in the past, and who will contribute again in the future," he proclaimed.[40]

After Kennedy assumed the presidency, Harry M. Caudill's *Night Comes to the Cumberlands* became the catalyst for the administration's efforts in the region. Written by a longtime lawyer and journalist who resided in the mountains of eastern Kentucky, the book detailed the effects of economic exploitation by timber companies, strip-mining coal companies, and the big banks that supported them. They hired men to work in the timber mills and coal mines and then left them destitute when they pulled out after ravaging the countryside and taking its natural resources. The result was a debilitating web of minimal education, worthless land, and poverty. As Arthur Schlesinger noted, "Caudill's book came out with a foreword by Stewart Udall and was widely read in New Frontier Washington."[41]

Night Comes to the Cumberlands saw the problem of rampant Appalachian poverty in Kennedyesque terms: a case study of the modern degeneration of a manly, independent, pioneering spirit. It argued that in the eighteenth and nineteenth centuries, the region had been settled by "Southern mountaineers," hardy individualists whose "inurement to primitive outdoor living made them almost as wild as the red man and physically near as tough." In Caudill's words, "It is unlikely that history will ever again record the appearance of a man who, as a type, will possess the hardihood, the sturdy self-reliance, and the fierce independence of the American frontiersman." Sadly, timber deforestation and the strip mining of coal had destroyed this manly spirit of fortitude as the "old fierce pride and sensitive spirit of independence have died from the continuing social trauma of a half-century." This parable of masculine decline in Appalachia was reiterated in Michael Harrington's *The Other America,* the other great antipoverty tract of the era. Its people were "of old American stock, many of them Anglo-Saxon, and old traditions still survive among them," Harrington wrote. They still harbored "a romantic image of mountain life as independent, self-reliant, and athletic," but the reality of a devastated landscape, decaying buildings, unemployment, and poverty clearly made this a portrait of the past. "Perhaps this myth once held a real truth. Now it is becoming more false every day."[42]

In May 1961, Kennedy signed legislation creating the Area Redevelopment Administration (ARA) to provide $75 million annually to deal with unemployment in Appalachia. In 1963, after reading a long review of Caudill's book, JFK summoned ARA officials to the White House, and in the words of an attendee, "The President wanted us to throw the book in there, everything we could do, in effect, to make these programs work." Shortly thereafter, the president, working with the governors of several states in the region, formed the Appalachian Regional Commission to funnel federal money into the region to create jobs, improve the infrastructure, and build highways. These important initiatives of the New Frontier offered a precursor to the later War on Poverty. They sought to improve the economic fate of the region, but equally important for JFK and his New Frontiersmen they promised to regenerate the hardy masculine spirit of an earlier age.[43]

The masculine mystique of the Kennedy administration appeared even more vividly in the Cold War struggle over Cuba. As president, JFK quickly came face-to-face with a volatile situation regarding this island nation that would torment him throughout much of his time in office. The Marxist revolutionary Fidel Castro had come to power in the island country only ninety miles off the southeastern coast of the United States in the late 1950s. His alliance with the Soviet Union, and his inflammatory rhetoric about spreading Communism throughout Latin America, deeply concerned American policy makers and military strategists, who, in President Eisenhower's last months in office, put together a plan for assisting exiled Cuban citizens who wanted to return to Cuba and overthrow the Communist regime. Primarily a creation of the CIA and signed off on by the Joint Chiefs of Staff, this scheme was presented to Kennedy after a few weeks in office. In several meetings, the new president asked many questions and expressed apprehension about direct, visible American involvement but finally authorized the campaign. What followed from April 17 to 19, 1961, was an unmitigated disaster and probably the greatest setback for American foreign policy since World War II. A force of some fourteen hundred anti-Communist Cubans landed at the Bay of Pigs and was immediately hemmed in by Castro's military forces. Things quickly unraveled. An uprising against the Communist dictator, which the CIA had predicted, failed to materialize; American airpower was not deployed to save the undertaking; and the invasion was crushed with hundreds of casualties and the capture of nearly all the remaining force. This humiliating fiasco produced a severe blow to American prestige and position in the larger Cold War struggle.[44]

The Kennedy administration tried to limit damage by suggesting that the president had been handed a plan preapproved by the Eisenhower administration and that he was deceived by the CIA and the Joint Chiefs of Staff, who provided faulty information and blithely assured him of success.

According to this version of events, JFK learned to never again fully trust military and intelligence experts. "John Kennedy was capable of choosing a wrong course, but never a stupid one," Ted Sorensen noted. "[He] inherited the plan, the planners, and most troubling of all, the Cuban exile brigade." The new president set aside his own misgivings to approve it. After the disaster, Sorensen claimed, an embittered Kennedy declared, "All my life I've known better than to depend on the experts. How could I have been so stupid, to let them go ahead?" Arthur Schlesinger reinforced this interpretation, writing that JFK declared to him, "My God, the bunch of advisers we inherited," and vowed in the future "never to rely on the experts."[45]

This official version, however, masked a crucial factor: JFK, while reluctant to directly commit American military forces to the venture, willingly embraced the CIA's Bay of Pigs campaign as a demonstration of his administration's vigorous, nontraditional approach to the Cold War. It was precisely the kind of New Frontier undertaking—circumventing bureaucracy, enamored of clandestine techniques, contemptuous of traditional military procedures—that the young president envisioned as a welcome departure from the Eisenhower-era dependence on clunky committees and nuclear deterrence. In the meetings and briefings that led up to the invasion, the CIA's Richard Bissell, according to Kennedy's adviser Harris Wofford, took advantage of this sensibility. He brilliantly explained the plan in a way that appealed to "Kennedy's yearning for adventure, a vicarious form of which was his fondness for James Bond stories. . . . Bissell was like a character out of literature, a figure larger than life, engaged in plots more important than any James Bond fantasy."[46]

The Kennedy stress on avoiding the organization man's tedious procedures and reviews and relying on the judgment of the insightful individual also predisposed acceptance of the plan. "The witty, rough, sardonic language that Kennedy liked was stimulating, but the degree to which this style dominated the White House and became the common denominator of those to whom the President listened was self-defeating," observed Wofford. The New Frontier compulsion to be irreverent and incisive tended to favor action over reflection, brilliance over wisdom, at the Kennedy White House and produced a syndrome that "inhibited questions of principle and purpose, and strengthened the hand of those who knew how to talk

LEFT: JFK's heroic masculine image depicted on the cover of *Man's Magazine* in May 1960.

BELOW: Kennedy's celebrity appeal on the campaign trail in the 1960 presidential election. CORBIS IMAGES

ABOVE: The Rat Pack in Las Vegas in 1960 (*left to right*): Peter Lawford, Sammy Davis Jr., Frank Sinatra, Joey Bishop, and Dean Martin. GETTY IMAGES

RIGHT: Frank Sinatra and JFK at the Sands Hotel in Las Vegas in 1960. GETTY IMAGES

Novelist Norman Mailer posing as an existential tough guy in the early 1960s. INGE MORATH/MAGNUM IMAGES

James Bond as depicted by actor Sean Connery in a poster for the 1963 movie *From Russia With Love*.
THE ADVERTISING ARCHIVE/ALAMY STOCK PHOTOS

Playboy's Hugh Hefner with his party at JFK's
1961 Inaugural. HUGH HEFNER

Ian Fleming, popular author and creator of Agent 007.
GETTY IMAGES

Jack and Jacqueline Kennedy with children Carolyn and John, Jr., as they broadcast a wholesome family image. JOHN F. KENNEDY LIBRARY

The new President and First Lady embodied the New Frontier's spirit of sophisticated elegance.
JOHN F. KENNEDY LIBRARY

One side of JFK's masculine image as president: The proud father claps as his young children romp around in the Oval Office. JOHN F. KENNEDY LIBRARY

The other side: JFK the sex symbol as he emerges from an ocean swim in Malibu, California, to be mobbed by female passersby. Bill Beebe/*Los Angeles Times* Photographic Archive, UCLA, https://creative commons.org/licenses/by/4.0legalcode

BELOW: Ben and Tony Bradlee socializing with Jack and Jackie Kennedy in the family quarters at the White House. JOHN F. KENNEDY LIBRARY

President Kennedy consults with General Maxwell Taylor (*left*) and Secretary of Defense Robert McNamara (*middle*). JOHN F. KENNEDY LIBRARY

Counterinsurgency icon, General Edward Lansdale, USAF.

Kirk Douglas (*center*) and Tony Curtis (*to his right*) as ancient freedom fighters against Rome in Spartacus. ALAMY STOCK PHOTOS

President Kennedy and a group of Green Berets during the presidential visit to Fort Bragg, North Carolina, in 1961. JOHN F. KENNEDY LIBRARY

The Mercury Seven astronauts as modern male heroes *(front row, left to right)*: Walter M. Schirra, Jr., Donald K. "Deke" Slayton, John H. Glenn, Jr., and M. Scott Carpenter *(back row)*: Alan B. Shepard, Jr., Virgil I. "Gus" Grissom, and L. Gordon Cooper, Jr. NASA

A buoyant JFK and John Glenn in a Cape Canaveral motorcade giving the "thumbs- up" sign to onlookers. GETTY IMAGES

about power with wit and sophistication." While Eisenhower had given Cuba a low priority and approved only American training of guerrilla fighters while withholding final approval of a broader plan, Kennedy embraced the CIA scheme. "Later, the plan would look so crazy that people could not credit its acceptance in the first place. But it made sense to a James Bond fan," one historian has contended. "No, the Cuban invasion was taken to heart because it was so clearly marked with the new traits of Kennedy's own government. . . . It was a chess game backed by daring— played mind to mind, macho to macho, charisma to charisma. It was a James Bond exploit blessed by Yale, a PT raid run by Ph.D.'s. It was the very definition of the New Frontier."[47]

More specifically, the CIA plan expressed the virile, manly sensibility of Kennedy and his youthful administration. Arthur Schlesinger Jr. labeled the daring CIA plan to overthrow Castro "Operation Castration" in a memo to the president. Kennedy, according to Wofford, quashed criticism of the CIA scheme by suggesting that some of his advisers were more fearful of a fight than real men should be. "I know everybody is grabbing their nuts on this," he commented sharply. In fact, throughout the preinvasion deliberations, an attitude of manly toughness prevailed as advocates of the invasion struck "virile poses and talk[ed] of tangible things—fire power, air strikes, landing craft, and so on," reported Schlesinger. Kennedy and his New Frontiersmen exuded a "desire to prove to the CIA and the Joint Chiefs that they were not soft-headed idealists but were really tough guys, too." The president seemed determined to back up his stern campaign rhetoric with action. "Machismo was not a minor factor in Kennedy's makeup," Wofford concluded. As even Sorensen admitted, Kennedy felt that "his disapproval of the plan would be a show of weakness inconsistent with his general stance."[48]

When the Bay of Pigs proved a disaster, Kennedy did not shrink from facing the situation. Refusing to publicly blame anyone among the cabinet, staff, military, or intelligence wings of the government, he accepted responsibility for the debacle. At a press conference, he noted, "There's an old saying that victory has a hundred fathers and defeat is an orphan," before bravely shouldering the blame: "I am the responsible officer of the government." Within his administration, Kennedy took much the same approach. Among his closest confidants such as Robert Kennedy and Ted Sorensen, he bitterly complained about the bad advice he received from the intelligence people and the Joint Chiefs. But when JFK heard Lyndon Johnson attacking the CIA to another administration official, he said sharply, "Lyndon, you've got to remember we're all in this and that when I accepted the responsibility for this operation, I took the entire responsibility on myself and I will have no passing of the buck or backbiting, however justified." Such a stance earned the admiration of Kennedy's associates. Charles Bohlen, an old hand in American foreign affairs councils, confessed, "I was very much impressed with the calmness, the coolness with which the President . . . [absorbed] a defeat. There is certainly no better test of a man's basic quality than the ability to face adversity and to come through it with everything intact."[49]

In fact, after the Bay of Pigs disaster, Kennedy bolstered his standing by insisting on the need to stand up to the Communist menace of Castro. On April 20, the day after the final surrender and capture of the invasion force in Cuba, the president appeared before a national convention of newspaper editors and cast the American struggle with Cuba as a test of national purpose and masculine fortitude. The failed invasion, he argued, was a campaign of freedom-loving Cuban patriots against a police state dictatorship and part of a larger struggle against the forces of Communism around the world. Victory would come to those demonstrating toughness, vigor, and determination. "If the self-discipline of the free cannot match the iron discipline of the mailed fist—in economic, political, scientific, and all the other kinds of struggles as well as military—then the peril to freedom will continue to rise," Kennedy proclaimed. "The complacent, the self-indulgent, the soft societies are about to be swept away with the debris of history. Only the strong, only the industrious, only the determined, only the courageous . . . can possibly survive."[50]

Appreciative of his manful acceptance of responsibility and tough-minded opposition to Communism, the American public rallied around Kennedy's administration after the Bay of Pigs. JFK's popularity in the polls spiked noticeably, with his approval rating rising to 82 percent. (The president noted wryly, "It's just like Eisenhower. The worse I do, the more popular I get.") Many commentators in newspapers and magazines agreed. While

the president's inexperience and the amateurish quality of the Cuban invasion earned much criticism, they praised the young leader for owning
up to his mistakes, demonstrating courage, and making a powerful case
for taking on Communist expansion. As *Life* noted, "Having manfully
taken the blame, he is entitled to a few more months to figure out how to
remedy it." The *New York Times* praised Kennedy for offering a "ringing
challenge" and "mincing no words" in proclaiming America's determination to oppose Communist expansion in the Western Hemisphere.
Kennedy's stance during the first great crisis of his administration seemed
to embody the masculine ideal of courage, conviction, and strength that
had been such an important part of his campaign for the presidency. It
promised dividends in the future, despite the travail of the present situation, and Kennedy emerged with his manly image even more sharply
defined.[51]

JFK's masculine mystique grew even more during a far more dangerous imbroglio with America's troublesome Caribbean neighbor: the
Cuban missile crisis. This episode in late October 1962 involved a nuclear
standoff between the United States and the Soviet Union over the latter's
secret deployment of offensive warhead missiles in Cuba. When aerial sur-
veillance disclosed these installations, Kennedy began a series of lengthy
consultations with his closest advisers, convened in what was called the
ExComm. They considered various courses of action: bombing the missile sites, invading the island with American forces, or simply calling for
their removal. Kennedy decided to pursue a firm middle course: demanding that the Russians dismantle the nuclear weapons while establishing an
American naval blockade, or "quarantine," around the island to stop any
Russian ships that were carrying military armaments to Cuba. After several extremely tense days facing the prospect of a nuclear exchange, the
Russian premier, Nikita Khrushchev, backed down and agreed to remove the
missiles. (Behind the scenes, Kennedy also secretly agreed to remove American missiles from Turkey, but knowledge of this agreement would remain
unknown for some twenty years.)[52]

From this closest scrape with nuclear warfare in the postwar world,
JFK emerged as a leader of heroic proportions. He appeared as an unflinching, manly figure who had faced down the Russian threat with a perfect

combination of courage and cool judgment, resolution and vigor, determination and clarity. The Cuban missile crisis, indeed, shone a spotlight
on Kennedy as the masculine ideal of the New Frontier who embraced
neither wild-eyed military bombast nor weak-kneed capitulation but calm,
pragmatic, valiant discernment. It enhanced the popular image of Kennedy
as a man who had been under fire and could handle the most enormous
pressure imaginable with grace, shrewdness, and a sense of proportion.

A torrent of praise for this manly stand engulfed President Kennedy in
the aftermath of the crisis as Americans breathed a sigh of relief. The dean
of national political commentators, Walter Lippmann, described JFK as
having "not only the courage of a warrior, which is to take risks that are
necessary, but the wisdom of the statesman, which is to use power with
restraint." The columnist William S. White, a rock-ribbed conservative,
praised Kennedy's stand against the Russians and commended him for
avoiding "an unmanly betrayal of the nation." Walter Trohan, writing in
the *Chicago Tribune,* asserted that "Americans were proud when youthful
Mr. Kennedy thrust out his jaw in a fighting attitude and faced up to the
bully in the Kremlin." Joseph Alsop and Charles Bartlett, in a long analysis in *The Saturday Evening Post,* praised the president's cool demeanor
during the crisis. "John F. Kennedy is not an outwardly emotional man,
and in the bad days there were few signs that he was passing through the
loneliest moments of his lonely job," they wrote. A couple of times he lost
his temper over minor matters. "But he never lost his nerve." Joseph Kraft
simply noted that after earlier setbacks at the Vienna Summit and the Bay
of Pigs, the Cuban missile crisis saw JFK "finally win his manhood from
the Russians."[53]

But the clearest explanation of Kennedy's masculine achievement dur-
ing the Cuban missile crisis came in a *Newsweek* postmortem. Titled
"When One Man Sizes Up Another," the piece noted that Khrushchev had
run roughshod over the young president a few months earlier at the Vienna
Summit, gloating over the Berlin Wall and the Bay of Pigs disaster. But
JFK's stalwart conduct during the missile crisis "changed all that. Suddenly,
Khrushchev was shown that the Presidential fiber was as tough as his own,"
said *Newsweek.* "With this new appraisal of one man by another, a new
phase of the nuclear age seemed to have opened. . . . Fidel Castro has been

emasculated as a threat to the Western Hemisphere. . . . Out of a month of crisis, President Kennedy had won a great personal triumph. In Mexico and other Latin American countries he was being called *muy macho*—a real man—the highest compliment a Latin can pay to another man."[54]

While the cascading Cuban crises both reinforced Kennedy's masculine mystique, so, too, did a quieter endeavor in foreign affairs. During the 1960 presidential campaign, the Democratic candidate had endorsed the idea of the Peace Corps, a government-backed project that would send young volunteers abroad to underdeveloped countries to provide skilled manpower and technical assistance for economic projects. As president, he established the agency by executive order in March 1961. Over the next two years, over five thousand volunteers were trained and set to work in some forty-six countries in Asia, Latin America, and Africa. The Peace Corps became a signature undertaking of the New Frontier, reflecting its idealistic spirit of public service and unconventional approaches to solving problems.

But it was also a symbol of Kennedy's regenerative masculine ideal. While an exercise in altruism, the Peace Corps was also a weapon in the global struggle against Communism. It provided a fresh field of endeavor for young men—women were admitted to the program but in much smaller numbers, and their endeavors were more restricted—to demonstrate manly vitality and dedication outside the normal comfort zone of suburban, bureaucratic life. JFK and other New Frontiersmen saw the Peace Corps as an antidote to the problems laid out in *The Ugly American*—instead of sending soft, reception-loving, uninformed bureaucrats abroad to represent American values and interests, it put self-sacrificing, tough, practical-minded young men into the field to embody notions of freedom, enterprise, and democracy.[55]

Under the direction of Sargent Shriver, President Kennedy's brother-in-law, this enterprise quickly emerged as a showpiece for the tough, individualist, manly spirit of the New Frontier. "Like many other Americans, I have wondered whether our contemporary society, with its emphasis on the organization man and the easy life, can continue to produce the self-reliance, initiative, and independence we consider our heritage," Shriver wrote. "The Peace Corps is truly a new frontier in the sense that it provides the challenge to self-reliance and independent action which the vanished frontier once provided on our own continent." To that end, boot camps for the project were established in Puerto Rico that roused participants at 5:00 A.M. and placed them in a demanding regimen of calisthenics, running, rappelling, camping, and swimming. As one of the camp directors observed, "We will use physical training as a vehicle to measure a man's stamina, courage, and resourcefulness." Volunteers received instruction in the language and culture of their designated country and were given tips on how to prepare for serving a two-year tour of duty living plainly and austerely in some of the poorest cities, villages, and rural areas in the world. An understated but proud ethos of toughness became a hallmark of the organization. "This won't be a moonlight cruise on the Amazon," Shriver reassured those who perceived the Peace Corps as a way to dodge the draft. "The military life may not only be more glamorous, but it may be safer."

A public relations effort buttressed the image of the Peace Corps' masculine hardihood. The Kennedy administration publicized the types of people attracted to the program: a University of Michigan boxing coach, a member of the Football Hall of Fame, mountain climbers, physicians, Ph.D.'s, successful businessmen. Shriver proudly reported that a Peace Corps volunteer had participated in a "Thai-style boxing" match with a native Thai opponent and fought him to a draw. In Colombia, two volunteers had upheld the honor of the Peace Corps by completing a fifty-mile hike during a rest day. Shriver arranged for the African American Olympic decathlon champion Rafer Johnson to consult with volunteers in Nigeria and Ghana and secured the services of William Lederer and Eugene Burdick, authors of *The Ugly American,* as consultants on training issues. In other words, the Peace Corps drew upon the same combination of physical vigor, high achievement, and determination that characterized "the best and the brightest" recruited at the highest councils of the administration. The agency, in Shriver's words, formed the "point of the lance" in America's fight against Communism in the third world and fulfilled Kennedy's instructions "to create a New Frontier image abroad."[56]

Thus many of the policies, as well as the imagery, of the Kennedy administration exuded the virile, pragmatic, cool male impulses of its leader.

In a public sense, this ethos promised to overcome the crisis of masculinity prevalent in 1950s America. Just as powerfully, it also permeated the private image of JFK that steadily saturated the country during the early 1960s.

From the welter of complex political issues and policy conundrums confronting the New Frontier in the early 1960s, the glowing personal aura of President John F. Kennedy shone through consistently. Surveys reflected his personal popularity. According to Gallup, during his time in office JFK won a higher approval rating than any other American president in the six decades after World War II. His average job approval rating during his roughly thousand days in office was 70 percent. (His nearest competitor was Dwight Eisenhower, with a rating of 65 percent, while George H. W. Bush stood at 61 percent, Bill Clinton at 55 percent, Ronald Reagan at 53 percent, Barack Obama at 49 percent, and Jimmy Carter at 46 percent.) JFK's contemporary standing among his fellow citizens was impressive.[57]

But President Kennedy's extraordinary popularity seemed to flow more from his personal appeal than from his political positions or achievements. A leading national magazine concluded that his phenomenal appeal after one year in office "was an accolade to his personality, rather than to his New Frontier policies." Another concluded that the chief executive was "a compelling public personality. But his appeal seemed to remain in part a kind of celebrity pulling-power." Perhaps the most thoughtful analysis of this phenomenon appeared in a long piece in *Harper's* titled "The Cult of Personality Comes to the White House." The public, it argued, loved President Kennedy but seemed to be "reacting to him largely as a personality." People had been charmed by the unique Kennedy combination of "martial heroism, high fashion, dashing international society, the scholarly-literary-artistic world . . . the tenderness of young parents shown in the women's magazines, and the glamour of sports, stage, and movie stars." This trend, the article suggested, was creating a "personalized Presidency" so divorced from Congress, the political parties, and policy making that it was unique in American history.[58]

President Kennedy's compelling personal appeal, it seems clear, was rooted more deeply in cultural factors than in political ones. It reflected the vibrant masculine ideal that he had been promoting since his emergence on the national stage in the mid-1950s. Moreover, it was multidimensional, bowing toward the postwar family ideal while at the same time portraying the national leader as a masculine sex symbol and a celebrity. It was a powerful combination.

From the earliest days of his presidency, Kennedy was portrayed as the head of an attractive, modern American family. Warm images of Jack, Jackie, and their children became mainstays in magazine and television stories as Americans chuckled at the photographs of Caroline riding her pony, Macaroni, and John junior running to throw himself into the arms of his proud, smiling father as he descended from a helicopter. Two weeks after Kennedy's electoral victory, *Life* started the trend with an article describing the president-elect as "a family man with a big job to do." After the inauguration, *Look* offered a cover story titled "Our New First Family" that introduced readers, with the help of photographs from the famed photographer Richard Avedon, to the warm domestic life of the First Family. It described three-year-old Caroline's "loving, imaginative relationship with her parents" while hovering protectively over her newly arrived little brother, John junior, whom she dubbed "the kissing baby." The article quoted Jacqueline Kennedy on her determination to not be bound by theories in raising her children: "The personality of the child seems to guide you. Children have imagination, a quality that seems to flicker out in so many adults." The story stressed most strongly the benevolent paternal role of JFK, whom the First Lady described as falling in love with children after Caroline's birth and even adopting a new favorite quotation: "He who has a wife and child gives hostages to fortune." The president, the article claimed, bequeathed to Caroline many of his own qualities. "In many ways she is her father's child—blond, restless, electric with energy. They often have the same expression, eyes slightly narrowed, with a keen, questing, quizzical interest in the world. She is a child of strong will who knows what she wants when she wants it." When Jackie was hospitalized to give birth not long after the election, a children's party went on as planned because "overseeing the festivities, in his wife's absence, was none other than John F. Kennedy himself."[59]

Adoring features on the president and his domestic role poured forth over the next three years. *Newsweek* ran a cover story titled "Caroline in the White House" full of anecdotes about the warm Kennedy family life in the presidential residence, such as when the First Daughter burst in on her father when he was taking a bath. Holding a magazine with his photograph on the cover, she pointed and squealed, "Daddy!" before tossing it into the bathtub. *Time* detailed a joint birthday party for Caroline and John junior that featured fifteen friends and cousins as guests, a black woolly monkey, ice cream and cake, and boisterous tricycle riding on the marble halls of the White House. "With the Kennedys on Vacation" in *Ladies' Home Journal* portrayed a First Family sojourn to the seashore in halcyon terms: "This is a summer day—family style—in the USA: salt air, wind, and a child's sweet laughter." *Good Housekeeping* examined "how the Kennedy marriage has fared," noting that the president and his wife, like most young couples, had overcome rocky patches early in their partnership and now enjoyed "a particularly warm relationship." *Look* magazine offered a striking portrayal of Kennedy as a family man in a special January 1962 issue. It showed JFK in a golf cart at Hyannis Port surrounded by children—his daughter and numerous nieces and nephews shrieking, "Uncle Jack"—as he happily raced them around the compound before going to the local candy store for treats. "Caroline's father," the article informed readers, grappled daily "with problems that threaten all the world's children."[60]

The most poignant stories on the young president's family role appeared with the death of his infant son, Patrick Kennedy. In August 1963, Jacqueline Kennedy entered the hospital in Boston and gave birth to a child who was five weeks premature and weighed less than five pounds. The president rushed to his wife's side as the boy struggled to maintain his precarious hold on life. *Life* magazine showed masked doctors and nurses huddled around the infant's bed trying to treat his severe respiratory problems as "a compassionate nation watched." Another photograph depicted JFK emerging from the hospital elevator over the caption "A worried father visits his stricken son." The story's final sentence noted somberly that "neither the devoted care nor the nation's prayers could save the President's son" as the infant died two days after his birth. These melancholy images, in concert with the usual glowing ones, worked to enhance a common motif in the early 1960s: the Kennedys as an exemplary modern family and the president as a committed father and husband.[61]

At the same time, however, subtly surrounding this family narrative was an equally powerful image of JFK as masculine sex symbol. Somehow, he succeeded in having it both ways. During his presidency, he appeared, simultaneously, as both the devoted family man and the physically alluring male who set feminine pulses fluttering. Following his inauguration, President Kennedy consistently appeared before the American public as a handsome, glamorous, even erotic figure whose appeal to women far surpassed that of the ordinary suburban organization man. A receptive public ate it up. *Newsweek,* in a story on the president's campaigning in the 1962 congressional elections, covered a trip to Minneapolis and noted that the four thousand people greeting him at the airport "was the kind of crowd that might swarm around a movie star" and quoted a stewardess who declared, "You don't realize he's that good looking until you really see him."[62]

Women who saw the president in a private setting confirmed his powerful sexual appeal. The writer Diana Trilling, after observing and talking briefly with JFK at a White House dinner, reported breathlessly, "The President was handsome and exuded energy—I could feel it even at my distance from him.... [His face] radiated strength, power so compressed that you felt it was about to explode." Laura Bergquist, a reporter for *Look* who had many conversations with JFK, noted his combination of masculine appeal and superiority. "I think Kennedy liked women very much. He was very male, or what the Latins call 'macho.' . . . Maybe it was the Irish mick in him, but I don't think he took women seriously—as human beings, for instance, that you work with casually," she reflected. "He was beguiled by women, he loved being around them. But when it came to serious talk, he preferred talking to the guys about politics. He was kind of a man's man."[63]

JFK's sex appeal constantly appeared in the public spotlight. In a famous incident on the Santa Monica beach during a presidential visit to Peter Lawford's ocean-side home on August 19, 1962, Kennedy decided to break free from the usual restraints on presidential behavior by leaving the house for a swim in the Pacific. Clad only in blue swim trunks, he strode out of the house and headed across the sand into the ocean. Beachgoers spotted him, and a crowd gathered, shouting, "Here he comes! It's him! Look how handsome!" According to the *Los Angeles Times*, "several women went into the water with him fully dressed," and one was overheard commenting on how "big and powerful looking" JFK was. A staff photographer for the newspaper, who had been staking out the Lawford home, quickly snapped a photograph of Kennedy as he returned to the beach to be mobbed by an enthusiastic crowd. It showed a tan and shirtless president, a wide grin on his face, as he emerged dripping from the ocean and was surrounded by a group of exhilarated, middle-aged females. Kennedy shook hands with many and patted children on the head, the *Times* continued, as "women clung to him and everybody wanted to touch, talk, and see him up close." The beach photograph of Kennedy and his admirers was reprinted in newspapers throughout the United States.[64]

Recurring depictions of President Kennedy as a handsome leading man—often alongside famous, beautiful Hollywood actresses—illustrated his powerful sex appeal even more sharply. In June 1961, *Life* ran a photograph of a recent White House luncheon showing Princess Grace of Monaco, the gorgeous former movie star, standing next to the president and adoringly gazing up at him with warm eyes and the hint of a seductive smile. *Esquire*, in January 1963, used its cover to pair the president alongside Anita Ekberg, the legendary Swedish sex symbol. On the left side appeared a photograph of Ekberg cavorting in the Trevi Fountain in *La dolce vita* (1960), the famous Federico Fellini film, with blond hair flying and dressed in a tight, short black dress that exposed her impressive décolletage and legs. On the right side of the cover appeared Kennedy in his iconic Santa Monica beach photograph, shirtless and dripping water, with several women hanging on him. Ekberg seemed to be staring appreciatively at the president in a tribute to JFK's sexy star power.[65]

Perhaps the clearest public sign of JFK's sexual charisma came in a notorious episode on May 19, 1962, when Marilyn Monroe appeared before a large gathering at Madison Square Garden. The president and the actress, of course, were widely rumored (and correctly so) to be involved in a sexual relationship. Now at this $1,000-a-plate birthday celebration for the president that was also a Democratic Party fund-raiser, America's reigning female sex symbol slithered onstage in a formfitting, glittering, flesh-colored sequined gown. The dress was so tight that she had been sewn into it and could barely move. Monroe scanned the audience to locate Kennedy before launching into a sultry, seductive version of "Happy Birthday" that triggered peals of knowing laughter in the audience. After this performance, the president took the stage and delivered one of his trademark quips: "I can now retire from politics after having 'Happy Birthday' sung to me in, ah, such a sweet, wholesome way." The crowd, sensing that it had been let in on an inside joke, roared. *Time* magazine, describing Monroe's scanty apparel and sexy delivery, noted archly, "It was Marilyn who was the hit of the evening." Dorothy Kilgallen, a columnist for the *New York Journal-American,* was more frank, writing, "It seemed like Marilyn was making love to the President in front of 40 million Americans." This highly symbolic episode clearly displayed JFK's appeal as a masculine sex symbol.[66]

In fact, much more than symbolism was at work. While occupying the Oval Office, Kennedy continued his lifelong pattern of behavior by engaging in numerous trysts and sexual flings with women. Lots of them. While serving as president, and while the First Lady was frequently absent at their country home in Virginia, JFK brazenly bedded (sometimes together) a pair of free-spirited White House secretaries, Priscilla Wear and Jill Cowen, nicknamed Fiddle and Faddle, as well as Jackie's press secretary, Pamela Turnure. He had long-term affairs with Helen Chavchavadze, a beautiful Georgetown graduate and divorcée whom he had met in 1959, and Diana de Vegh, an elegant Radcliffe graduate in her early twenties whom he had met in 1958 and then placed on McGeorge Bundy's staff. He had several liaisons with Ellen Rometsch, a call girl and suspected East German spy, whose potential to compromise national security and the administration caused J. Edgar Hoover, director of the FBI, to warn the president about the danger accruing to this situation. And, of course, the president continued periodic dalliances with Marilyn Monroe, meeting her in Lawford's California home and at a hotel in New York.[67]

More disturbingly, Kennedy also cast his sexual net in a much wider and less discerning manner. According to Traphes Bryant, a longtime White House employee who kept a diary—he cared for the presidential dogs and performed a variety of handyman tasks at the residence—JFK indulged in a host of casual dalliances throughout his time as president. Bryant claimed that staffers at the executive mansion would scour its private rooms for hairpins and other personal items to discard after one of the president's many "feminine friends" departed the premises. He overheard JFK comment to one of his friends, "I'm not through with a girl until I've had her three ways." Another time, he recorded in his diary this exchange: "Dave Powers once asked the President what he would like to have for his birthday. He named a TV actress from California. His wish was granted." Once on a job assignment, Bryant stepped out of the elevator on the second floor just as "a naked blond office girl ran through the hall between the second-floor kitchen and the door leading to the West Hall. Her breasts were swinging as she ran by." A bizarrely comical episode occurred when Jacqueline Kennedy left the White House for Virginia and a short time later a tall, beautiful blond girl arrived and was escorted immediately to the swimming pool, where she proceeded to disrobe and frolic with a number of other young women, the president, and several male friends. Everyone was naked, including Kennedy, who sat poolside sipping a daiquiri. Bedlam ensued, however, when the First Lady unexpectedly returned to the residence to retrieve an item she had forgotten. According to Bryant, White House employees sounded the alarm and "naked bodies were scurrying every which way. . . . [T]he help had a time clearing away the evidence— like highball glasses. Only the President remained in the pool."[68]

Several Secret Service agents—Lawrence Newman, Anthony Sherman, William McIntyre, and Joseph Paolella—observed similar episodes of presidential philandering. Unknown young women constantly appeared for visits with Kennedy, often being escorted into his presence by Dave Powers, and the agents continuously worried about security breaches or the potential for blackmail when they were not allowed to interview or identify them. But they were instructed "to keep their eyes open and their mouth shut." Newman related that on a trip to Seattle he was outside the president's hotel suite standing watch when a senior staffer got off the elevator with two females who were obviously prostitutes. The staffer instructed the agent to stand aside and let them pass. A deeply troubled

Newman commented, "You've received the most elite assignment in the Secret Service. You were then watching the elevator door because the President was inside with two hookers." Kennedy's reckless womanizing, Sherman continued, "continued constantly. Not just once every six months, not every New Year's Eve. It was a regular thing." The agents found this behavior deeply disturbing, but as Sherman put it, "We protected the President in many ways."[69]

Amid this torrent of casual sexual activity, President Kennedy maintained a trio of long-term affairs during his term in the White House. First, he continued a relationship with Judith Campbell, the beautiful young woman introduced to him by Frank Sinatra during the election campaign. Log sheets at the executive mansion indicate that Campbell called JFK some seventy times in 1961 and 1962, and she claimed that she visited him more than twenty times for intimate lunches during this same period. This became deeply problematic when the FBI discovered that Campbell also had a sexual relationship with the notorious Mafia figure Sam Giancana, and J. Edgar Hoover visited Kennedy for lunch on March 22, 1962. Presumably, he warned the president about the seriousness of this indiscretion because the last known phone call with Campbell occurred later that afternoon. In addition, the president pursued a lengthy affair with Mary Meyer, a Washington artist (and sister-in-law of one of his best friends, the journalist Ben Bradlee) whom he had known casually for many years. They commenced a sexual relationship in 1961—she also became a frequent White House guest in Jacqueline Kennedy's absence—that lasted until his assassination in late 1963.[70]

More disturbingly, President Kennedy commenced an affair with a nineteen-year-old intern in the White House press office, Mimi Beardsley, that lasted throughout 1962 and 1963. Coming from a prosperous New Jersey family and attending the exclusive Miss Porter's School in Connecticut—Jacqueline Kennedy was an alumna—she wrote an impressive article in the student newspaper that won her a student internship for the summer. Tall, lithe, and pretty, Beardsley attracted the president's attention, and he seduced her on her fourth day at work. Invited to the White House swimming pool by Powers, she was joined by Kennedy, who

then offered to give her a tour of the private residence. Then, after ushering her into the First Lady's bedroom, he smoothly steered her into bed,
and the starstruck teenager complied. After that, JFK and Beardsley had
regular sexual liaisons, including in his children's bathtub and on presidential trips around the United States. Their relationship also included
several degrading episodes where Kennedy asked her to perform oral sex
on Powers (she reluctantly agreed) and then later on his brother Teddy
(she angrily refused). For Beardsley, it was a dazzling if somewhat mysti-
fying adventure. She worried about the implications of his being married
but found a rationalization for the situation: If the president "wasn't troubled about his wife, why should I be?"[71]

Jacqueline Kennedy, of course, was well aware of her husband's enormous sexual appetite and largely tolerated his extramarital escapades. But
occasionally she displayed flashes of bitterness. In Canada, a furious First
Lady turned on Dave Powers when she observed a "blond bimbo" standing in the receiving line and burst out, "Isn't it bad enough that you solicit
this woman for my husband, but then you insult me by asking me to shake
her hand!" Another time, while taking a visiting French journalist around
the White House, she shocked him by remarking in French, as they passed
Fiddle's desk, "This is the girl who is supposedly sleeping with my husband." Such comments merely acknowledged the obvious. Even in far-
away Chicago, Hugh Hefner reflected the common wisdom that circulated
among powerful friends of the new administration: "Kennedy was married, but he wasn't."[72]

Thus President John F. Kennedy represented a new kind of American
leader, one who fully realized the masculine mystique of sexual power, assertive individualism, and sophisticated independence projected during
his campaign for the office. As Arthur Schlesinger remarked, "His 'coolness'
was itself a new frontier. It meant freedom from the stereotyped responses
of the past. It promised the deliverance of American idealism, buried
deep in the national character but imprisoned by the knowingness and
calculation of American society in the fifties." But JFK's male charisma
was once again not the result of his solitary labors but rather an image
that was shared, supported, promoted, and polished by a cadre of associates.

In 1961, after the youthful senator assumed the mantle of national leadership, the Kennedy Circle expanded to include a new galaxy of figures.
Converging from the worlds of journalism, the military, Hollywood, and
the space program, they served to enhance the powerful masculine aura
of the man in the White House. [73]

EIGHT

CELEBRITY JOURNALIST:
BEN BRADLEE

On the evening of the West Virginia primary in May 1960, an anxious John F. Kennedy waited for the returns to dribble in. This was a stringent test for the Democratic senator, who, as a Catholic candidate, had yet to prove that he could pull votes in a pervasively Protestant state. So he sought respite from the tension by corralling the Washington bureau chief for *Newsweek*, Ben Bradlee, along with their wives—the couples had enjoyed dinner together—to see a movie. They originally went to see *Suddenly, Last Summer*, a popular new film, but when it was sold out, Kennedy chose a stag film showing at a rather run-down Washington theater across the street. It was, in Bradlee's words, "a nasty thing called *Private Property*, starring one Katie Manx as a horny housewife." The journalist later discovered that the movie was on "the Catholic Index of forbidden films." After the movie, the Kennedys and Bradlees returned to the senator's home to learn that he had won a big victory. After a bottle of champagne was opened, JFK invited the reporter and his wife to fly down to West Virginia on his private plane, the *Caroline*, for a victory appearance, and the Bradlees happily accepted.[1]

This politically significant evening provided a glimpse of how Kennedy's legendary libido lay intertwined with his political success. But the events of that night revealed even more about Ben Bradlee. They exhibited the bond of forthright male sexuality that linked the aspiring president and the up-and-coming young reporter. It also disclosed an unusually close friendship between a journalist and his subject, one that would eventually raise eyebrows over its impropriety even as it launched a fabulous career that made Bradlee the most famous and influential newsman in Washington, D.C., within a few years. That spring evening in 1960 captured the symbiotic relationship of two like-minded young men in the heady days of a new era in Washington, one held together with a bond of commingled affection and self-interest that would go far to burnish JFK's masculine mystique.

Bradlee had met Kennedy two years before when they became neighbors in a Georgetown neighborhood and, along with their spouses, passed on the sidewalk pushing baby carriages. Stopping for a conversation, the couples ended up talking in the Kennedys' backyard and discovered that they were attending the same dinner party later that evening, where they had been assigned to sit next to each other. Like their husbands, Jackie Kennedy and Tony Bradlee hit it off, and as they all uncovered many common interests, including the magnet of young children, the two couples soon became close friends. They socialized frequently, traveled together to campaign functions after the senator launched his bid for the Democratic nomination, and even spent time at the Kennedy family compound in Hyannis Port and, later, Camp David. But the relationship involved more than friendship. It involved the entanglement of politics and journalism, two key parts of a larger culture of celebrity, information, and entertainment in America's postwar mass society. As Bradlee confessed, "This thing I had going with the junior senator from Massachusetts was very seductive. He had the smell of success, and my special access to him was enormously valuable to *Newsweek*." He put it more bluntly in a memoir penned many years later: "When I got to know Kennedy, I kind of staked him out as part of my own territorial imperative, and as he prospered, so did I."[2]

As their relationship developed, it became clear that the two young men shared more than just professional ambition. Frustrated with the stagnant social milieu of Eisenhower's America, impatient with the restrictive demands of the organization man, and appreciative of beautiful women, Kennedy and Bradlee embodied the spirit of manly regeneration that had welled up with the New Frontier. One, stationed at the pinnacle of the national government, and the other, stationed in a crucial job in one of the nation's leading national magazines, collaborated in shaping the vibrant, masculine mystique that would become a hallmark of American public life in the early 1960s.

The powerful bond between Jack Kennedy and Ben Bradlee stemmed in part from a shared background. Like the politician, the journalist was a Bostonian who had attended boarding schools as a boy, Harvard as a young man, and then served in the navy in the Pacific theater during World War II. In early life, each had displayed a native intelligence stirred with a tonic of great personal charm and a certain aristocratic sense of insouciant privilege. But while Kennedy came from a clan of Irish politicians and parvenus and veered into the world of elections and lawmaking after the war, Bradlee was a scion of the Brahmin caste who found his footing in the world of newspapers and magazines. As events would prove, the intersection of their efforts in the national capital in the late 1950s would play a shaping role in the cultural politics of the New Frontier.

Benjamin Crowninshield Bradlee was born on August 26, 1921, to a prominent Boston family with roots in the city going back three hundred years. His father had been an all-American football player at Harvard before carving out a comfortable career as an investment banker. Young Bradlee grew up in a prosperous atmosphere, complete with a spacious house and a series of governesses who looked after him and his older brother and younger sister. At age fourteen, the boy suffered the biggest trial of his early life. He contracted polio and developed paralysis in both of his legs. Outfitted with braces and undergoing a grinding regimen of therapies and treatments, he gradually rehabilitated his legs. Decades later, he still remembered the night when they called his mother and father up to his bedroom "and there I was, grimacing from the pain of the braces, but standing. We all cried our different tears of relief." Eight weeks later, he was walking and ready to go back to school.[3]

Bradlee attended St. Mark's, an exclusive prep school that was "a citadel of WASP culture" in New England. He excelled in subjects such as history, government, and classics and lettered in football, hockey, and tennis. Baseball, however, was his first love, and he became a star first basemen for the school team. Bradlee served on the debating team, sang in the school choir, and edited the yearbook and overall received a "top of the line education," he recalled later. But he also came to realize that while St. Mark's specialized in "fitting round pegs into round holes, fine-tuning good students and good athletes into better students and better athletes," the school did little to acquaint him with the wider world and pressing social issues.[4]

In 1939, Bradlee, like earlier generations of his family dating back to the late eighteenth century, entered Harvard University. While intelligent and capable, he was a lackluster student. He slid by in his courses and devoted most of his considerable energy to pranks, conviviality, drinking, and chasing girls. In fact, the school administration eventually placed him on disciplinary probation for cutting too many classes. He played on Harvard's baseball team but came to the unfortunate realization that he could not hit a curveball, a discovery that planted him on the bench. In his last year as a student, Bradlee also began dating Jean Saltonstall, a pretty young woman from a proper, aristocratic Boston family, and their relationship became serious. Then, like many young men, he was swept up in war fever after the Japanese attack on Pearl Harbor and yearned to enter the armed forces. Thus August 8, 1942, was a red-letter day in Bradlee's life: he graduated from Harvard at 10:00 A.M., became a commissioned ensign in the U.S. Navy at noon, and married Jean Saltonstall at 4:00 P.M.[5]

A few days later, Bradlee left his new bride for the Pacific theater and spent the next two years aboard a destroyer, the U.S.S. *Philip,* escorting cruisers and aircraft carriers in the South Pacific and spending considerable time in the Solomon Islands, the Marianas, Australia, and New Zealand. He rose to become officer of the deck within a year and then worked in communications managing Combat Information Centers that imparted crucial technical information to ships before they headed off to combat in the Philippines and Okinawa. After the surrender of Japan, he mustered out of the navy in October 1945 and returned to Boston to take up civilian life. His wartime experience, Bradlee believed, had taken him from boyhood to manhood and forged certain characteristics: "enthusiastic, tactful, hardworking, constructive, practical, diligent, consistent, resourceful, cooperative, realistic, able to inspire those below him and to impress those above him—when he knows what he is talking about."[6]

Like many ex-servicemen, young Bradlee faced the postwar future with uncertain prospects. He bounced around before drifting and joining a small group of veterans who founded an independent newspaper, the *New Hampshire Sunday News*. He also moonlighted at a Manchester radio station and worked as a stringer for *Time-Life* and *Newsweek*. In the late summer of 1948, the young newspaper went under, but Bradlee described this period as "a glorious, happy two and a half years, exciting, rewarding, unbelievably educational, and great fun from beginning to end." And it had revealed to him his life's work.[7]

A few weeks later, Bradlee got a job as a staff reporter on the night shift at *The Washington Post*. He and Jean and their infant son, Benjamin junior, moved into a small house in Georgetown. Bradlee, as the new kid on the block at the *Post*, covered local stories on the municipal court, civic associations, gambling scandals, and minor crime sprees. Occasionally, he stumbled upon a national story, such as the day in 1950 when two armed Puerto Rican extremists attacked Blair House and attempted to assassinate President Truman, who was staying there while the White House was being repaired. Bradlee, who accidentally came upon the scene while riding a trolley car, crawled on his stomach past the bodies of a police officer and one of the assailants to get the story, which ended up on the front page. The young reporter later credited his early days at *The Washington Post* for giving him an eye for a good newspaper story and teaching him "how to write tightly and with some flair."[8]

After a few years, however, Bradlee leaped at the opportunity when the United States Information Service offered him a position as a press attaché in Paris. He headed off to France with his wife and young son and spent the next few years making summaries of French press stories for the State Department, covering stories in Western Europe and North Africa, serving as a liaison with American correspondents on the Continent, and helping organize social functions for visiting government dignitaries. Then, at the beginning of 1954, he took a position as the European correspondent for *Newsweek*. Bradlee loved the work. "The sheer joy and romance of being a foreign correspondent is hard to explain, even harder to exaggerate," he wrote. "Even when it's dangerous—a war, a revolution, a plane ride in an uninsurable vehicle, the adrenaline high is incredible, and long-lasting."[9]

As a young journalist, Bradlee developed several lifelong characteristics. Intelligent, tough, and ambitious, he displayed considerable charm and charisma with his gravelly voice, cheerfully profane vocabulary, broad smile, and cool demeanor. He lived adventurously, traveling to great national capitals and war zones alike in the early 1950s, and gained a certain celebrity status by getting himself arrested and threatened with expulsion from France after officials believed he had gotten mixed up with the Algerian liberation movement. Bradlee relished French cuisine and drink. "When you start sucking air on a story, there's always a little one-star restaurant within easy reach where journalistic frustrations can be overwhelmed by food and wine," he noted. A man's man, he delighted in hanging out with other reporters at seedy bars, trading war stories, drinking, and playing cards late into the night. Handsome and debonair, Bradlee was drawn to beautiful women and attracted their attention in turn. "I couldn't get over the French women, pretty or plain, in cafés, on the street, looking you up and down with confidence and interest," he related. He often reciprocated.[10]

Moreover, Bradlee's marriage started to unravel. He and Jean had married young, and it proved an unsuitable match. Things slowly came apart in Paris as they separated and then got back together. Meanwhile, Bradlee indulged in a number of sexual dalliances and affairs. They ranged from a saleswoman at a New York department store to the attractive wife of a Dutch couple the Bradlees met on the ski slopes in the Alps. Then, in Paris, Bradlee began a months-long affair "with someone full of joy, humor, and adventure. I became overwhelmed by sex itself, and the sexual excitement that gave my relationship with her a vitality I had not known before."[11]

Bradlee's marriage disintegrated when he was swept away by a whirlwind romance. In August 1954, two sisters whom he had known casually in Washington—Mary Pinchot Meyer, wife of the CIA man Cord Meyer, and Antoinette "Tony" Pinchot Pittman, wife of the Washington lawyer

Steuart Pittman—visited Paris on a leg of their longer European tour. Bradlee and Tony, the mother of four children, became infatuated with each other and spent the night together at a romantic hotel outside the city. They soon fell in love. Over the next two years, they conducted a secret romance, flying back and forth between Washington and Paris when they could get away. After finally divorcing their spouses, the two were married on July 6, 1956, in Paris, and he wrangled a new position with *Newsweek* covering national news in Washington.[12]

Bradlee returned to the United States and launched a new stage in both his personal life and his career. His duties at *Newsweek* involved covering minor stories the regular beat reporters had turned down: minor international agreements and foreign aid, forgettable political disputes in the House of Representative or the Senate, utilities regulation, and the campaign for Alaskan statehood. At the same time, in Bradlee's words, "I was getting a crash course in what makes Washington tick." Finally, in the summer of 1958, Bradlee broke a front-page story about congressional corruption in several federal regulatory agencies—the Federal Communications Commission, the Securities and Exchange Commission, and the Federal Trade Commission—that eventually reached into the White House itself. His reporting revealed that Sherman Adams, President Eisenhower's chief of staff, had been the recipient of numerous financial gifts and favors from a wealthy New England industrialist. Adams was forced to resign, and Bradlee's journalistic stock at *Newsweek* soared.[13]

Meanwhile, the Bradlees had purchased a house on the 3300 block of N Street NW in Georgetown and had another child. Then, in 1959, Bradlee had the serendipitous experience that changed his life. He and Tony made the sidewalk acquaintance of a young Massachusetts senator, Jack Kennedy, who, along with his wife, Jacqueline, had purchased a house on the same block. As the Bradlee-Kennedy friendship grew steadily over subsequent months, it became a catalyst in the professional evolution of both the politician and the journalist. Kennedy had determined to run for president, and Bradlee sensed an opportunity to bolster his career by covering the attractive young candidate. In the reporter's words, "Little by little it was accepted by the rest of the *Newsweek* bureau and by New York that Kennedy was mine." Within a few weeks of the start of the Democratic

primaries in 1960, the magazine assigned Bradlee to cover the Massachusetts senator full-time.[14]

The newsman was thrilled about Kennedy's candidacy. In his words, it
was "exciting to consider the prospect that a friend and neighbor might,
just possibly, become president of the United States." At the same time,
however, it was also a bit disorienting when that friend might actually
become the most powerful individual in the world. It once caused Bradlee
to ask JFK if running for the office ever seemed strange or gave him pause.
He replied that he had wondered about his own qualifications "until I stop
and look around at the other people who are running for the job. And then
I think I'm just as qualified as they are."[15]

As the 1960 election unfolded, Kennedy slowly gave Bradlee inside
access to his life and activities and thoughts. The two men, and often their
wives, became boon companions, sharing many experiences during the
electoral process. Ben and Tony Bradlee sat next to Jacqueline Kennedy in
the audience when her husband announced his candidacy in the Senate
Caucus Room on January 3, 1960. Over the following months, Bradlee
followed Kennedy on the campaign trail, regularly talked with him privately
about issues and personalities, and even celebrated his successes. The
Bradlees accompanied the Kennedys to primary victory celebrations; Tony
flew to Los Angeles for the Democratic nominating convention, sitting
next to JFK on a commercial airliner (Ben had gone out a few days earlier);
on the night of the general election, the Bradlees flew to Hyannis Port to
follow the returns, and the following evening they were invited for a private
dinner at the president-elect's home on the compound.[16]

This arrangement raised a troubling conflict of interest for this ambitious journalist. The conundrum was relatively simple: Could Bradlee report fairly and objectively on a man with whom he was a close personal
friend? Could he analyze an election process and provide unbiased information to millions of American citizens in Newsweek when he was the recipient of considerable inside information from one of the candidates? Bradlee
was well aware of his precarious position and reflected upon the ethical
bind in which he had entangled himself. "What is the dividing line between friendship and professionalism? Closeness brings the access that is
essential to understanding, but with closeness comes potentially conflict-

ing loyalties," he observed. His relationship with JFK prompted a question that "plagued us both: what, in fact, was I? A friend, or a journalist? I wanted to be both." Bradlee never provided a satisfactory answer to his own question. He admitted that while "Kennedy valued my friendship—I made him laugh, I brought him the fruits of contact with an outside world from which he was now shut out—he valued my journalism most when it carried his water." Yet this recognition that JFK clearly manipulated the journalist to support his efforts and enhance his image did not cause Bradlee to modify his behavior.[17]

For Bradlee cherished his privileged position as an insider. "This thing I had going with the junior Senator from Massachusetts was very seductive," he confessed. "He had the smell of success, and my special access to him was enormously valuable to *Newsweek*." And enormously valuable to himself, the journalist neglected to add. When JFK asked Bradlee and his wife to fly down to West Virginia with him on his private plane for a celebration after the primary victory, he did not hesitate at accepting. He enjoyed triumphing over other reporters, noting how he relished seeing "Hugh Sidey's expression after my opposite number at *Time* watched me get off the plane at the Charleston airport behind the candidate." Bradlee offered a pretense of objectivity by spending some time with Richard Nixon during the 1960 campaign. Not surprisingly, he came away unimpressed. After enjoying the personal charm of the Massachusetts senator on numerous occasions in Georgetown and Hyannis Port, he predictably concluded that "while Kennedy was instinctively graceful and natural, Nixon was instinctively graceless and programmed."[18]

On at least two occasions during the 1960 election, Bradlee clearly crossed a line from reporting on Kennedy's effort to assisting it. In the run-up to the Democratic Party primaries, the journalist sent a memorandum to the Massachusetts senator on one of his likely opponents, Senator Lyndon B. Johnson. It critiqued a recent Johnson speech that Bradlee had heard and analyzed the Texas senator's potential as a candidate. On the one hand, Bradlee reported to Kennedy, Johnson "could never make it. The image is poor. The accent hurts. . . . He is hard to take seriously even when he is being desperately serious. . . . Johnson really does not have the requisite dignity. He's somebody's gabby Texas cousin from Fort Worth." On the other hand, even though the speech was a "masterpiece of corn," it indicated that Johnson was going to enter the race. "I think your present assumption, that he is a candidate, has to be the [correct] one." Bradlee counseled preparation for the real danger, which was that Johnson could control enough delegates to deny Kennedy the nomination and thereby throw it to someone else. "He's to be feared, not as a potential winner," Bradlee told Kennedy, "but as a game-player who might try to maneuver you right out of the contest." This picture of a reporter covering the presidential election for a major national magazine advising one of the candidates on how to defeat an opponent was audaciously inappropriate.[19]

Bradlee also crossed an ethical line by assisting Kennedy in the West Virginia primary. According to William L. Jacobs, the state cochairman for Senator Hubert Humphrey, JFK's leading opponent in that contest, the *Newsweek* reporter interviewed him about the Humphrey campaign and its prospects for success. After they were done, Bradlee asked him, several times, "off the record, just between the two of us," what he really thought of Humphrey's chances in the state. Jacobs finally replied, "strictly off the record," that Kennedy's personality appeal and ample spending had hindered Humphrey and that "the campaign is not progressing as well as I had hoped." A couple of days later, Jacobs was astounded when another reporter called to get his reaction to the "explosive paragraph" in a *Newsweek* article that had boosted Kennedy and predicted his victory over a fading Humphrey. When the campaign manager read it, he was astonished to see his own words quoted at some length. The clouds cleared some weeks later when he saw a newspaper piece that described an intimate social affair hosted by the Kennedys where among the handful of attendees was "Ben Bradlee, a former neighbor who had lived on the same block as John F. Kennedy when they were neighbors in Georgetown." Jacobs realized that the *Newsweek* journalist, by double-crossing him, had done more than simply report on the election process. He had intervened in it on behalf of his good friend, one of the candidates.[20]

Bradlee, remarkably, did not grasp the irony when he chastised Nixon and his staff for accusing the press of bias in favor of Kennedy. The Republican candidate, Bradlee claimed, was plagued by an irrational distrust of journalists covering his campaign and was "annoyed by them," while the

Democrat enjoyed reporters and "liked to shoot the breeze" with them. Nixon and his inner circle treated the press with suspicion, while Kennedy and his people were always available "often for a drink, always for a bull session." Bradlee noted, for example, that when reporters challenged the Kennedy campaign for inflating crowd estimates at rallies, JFK joked that the figures had been arrived at when Pierre Salinger "counts the nuns and multiplies by 100." The reporters laughed and nixed any stories about crowd inflation. Such challenges to Nixon's crowd numbers, Bradlee continued, "usually brought a lecture about bias" so sullen that reporters reported the inflation. As a result, Bradlee confessed, "the press appreciated Kennedy for his openness and protected him, while the press reacted skeptically to other candidates." The journalist seemed unable, or unwilling, to grasp the skill with which JFK played him and his cohorts or to appreciate any justification for Nixon's resentment. Kennedy's bewitchment of Bradlee, and much of the national press, simply swept all before it.[21]

Bradlee eventually came clean—at least to himself—near the end of the 1960 campaign. He admitted privately that "however much I had tried to be fair and objective in my reporting of the campaign, I now wanted Kennedy to win. I wanted my friend and neighbor to be president." This conclusion surprised no one. Bradlee had recognized the dangers posed by access journalism but easily overcame any qualms. He simply decided that closeness to power through a friendship with John Kennedy was more important than misgivings about its tainting his ability to judge that power. Bradlee made a deal with the devil, and it would carry him far.[22]

With John F. Kennedy's assumption of the presidency in early 1961, the Bradlees and the new First Family intensified their friendship. The couples met regularly for dinners, parties, and movies at the White House, and the bond between the two talented, ambitious, dynamic young men grew even stronger. Ben Bradlee, realizing his special position as an intimate friend of the president's with an inside view of his administration, began to make notes and Dictaphone tapes about their social interactions and political discussions. When published over a decade later as *Conversations with Kennedy,* it revealed the casual intimacy between the two couples as they gossiped about the issues and personalities of the day, compared notes on their children, went for cruises on the Potomac aboard the presidential yacht, and spent weekends together at Hyannis Port, Newport, the Kennedy farm in Virginia, and Camp David. The two men played golf at Washington-area courses and at the Newport Country Club, and the couples spent much time together in the White House's family quarters. Bradlee reported, "We watched NBC's special on the Kremlin in Jackie's bedroom, while the president walked around in his underdrawers and wondered what life must be like in that mausoleum." After one of their evenings together not long after the death of the infant Patrick Kennedy, an emotional First Lady acknowledged the close bond. "Just before we re-tired Jackie drew me aside, her eyes glistening near tears, to announce that 'you two really are our best friends,'" Bradlee reported. "She repeated the message a couple of times to Tony."[23]

This intimacy prompted Bradlee to become a journalistic cheerleader for the New Frontier. From 1961 through 1963, he wrote numerous stories on Kennedy and his administration for *Newsweek*, and they were almost unfailingly positive, even glowing assessments that stressed their ener-getic, stylish qualities. Of the inaugural, Bradlee described the new presi-dent's "restless energy," the "sudden flash of his eyes," and "the spontaneity of his laughter" along with "a new seriousness, a palpable sense of the awe-someness of his position." In subsequent weeks, Bradlee and *Newsweek* took readers on an admiring tour of the New Frontier. He observed that JFK did not shrink from challenges but faced them directly and "in a daz-zling display of energy and versatility, he sent around the world the image of a country on the move." Bradlee claimed that a pair of recent JFK speeches on the need to halt nuclear testing and promote civil rights fol-lowed the dictum that "all of our great Presidents" had taken the lead "when certain historic ideas in the life of the nation needed to be clarified." With these "bold initiatives to lower tensions in the cold war and assume moral leadership in the racial crisis, the President . . . had ascended Theo-dore Roosevelt's bully pulpit."[24]

Bradlee praised Kennedy's "masterful U.N. address" on the United States' position in world affairs and described how that "articulate and politically sensitive man in the White House" genuinely communicated with the American people. He painted a picture of JFK's triumphant tour .around the country where he charmed local dignitaries and eloquently defended the fight for freedom as "a shirtsleeve crowd of 30,000 cheered him." Bradlee reported on JFK's speech in Berlin, suggesting that "never has John F. Kennedy sounded more like a President." He described how in another address Kennedy "vigorously and eloquently sketched his vision of a new frontier that had as its purpose the strengthening of freedom around the globe. . . . [A] virtuoso performance." He praised Kennedy's "light-touch timing" and humor in a speech to amateur athletes, where he compared his close election victory in 1960 to a recent football game won by Notre Dame over Syracuse on a last-minute disputed penalty: "I'm like Notre Dame. We just take it as it comes along. We're not giving it back."[25]

On a personal level, Bradlee reveled in the flashy new social scene at the White House. He marveled at the sophistication of the New Frontier and "the dawn of the celebrity culture" that began to sweep through the United States. The president and First Lady, he asserted, "were glamorous in a way that no American leader had ever been. The country rhapsodized over their clothes, their look, their style, and their children." As close friends of the First Couple, the Bradlees were invited to nearly every significant soiree hosted by the Kennedys, often mingling with famous guests at preparty or postparty gatherings in the mansion's private quarters. "This was the third of the White House dances, like the rest a dazzling picture of 'beautiful people' from New York, jet setters from Europe, politicians, reporters (always reporters) who are friends, and Kennedy relatives," he reported in early 1962. "The crowd is always young. The women are always gorgeous, and you have to pinch yourself to realize that you are in the Green Room of the White House." The youthful president and First Lady were changing the face of Washington, Bradlee believed, and "nothing symbolized this change more than the parties, for the Kennedys were party people. He loved the gaiety and spirit and ceremony of a collection of friends, especially beautiful women in beautiful dresses. . . . Jackie was the producer of these parties. Jack was the consumer." Overall, Bradlee concluded, "the Kennedy magic was growing on the country."[26]

But Bradlee's personal involvement with the new president went beyond social matters. In private discussions, he and Kennedy frequently talked politics—problems, personalities, and policies. They worked out an ar-rangement that the reporter convinced himself resolved any tension be-tween the personal demands of friendship and the professional requirements of journalism. The president fed Bradlee information for articles, which he expected would be used for favorable portrayals of his administration. They also agreed that Kennedy "could keep anything he wanted off the record," but if he did not explicitly indicate such, it would be fair game for the journalist's stories. Bradlee admitted that Kennedy "was much more apt to tell me what to put in my notes than what to keep out," but this ar-rangement seemed to allay any discomfort he felt about his duty as a jour-nalist.[27]

In fact, this arrangement only intensified the troubling issue of access journalism that had first arisen during the 1960 campaign. Whether he liked it or not, or even admitted it or not, Bradlee's special link with the president made him an extension of, even a publicist for, the Kennedy ad-ministration. It was not a question of the reporter's naïveté. "Did he use me? Of course he used me," Bradlee declared defensively to an interviewer years later. "Did I use him? Of course I used him. Are those the ground rules down here in Washington? Hell, yes." But this blustery assertion ignored the larger, persistent question: Could Bradlee be objective, fair, and honest in reporting the issues surrounding the president and his administration in light of their close friendship?[28]

Bradlee frequently noted this dilemma, but he failed to confront it fully and evaded its implications. After Kennedy had fed him an inside story of a just-completed deal with the Soviet Union to exchange a Russian spy for the captured American pilot Gary Powers, the journalist noted only, "It was the kind of thing that made Kennedy nervous about me, and the kind of thing that made me nervous about the personal relationship, but not nervous enough to sacrifice the professional challenge and thrill." Later, when JFK lashed out at accusations that he managed the news and chal-lenged Bradlee to cite one single case, the reporter reacted similarly: "I felt I was a potential example, but it seemed almost impolite to bring it up. . . . [I] will not look this gift horse in the mouth."[29]

Bradlee's uneasy position mirrored a broader issue among the national press corps. During his presidency, Kennedy patently, self-consciously, and skillfully manipulated the legion of reporters who covered him and the White House. He understood their needs, their desires, and their vanity. As Bradlee frequently observed, JFK had immersed himself in the world of journalism and its practitioners and talked constantly about the competition among various newspapers and magazines, whose stock was rising or falling among reporters and columnists, and who was describing his efforts favorably or unfavorably. "The conversation turned to journalists—one of the president's all-time favorite subjects," Bradlee wrote of one White House encounter. "It is unbelievable to an outsider how interested Kennedy was in journalists and how clued in he was to their characters, their office politics, their petty rivalries." Bradlee noted at another point, "He sops up newspaper gossip like a blotter." Moreover, JFK worked hard to create a sense of communion with the press and went out of his way to massage reportorial egos. "Kennedy had the delightful habit of remembering something you had written," an editor for *The Reporter* noted. "And nothing so puffs up a reporter as to have him be quoted to himself."[30]

There was some awareness of this situation in the national press corps. *Look,* in a lengthy analysis of the president and the press, pointed to "Kennedy's own genius for public relations" and described him as "the most accessible president since Teddy Roosevelt." But as *Look* recognized, this accessibility came at a price. "Having thrown the door wide, the President does not take kindly to those who cross the threshold armed with a harpoon instead of a bouquet," the magazine noted. "'They want us as a cheering squad, as an arm of the executive branch of government,' says one White House reporter." Arthur Krock, longtime columnist for *The New York Times*, complained that Kennedy "cynically and boldly" managed the news, both by concealing and distorting and by arranging meetings and briefings with reporters from which they "emerge in a state of protracted enchantment evoked by the President's charm and the awesome aura of his office." It was troubling, Krock concluded, to see the positive stories that emerged from "John F. Kennedy's devoted wooing of the press."[31]

The vast majority of national journalists, however, ignored such manipulation and competed to create favorable portrayals of Kennedy and the New Frontier. In Bradlee's words, "The press appreciated Kennedy for his openness and protected him, while the press reacted skeptically to other candidates." He described JFK's lengthy cultivation of Theodore White, the longtime journalist, whose laudatory book, *The Making of the President, 1960,* "had benefitted enormously from his friendship with Kennedy." Sir Isaiah Berlin gave an account of a dinner party attended by Kennedy, himself, the columnist Joseph Alsop, and Phil Graham, owner of *Newsweek* and *The Washington Post.* After the president returned to the White House, Berlin noted that the two journalists "said how much they liked him. Phil went on and on. . . . It is difficult to describe his and Joe's absolute devotion to the President. It was almost as if their lives had been completely transformed by him. They felt like young men, which they no longer were in the technical sense, about to march . . . to conquer new lands under a great new leader, who would be bound to transform them and the world."[32]

Another revealing case appeared with the press's protection of Kennedy for his philandering. The president's womanizing ways were widely known among reporters for the big national magazines and newspapers and television networks, but they unanimously refused to report on the subject, even in a period when the Profumo scandal in Great Britain and Bobby Baker's shocking escapades with call girls and congressmen had attracted much press attention. The CBS newsman Roger Mudd, for instance, later recalled President Kennedy's longtime friendship with the Florida senator George Smathers. "Together or singly, they were wolves on the prowl, always able to find or attract gorgeous prey," he wrote. On a Saturday afternoon in Palm Beach, Mudd remembered, he was in a press pool boat that followed the Kennedy yacht. "It was a joke, our pretending to cover the president, bobbing around in the ocean, squinting through binoculars to find out who was coming and going but always having our view blocked by a Secret Service boat just as another long-legged Palm Beach beauty climbed aboard," he noted. "What would today be called the 'mainstream media' didn't and wouldn't touch the story." Barbara Gamarekian, an official in the White House press office, recalled how reporters observed Mimi Beardsley and "Fiddle and Faddle" accompanying Kennedy on a presidential trip with no apparent duties. They drew the obvious conclusion, and many "thought it was going to blow up eventually," she admitted. "It was kind of a big joke. Everyone knew about it and there were lots of sly remarks made. And everyone knew." In her view, JFK acted so recklessly because "he must have felt that his position was pretty secure and that there was no possibility that this would ever hit print."[33]

In terms of press favoritism toward JFK, however, Bradlee stood in a class by himself. A vivid example of Kennedy's manipulation of the *Newsweek* reporter, and the journalist's willingness to be manipulated, came in the summer of 1962. Bradlee, in a *Look* article on Kennedy and the press, had mildly complained about presidential sensitivity to criticism by journalists, noting that both the president and the attorney general had taken him to task for stories they saw as unfavorable to the administration. "It's almost impossible to write a story they like," he noted. "Even if a story is quite favorable to their side, they'll find one paragraph to quibble with." Bradlee's comments infuriated JFK, and he retaliated by cutting him off for three months as an object lesson—no more invitations to White House parties, no more drinks and dinners in the family quarters, no more movies and late-night conversation. A distraught Bradlee suffered during his banishment. Kennedy finally gave the journalist a chance to escape the doghouse and contacted him to write about a recent charge that accused the president of hiding an earlier, annulled marriage to a Florida woman. Pierre Salinger offered Bradlee a deal: if he came to Newport, where JFK was vacationing, he would be given a collection of documents to examine for twenty-four hours, and then the president would have "the right of clearance," or final approval, over the resulting article. Journalists rarely, if ever, give their subjects this kind of editorial control, but Bradlee eagerly made the deal. After JFK approved the contents, he ran a story in *Newsweek* scuttling the rumors of an earlier presidential marriage. As Bradlee admitted, "I wanted to be friends again. I missed the access, of course, but I missed the laughter and the warmth just as much." So Kennedy readmitted the journalist and his wife to the inner sanctum of the White House, inviting the Bradlees for a dinner and dance where the Kennedys conversed with them at length. "Everybody loves one another again," Bradlee noted gratefully. Admitting that "the information Kennedy gave me tended to put him and his policies in a favorable light," the *Newsweek* reporter nonetheless reached another untroubled conclusion: "If I was had, so be it."[34]

For all of its complex political and journalistic dimensions, the Jack Kennedy–Ben Bradlee relationship also reflected a broader impulse in early 1960s America: the assertively manly ethos of the New Frontier. The journalist and the president were cut from the same bolt of cloth as representatives of a cultural movement celebrating tough, debonair, vigorous masculinity. In fact, Bradlee offered the journalistic version of the ideal New Frontiersman. He was highly intelligent and handsome—an observer once described the dapper, dashing newsman as having the face of "an international jewel thief"—and full of wit and engaging masculine charm. An Ivy League graduate who had lived abroad, Bradlee eschewed ideological rigor in favor of pragmatic problem solving and an elegant, worldly persona. He dined with elite figures in the national capital, not only the First Couple, but Walter Lippmann and Phil and Katharine Graham. By the early 1960s, the journalist had emerged as a celebrity in his own right with a considerable sheen of glamour.[35]

Bradlee's oversize, multifaceted personality perfectly matched the masculine ethos of the Kennedy administration. He had played varsity baseball at Harvard, was a downhill skier as an adult, and remained a man-about-town whose powerful presence and salty vocabulary became legendary. A man of considerable sophistication and flair, he spoke French fluently, somewhat to the chagrin of Kennedy, who had no facility with foreign languages. The president admired Bradlee's linguistic skill, as well as Jacqueline's, especially in light of his own hapless efforts. "His French can only be described as unusual," the journalist reported of JFK. "One French friend says he speaks it 'with a bad Cuban accent.'" Even many years later, a long biographical article in *The New Yorker* described Bradlee as the "last of the red hots" with "something of the movie star about him" and "the very model of the devil-may-care WASP." Another observer described how Bradlee "camouflaged his pedigree behind a streetwise front. With his macho manner, savvy, and profanity, he epitomized the finger-snapping cool of the Hollywood Rat Pack."[36]

In fact, this cool, vigorous, cosmopolitan personal style formed one of the key bonds between the newsman and his presidential patron. Mc-

George Bundy, who had ample opportunity to observe both men, noted that "what made Bradlee and President Kennedy friends was a shared coolness and irony and detachment." According to another observer, "Bradlee and Kennedy, as types, were much the same. If Bradlee had been President, he would have been much like Kennedy: without ideology, mindful of style, reliant on expert elders, intelligent but hardly intellectual, long on vision and wit, short on temper and attention span," he wrote. "They shared a sense of privilege and fortune; they shared Harvard, the war, and an understanding of class; and they shared a penchant for gossip, detachment, irony, and courage." Bradlee also sensed this stylistic connection. "John Fitzgerald Kennedy was about the most urban—and urbane—man I have ever met," he wrote. "He was a product of big city life, and the comforts and conveniences that his family fortune had provided." The journalist could have been describing himself.[37]

This pair of vigorous, sophisticated young men also shared a final trait that was key to the New Frontier's strongly masculine image. The president and the celebrity journalist radiated an overt, magnetic sex appeal, a trait that would entangle their lives in ways that neither could imagine when they first became friends in 1959.

John F. Kennedy and Benjamin Bradlee personified the strong element of sexual power pervading the masculine atmosphere of the New Frontier. A profound appreciation for good-looking women and the projection of a vigorous manly air were key elements in their common sensibility. While not in Kennedy's league as a womanizer, Bradlee had a considerable reputation as a ladies' man that had emerged in Paris in the early 1950s while his first marriage was crumbling. As he explained, "All those cumbersome Puritan legacies about sex and joy—laid on me by my heritage—slipped from my shoulders, and the world has looked different to me ever since."[38]

Bradlee entered what he termed a "swashbuckling phase," and a friend quipped, "We used to kid him that there were women queuing up in front of his apartment for fifteen minutes of his time." In Paris, while he was separated from Jean and waiting for Tony Pinchot to decide whether to marry him, his life became an ongoing sexual adventure where a constant stream of women attracted his attention: "A shared ride home would turn complicated. Sudden knee pressure could not be explained as accidental. Dinner partners would appear less interested in food than me. Eye contact across crowded rooms could develop in ways new to me. One woman, the wife of a friend, ambushed me one night in the shadows of the arcades under my apartment in the Place des Vosges. Even two of Tony's friends tested the waters, to my astonishment."[39]

After he moved to Washington and became a celebrity journalist, Bradlee's rating on the virility meter continued to rise. He garnered a widespread reputation as a charismatic, attractive male figure with an eye for the ladies. Numerous public accounts of the famous newsman paid tribute to this quality while not delving into details. The *New Republic* referred to Bradlee as "a vocal and enthusiastic heterosexual" with "countless one-night stands," while the *American Journalism Review* described the rakish journalist as "a lusty inamorato who romped through flings and flirtations on several continents." The *New York Times* referred to the newsman as "the virile king of the Washington jungle." The *New Yorker* observed that he was "the one newspaperman routinely compared to Errol Flynn," the legendary film Lothario.[40]

Bradlee's notorious use of sexual metaphors reinforced his virile persona. When Katharine Graham asked him if he wanted to become editor of *The Washington Post*, he replied that he would "give my left one" for the opportunity. As one observer quipped, "He probably would have gotten along fine on the remaining testosterone." Bradlee typically expressed admiration for a colleague's courage by noting his brass balls, or contempt for his weakness by noting "nothing clanks when he walks." As *The New York Times* assured readers, there was no doubt about the famous journalist's manliness: he unquestionably "clanked when he walked." In the macho world of Ben Bradlee, a loud metallic din filled the air where public figures traversed the nation's capital as modern, well-endowed, armored knights rattling their oversize codpieces.[41]

As Bradlee became close friends with JFK, the two young men shared their keen interest in attractive women. Many exchanges between them revolved around sexual themes and female attributes. Bradlee noted conversations with the president on how a White House party brought "a stable of pretty women from New York" or how certain "women . . . castrate their husbands for various reasons." Once, JFK noted that an upcoming White House gathering would have not the usual one hundred guests but "about thirty-five real swingers." The president appreciated the sexual sophistication of the New Frontier atmosphere. As Bradlee recounted of one party, "The females imported from New York for the occasion had been spectacular again, and at one point Kennedy had pulled me to one side to comment, 'If you and I could only run wild, Benjy.'" At one point, JFK even commented on the future sexual conquests of Bradlee's young son. "'My God, he's a good looking child,' he said. 'Those eyes. He's going to do a helluva business.'" As Garry Wills, a shrewd student of the thirty-fifth president, once observed, Joseph Kennedy and his close friend the journalist Arthur Krock had "cemented their joint purposes with a male camaraderie of conquest—exactly the relationship John Kennedy would later have with *Newsweek*'s Ben Bradlee."[42]

Bradlee clearly valued the manly ethos that cemented his relationship with JFK. Like many males of his generation, he shared with the president a high regard for military service during World War II and a disparagement of those who had avoided it. "It is interesting how often Kennedy referred to the war records of political opponents," Bradlee noticed. "Now he was at it again with [New York's governor, Nelson] Rockefeller. 'Where was old Nels when you and I were dodging bullets in the Solomon Islands?' he wondered aloud." Bradlee also appreciated, indeed shared, JFK's habit of using crude sexual metaphors in describing issues, people, and power relations that confronted him in public life. During Kennedy's famous dispute with American steel companies when they raised prices and doublecrossed his administration, the president, Bradlee noted, burst out, "They kicked us right in the balls. And we kicked back. The question really is: are we supposed to sit there and take a cold, deliberate fucking?" After JFK's announcement that the United States had resumed nuclear testing, Bradlee asked him if everyone in the administration was behind this. The president replied in the affirmative but added, "I suppose if you grabbed Adlai by the nuts, he might object." Kennedy, in describing his difficult summit meeting with Khrushchev in Vienna, related that there was particular tension over the issue of Berlin. " 'This was the nut-cutter,' Kennedy said more than once later," the journalist observed.[43]

The male camaraderie between Kennedy and Bradley also featured a certain amount of competition and one-upmanship. In an interview at Kennedy's Georgetown home on January 5, 1960, with both wives present, a manly contest ensued between the two. When Kennedy was asked about his reasons for seeking high office, he responded with some boilerplate about solving the world's problems. Then he confessed that he was attracted to the competitive aura of high-level politics. "Life is a struggle and you're struggling in a tremendous sort of arena," he mused. "It's like playing Yale every Saturday, in a sense." Then the alpha male asserted his primacy over Bradlee, saying, "My scope is far greater than Ben's. He works extremely hard on his effort, but my scope is unlimited. His scope is somewhat limited because he goes to press every week. . . . But my scope is really dependent on my judgment now and energy and tactical and strategic sense. And then the scope is unlimited." When Bradlee later mentioned speaking French, Kennedy jabbed again, accusing the journalist of speaking the language with a shoddy "French Canadian accent." Bradlee protested that he spoke in a "flawless Tours accent" as everyone giggled. While the tone was kidding, the subtext of masculine rivalry was not.[44]

Despite their common sensibility and style, especially regarding sex and women, Bradlee professed complete ignorance of JFK's legendary philandering. He recognized the "fundamental dichotomy in Kennedy's character: half the 'mick' politician, tough, earthy, bawdy, sentimental and half the bright, graceful, intellectual Playboy of the Western World." But Bradlee insisted that he never discussed JFK's "playboy" image with him, either as a close friend or as a journalist. "You're all looking to tag me with some girl, and none of you can do it, because it just isn't there," JFK once told him. "And that is the closest I ever came to hearing him discuss his reputation as what my father used to call 'a fearful girler,' " Bradlee said. The journalist maintained throughout his life that he stood completely in the dark about JFK's sexual dalliances both as a candidate and during his presidency. When he learned about it after Kennedy's death, he professed utter shock. In his words, "During the five years that I knew him,

I heard stories about how he had slept around in his bachelor days. . . . I heard people described as 'one of Jack's girlfriends' from time to time. It was never topic A among my reporter friends, while he was a candidate. Since most of the 125 conversations I had with him took place with Tony and Jackie present, extracurricular screwing was one of the few subjects that never came up."[45]

Bradlee even went further and condemned JFK's behavior when he professed to learn about it. Only many years later, he claimed, did he become aware that "Kennedy screwed around. A lot." This discovery might have been interesting to "those of us who know something about screwing around, but it is hardly disqualifying." Bradlee continued, "My friends have always had trouble believing my innocence of his activities. . . . So be it. I can only repeat my ignorance of Kennedy's sex life, and state that I am appalled by the recklessness, by the subterfuge that must have been involved." But it is, indeed, hard to believe the journalist's professions of ignorance and outrage. Not least because of the masculine sexual agenda that colored the Kennedy-Bradlee friendship and two intimate situations that complicated it in fascinating ways.[46]

First, JFK engaged in a serious, ongoing flirtation with Bradlee's wife. During their friendship in the late 1950s and early 1960s, Kennedy made no secret of his great attraction to Tony Pinchot Bradlee. While the Bradlees dined with the First Couple in the private quarters of the White House, the quartet was discussing the complicated relations between men and women when Jackie Kennedy said suddenly, " 'Oh, Jack, you know you always say that Tony is your ideal.' The president replied, 'Yes, that's true.' " But then, Ben Bradlee related, JFK thought better of his answer and quickly added, "You're my ideal, Jacqueline." The president's admiration was not restricted to words. According to Tony, Kennedy made several passes at her during the course of the couple's friendship, but she rebuffed him. "Jack was always so complimentary to me, putting his hands around my waist. I thought, 'Hmmmm, he likes me,' " she recalled many years later. "I think it surprised him I would not succumb. If I hadn't been married maybe I would have."[47]

On one occasion, Kennedy went much further. At his forty-sixth birthday party in May 1963, thrown by Jackie aboard the presidential yacht,

Sequoia, as it sailed down the Potomac, the First Couple and a group of family and close friends enjoyed a boisterous, even rowdy time. The attendees included Bobby and Ethel Kennedy, Teddy Kennedy, the Shrivers, William Walton, Mary Meyer, the Smatherses, the Bartletts, the Fays, and the actor David Niven and his wife. Dinner and a number of teasing toasts were followed by JFK's opening presents, then singing and dancing and much shouting and laughing as the gathering became ever more lubricated with liquor. Drinking 1955 Dom Pérignon champagne, the participants did the twist to the music of a live trio as the party went into the early hours of the morning. Escapades abounded. At one point, an intoxicated Boston politico stumbled into the president's pile of gifts and put his foot through a rare old engraving that had been Jackie's present. A bit later, Teddy somehow had the left leg of his trousers ripped off, revealing his underwear as he danced around the yacht.[48]

The president added his own shenanigans to the revelry. At the height of the merrymaking, Tony Pinchot left the deck of the *Sequoia* to go below to the ladies' room and JFK followed her. "He chased me all around the boat," she related. "I was running and laughing as he chased me. He caught up with me in the ladies' room and made a pass. It was a pretty strenuous attack, not as if he pushed me down, but his hands wandered. I said, 'That's it, so long.' . . . I guess I was pretty surprised, but I was kind of flattered, and appalled, too." Many years later, Tony told her children another version of this incident—that Kennedy had pushed her up against a wall and had been rather aggressive and that it had upset her.[49]

Ben Bradlee's reaction to JFK's play for his wife was not anger or resentment but a curious kind of acceptance, even satisfaction. While he did not learn about the president's aggressive pass at Tony on the *Sequoia* until she told him years later, at the time he sensed their mutual attraction. The journalist reported that President Kennedy asked Tony twice to accompany him on a European trip on Air Force One, but he, Ben, quickly objected to it as being improper. But in later years, as one of his children reported, "I know he was proud of the fact that the President had a kind of crush on his wife." Bradlee even told Arthur Schlesinger about JFK, "I think he was rather in love with Tony." In the sophisticated world of the

New Frontier, it seems, coveting your neighbor's wife was not a matter of immorality or bad manners but an act of masculine achievement.[50]

JFK became even more intimately involved with another member of the *Newsweek* journalist's family. After assuming the presidency, Kennedy took Mary Meyer, Tony's sister and Ben Bradlee's sister-in-law, as a mistress. In the presidential psyche—or perhaps a more primal region—there lurked some kind of basic attraction to the blond, sophisticated Pinchot sisters. "I always felt he liked me as much as Mary," Tony once confessed. "You could say there was a little rivalry." In fact, at a White House dinner in March 1961, JFK arranged for the two sisters to be seated on either side of him. In Bradlee's words, upon witnessing this tableau "the Beautiful People from New York seethed with disbelief." Then, after dinner, the president linked arms with both Mary and Tony and exclaimed as they entered the Blue Room, "Well, girls, what did you think of *that*?" So while Kennedy periodically made plays for Tony's affections, it was her older sister who began to share his bed not long after he moved into the White House.[51]

Mary Pinchot Meyer and Kennedy had known each other since their student days, when they met at a Choate dance. Their paths crossed periodically thereafter until the early 1950s, when both were living in the national capital—Kennedy as a senator and Meyer as the wife of a CIA official—where they moved in the same Georgetown social circles. In the spring of 1959, Meyer dropped by the home of Ben and Tony Bradlee for drinks, and their neighbor the young senator from Massachusetts was also in attendance. As the small group sat there talking and enjoying their cocktails, an observer noticed a "stirring" between Kennedy and Meyer. This spark of attraction burst into flame, and the elder Pinchot sister later became a regular invitee to White House functions. In October 1961, while Mrs. Kennedy was away in Newport, Meyer made the first of many visits to the executive mansion to spend the evening alone with the president.[52]

Mary Meyer's privileged background made her a comfortable social fit with the president. Born in 1920, she came from a wealthy, distinguished family, and her uncle, Gifford Pinchot, was a close friend and political ally of Theodore Roosevelt's. Meyer's father, Amos Pinchot, supported socialism and circulated among New York's bohemian, left-wing radical set, eventually marrying Ruth Pickering, a much younger Greenwich Village writer and poet. The Pinchot household became a stopping point for activist intellectuals such as Max Eastman, Sinclair Lewis, Edna St. Vincent Millay, Mabel Dodge, Louis Brandeis, and Robert La Follette.[53]

As the daughter of aristocratic radicals, Mary Pinchot grew up in luxurious, upper-class circumstances. The Pinchots lived for part of the year in a Park Avenue apartment in New York, and the rest at Grey Towers, the three-thousand-acre family estate in Milford, Pennsylvania, with a French château-style mansion, tennis courts, swimming pool, horses, and a private waterfall. Mary attended an exclusive preparatory school, appeared at debutante balls, and matriculated at Vassar College. In other words, Mary Pinchot represented the kind of privileged class background that both Ben Bradlee and Jack Kennedy inhabited. This position also reflected a key impulse in the New Frontier: galvanizing the better sort of people from the upper echelon of American society who promised to overturn the boring bourgeois standards and values of Truman and Eisenhower's America.[54]

After college, Mary worked for a short time as a journalist before marrying Cord Meyer, a Yale graduate who had fought heroically in World War II as a marine officer and lost an eye. Persuaded to join the CIA by Allen Dulles, Cord moved to Washington with his wife and settled into life in the national capital. They had three sons and became close friends with several other couples where the husbands worked for the CIA or other government agencies: James and Anne Truitt, Wistar and Mary Janney, James and Cicely Angleton, Jack and Scottie Lanahan. But the Meyer marriage slowly unraveled as Cord's obsession with his work and Mary's growing discontent with the restrictions of female domestic life began to separate them. Then, in late 1956, the Meyers' middle son was tragically killed by an automobile, an emotional trauma that drove a larger wedge into their marriage. Within a year, Mary and Cord separated, and she immersed herself in the world of art as a painter and had several affairs. They divorced in 1958. As a consequence, Cord Meyer and Ben Bradlee developed an intense dislike for each other over the Pinchot sisters' visit to Paris, which had done much to break up both of their marriages. This animosity once caused an intoxicated Meyer to come across the table at a Georgetown dinner party and try to grab Bradlee by the throat.[55]

By the late 1950s, Mary Meyer had broken free from her role as wife and mother. With short, windblown, blond hair and an attractive figure, she exuded a free-spirited yet very feminine spirit. Highly intelligent with an aristocratic bearing, she appeared graceful, poised, and dignified. She had an iconoclastic yet striking sense of style and often wore loose, comfortable clothes—peasant blouses, tights, colorful skirts—and had a knack for making a distinctive, sometimes dramatic impact. "She was kind of fey, very soft-appearing and soft-voiced and delicate and mannered in the way privileged women sometimes are," according to one close friend. But she also had a very strong will, and according to a close friend, Cicely Angleton, "The secret to Mary's personality is that she didn't care about convention." Having jettisoned her marriage and increasingly willing to take risks to experience a wider range of life, she "lived to give and take pleasure," said a friend, Anne Truitt. In the words of another observer, she was "a well-bred ingénue out looking for fun and getting into trouble along the way."[56]

Mary Meyer's social position, like much else in the New Frontier, reflected the influence of what one historian has called "the Georgetown set." Located in the northwest section of the American capital city, the Georgetown area was notable for its influential residents: men who were important figures in the national government or media and their influential wives, who became dominant figures in the social scene. This residential power center featured figures such as Phil and Katharine Graham, publishers of *The Washington Post,* the foreign policy gurus Dean Acheson and Chip Bohlen, the Supreme Court justice Felix Frankfurter, the CIA's chief of covert operations, Frank Wisner, the newspaper columnists Joseph and Stewart Alsop, Jack and Jacqueline Kennedy, and Ben and Tony Bradlee, among many others. It also featured influential hostesses such as Evangeline Bruce, wife of Ambassador David Bruce, and Joan Braden, wife of Tom Braden of the CIA, who organized the dinners and cocktail parties where Georgetown luminaries discussed policy and spun webs of influence. Participants even coined a word—"salonisma"—to describe how Georgetown's influence radiated from these social gatherings, which one defined as "a form of government by invitation." These doyennes, according to one analyst, "had their own code of behavior. They were skillful flirts, practitioners of a lost art. They had to be. Men were the only route to economic and social power. Without a powerful man, a woman would almost certainly fall out of the circle. Certain women became leaders, and their whims and behavior were copied the way girls do a high school clique."[57]

By the dawn of the Kennedy era, Georgetown had become a sophisticated sexual nexus for the privileged classes in America. An aura of "sexual adventurousness" permeated the atmosphere as many of its sophisticated residents, having lived in Europe for stretches in the postwar era, "thought that wife swapping separated them from the country folks," in the pointed words of one observer. When JFK came into office, Georgetowners saw it as a sociosexual revolution that ended the reign of midwestern provincials and installed a new order. As one journalist put it, "The new social arbiters in the capital elevated 'swingers,' men and women who were sophisticated about world travel, art, politics, and sex. . . . A quick act of love shared between a willing man and a willing woman, whether married or not, was one of the small pleasures of a life well lived. It was accepted that one code of behavior applied to the peasants and the middle class, another to the sophisticates." President Kennedy stood as a central figure in this vibrant, morally liberated new atmosphere. His sexual escapades were legendary in Georgetown and served as a regular topic of conversation. A prominent Georgetown hostess was in a car with several women after JFK's election when she commented that his behavior with women was unbelievable and that many of the stories must be exaggerations. Then, she related, "there was a great giggle—every woman in the car had either had an affair or been propositioned by him."[58]

In one sense, Mary Meyer typified the New Frontier ethos with her Georgetown residence, prestigious family background, CIA ex-husband, and personal style of casual elegance and sexual daring. But she also had an ambiguous relationship with the "Georgetown set"—she was part of it yet expressed a different sensibility, especially in terms of social expectations regarding women. Meyer avoided the social whirl, was deliberately unconventional, and refused to play the role of Georgetown hostess. Treating the social rituals of this influential caste as frivolous, she cultivated a fierce independence and embraced the role of artist with emotional experience and serious expression as her métier. She became a devoted painter after her divorce, embracing the abstract "Color School" in Washington and spending much of her time with her paintings.[59]

As she emerged from the Georgetown milieu with this idiosyncratic image—part sophisticated product of a wealthy background and part rebel ingenue—it seems almost inevitable that Mary Meyer would catch the eye of JFK. After becoming close friends over a two-year period, she and the president began an extended affair. She would visit the White House about thirty times when Jacqueline Kennedy was absent, usually at the First Couple's Virginia farm. Typically, Kennedy and Meyer would spend several hours together in the evening, and a White House car would take her home around midnight. But unlike the president's other paramours, she also spent time in the Oval Office and in the family's private quarters when others were present. In other words, Kennedy made little attempt to hide his close relationship with Meyer, causing friends and government officials alike to conclude that she had the president's ear in an unusual fashion.[60]

For her part, Meyer had a curiously casual view of her affair with the president. She saw it as a great adventure, a source of fun and emotional fulfillment. "She and Jack understood each other. Mary didn't want to marry anyone. In that sense the relationship was superficial," said Anne Truitt, a very close friend to whom she confided. "They were two very sophisticated people who formed a friendship with no intention of it being forever. It was for mutual friendship and pleasure and enlightenment. It was a matter of lifting each other." Truitt described the Kennedy-Meyer liaison as a "romantic friendship." "He saw that she was trustworthy. He could talk to her with pleasure, without having to watch his words," she concluded. "Mary brought him a whiff of the outdoors, the quick interchange of lightheartedness. He needed entertainment of various sorts. Mary was very entertaining."[61]

JFK took Meyer more seriously than any other woman (which is to say, not much) and seems to have approached this relationship with more respect than the others. He genuinely enjoyed her company and apparently engaged her in serious conversation. Kennedy did not ask her to leave when he discussed political business, the White House counsel Myer Feldman noticed, and he concluded that the president "had a great attachment to her" and "discussed things that were on his mind, not just social gossip." Dave Powers observed the same thing: "Jack loved to talk to her and he talked to her about just about everything." Blair Clark, vice president of CBS News and Kennedy friend who occasionally served as a beard for Meyer at White House functions, even contended that "JFK's affair with Mary was serious in nature. Unlike the preponderance of his lovers—and there seemed to be no end to them—Mary was his intellectual equal. He regarded her as more than a roll in the hay."[62]

A sign of the president's esteem for Mary Meyer, as well as for her sister, Tony, came in September 1963. He toured the northern section of the United States to support the conservation of natural resources, and he included the Pinchot family home in Milford, Pennsylvania, in his itinerary. The occasion was to accept, on behalf of the United States, the gift of Grey Towers, several hundred acres and a stone mansion, from the Pinchot family. Ben Bradlee, who covered the trip for *Newsweek,* noted that both Mary and Tony flew to Milford on the presidential helicopter with JFK, who was eager to see where the Pinchot sisters had grown up. He also wanted to meet their mother, Ruth Pinchot, whose libertarian leanings had made her a Goldwater Republican by the early 1960s. She was cordial to Kennedy, who enjoyed charming her, and showed him baby pictures of her two daughters. But the mother could not overcome her political disapproval of the president and grimly posed for a photograph on the porch with her daughters and the famous visitor that Bradlee described as "one of history's most frozen shots."[63]

A final complication in the Jack Kennedy–Mary Meyer relationship came about a year after the president's assassination, and it involved Ben Bradlee directly and seriously. On October 12, 1964, while walking at midday on a canal path in Georgetown, Mary Meyer was murdered. She was attacked a little past noon, and people in the vicinity heard a female voice yell, "Somebody help me," followed by a gunshot. Although wounded in the head and bleeding profusely, Meyer apparently summoned the strength to try to run away, but after only a few yards she fell to the ground near the canal. The assailant then put the gun to her back and again pulled the trigger, shattering her shoulder blade before the bullet exited through the heart. A witness glimpsed a man leaning over the body, and the man was later identified, arrested, and brought to trial. The man was acquitted, however, and the case remains unsolved.[64]

The murder quickly became entangled with the Kennedy-Meyer affair, and Ben Bradlee was at the center of things. The evening after Mary's murder, he and Tony received a phone call from Anne Truitt, Meyer's closest friend then living in Tokyo, who told them that Mary had asked her to take possession of a private diary should anything ever happen to her. Truitt urged the Bradlees to find the diary and take possession. So the next morning, the Bradlees walked over to Meyer's house to begin their search but were surprised to discover James Angleton, a friend and high-ranking CIA official, already inside the house and also looking for the diary. They joined forces but had no success in finding it. Later that day, the Bradlees realized they had not searched in Mary's studio, which was in a converted garage near the garden in back. They decided to search there and once again found Angleton in the process of picking the lock to get in. He left with barely a word. Once inside, Ben and Tony went through Meyer's things and found the diary after about an hour.[65]

When they read the diary, the reason for Meyer's and Truitt's concern appeared clear. Although most of its fifty pages were covered with color swatches related to Meyer's painting efforts, about ten pages were filled with her handwriting. In Bradlee's words, the words "described a love affair, and after reading only a few phrases it was clear that the lover had been the President of the United States, although his name was never mentioned. To say we were stunned doesn't begin to describe our reactions." Bradlee claimed that while he had heard rumors about Kennedy's womanizing and girlfriends, he had never seen it nor talked with him about it, so "I was truly appalled by the realization of the extent of the deceit involved." He also thought back to several presidential remarks, when JFK observed offhandedly, "'Mary would be rough to live with' . . . not for the first time. And I agreed, not for the first time." Or when Kennedy greeted Tony and inquired, "'How's your sister?' presumably including those occasions when he had just left her arms." In hindsight, Bradlee couldn't decide if Kennedy had been trying to cover his tracks or was leaving tantalizing hints of the relationship. In any event, the journalist concluded that the affair did not fundamentally change his opinion of either party. "They were attractive, intelligent, and interesting people before their paths crossed in this explosive way, and they remain that way in my mind," he wrote. "There was a boldness in pulling something like that off that I found fascinating. . . . I resented the deception by Mary and Jack, but with both of them gone from my life, resentment seemed selfish."[66]

What Bradlee did with the information about the JFK-Meyer relationship, however, was revealing. Once again the journalist's instinctive protection of his late friend President Kennedy trumped any professional considerations. Bradlee decided that the diary "was in no sense a public document, despite the braying of the knee jerks about some public right to know. I felt it was a family document, privately created by Mary, privately protected by her." So Ben and Tony decided to give the diary to Angleton because of the CIA's expertise in the destruction of documents (several years later, they would discover that Angleton did not destroy the diary, so they demanded it back and Tony burned it in the fireplace). "I never for a minute considered reporting that it had been learned that the slain president had in fact had a lover, who had herself been murdered," Bradlee explained in his memoir. "Mary Meyer's murder was news, not her past love affair, I thought then, and part of me would still like to think so now." Even in 1976, when James Truitt went public with his knowledge of the affair, Bradlee, who was then editor of *The Washington Post,* refused to cover the story until he was overruled by other editors at the newspaper.[67]

Thus JFK and Mary Meyer's tangled relationship remains shrouded in mystery. But Ben Bradlee's indignant claims of innocence about his sister-in-law's sexual affair with JFK—indeed, about Kennedy's larger track record of womanizing—ring hollow. Given several key factors—the strength of the Kennedy-Bradlee friendship, the journalist's frequent and close observation of the president and his habits, the proximity of Meyer's home to his, the closeness of the Pinchot sisters, and his key position with Washington journalists among whom knowledge of JFK's womanizing was widely known—Bradlee's claims simply strain credibility. They recall the famous scene in *Casablanca* where the French commander, Captain Renault, with just a hint of a sardonic smile, tells Humphrey Bogart he is closing down his establishment and announces, "I'm shocked, shocked to find that gambling is going on in here!" just before accepting his own winnings for the evening from the croupier.

Skepticism about Bradlee's claims of ignorance also arises from a simple, if broader, fact: the trysts between President Kennedy and Mary Meyer reflected the larger masculine vigor and heated sexual atmosphere of the new administration of which the celebrity journalist was a key part. Ben Bradlee stood as an important figure in the Kennedy Circle during the heyday of the New Frontier. He exemplified the press's love affair with JFK during the halcyon days of the early 1960s and personally helped shape the chief executive's compelling masculine image. Relying on his insider status, the *Newsweek* reporter did yeoman work in presenting to the public an attractive portrait of the youthful leader's manly vigor as he directed the affairs of the nation from the White House. In his own endeavors, of course, Bradlee presented the same image. So while one might believe that the journalist and the president never talked about specifics, one simply cannot believe that this national reporter, White House insider, and keen observer blithely overlooked in Kennedy's behavior and worldview what a host of less connected figures saw clearly.

But the enhancement of President Kennedy's masculine image relied on more than media effort, no matter how influential the celebrity journalist who stood as its key purveyor. It also emerged from a self-conscious campaign emanating from the White House itself. One of its most significant initiatives came from JFK's successful association with a new military ethos. It rejected what the New Frontiersmen saw as an old-fashioned, World War II–era, Eisenhower-style design that relied on vast organization, ponderous strategic thinking, and massed forces. Instead, the new president embraced an unconventional, innovative approach that embodied the tough-minded, flexible pragmatism of his administration. Its incorporation of Kennedy's vigorous, manly sensibility promised to make America safe in the ever more threatening world of the Cold War.

NINE

MODERN WARRIORS: MAXWELL TAYLOR AND EDWARD LANSDALE

On October 12, 1961, President Kennedy, Secretary of Defense Robert McNamara, several members of the Joint Chiefs of Staff, and the entire White House press corps journeyed to Fort Bragg, North Carolina. As the observers looked on, the army's Special Forces presented an impressive show of counterinsurgency tactics. Hundreds of commandos staged ambushes and counter-ambushes, ate snake meat, deployed rapidly by helicopter, deftly handled high-powered automatic weapons, and rapidly traversed lakes and streams. JFK and other high-level figures in his administration might not have known, however, the meticulous planning that had been done for his benefit.

A member of the Special Forces later described how this "dazzling show" had been as elaborately staged and meticulously rehearsed as any Broadway production, with weeks of "talkthroughs, walkthroughs, and, finally, dress rehearsals." First came floats depicting various aspects of counterinsurgency warfare. Then a twelve-man team gave a demonstration with each trooper explaining his particular role, special skills, and ability to speak a foreign language. Next, judo teams displayed their skills while troopers traversed water on cables at breakneck speed and skydivers trailing colored smoke parachuted in from transport planes. Finally, as scuba divers swam to shore from a dummy submarine, a soldier with a special rocket contraption on his back flew across the lake and landed in front of JFK. To top off the demonstration, the psychological warfare battalion dropped thousands of leaflets over the area, all printed with the president's pictures. The message was clear, wrote the trooper: "We are yours. Use us. . . . [It was] one of the most magnificent, impressive, bald-faced, complex, and expensive snow jobs in history."[1]

The president loved it. At the conclusion of the show, Kennedy asked the Special Forces commander, General William Yarborough, if his men liked the special hats that they had worn by presidential request. He replied, "They're fine, sir. We've wanted them a long time." Thus the president authorized the green beret as the official headgear for the Special Forces (the army command had taken away the distinguishing hats years before) and wrote to Yarborough, "I know that you and the members of your command will carry on for us and the free world in a manner which is both worthy and inspiring."[2]

The Fort Bragg visit revealed President Kennedy's deep affinity for the Special Forces, a fact that mirrored not only the new military mind-set of his administration but the broader masculine mystique of the New Frontier. Soon after taking office, JFK began reorienting the basic military posture of the United States. Facing a global prospect of Communist expansion from Cuba to Laos, Africa to the Middle East, noted the new defense secretary, Robert McNamara, the Kennedy administration initiated "a shift in strategy—a shift from a complete and sole reliance on massive retaliation with strategic nuclear weapons to a controlled, flexible response tailored to the level of the political or military aggression to which it was responding." Like much else in the new American government, this approach to fighting the Cold War lay rooted in an ethos of young, assertive, and sophisticated masculine energy. JFK's beloved Green Berets became the most powerful symbol of the Kennedy commitment to these fresh tactics.[3]

As the New Frontier strategy took shape, two figures emerged as key advisers in shaping its basic thrust and defining characteristics. Both mavericks, they emerged as important influences on JFK in this strategic reorientation. One of them, General Maxwell Taylor, a former army chief of staff, had split with the Eisenhower administration and the Joint Chiefs of Staff over the policy of massive nuclear retaliation in combating the Communist threat. He believed it was too rigid to meet the varying and complicated demands of the modern global situation. The second figure, General Edward Lansdale, a colorful and mysterious air force officer and CIA agent, had become a controversial spokesman for jettisoning bureaucracy and brute military power in favor of indigenous programs, creative subversion, and guerrilla training for underdeveloped nations seeking to rebuff Communist aggression. In their military thinking, Taylor and Lansdale represented two aspects of Kennedy's masculine mystique in the military arena: one a paragon of cool, sophisticated, pragmatic intellectualism and the other a symbol of romantic, daring, unconventional vigor. One was a strategic military thinker and the other James Bond in the jungle. But both would play crucial roles in creating and implementing the president's new approach to the Cold War struggle.

As John F. Kennedy settled into the Oval Office, he immediately began revising the American doctrine of overwhelming nuclear retaliation formulated during the Eisenhower administration. As a senator, JFK had worried about the rigidity of large-scale nuclear response, a posture that had led to the development of ever more powerful nuclear warheads and elaborate delivery systems. Kennedy believed that "massive retaliation" was inadequate to a global struggle increasingly characterized by brushfire wars, social agitation, and guerrilla insurgencies in third world countries. Thus in a "National Security Memorandum" in the early days of his administration, the president directed the secretary of defense to "examine the means for placing new emphasis on the development of counter-guerilla forces" in the U.S. military.[4]

Kennedy elaborated his position on numerous occasions. In a commencement speech at West Point, he argued that the American military faced an exacting situation in the modern world. In the Cold War of the 1960s, he told graduating cadets, it was misleading to call this "the nuclear age" because of the persistence of "another type of warfare—new in its intensity, ancient in its origin—war by guerillas, subversives, insurgents, and assassins—war by ambush instead of combat, by infiltration instead of aggression—seeking victory by eroding and exhausting the enemy instead of engaging him." This required new training, new weapons, and a new mind-set that was willing to confront diplomatic, economic, and political problems. "What they are doing at Fort Bragg is really good," he told the journalist Stewart Alsop, but "in the final analysis what is needed is a political effort." Privately, Kennedy insisted to Roger Hilsman, an assistant secretary of state, that the main Communist threat lay in "the subtle, ambiguous threat of the guerilla. To meet this threat, new military tactics had to be developed, which he hoped the Special Forces would do. But new political tactics also had to be devised, and, most importantly, the two—the military and the political—had to be meshed together and blended."[5]

Kennedy's desire for a military strategy of flexible response came from several sources. Most obviously, it stemmed from his belief that massive nuclear retaliation was applicable only to a large-scale confrontation with the Soviet Union, or perhaps Red China, but unsuited to dealing with the numerous, smaller Communist insurgencies around the globe. Moreover, the constant threat of nuclear holocaust gave thoughtful people pause. In addition, JFK and his advisers saw massive retaliation as the product of the stodgy bureaucratic thinking that prevailed in the U.S. military. As Arthur Schlesinger explained, under Eisenhower the American military had fallen into the hands of "organization generals"—the counterpart of the organization man in civilian life—who valued bureaucratic attachment, committee consensus, and group loyalty over bold, effective, innovative individual action. These military leaders, heavily invested in nuclear technology, were hostile to "the rude weapons, amateur tactics, hard life, and marginal effects of guerilla warfare." This bureaucratic thinking was the same one denounced in one of JFK's favorite books, *The Ugly American*, which had urged getting Americans out of embassies and diplomatic receptions and into the countryside, where they would win the loyalty of the natives. So in the same way that the New Frontiersmen sought to overturn the stifling influence of the organization man in American social life, they sought to overturn the restricting, stuffy paradigm established by the organization generals.[6]

A strong element of masculine vigor permeated President Kennedy's desire for a strategy of flexible response. As in many other areas, the manly sensibility of the New Frontier with its emphasis on toughness, virility, and antibureaucratic individualism shaped his reflections on this Cold War topic. JFK sought a strategic vision that pivoted less on the axis of large-scale nuclear weaponry with its elaborate governmental structure and more on the axis of the lone man of fortitude, judgment, bravery, and sophistication who was determined to make a difference. Fighting Communism, the new administration believed, offered a rich opportunity for displaying the masculine virtues that its leader had played such a strong role in regenerating. It was the ultimate arena for "vigor."

As Kennedy began rethinking America's global military strategy, he turned for advice and leadership to a respected, if controversial, military man. General Maxwell Taylor, an experienced and heroic commander in World War II, had risen to become army chief of staff in the 1950s. But the general had clashed with the Eisenhower administration over the policy of massive nuclear retaliation as a response to Communist aggression. In Taylor's view, this one-size-fits-all approach was unsuited to meet the varied challenges of the Cold War struggle, and the United States also needed to be prepared to fight brushfire wars, third world insurgencies, and limited conflicts that demanded conventional armies. Different situations demanded different forces and weaponry. Taylor's position made him unpopular in Eisenhower's circle, and a series of frustrating clashes finally prompted his retirement in 1959. But it made Taylor a natural fit with the new president and his thinking, as did his impressive military résumé.

Maxwell Taylor had been born in 1901 in rural Missouri and won an appointment to West Point, where he graduated fourth in his class. After training at the Engineer School, the Artillery School, and the General Staff School, he taught for several years back at West Point. During World War II, Taylor served with great distinction in the European theater. As chief of staff for the Eighty-Second Airborne Division under General Matthew B. Ridgway, he fought in North Africa, Sicily, and Italy. Taylor was appointed commander of the 101st Airborne Division and led it in the D-day invasion and then in campaigns in Holland, France, and Germany.[7]

After the war, Taylor was superintendent at West Point from 1945 until

1949 and then commanded American troops in Berlin. After leading the Eighth Army during the Korean War, he was army chief of staff from 1955 to 1959. He retired from the military at the end of his term, worked for a year in Mexico City as chairman of the board of the Mexican Light and Power Company, and then returned to the United States in 1960 to become president of the Lincoln Center for the Performing Arts in New York. He was in that position when President Kennedy approached and asked him to enter his administration.[8]

What attracted JFK's attention was Taylor's book *The Uncertain Trumpet* (1959), which outlined his views on the need to reformulate America's military posture. "We are faced with declining military strength at a time of increasing political tension," he wrote. "The permanent remedy calls for a complete reappraisal of our strategy." Citing a Bible verse from 1 Corinthians—"For if the trumpet gives an uncertain sound, who shall prepare himself to the battle?"—Taylor took apart the prevailing doctrine in precise, dispassionate language. While a robust nuclear force was necessary, he argued, actual Cold War conditions demanded a more versatile strategy. In Taylor's words, a new program of "Flexible Response should contain at the outset an unqualified renunciation of reliance on the strategy of Massive Retaliation. It should be made clear that the United States will prepare itself to respond anywhere, any time, with weapons and forces appropriate to the situation." This meant an upgrading of conventional land forces, air and naval defense forces, and counterinsurgency forces. For Taylor, an enhanced capability for waging limited war would sound "the sure notes of a certain trumpet, giving to friend and foe alike a clear expression of our purpose and our motives."[9]

The Uncertain Trumpet attracted the attention of the new president, who had vowed to "pay any price, bear any burden, meet any hardship, support any friend, oppose any foe, to assure the survival and success of liberty." JFK wrote an endorsement to Taylor's editor in 1959: "This volume is characterized by an unmistakable honesty, clarity of judgment, and a genuine sense of urgency. It is free of rancor and recrimination, but it leaves no room for doubt that we have not brought our conventional war capabilities into line with the necessities. We have allowed important aspects of our national military strength to erode over the past years. . . . It is a book that deserves reading by every American." Taylor dropped Kennedy a note of appreciation, and the presidential candidate replied, "I was more than happy to give your book my endorsement. Its central arguments are most persuasive . . . and it has certainly helped to shape my own thinking."[10]

So when he began reformulating American military strategy as president, JFK turned to Taylor. Kennedy asked him to head an investigation of the Bay of Pigs debacle and identify the causes of its failure. But the president also had a broader agenda in mind, as he noted in his appointment letter to Taylor. "It is apparent that we need to take a close look at all our practices and programs in the areas of military and paramilitary, guerilla and anti-guerilla activities which fall short of outright war," Kennedy wrote. "I believe we need to strengthen our work in this area." After several weeks of investigation, Taylor reached two conclusions. First, from a military point of view the operation was flawed from the outset with inadequate strategy, numbers of men, air support, and ammunition. Second, the CIA was ill-suited to direct such a large-scale action, and military operations should be left to the Pentagon.[11]

Kennedy asked Taylor to stay on. He invited the general to become a personal military adviser with the title of military representative to the president. Taylor accepted, in his own words, because the president was "a sincere convert to the need for a strategy of Flexible Response to replace the dependence on Massive Retaliation of the Eisenhower Dulles era." Taylor described his task as "one of anticipating problems of the President in the areas of my responsibility and of being ready to help the President when they came before him. This requirement meant that I must be aware at all times of the important issues as they were taking shape in State, Defense, and the intelligence community." When a pressing issue arose for Kennedy's formal consideration, Taylor tried to have in the chief executive's hands "an analysis of the issue, the contending arguments, and the key points which he must eventually decide."[12]

Taylor also became a key player on another front. Kennedy, deeply struck by Nikita Khrushchev's January 6, 1961, speech calling for wars of national liberation around the globe, moved quickly in the direction of counterinsurgency preparations. He issued a National Security Memorandum to the Department of Defense and requested that the State Department take the lead in developing a counterinsurgency policy document that would guide both the American military and civilian agencies of the government. Kennedy read the latest issue of the *Marine Corps Gazette,* which was devoted entirely to guerrilla warfare and counterinsurgency, and discussed it at length with Roger Hilsman, assistant secretary of state.[13]

Eventually, however, JFK felt the need to go beyond such piecemeal efforts. So in January 1962, he issued a presidential directive establishing the Special Group (Counterinsurgency). The president appointed Taylor chairman and added Attorney General Robert Kennedy, Deputy Undersecretary of State Alexis Johnson, Deputy Secretary of Defense Ros Gilpatric, Chairman of the Joint Chiefs Lyman Lemnitzer, Director of the Central Intelligence Agency John McCone, and National Security Adviser McGeorge Bundy. The president directed the group to "insure proper recognition throughout the U.S. Government" that wars of liberation rivaled conventional warfare as threats in the Cold War. The directive also instructed the group to marshal all available resources to ensure the proper training of U.S. military forces and embassy personnel, government agencies, and aid programs staff to meet the threat of "subversive insurgency and related forms of indirect aggression."[14]

Taylor and Special Group (Counterinsurgency) set a number of projects in motion. The group produced a statement that became the basis for new training programs established by Kennedy in National Security Memorandum No. 131, titled "Training Objectives for Counter-insurgency." It supervised these programs in unconventional warfare, which soon involved some fifty thousand men. This included the preparation of new courses in the curricula of the nation's war colleges. The Special Group (Counterinsurgency) promoted police training and civic action initiatives in the governments of countries threatened by Communist rebellions. While Taylor made clear "it was President Kennedy himself who put the great drive behind the so-called counterinsurgency program to prevent wars of national liberation," the president held Taylor in such high regard that he appointed him chairman of the Joint Chiefs of Staff in October 1962. The general had some misgivings, but he accepted because "the strategic heresy of Flexible Response which I had advocated to little avail had become the orthodoxy of the Kennedy Administration."[15]

While Taylor's cogent strategic thinking constituted part of his appeal for President Kennedy, equally important was his personal image that fit perfectly with the masculine mystique of the new administration. Had he not existed, Maxwell Taylor would have needed to be invented as the ideal "Kennedy general." He appeared as the martial version of the ideal New Frontiersman: educated, articulate, cultured, handsome, athletic, tough, and pragmatic. He was a war hero who knew four languages, authored books, played a vigorous game of tennis at age sixty, and had left a military career to serve as president of the Lincoln Center for the Performing Arts in New York. "Taylor is something special in American military history—a fighting hero, an acknowledged intellectual and keenly political person with no apparent personal political ambitions," wrote Jack Raymond of *The New York Times*. "He runs counter to the prevailing image of professional soldiers as inarticulate men of narrow interests."[16]

Taylor's New Frontier image was projected vividly when he appeared on the cover of *Time* on July 28, 1961. In a feature article titled "A Soldier and the White House," the magazine described him as a representative of the Kennedyesque masculine image: "an aloof, handsome man with cool china blue eyes, a knack for sketching a problem in broad perspective, and a talent for hammering out explicit courses of action." This brilliant general "has shown the Kennedys that he can handle himself agilely in any social situation—from humorously barbed, dinner-party small talk to the more energetic competition of the tennis court. . . . Taylor is fluent in Japanese, German, Spanish, and French." His wartime laurels had led to an appointment as head of West Point, where he expanded the liberal arts and had cadets studying the poetry of T. S. Eliot and the judicial opinions of Oliver Wendell Holmes while also stressing athletic training and fitness. "No pot belly will ever lead the corps of cadets," he declared. Taylor himself cut an imposingly manly figure. When a White House staffer chirped, " 'Good morning, Max,' the glint of steel flashed in the general's eye" over this presumption of first-name familiarity. A congressman who had observed Taylor over the years stressed that he was not a bureaucratic backslapper but a reserved, intellectual, tough-minded thinker. "He was always a loner.

He'd never mix with the fellows when we went on trips, drink a beer, or join in chitchat. He'd go over in a corner of the plane and read a book."[17]

Taylor polished his Kennedyesque image as a warrior-intellectual with a much-publicized commencement address at West Point in June 1963. Titled "The American Soldier," the speech took as its starting point Ralph Waldo Emerson's famous "The American Scholar," an 1837 oration to the Phi Beta Kappa Society that had proclaimed the independence of American thinkers from the thrall of European tradition. Now, Taylor told the cadets, a similar day had dawned for the American soldier. He had emerged victorious from two world wars and helped make the United States the preeminent global power, but now he faced new challenges. The American soldier must be not only a fighter and a man of character but a man of "wisdom" who understood the principles of democratic government, the nature of American objectives, and the proper role of the military in a complex global environment. Properly armed with ideas as well as weapons, he would embody the ideal of the military man on the New Frontier—a sophisticated, literate, and cultured warrior prepared to fight fiercely in defense of freedom.[18]

Taylor's New Frontier image gained considerable luster from his personal relationship with President Kennedy and his family. JFK publicly praised the general as "absolutely first class" and in possession of "a definitive, tough mind." Bobby Kennedy and Averell Harriman confirmed the president's reliance on his advice. Kennedy invited Taylor to the family compound at Hyannis Port on several occasions, and the general reported that his moderately strenuous schedule included "tennis morning and afternoon, a swim, a boat ride, a walk on the beach, and several jogs to the house where we were staying located about a mile from the center of the community. Had I taken the 'A' course, I would have done the same plus a round of golf and a game of touch football."[19]

Taylor not only respected JFK but liked him personally. He enjoyed the president's wry sense of humor, cool judgment, and considerable patience. Unlike Eisenhower, whom Taylor saw as reluctant to resolve disputes or take actions that might have adverse consequences, JFK wanted to be involved in the decision making and take action after considering all of the options. For all of his self-possessed reserve, the intellectual general also found himself caught up in the youthful excitement and innovation of the new administration. "The Kennedy White House generated a certain electricity," he observed. "It was a stimulating environment." In fact, when Taylor agreed to become chairman of the Joint Chiefs, he claimed that his greatest misgiving concerned a greater distance from President Kennedy. "I knew that of all the changes resulting from my move to the Pentagon, the one which I would feel most was the loss of daily association with him," he reported. "I told him that I hoped to retain as much as possible of this closeness in my new assignment and was pleased when he invited me to telephone him directly whenever it seemed necessary."[20]

Taylor might have become even closer to Robert Kennedy. He first met the attorney general on the Cuba committee, and they became warm friends. He wrote of the younger Kennedy, "I was impressed by his ability as a thorough and incisive interrogator of witnesses, always on the lookout for a snow job, impatient at any suggestion of evasion or imprecision, and relentless in his determination to get at the truth, particularly if it bore on a matter affecting John F. Kennedy." The general became a frequent visitor to Hickory Hill, the estate of the attorney general and his large family in McLean, Virginia. Taylor enjoyed its boisterous informality, once quipping, "You never knew who would be there for tennis. You could end up with either Donald Dell or Donald Duck."[21]

Thus Maxwell Taylor, the ideal New Frontier general, became the chief military strategist in the Kennedy administration. Not only did his ideas and strategic vision match JFK's rethinking of American policy, but his personal style reflected the vigorous, individualist masculinity of the youthful leader and his program. But this handsome, articulate, tough-minded military adviser was not the only figure who played an important role in shaping Kennedy's new approach to fighting global Communism. Also appearing frequently in the president's councils was another military figure who created even more controversy with his shadowy celebrity image as an iconoclastic cold warrior.

In the process of refashioning America's overall strategic military thinking in the early days of his administration, President Kennedy was especially concerned about Communist insurgencies in poorer countries around the globe. From unrest in Laos and Vietnam in Southeast Asia to turmoil in Africa and the Middle East to the possible export of Fidel Castro's Communist revolution to the rest of Latin America, a host of volatile and murky situations faced the young American leader. Determined to find innovative, effective solutions, JFK turned to another unorthodox military figure for guidance. General Edward Lansdale was a romantic Cold Warrior who had ruffled many feathers in Washington and the Pentagon in the postwar period. Well versed in the social and political issues roiling underdeveloped countries around the globe, he had pushed hard for unconventional approaches that ran against the grain of President Eisenhower and his generals. For just that reason, however, he appealed mightily to the youthful new president.

Edward Geary Lansdale had spent much of his youth moving about the country as his father, an auto executive, took a succession of positions. The family finally settled in Los Angeles, where the youth eventually enrolled at UCLA and joined ROTC. Bored with academic subjects, he left college before graduating and worked at several jobs before drifting into advertising. Lansdale demonstrated a knack for the work and was soon working at a big ad agency with accounts at several large companies. Then, on the fateful day of December 7, 1941, with the attack on Pearl Harbor, Lansdale's life changed forever.[22]

Lansdale was able to procure a commission in the Military Intelligence Service and soon made the acquaintance of William "Wild Bill" Donovan, head of the Office of Strategic Services (OSS), the primary intelligence-gathering organization for the national government. The OSS took Lansdale on, and he became involved with establishing training courses, writing intelligence summaries, and collecting information on beaches, airstrips, and native populations that could be invaluable for military campaigns. By 1945, he was working in the OSS office in New York City.[23]

After the surrender of Germany and Japan, Lansdale decided upon a career as an intelligence officer. In late 1945, he was assigned to the Philippines, where he remained for the next three years advising the government, helping the army rebuild its intelligence service, and sorting out complex prisoner of war issues. Lansdale demonstrated a characteristic trait: a deep sympathy for the common people of Asia, the villagers and farmers who were trying to eke out a living amid the wars and ideologies that were descending upon them from above. With almost anthropological intensity, he studied their customs, values, culture, and folklore. "Filipinos and I fell in love with each other," he said. "There was tremendous brotherly love on both parts." He returned to the Philippines in 1950 to play a crucial role in defeating the Communist Huk insurgency by setting in motion a successful movement—Lansdale described it as "a social revolution which would have delighted Thomas Jefferson"—led by Ramon Magsaysay, who was then elected president.[24]

Meanwhile, Lansdale had become linked to the intelligence world. While Lansdale was paid by the air force, where he became a general, he also worked for the CIA, thus inhabiting a kind of shadowy space with a double identity: one foot in the regular military and one foot in covert operations. For most of his career, this counterinsurgency expert denied or downplayed his CIA involvement, but in the 1980s he admitted, "I served part of my career as a military man as a volunteer on CIA duties," duties that also took him to Vietnam. Lansdale served as a military liaison to the French forces and helped train the Vietnamese National Army and its various militia allies.[25]

Throughout the 1950s, Lansdale became notorious as a critic of American military bureaucracy in the Cold War struggle. Instead of rigid, top-down, weapons-heavy tactics, he urged the development of unconventional, decentralized, covert anti-Communist operations run by imaginative officers who knew local languages, understood local mores, and sympathized with local needs. He criticized American diplomatic and military officers in the Philippines for remaining isolated in embassies or among wealthy elites in big cities while ignoring ordinary people. "When was the 'expert' last invited to be a guest in an 'average' Filipino household to share a meal? When did he last spend a night with Filipinos in the provinces?" Lansdale asked sharply. "Working close up is one hell of a lot better than sitting in an office reading information . . . second-hand through a few selected contacts who specialize in scandal and gossip."[26]

Lansdale urged a spirit of friendly openness to native people, respect for their customs and values, and recognition of a common humanity. He established a reputation for such unorthodox tactics. One day, while driving in a rural province of the Philippines, he came across a Communist insurgent haranguing a crowd as he blamed a host of social and economic problems on American imperialism. "Impetuously, I got out of the jeep from where I had parked it at the edge of the crowd, climbed up on its hood, and when the speaker had paused for breath, I shouted, 'What's the matter? Didn't you ever have an American friend?'" he recalled. "The startled crowd turned around and saw an American in uniform standing up on his jeep.... But the people immediately put me at ease.... They clustered around me naming Americans they had known and liked and asked if I was acquainted with them. I teased them with the reminder that these folks they had known were 'American imperialists' they had been denouncing." Lansdale spent many hours in favorite pastimes: visiting and eating with native people in their homes, listening to their stories and telling jokes, and playing local folk songs on his harmonica. "The U.S. political warrior is actually extending the Pax Americana when he works effectively" through such tactics, he insisted in a 1954 lecture.[27]

In a series of talks and articles, Lansdale began to formulate a full-blown counterinsurgency strategy that combined political, socioeconomic, and military elements. Mimicking Mao's ideas, he urged a program of "civic action" that "makes the soldier a brother of the people, as well as their protector. The Communist guerilla will claim his dogmatic kinship to the people, to gain their support and hide among them.... You, and the free citizens in uniform with you, must demonstrate a *closer* kinship to the people." This meant being polite and kind to civilians, honoring their property, respecting their customs, and encouraging a "spirit of freedom" at every opportunity. Civic action promised to enlist the hearts and minds of the natives.[28]

In particular, Lansdale stressed an ideological component, particularly a defense of ideals of personal freedom and democratic government, in the struggle against Communist insurgency around the globe. In his words, counterinsurgency demanded "a forceful, positive ideological base from which to combat and surpass the dynamic ideas of the Communist side.... Against those Communist beliefs, rooted in nineteenth-century philosophy, we should at least pit our own ideals, rooted in eighteenth-century philosophical concepts, to show that we are *for* something and not just fighting a negative, defensive battle." While Communists employed fear and intimidation to tear down existing structures, Americans must embrace the harder task of promoting freedom, opportunity, and democratic participation "so that we can be brothers to a world family of free people." They needed to trumpet the ideals of the Declaration of Independence, the British Magna Carta, and the French "Liberté, Égalité, Fraternité" to make a stronger appeal than the Communist cause.[29]

This battle of ideas needed to be supported with real political and economic reforms. To successfully defeat insurgencies in poorer countries, Lansdale contended, the United States should promote democratic practices in governments it supported, use aid programs to help provide people with an opportunity to earn a decent living, and encourage land reform so peasants would have a stake in defending their own well-being and way of life. Such a strategy, he never tired of emphasizing, demanded that Americans leave their diplomatic and military enclaves and actually engage with ordinary people. When the American ambassador to Vietnam asked Lansdale how to make the American effort more effective, he recommended that "the number of cocktail parties and evening dress affairs be cut down in favor of using the time and energy to give more help to the Vietnamese, who were fighting and dying just outside of town."[30]

Lansdale also strayed off the beaten path to urge unorthodox approaches on the battlefield. He urged training in counterinsurgency warfare where Americans and natives worked together in teams; using actual case studies instead of theory to teach antiguerrilla tactics; and expanding the Special Forces training center at Fort Bragg while liberating it from the military bureaucracy. He also endorsed tactics such as ambushes, clandestine operations, hit-and-run tactics by irregular troops, counterinsurgent hit squads, and acts of sabotage such as blowing up power plants and disrupting water supplies.[31]

Finally, Lansdale advocated "psywarfare" tactics that would demoralize enemy forces in imaginative ways. In the Philippines, he played upon local fears of vampires by arranging for government forces to take the corpse of a Communist insurgent, poke two holes in the side of the neck, drain it of blood, and carefully place it on a trail much followed by the rebels. After finding the body, the Huk insurgents vacated the area in terror. Another time Lansdale employed what he called "the eye of God" technique. Drawing upon the ancient Egyptian practice of placing a highly stylized image of a baleful, warning eye near tombs to scare away grave robbers, he and his team snuck into villages in the middle of the night and silently painted this forbidding image on walls facing the abodes of Communist suspects. Peasants frightened by this mysterious, malevolent symbol subsequently treated rebels with great suspicion.[32]

Lansdale's reputation swelled when he became an inspiration for the bestselling novel *The Ugly American* (1958). This book, a favorite of Senator Kennedy's, contrasts elite, effeminate, luxurious Foreign Service officers who while away the time in big cities with "hard and muscular" men in the field who understand the struggling peasantry and seek to help them resist ruthless Communist insurgents. One of the most heroic figures is Colonel Hillandale, a committed military officer who immerses himself in Sarkhan culture to understand the native people and win their loyalty. He was based on Edward Lansdale. Hillandale, like his real-life counterpart, eats meals and jokes and socializes with peasants on their own turf, plays folk tunes on his harmonica, promotes a message of liberty and freedom that helps thwart Communist propaganda, and encourages counterinsurgency tactics to defend against insurgent attacks.[33]

Lansdale, many believed, also inspired the protagonist in a much darker fictional portrait of American efforts in Southeast Asia, Graham Greene's *Quiet American*. Its protagonist is Alden Pyle, an intellectual, idealistic, but innocent young American CIA agent working undercover in Vietnam. He believes that an American-backed "third force," neither colonialist nor Communist but advocating a message of freedom mixed with native traditions, offers the best hope for Vietnam's future. But his naïveté leads to involvement with a renegade military officer who is subsequently implicated in a car bombing in Saigon that kills many innocent people, including women and children. As a cynical observer notes, "I never knew a man who had better motives for all the trouble he caused." While Greene denied modeling Pyle on Lansdale, the two had much in common, particularly an affinity for idealism, ideology, and intrigue, and many saw a resemblance. Thus *The Quiet American*'s rendering of an American similar to Lansdale further enhanced his reputation by making it an object of controversy.[34]

The military establishment tended to view Lansdale as an iconoclastic wheeler-dealer and oddball, but he attracted many younger military and intelligence officers with his counterinsurgency creed and unconventional activities. His success in the Philippines and his exploits in Vietnam in the 1950s created a legendary persona. With a reputation for living in the countryside among the people and beating Communist insurgents at their own game, Lansdale became larger than life. Equal parts charisma and controversy, this swashbuckling general who bucked the bureaucracy emerged as a vigorous, manly figure. "Solitary in his methods, disinclined toward bureaucratic empires, Lansdale has been a legend in Asia for almost twenty years, America's version of T. E. Lawrence," wrote one journalist. *Saga: The Magazine for Men* presented a highly embellished account titled "Our Mysterious Edward G. Lansdale: America's Deadliest Secret Agent," wherein Ho Chi Minh, leader of the Communist forces, urged his minions to kill the officer at any cost. A newspaper writer put it bluntly in 1961: "If there's any one American whose name rouses Asia's commies to fury it is Ed Lansdale."[35]

The Lansdale legend was enhanced by his flair for publicity and salesmanship, something he had sharpened during his early career as an advertising man. "Ed was low key but he could always convince people. . . . God! The way he explained the situation in Vietnam," declared a fellow officer. "If we gave up, all of Asia would go down the drain. It was just remarkable [how he made this case]. . . . Of course, he was an advertising man, a salesman, very soft-spoken, very quiet, very smooth." Ros Gilpatric, deputy secretary of defense, described Lansdale as "a freewheeler, entrepreneur type of operator, and he would go around with an idea and sell it to somebody in the hopes that they would take him on as sort of project director." In other words, he excelled at promoting his activities, his country, and himself. An observer pictured this superb salesman: "Lansdale selling America and himself to Magsaysay and to Diem; Lansdale selling America and himself to the Dulles brothers; Lansdale appearing on television news programs or coordinating mass circulation articles selling the Cold War to the American public; Lansdale playing his harmonica or using the 'eye of God' tactic to influence Filipino and Vietnamese peasants."[36]

Lansdale's communication skills became evident in the late 1950s when he persuaded the Hollywood director Joseph Mankiewicz to revise his movie version of *The Quiet American*. Where Graham Greene's novel had been highly critical of American efforts in Southeast Asia, Lansdale influenced the filmmaker to create a pro-America rendering of the book. When it appeared in 1958, the movie starred the World War II hero Audie Murphy as an admirable Alden Pyle, who is not a CIA agent but a private citizen working for a U.S. foundation who is spreading homespun truths. The movie made the Communists responsible for the bombing carnage in Saigon. Mankiewicz's *Quiet American* supported the U.S. effort in Vietnam and excoriated the Communists, causing a satisfied Lansdale to declare that it represented "an excellent change from Mr. Greene's novel of despair."[37]

By the time of Kennedy's election, Lansdale had become a celebrity, albeit a controversial one, in the American military. He entered the councils of the New Frontier in typical fashion. As the new administration settled in during late January 1961, the maverick general forwarded several memorandums on Vietnam to the national security team. These reports impressed Kennedy with their ideas about effective counterinsurgency tactics. In fact, he was so struck by one of them—the story of a Vietnamese village that successfully rebuffed insurgent forces—that he recommended it to *The Saturday Evening Post* for publication. It appeared as "The Report the President Wanted Published," by "An American Officer." In colorful and somewhat breathless prose, it told the story of Binh Hung, a small village in South Vietnam, that heroically fought off the Communist Vietcong, inspired by a vision of liberty and practicing their own guerrilla tactics. "The light in their eyes when they talked about freedom showed that it was not just oratory," wrote Lansdale. "Freedom is precious to them, a personal thing."[38]

It was a perfect fit: the individualist, innovative, antibureaucratic, vigorously masculine military officer and the youthful administration pushing many of the same values. It was as if General Lansdale had been tailor-made for the New Frontier. He wanted to do things "the right way, the modern way," wrote one historian of the Kennedy administration.

"[He] was against big, bumbling U.S. government programs run by insensitive, boastful, bureaucratic, materialistic racists, and for small indigenous programs run by folksy, modest American country boys who knew the local mores, culture, and language."[39]

Yet some New Frontiersmen had reservations. William Bundy, a foreign policy adviser to JFK, saw Lansdale as a secretive operator who left the feeling "he had three more angles he was playing," while Chester Bowles, the undersecretary of state, dismissed him as a juvenile advocate of "cops and robbers, cowboys and Indians, ambushing people." Roger Hilsman concluded that Lansdale had little real understanding of issues but took "great delight in manipulating personalities. He's very much a CIA type." Robert McNamara never recovered from his first encounter with the freewheeling general, who marched into the secretary of defense's office, introduced himself, and dumped a pile of Vietnamese rifles on his desk. This pile of weapons, Lansdale told him, symbolized the lesson that the Vietnamese needed something to believe in and defend if American efforts were to be successful. McNamara stared askance at this performance, which he saw as absurd, and never again took Lansdale seriously.[40]

But the man who mattered most in New Frontier circles, the president, took a great liking to Lansdale almost immediately. Shortly after the general's initial memorandum went to the White House, Walt Rostow forwarded to JFK a copy of Lansdale's recent comments to the Special Forces school at Fort Bragg, noting, "Here's a talk by your favorite current author. It underlines the strictly military reasons why the local armies should be encouraged by us to engage in economic development activities." Kennedy admired Lansdale's innovative military thinking and his stance as a vigorous, tough-minded, liberal anti-Communist. As two historians have observed, to the extent that the president "gained reassurance from a man's man, Lansdale and the solutions he proffered were extremely satisfying." The general's attraction was partly a matter of his counterinsurgency ideas and partly a matter of masculine style. As McGeorge Bundy noted, "Lansdale was temperamentally somewhat his kind of person." The president, in fact, signaled his approval when he described the unorthodox general as "America's James Bond."[41]

Lansdale had a high opinion of President Kennedy's strategic sense and commitment to fighting Communist insurgencies in new and innovative ways. In a 1961 lecture on the importance of "civic action" for a successful American strategy, he declared, "President Kennedy is apparently alert to this basic point as he seeks to win the peace with freedom." In a talk titled "The Insurgent Battlefield," Lansdale pointed out that "spurred by the personal interest of President Kennedy, the U.S. is discovering a new military term: 'counterinsurgency.'" In a private letter to a sympathetic friend, he disclosed that "President Kennedy had me in for a long talk on the subject [of Vietnam and counterinsurgency]. He was warmly interested and asked many questions. . . . It would have warmed your heart to have heard this conversation."[42]

So with Edward Lansdale, as with Maxwell Taylor, President Kennedy sought innovative ideas, fresh tactics, and revamped strategies as he reoriented the American approach to fighting the Cold War in the dangerous days of the early 1960s. This undertaking involved large-scale, overarching theories of flexible response and counterinsurgency. But it also demanded the development of actual initiatives. Here, too, the two generals—the cool, incisive, elegant commander and the unorthodox, mysterious operative in the jungle—would assume important roles.

President Kennedy outlined his new military approach, with its twin pillars of flexible response and counterinsurgency, in a series of speeches. In his "Special Message to the Congress on Urgent National Needs" in May 1961, he described the threat of Communist insurgencies: "They have fired no missiles, and their troops are seldom seen. They send arms, agitators, aid, technicians and propaganda to every troubled area. But where fighting is required, it is usually done by others—by guerillas striking at night, by assassins striking alone . . . by subversives and saboteurs and insurrectionists." The following year, he stressed that this type of guerrilla insurgency—"new in its intensity, ancient in its origins"—required "a whole new kind of strategy, a wholly different kind of force, and therefore a new and wholly different kind of military training."[43]

JFK moved to develop just such a strategy, force, and training. This approach incorporated a limited war perspective and counterinsurgency tactics while harnessing the individualist, antibureaucratic, manly spirit of the New Frontier. Both Taylor and Lansdale were intimately involved at nearly every turn. One of the first endeavors focused on South Vietnam, where American military advisers, weaponry, and economic aid to support the government of Ngo Dinh Diem was proving increasingly ineffective in stopping a Communist-led insurgency. This small Southeast Asian country had become a testing ground for Kennedy's new ideas about fighting the Cold War, and he was determined to shape a winning approach.

After going to Vietnam in early January 1961, Lansdale returned to Washington determined to try to revamp American strategy. In a lengthy report, he argued that the Communists had made significant gains and were extending their control in the countryside. "The U.S. should recognize that Vietnam is in a critical condition . . . an area requiring emergency treatment." Lansdale recommended that the United States continue to support President Diem while putting in new personnel with a fresh approach who "know and really like Asians, dedicated people who are willing to risk their lives for the ideal of freedom, and who will try to influence and guide the Vietnamese towards U.S. policy objectives with the warm friendship and affection which our close alliance deserves." This team, in other words, should be created in the Lansdale mold.[44]

President Kennedy, who closely read the report, was impressed. "This is the worst one we've got, isn't it," he commented to an adviser. "You know, Eisenhower never mentioned it. He talked at length about Laos, but never uttered the word Vietnam." JFK summoned Lansdale to the White House for a meeting of top-level foreign policy advisers, including Robert McNamara, Dean Rusk, Allen Dulles, and the chairman of the Joint Chiefs. Kennedy greeted the general, complimented him on his Vietnam analysis, and according to official notes of the meeting, "in response to the President's invitation, General Lansdale spoke at some length along the lines of his report." Afterward, Kennedy held him over for a private chat in the Oval Office and hinted that he might make him the new ambassador to Vietnam. This marked the beginning of Lansdale's meteoric ascendancy in the military councils of the new administration. As Rostow observed, "He knew more about guerilla warfare on the Asian scene than any other American. He had an extraordinary sensitivity and respect for the political problems of postcolonial nations and for the human beings caught up in them." It helped that Lansdale's reports on the Vietnam situation clothed serious ideas in typically colorful language. In a briefing paper on Diem for Lyndon Johnson in preparation for a visit, the general wrote, "When the Vice-President sees him, he will find him as interested in cattle as any Texan, and as interested in freedom as Sam Houston."[45]

Maxwell Taylor emerged to play an even larger role in the Vietnam conflict. In October 1961, President Kennedy sent his military adviser to Vietnam, along with his deputy national security adviser, Walt Rostow, and several minor officials, to assess the situation and make policy recommendations. The group included Edward Lansdale. In his charge, the president stressed the complex nature of the situation. "While the military part of the problem is of great importance in South Vietnam, its political, social, and economic elements are equally significant, and I shall expect your appraisal and your recommendations to take full account of them," he told Taylor. After a week of fact-finding, the general submitted a report arguing that Communist forces had made progress in their campaign to gain control of Southeast Asia through "subversion and guerilla war." Taylor called for a strengthening of the U.S. military role ("on the order of 6–8,000 troops") to demonstrate American seriousness and support of the Diem government, increased pressure for democratic reforms, a boost in economic assistance, and increased insurgency training for South Vietnamese troops. For Taylor, it was a classic case of fighting the limited conflicts that characterized the Cold War struggle.[46]

This task force to Vietnam also illuminated something else: Maxwell Taylor and Edward Lansdale did not get along. For all of their shared interest in innovative military strategies, they differed profoundly in emphasis. Taylor wanted to strengthen conventional forces as an alternative to nuclear response, while Lansdale favored unorthodox counterinsurgency tactics that involved social reform and psychological warfare. Each viewed the other, and his ideas, as misguided. "Lansdale was an idea man, and he could turn out ideas faster than you could pick them up off the floor, but I was never impressed with their feasibility," Taylor complained. In Lansdale's view, Taylor never really understood in Vietnam "who the enemy was or how he was trying to fight, the political basis behind their military activities, the political results they were trying to achieve." With military thinking as with religion or politics, it is often the people with the smallest differences in opinion who generate the nastiest clashes.[47]

Immediately upon landing in Saigon, Taylor froze Lansdale out of all high-ranking meetings and set him to a minor task: exploring the possibility of constructing an "electronic line" between North and South Vietnam and along the border with Laos and Cambodia to repel invaders. A resentful Lansdale did as he was ordered but described the project as "stupid." "A patrician, cold, short-sighted person," a bitter Lansdale said of Taylor. "I admire his charm, his manners, his language, his approach to life but he essentially turned me off at the same time. . . . There was also a coldness that came from command for a long time, which also turned me off." Taylor, like many officials in the State and Defense Departments, saw Lansdale as a loose cannon whose obsession with irregular forces and psychological warfare twisted his judgment.[48]

With Cuba, however, the situation was reversed. Taylor was involved to a certain extent with the Kennedy administration's confrontations with the government of Fidel Castro, especially during the Cuban missile crisis of October 1962, when he served as a key figure in the deliberations of the famous ExComm over thirteen tension-filled days. While he favored taking out the nuclear missile installations through bombing, Taylor's moderation and loyalty led him to support Kennedy's less aggressive decision to quarantine the island. This tactic proved successful, of course, when Nikita Khrushchev backed down and agreed to remove Russian nuclear weapons from the island. Taylor concluded that the confrontation affirmed the validity of flexible response. "Khrushchev eventually retreated not because of SAC aircraft aloft and Polaris submarines on station but because Cuba was beyond the range of his conventional forces and Kennedy had called his bluff," he wrote. "The decisive factor was our conventional military forces in Florida, which convinced Khrushchev that his opponent was quite serious about invading Cuba if he did not yield."[49]

However, Taylor remained on the margins of Kennedy's broader strategy to change the government in Cuba. In the fall of 1961, JFK, still smarting from the Bay of Pigs debacle, summoned the CIA's assistant director Richard Bissell and chewed him out for "sitting on his ass and not doing anything about getting rid of Castro and the Castro regime." Shortly thereafter, the president called Lansdale into his office and asked him to look into America's anti-Castro actions there to determine their effectiveness. The general reported that most activity was merely of the "harassing" variety, and he pressed for a more active program to guide and assist dissident Cubans in undermining Castro. Kennedy agreed and asked Lansdale to "go ahead and see what could be done" to coordinate the agencies of the U.S. government to that end.[50]

To provide a structure for this endeavor, on November 30, 1961, President Kennedy issued a top secret memorandum on the Cuba operation. It announced a program to marshal "our available assets . . . to help Cuba overthrow the communist regime" and gave notice that it would be "under the general guidance of General Lansdale, acting as Chief of Operations." Representatives from the Departments of State and Defense as well as the CIA would serve, and Robert Kennedy would function as a liaison to keep the president informed. The memorandum also stressed that "knowledge of the existence of this operation should be restricted" to recipients of the memo and the highest-ranking officials concerned with national security. Officially named Special Group (Augmented), the committee became known by the code name created by Lansdale: Operation Mongoose.[51]

A full-scale covert action program ensued as Lansdale brought suggestions to the committee table, usually after consulting with Robert Kennedy. His schemes for removing the Cuban dictator—by psychological subversion, economic sabotage, or even assassination—drew upon his fertile counterinsurgency imagination. In a top secret "eyes only" memo on February 20, 1962, Lansdale discussed the overall Mongoose plan for bringing down the Castro government and warned the recipients of the need for secrecy: "Any inference that this plan exists could place the President of the United States in a most damaging position." He then proposed a series of moves designed to unfold over the next year: covert operations, a barrage of anti-Castro broadcasts, the creation of "bases for guerilla operations," the sabotage of military, communication, and transportation systems, the training of "Cuban paramilitary teams," the liberation of "political prisoners," and the elimination of "key leaders of the regime" by employing "gangster elements." It would culminate with a "declaration of revolt" to establish a new Cuban government. Lansdale's most outlandish scheme was called "Illumination by Submarine." He proposed that after dark on All Souls' Day, a U.S. submarine should fire star shells to illuminate the Havana sky, followed by a campaign declaring it was a "portent signifying the downfall of the regime and the growing strength of the resistance." When a colleague in Operation Mongoose later testified to Congress, he sardonically described the bizarre plan as "Elimination by Illumination."[52]

By the fall of 1962, President Kennedy had grown impatient with meager results from the Cuba project. At a meeting of the Special Group (Augmented) on October 4, Robert Kennedy conveyed that his brother was "concerned about progress on the Mongoose program and feels that more priority should be given to trying to mount sabotage operations." The attorney general urged the group to mount "massive activity" against the Communist government in Cuba. The group agreed and after much discussion concluded that "all efforts should be made to develop new and imaginative approaches to the possibility of getting rid of the Castro regime."[53]

But such ambitious plans never panned out. Although a number of small operations and initiatives took place, Operation Mongoose faded with the onset of the Cuban missile crisis in October 1962. As the confrontation with the Soviet Union intensified, Robert Kennedy, reflecting the wishes of the president, instructed that clandestine operations against Castro cease so as to give Khrushchev no excuse for maintaining nuclear warheads in Cuba. In early 1963, however, the CIA created a new group called the Special Affairs Staff, headed by Desmond FitzGerald, which plotted the removal of the Cuban dictator with even more outlandish ruses: exploding seashells planted near his favorite diving sites, a wet suit impregnated with toxins, a poison pen to be deployed by a turncoat Cuban army officer. While none of these schemes came to fruition, they reflected the Kennedy administration's determination to rid Latin America of Castro and Communist influence by covert action.[54]

The supreme example of JFK's counterinsurgency vision, however, lay not in a geographical area but in an elite American military unit that became a key symbol of the New Frontier's vigorous, tough-minded masculinity. Early in his administration, Kennedy urged the army to expand its training of elite Special Forces units—the Green Berets—as the cutting edge of America's unconventional, antiguerrilla forces. A few months after his famous trip to Fort Bragg, where he witnessed that dazzling display of commando expertise, Kennedy wrote a letter to the U.S. Army insisting that Communist insurgency around the globe called for new techniques and tactics. "Pure military skill is not enough," he said. "A full spectrum of military, para-military, and civil action must be blended to produce success." The president believed that the Special Forces were best suited for this enterprise, proclaiming, "The 'green beret' is again becoming a symbol of excellence, a badge of courage, a mark of distinction in the fight for freedom."[55]

The Green Berets became closely identified with JFK. Stewart Alsop, the influential journalist, interviewed Kennedy at length on the principles and parameters of his global strategy and was struck by his commitment to counterinsurgency. "Kennedy has something approaching an obsession about guerilla warfare, and he has studied closely the extensive literature on the subject," he wrote. *Newsweek* agreed, reporting that "the Special Forces suddenly found a new champion: Commander-in-Chief John F. Kennedy. . . . [He instructed the Joint Chiefs that] the Special Forces would no longer languish in the shade of the atomic missile, and they would, in fact, take on a whole series of new duties." JFK's support for the Green Berets became a hallmark of his public image. As one observer noted, "Kennedy's well-publicized interest in the Special Forces made them extensions of the commander-in-chief, just as the Hunters of Kentucky and the Rough Riders had once magnified the respective images of Andrew Jackson and Theodore Roosevelt."[56]

Publicity for the Special Forces exploded. A host of articles appeared in *Time, Newsweek, The Saturday Evening Post, Commonweal, Esquire,* and even *Popular Science* that examined in detail the Green Berets' exhaustive training that included arctic duty in Alaska, jungle duty in Panama, mountain climbing in North Carolina, amphibious tasks off the coast of Virginia, underwater demolition in Key West, and ski duty in Utah. Many of the treatments focused on what one analyst described as "the romantic, movie-script ideas of Special Forces: the behind-the-lines drop, the sub-marine launched rubber raft paddling ashore at midnight." In fact, so many journalists and public figures came to Fort Bragg that the army appointed a special public information officer and set up a standard show for visitors that showed Green Berets blowing up a bridge. The scene occasionally turned bizarre. As the commandos moved stealthily up a creek to overcome two guards, for example, photographers yelled for them to hold up their knives so they would glint in the sun and enhance the shot. When the commandos detonated a large charge of black powder, the bridge did not actually come down, and some reporters complained. If the Green Berets really blew it up every time, the public information officer patiently explained, the army would have to rebuild it repeatedly at great expense. The flood of visitors was overwhelming. "We had Cardinal Spellman last week," he reported wearily.[57]

Kennedy's Green Berets, as they gripped the public imagination, clearly reflected several powerful impulses in the New Frontier. They provided a vivid symbol of JFK's determination to replace a strategy of nuclear confrontation with one of flexible response and counterinsurgency. They were living, breathing answers to the problem of Communist insurgency, which, in his words, demanded "a wholly new kind of strategy, a wholly different kind of force, and therefore a wholly new and different kind of military leadership and training." The *Saturday Evening Post* concurred, noting that through "its special forces, the U.S. Army is developing in all corners of the world the capacity to organize, train, and guide low-level but effective resistance to penetration by Communist guerillas." *Commonweal* described how the Green Berets assisted common people in villages who were resisting insurgency, providing not only medical care but instruction in "the rudiments of self-defense" and the use of firearms and expertise in "techniques of ambush and surprise which enable them to clear guerilla bands from surrounding jungle."[58]

The Green Berets also appeared as intelligent, sophisticated, tough, highly trained modern warriors cast in the mold of Kennedyesque masculinity. Intonations of manliness consistently colored treatments of the Green Berets, with articles describing them as hardy and self-reliant men who balanced courage with maturity and as warriors able to "take care of themselves in a pinch." Observers stressed their facility with languages and range of knowledge, noting that a Special Forces group in South Vietnam included "a Swiss international lawyer, an ex-CIA Harvard man who was fluent in Russian, Japanese, and several other languages, two Yale men with language training . . . a recent ROTC graduate of a Southern college and a former New York City policeman." Much like President Kennedy, the Green Berets became noted for their coolness, intelligence, and strength under pressure. As a Special Forces commander emphasized, "This is no place for the hot-blooded hero type." Major General William B. Rosson, appointed head of the Special Forces in early 1962, served as a model: "One of the Army's toughest combat soldiers, Rosson, at age 43, is also its youngest major general, a Phi Beta Kappa from the University of Oregon, DSC from the Anzio beachhead, and a qualified paratrooper." A lengthy journalistic analysis of the Green Berets summarized their New Frontier masculinity when it described them as "the Harvard Ph.D.'s of the Special Warfare art."[59]

Finally, the Special Forces emerged as Kennedyesque symbols of anti-bureaucratic individualism. Analysts placed them in a long tradition of irregular but potent military groups. "From the French and Indian Wars through Francis Marion in the Revolution, Mosby's Rangers in the Civil War and Merrill's Marauders in World War II, Americans have always shown a gift for unconventional tactics," noted one article. The training of Green Berets, said another, aimed to create "a unique kind of soldier . . . [with] jack-of-all-warfare capabilities" who would be suited to "unconventional warfare, and the thing that makes it any good at all is that it has to attract unconventional guys. . . . [I]t must attract the talented, unconventional soldier, and foster his enthusiasm." The Special Forces would work outside the usual restraints of the military bureaucracy. As Adam Yarmolinsky, an official in the Department of Defense, contended, Kennedy and the New Frontiersmen envisioned a man-to-man scenario where a crack Green Beret would enter the jungle to meet a Communist guerrilla "and they would have a clean fight, and the best man would win, and they would both get together and start curing all of the villagers of smallpox."[60]

Thus the Green Berets emerged as a powerful symbol of the New Frontier's call for manly regeneration. This special group, in concert with the initiatives of Generals Maxwell Taylor and Edward Lansdale, represented not only a reconception of Cold War strategy but a new cultural mind-set. They constituted a military variant of the New Frontier's masculine mystique—the vigorous, pragmatic, anti-organizational, tough-minded male who combined a penchant for physical vigor with intellectual acuity, a yen for cerebral contemplation with a determination to be immersed in the action. Even in the massive bureaucracy of the postwar military establishment, as Taylor and Lansdale and the Special Forces suggested in their own ways, there was room for manly assertion.

This new male ideal also received powerful reinforcement from popular culture during the Kennedy presidency. JFK, a lifelong fan of the movies, embraced this medium as a natural way to enhance his masculine image making. No film played a bigger role in this regard than a Hollywood epic that took the country by storm early in his administration.

TEN

THE SPARTACUS SYNDROME:
KIRK DOUGLAS AND TONY CURTIS

P resident John F. Kennedy, throughout his life, was an enthusiastic fan of the movies who was fascinated by the public and private lives of the stars. As a boy he grew up in a household where the culture of Hollywood played an important role, while as a young man he spent time in Los Angeles mingling with famous actors and dating several beautiful young actresses. After becoming a player on the national political stage, he cultivated numerous connections with figures in the world of entertainment and films and kept abreast of the latest Hollywood gossip. Thus it was no great surprise when the new chief executive, on the third weekend of his presidency, snuck out of the White House on a whim to see a popular new movie playing at the Warner Theatre a few blocks away.

JFK had called Paul "Red" Fay, an old friend and now undersecretary of the navy, a few days earlier and asked him to quietly purchase a couple of tickets in advance. He outlined a plan: eat a quick dinner at the presidential residence, then surreptitiously go to the theater for the show and enter a few minutes after the lights had gone down to avoid disrupting the audience. But the Secret Service got wind of the ploy and pried the details out of Fay. So when he and the president showed up at the theater, a comic episode unfolded. The manager of the Warner was waiting at curbside to greet them. Then the movie, which had already begun, was stopped and rewound to replay it from the beginning for JFK as the audience, unaware of what was going on, hooted and clapped in unison. When the pair sat down, they noticed that all of the seats behind them were empty and roped off (at the instruction of the Secret Service). During the intermission, the theater manager escorted them into his office, where he had laid out a huge spread of liquor and hors d'oeuvres, for some uncomfortable small talk. To complete the farcical atmosphere, upon returning, the president spotted Secretary of Agriculture Orville Freeman and his wife seated in the row in front of them. Leaning over, he joked, "Haven't the leaders of the New Frontier got anything better to do with their time than spend it going to the movies?" Freeman replied, "I wanted to be immediately available on a moment's notice if the President wanted me." Both men laughed.

The movie was *Spartacus*. This Hollywood epic was on its way to becoming a blockbuster hit, widely acclaimed by popular audiences and destined to win four Academy Awards and three Golden Globes, including as best dramatic picture of the year. It would also become Universal Pictures' most profitable film for the next decade. Bobby Kennedy had seen *Spartacus* previously and recommended it to his brother, and the president loved the film. As the theater lights came up and the crowd turned around to leave, they saw President Kennedy and applauded vigorously as he smiled and waved and said, "It was a fine picture, don't you think?" Upon leaving the theater, he told a *New York Times* reporter, "It was fine." Privately, his reaction was much more enthusiastic. According to Fay, JFK's "total absorption" was obvious during the viewing, after which he talked about it at length. Later, Kennedy would list *Spartacus* among his very favorite movies.[1]

It is little wonder that the president loved the film. *Spartacus*, in the vein of popular culture, brilliantly expressed many aspects of JFK's worldview. Its story of a rebellious slave army striking blows against the authoritarian empire of Rome offered an allegory of the contemporary Cold War struggle for freedom against Communist tyranny. More directly, the movie projected key aspects of Kennedy's masculine mystique: a crusade for freedom led by a set of heroes in the prime of vigorous manhood, a group of individualist mavericks who excel in unconventional warfare and combine physical prowess with intellectual aspiration, keen pragmatic judgment with an ethos of action. In addition, the two movie stars who played the most heroic characters—Kirk Douglas and Tony Curtis—were themselves enthusiastic Kennedy supporters. In real life as well as on the silver screen, these two influential actors presented a striking Hollywood representation of the president's new masculine ideal. *Spartacus*, in several aspects, offered a cinematic representation of many of the deepest cultural impulses of the New Frontier.

In a broader sense, however, JFK's jaunt to see this popular movie transcended the particulars of the occasion. It reflected his larger love of Hollywood, its acolytes, and its creations. In many respects, the young president was a creature of American filmmaking, both as a consumer of its products and as a public figure who embodied much of its flavor and style. The mingling of the politician and the silver screen offered a seductive package.

Jack Kennedy grew up immersed in the lore and imagery of Hollywood films. His father, Joseph P. Kennedy, had earned a fortune in the 1920s and early 1930s when he branched out from financing and investment banking and entered the world of moviemaking, where he would end up running three film companies, two studios, and a national chain of theaters. He also became a powerful producer who oversaw a number of film projects. As the elder Kennedy cut a swath through the power structure of the film world, he also embraced its glamorous, uninhibited spirit by beginning a lengthy affair with the actress Gloria Swanson. This powerful film mogul was able to secure early copies of new films to show (and impress) family and friends. When he became the American ambassador to Great Britain for the Franklin Roosevelt administration, he procured first-run films for private showings, once even doing so for the royal couple. As one observer concluded, Joe Kennedy was "dazzled by Hollywood, and loved to use its glitter on others."[2]

For the second Kennedy son, as for his siblings, the movies were a powerful influence on his development. At Hyannis Port, the children saw a movie nearly every night, which thrilled them and impressed their visiting friends. "I remember the Kennedys had a movie theater down in the basement of the house," recalled one of them. "The paterfamilias [Joseph P. Kennedy Sr.] used to get films as soon as they were ready. I mean first run films, and he'd show them in the basement." The children were well aware of their father's special "friendship" with Swanson, who would grandly sweep into the Kennedy compound for visits in a Rolls-Royce driven by a chauffeur in a wine-colored coat. But of all the Kennedy offspring, Jack seemed most smitten by the allure of Hollywood. He was excited when his father returned home with the newest movies, especially cowboy films, and was absolutely thrilled when they were accompanied by the outfits of Tom Mix (one of the cowboy stars of the age). Joe's stories of Hollywood life entranced his son and cultivated an interest that grew stronger in succeeding years.[3]

In the fall of 1940, after graduating from Harvard, Kennedy enrolled at Stanford University. While blasé about his courses in the business school, he showed great enthusiasm for traveling to Southern California to spend time in Hollywood. His good friend Chuck Spalding was working for Gary Cooper, and Kennedy would talk with Spalding for hours about how the famous actor had achieved stardom and maintained his charismatic persona. Kennedy attended several Hollywood parties and chatted with Clark Gable and Spencer Tracy. He even shared an apartment for a time with a young actor named Robert Stack, who later went on to star in the hit television show *The Untouchables*. Stack later related how Kennedy was effortlessly attractive to women: "I've known many of the great Hollywood stars, and only a very few of them seemed to hold the attention for women that Jack Kennedy did. . . . He'd just look at them and they'd tumble."[4]

A few years later, after World War II, JFK again visited the movie capital in the spring of 1945 along with his friend Pat Lannan. The two checked into a suite at the Beverly Hills Hotel and met Spalding in the lobby, where they learned he had sold his book, *Love at First Flight,* to Cooper for a movie. Young Kennedy and his friends had lunch with Walter Huston, the actor, and were invited to a party one evening hosted by Sam Spiegel, the producer. They also went to a party at Cooper's, where they met Sonja Henie and were taken on a tour of her palatial house. A short time later the trio was invited for afternoon cocktails at Olivia de Havilland's home, and

Spalding later recalled JFK's amorous behavior. "Jack was just fascinated with Olivia de Havilland. He put himself out to be as attractive as he could be. He leaned toward her and fixed her with a stare and he was working just as hard as he could, really boring in," he reported. "Then, taking his leave, Jack, unable to take his eyes off Olivia, put his hand on the doorknob and walked straight into the hall closet! Tennis rackets and tennis balls and everything came down on top of his head. We broke up."[5]

Kennedy's fascination with Hollywood soon became entangled with his rapidly developing taste for pursuing beautiful actresses. During his 1940s jaunts to Tinseltown, he flirted with Henie and de Havilland and had an affair with the actress Gene Tierney, who was married to the fashion designer Oleg Cassini. He also dated starlets such as Angela Greene and Peggy Cummins. This attraction to Hollywood women would become a lifelong compulsion. As one historian of Kennedy has concluded, "Like his father, he was strongly attracted to beautiful girls who were climbing the ladder in show business or Hollywood."[6]

Kennedy sensed the similarities between the charisma demanded of the movie star and the charisma demanded of the modern political candidate. In 1946, after his congressional primary victory in Massachusetts, the young politician again visited Spalding in Hollywood and was fascinated by image making among stars in the movie capital. "Why did Cooper draw a crowd? And the other people out there: Spencer Tracy and Clark Gable and others who were floating through that world," Spalding noted. "So even though he was terribly self-conscious about it, he was always interested in seeing whether he had it—the magnetism—or didn't have it. We'd spend hours talking about it." During this same trip, JFK met Charles Feldman, the powerful Hollywood talent agent and lawyer, and they became good friends. In subsequent years, he would see Feldman and often stay at his house. He met a number of movie stars through Feldman and dated several of the agent's clients.[7]

Throughout the 1950s, as Kennedy's advancing political fortunes took him into the U.S. Senate, his Hollywood connection grew stronger. His sister's marriage to the actor Peter Lawford provided new access to the movie star community, and JFK's subsequent friendship with the singer and movie star Frank Sinatra took him even deeper into the heart of

Hollywood. By the time of his 1960 candidacy for the presidency, Tinseltown had embraced the handsome, glamorous young senator as one of its own. A host of movie stars and entertainers hosted fund-raisers, appeared in commercials, and personally campaigned for his election.

Kennedy's own movie star aura became a key part of his appeal. A constant drumbeat of public commentary noted his "movie star good looks." Norman Mailer especially recited a litany of film images: "the matinee idol, the movie star come to the palace to claim the princess," and "a great box-office actor"; "he was like an actor who had been cast as the candidate"; "like Brando, Kennedy's most characteristic quality is the remote and private air of a man who has traversed some lonely terrain of experience, of loss and gain, of nearness to death, which leaves him isolated from the mass of others." Following his election, JFK's Hollywood ethos went on public display as a cavalcade of stars from Hollywood and Broadway entertained the new president and the victorious tribunes of the New Frontier under the directorship of Frank Sinatra. Two years later, the United Artists chief, Arthur Krim, organized the famous birthday bash at Madison Square Garden where Marilyn Monroe presented her seductive version of "Happy Birthday" to the president.

As he settled into the White House, Kennedy's preoccupation with the movies became evident in his screening of new films. Actually, it appeared one day after his election, when the president-elect greeted family and a few friends at Hyannis Port, accepted their congratulations, and then suggested heading off to the theater. Ben Bradlee described this as a characteristic impulse: "In the early moments of John Kennedy's great historical life, he went to the movies. When in doubt, go to the movies." Throughout his term in office, JFK screened forty-eight films in the small theater at the executive mansion. Because of his chronically bad back, aides first put a rocking chair in the front row of the White House theater and later a special bed where he could watch propped up on pillows. One of the presidential secretary Evelyn Lincoln's jobs was to keep a current list of movies available from the Motion Picture Association. But JFK made the choices, and they revealed not only his taste in films but the broader cultural sensibility that lay behind it.[8]

President Kennedy favored adventure movies, westerns, war films, dramatic mysteries, and an occasional romantic comedy. Not surprisingly, the chief executive's taste held sway. In November 1962, when Ben Bradlee and his wife were at the White House, JFK wanted to see a movie, and when Jackie read off the list of available choices, he selected "the one we had all unanimously voted against, a brutal, sadistic little Western called *Lonely Are the Brave.*" Throughout his years in office, Kennedy chose other westerns such as *Cimarron, Red River, Bad Day at Black Rock,* and *The Sundowners,* an Australian western starring Robert Mitchum. Kennedy also liked World War II films such as *The Guns of Navarone* with Gregory Peck, David Niven, and Anthony Quinn; *The Great Escape,* with Steve McQueen and James Garner; and the Humphrey Bogart classic *Casablanca.* Given his enthusiasm for the book, it was no surprise that the president asked to see the film version of *The Ugly American,* starring Marlon Brando, in February 1963.[9]

Sometimes JFK favored romantic comedies and lighter fare. In the middle of the Cuban missile crisis, he celebrated Khrushchev's conciliatory letter by watching the charming *Roman Holiday,* starring one of his favorite actresses, Audrey Hepburn. But he did not care for another winsome Hepburn showcase, *Breakfast at Tiffany's.* In August 1961, JFK screened the Cliff Richard musical movie *Expresso Bongo* with an unnamed female companion when Jackie Kennedy was out of town. Along with the Bradlees, the First Couple screened *The Seven Deadly Sins,* a comedic French movie with seven segments, each done by a different director, on the seven major sins enunciated in the Bible. The president clearly liked sexy movies, such as two films that dealt with the theme of an older woman's affair with a younger man: *Girl with a Suitcase,* with the Italian bombshell Claudia Cardinale, and *A Cold Wind in August,* starring Lola Albright as a stripper. (However, he left early from a Roger Vadim movie about a sexy vampire, *Blood and Roses.*) Kennedy also enjoyed "the cool and the sex and the brutality" of the James Bond movie *From Russia with Love.* On the last weekend of his life, in Palm Beach, Florida, at his father's house with his old friends Dave Powers and Torbert Macdonald, he watched the bawdy comedic romp *Tom Jones.*[10]

White House intellectuals tried valiantly, but with little success, to attract Kennedy to sophisticated art-house films. Arthur Schlesinger, who in addition to his duties as presidential adviser reviewed films part-time for *Show* magazine, alerted the First Couple to new releases that he judged meritorious. They were often cosmopolitan art films, a genre that appealed far more to the First Lady than to the president. Schlesinger succeeded in getting *L'avventura* on the schedule—this dense, reflective movie by Michelangelo Antonioni had enchanted the critics—but Kennedy found it so slow paced that he had the projectionist skip to the final reel. *Last Year at Marienbad,* a surrealistic critical triumph by the director Alain Resnais, caused a similar reaction as the president walked out after twenty minutes. William Walton, the artist, tried to pique JFK's interest in the films of the notable French new wave director François Truffaut. But the president quickly grew bored with the lack of excitement and drama, Walton reported, and would "yawn and get up and leave. He just didn't dig it at all." Jackie's relative Gore Vidal, the novelist and screenwriter, made some headway, however, in attracting him to European films with a sexual theme. According to one report, "A proud libertine, Vidal was delighted that Kennedy enjoyed Fellini's *La Dolce Vita*, the antithesis of Anglo-Saxon puritanism."[11]

President Kennedy also took a keen interest—indeed, he actively participated—in several Hollywood projects that veered close to the political world of Washington. He was fascinated with *Advise and Consent*, Otto Preminger's adaptation of the novelist Allen Drury's bestselling thriller about political maneuvering in the national capital. For several weeks in September 1961, the company was in Washington on location shooting scenes for the movie, which starred Henry Fonda, Charles Laughton, Walter Pidgeon, and Burgess Meredith, as well as Kennedy's brother-in-law Peter Lawford and an old girlfriend, Gene Tierney. Some White House staffers even appeared as extras. The president kept close tabs on the film's progress, and according to the journalist Laura Bergquist, "he got so excited he kept calling to find out what was going on. He didn't want to be left out, he was curious." On September 21, he and the First Lady hosted a large, elegant White House luncheon for Preminger and the cast where the stars of the New Frontier mingled with the stars of Hollywood.[12]

JFK played a key role in the genesis of *The Manchurian Candidate*. Adapted from Richard Condon's popular novel, this 1962 film starred

Frank Sinatra and was produced by his company, while John Frankenheimer directed. It tells the dark, complex story of a Korean War hero
who is captured by Chinese Communists and brainwashed and returns
home programmed to commit murder. He becomes the pawn in a scheme,
masterminded by his manipulative mother, to assassinate a presidential
candidate and sweep into the White House a right-wing senator who is
actually a Communist agent. The plan is barely foiled by the heroic efforts
of Sinatra's character. Because of the film's sensitive political content,
United Artists worried that Kennedy would oppose it and threatened to
cancel the project. Sinatra, still on good terms with the president at that
point, visited him in Hyannis Port and explained the situation. Kennedy
replied, "I love *The Manchurian Candidate*. Who's going to play the
mother?" He then called Arthur Krim, head of the studio, to reassure him
about his support for the film. According to Sinatra, the president kept in
touch about the production and "was really interested in the facts of the
project." After *The Manchurian Candidate* was completed, he arranged
a private screening at the White House on August 29, 1962, almost two
months before its official premiere.[13]

Kennedy became particularly absorbed in several films about himself.
He closely monitored the making of *PT 109*, the Hollywood rendering
of the famous World War II incident that had created his image as a war
hero. The president's involvement ranged from script control to approving
the actor who portrayed him. JFK's interest in his own screen image also
extended to real-life productions. On the weekend after his famous trip to
Berlin, where he delivered his famous speech in June 1963 to hundreds of
thousands of cheering Germans ("Ich bin ein Berliner"), Kennedy ran
three newsreels of the trip for family and friends. "He was watching the
Berlin speech, and he started clapping," one of his aides recalled. "He was
not being egotistical. He was transported outside himself to the movie
image."[14]

JFK became involved in a famous trio of documentary films that portrayed his efforts in landmark fashion. The filmmaker Robert Drew approached the candidate in 1960 and proposed a documentary that would
follow his primary contest with Senator Hubert Humphrey in the crucial
state of Wisconsin. Drew suggested that he and his crew would follow

Kennedy for five days on the campaign trail and then do the same with Humphrey to see how they handled the demanding grind. The filmmaker told Kennedy that he would not have to do anything—just go about his normal activity and try to forget that the camera was there. After obtaining both candidates' consent, Drew created a new kind of documentary that became known as cinema verité: using a handheld camera that filmed action in sync with the sound that was right in the middle of the action, no interviews, no requests to do things for the camera, events captured in real time, and minimal commentary and voice-over narration. *Primary* (1960) not only represented a groundbreaking approach that highlighted a "you are there" feeling but depicted Kennedy as a natural star who effortlessly projected charisma, personality, and a made-for-film image as he was greeted by adoring crowds.[15]

The success of this experiment prompted a lengthier working relationship. Drew approached Kennedy after his election and suggested they cooperate in creating a new kind of history of the presidency, one that would capture events in the moment and convey "the expressions on people's faces, the mood of the country, the tensions in the room." Imagine, said Drew, if you could see what Franklin Roosevelt went through with Pearl Harbor and the launching of World War II. Intrigued by the idea, JFK agreed to cooperate. So Drew and his team filmed portions of the inauguration and then set up in the Oval Office to record several days of the new president's day-to-day schedule and activities. The result was *Adventures on the New Frontier* (1961), an unprecedented look into the work of the chief executive. Kennedy's natural ease before the cameras paved the way for the last film in Drew's cinema verité trilogy, *Crisis: Behind a Presidential Commitment* (1963). It covered the president over two days, June 10 and 11, 1963, during the confrontation at the University of Alabama as he grappled with Governor George Wallace and his refusal to allow the enrollment of two African American students. The film's candid portrait of strain and drama was striking as the young president maneuvered against Wallace, federalized the National Guard, and succeeded in forcing the integration of the university.[16]

Kennedy's multifaceted immersion in the world of movies thus prepared the ground for his much-publicized viewing of *Spartacus* in the earliest days of his administration. This epic film set in ancient Rome, which was setting attendance records all over the United States, appealed mightily to the president's cinematic sensibility. More important, it projected in myriad ways the spirit and underlying values of the New Frontier.

Spartacus emerged from a tradition of epic Roman films that had appeared in the 1950s as part of Hollywood's response to television. These "toga and sandal" movies, with their emphasis on grand, sweeping, big-screen stories, often involving large casts and thousands of extras, included such popular efforts as *Ben-Hur* (1959), *The Robe* (1953), and *Quo Vadis* (1951). *Spartacus* took shape when Kirk Douglas, the famous Hollywood actor, became intrigued by Howard Fast's novel of the same name and bought the movie rights. He financed the project with his own production company, became the executive producer, took on the lead role, and struck a distribution deal with Universal Pictures. *Spartacus* premiered in October 1960 and went out to national theaters over the next few months. The critical reaction was mixed, but the popular response was overwhelmingly favorable as crowds flocked to see it. Audiences were thrilled by its dramatic gladiator fights, the grandeur of ancient Rome, panoramic battle scenes with thousands of extras, and a tender love story. It ended up with several Oscar nominations, robust attendance records, and record profits.[17]

    Spartacus tells the true (if cinematically embellished) story of a slave revolt in first-century B.C. Rome. Its protagonist, a fiery Thracian slave, leads his fellow trainees in an uprising at a gladiator school in Capua. These highly trained slave fighters sack several Roman estates to gain money as hundreds of escaped slaves who have learned about the rebellion flock to join their band. Soon Spartacus stands at the head of a ragtag army that badly frightens the leaders of the Roman state. The Roman leaders send out several military expeditions to defeat the slaves, but Spartacus, forced by circumstances to arm and train his men, proves to be an inspiring commander and shrewd tactician. He defeats every force sent against him. Deeply alarmed, the Roman Senate finally delegates Marcus Crassus, a powerful consul and aspiring dictator, to lead a crack Roman army against the rebels. Using great military force, utter ruthlessness, and unsavory tactics (he bribes the pirates who have agreed to convey Sparta-cus's force away from Italy), Crassus finally brings the insurrectionists to bay and defeats them in the climactic scene of the movie. At the movie's conclusion, Crassus crucifies several hundred surviving rebels along the Appian Way leading to Rome as Spartacus's wife and son escape to free-dom to keep alive the spirit of the slave leader.

Embedded in the narrative of *Spartacus* were several themes that took the film out of the historical context of ancient Rome and into the culture of modern America, where it resonated powerfully in the atmosphere of the New Frontier. As one analyst of the movie has written, "*Spartacus* is not a lesson in Roman history, but it is a lesson in how Americans con-ceive of history and themselves." Most notably, the film appeared as a Cold War allegory depicting a struggle for liberty by freedom fighters. It cast "the long twilight struggle" against Communism, as President Kennedy had termed it in his inaugural, back into the world of ancient Rome. Au-diences responded viscerally to the inspiring story.[18]

Yet the politics of the film proved tricky. Some feared that the leftist reputation of the author, Howard Fast, and the screenwriter, Dalton Trumbo, would make the movie a thinly disguised parable of revolution by the oppressed. When news of the film first broke, it was denounced by several conservative groups and Hollywood figures such as John Wayne and Hedda Hopper. But when *Spartacus* appeared, it offered little in the way of revolutionary rhetoric. Douglas's production company issued study guides, pamphlets, and press releases that stressed the film's advocacy of "the struggle for freedom, both physical and spiritual," its hero's "passion for human rights and dignity [that remains] an inspiration to this very day," and "man's eternal desire for freedom."[19]

In fact, *Spartacus* presented audiences with a mainstream defense of freedom against vast state power and tyranny. It demonstrated an American-style devotion to liberty posed against a Communist-style au-thoritarianism. The opening narration sets the stage by explaining for viewers the "pagan tyranny of Rome" and noting "the age of the dictator was at hand." Subsequently, as the gladiator leader and his followers strike blow after blow at the power of Rome, they movingly testify to the human desire for liberty. When Spartacus is asked why slaves are ready to die for freedom, he explains, "When a free man dies, he loses the pleasure of life. A slave loses his pain. Death is the only freedom a slave knows. That's why he's not afraid of it."

This message was not lost on reviewers of the film, who consistently commented on its Cold War implications. According to *Time*, *Spartacus*, despite its screenwriter's "personal predilection for the 20th century's most crushing political orthodoxy . . . has imparted a universal passion for freedom and the men who live and die for it." *Life* observed, "Antiquity was full of iniquity, the film says, but the fires of liberty flickered." The *New York Times* noted its "freedom-shouting script," while *Variety* described Spartacus as "driven by a desire to be a free man, to walk with his head held high." The *Hollywood Reporter* described it as a mainstream American film with "nothing more subversive . . . than is contained in the Bill of Rights and the Fourteenth Amendment." Even the Daughters of the American Revolution chimed in, hailing *Spartacus* as "a lesson in freedom and man's sacrifice in the name of it."[20]

The movie consistently depicts Spartacus's foe, the Roman state, as tyrannical and authoritarian. From the gladiator school owner to the political leaders in the Senate, the power brokers of Rome appear power hungry, manipulative, and greedy. The Roman army, the instrument of state power used to crush the rebels, marches through the film as regimented, almost robotic killing machines with no evidence of individuality or humanity. Crassus, the cynical and ambitious consul, best expresses the sinister power of Roman authority when he warns fellow senators in the middle of the slave revolt, "The enemies of the state are known. Arrests are in progress. The prisons begin to fill. In every city and province, lists of the disloyal have been compiled. Tomorrow they will learn the costs of their terrible folly, their treason." In the prevailing context of the Cold War, Roman tyranny suggested an obvious modern counterpart in Communist dictatorship. As one commentator on *Spartacus* has concluded, the movie presented American audiences with "a Cold War sermon in historical guise."[21]

Once again, the national media drew a clear parallel between the authoritarianism of Rome and that of modern Moscow. One magazine described a Roman leader as a demagogue who was "as hilarious and frightening as

Khrushchev in a bed sheet." In *Variety*'s words, "The desire for freedom from oppression that motivates Spartacus has its modern counterpart today in areas of the world that struggle under Communist tyranny."[22]

Spartacus rounded out its Cold War allegory by consistently evoking Christianity. In essence, it presents the leader of the slave revolt as a messianic precursor to Jesus and the power of Christian virtue. The film's opening narration observes that the slave uprising occurs in "the last century before the birth of the new faith called Christianity, which was destined to overthrow the pagan tyranny of Rome." In a key scene, Spartacus stands on a hill and addresses his rapt followers in a fashion similar to the Sermon on the Mount. At the film's conclusion, Spartacus is crucified. Suffering intensely, this Christlike figure promises from the cross a kind of resurrection to Varinia as his wife hurries to escape with their infant child: "Take care of my son. . . . Tell him who I was and what we dreamed of. . . . As long as one of us lives, we all live." For most viewers, the movie clearly mirrored the Cold War contest between American Christianity, with its holy cause of freedom, and the tyranny of godless Communism.

Spartacus, however, also conveyed another Kennedyesque theme. The film made clear that a certain kind of man was required to sustain the long, arduous struggle for freedom. Not surprisingly, given JFK's enthusiasm for the movie, the film unfurled a banner for the masculine mystique of the New Frontier. It presented a vision of the Kennedy ideal of manhood, only outfitted in the tunics and gladiator regalia of the ancient world instead of tailored suits or hiking boots. *Spartacus* showed previously despondent and downtrodden slaves gradually realizing their own manhood as they resist the power of an authoritarian Rome. The movie's portrait of full-blown, assertive masculinity took several forms.

Spartacus presents the band of ex-gladiators as fighters and poets who combine physical and mental powers, virility and reflection. The movie delighted in beefcake shots of the gladiators, frequently stripped down to their loincloths, as virile figures with muscular physiques and bulging muscles. Their fights in the training arena especially highlight the conditioning, vigor, and physical prowess of these manly figures. At the same time, Spartacus and his fellow fighters display considerable intelligence and even a kind of sophistication. The head trainer at the Capua school sets the standard when he explains, "A gladiator is like a stallion. He must be pampered. You'll be bathed, oiled, shaved, massaged, taught to use your heads. A good body with a dull brain is as cheap as life itself." This melding of mental qualities into the masculine equation becomes a crucial factor in the rebellion's record of success, particularly in its leadership. Although Spartacus broods about his meager education and illiteracy, his native intelligence comes to the surface, and he develops into a shrewd strategist and organizer as he forges his motley band of followers into an effective and victorious fighting force.

As the revolt gathers momentum, Spartacus and his fighters display another side of the Kennedy manly ideal as they develop irregular tactics and innovative approaches to warfare that help them vanquish their powerful foes. They organize a nighttime surprise attack that destroys the first Roman force sent against them. As the slaves train to become soldiers, they learn the individualist combat tactics of their gladiator trainers, not the highly organized, almost mechanical formations and tactics of the Roman legions. In the ultimate battle with Crassus, Spartacus's army temporarily gains the upper hand when they send flaming logs rolling downhill into the massed legions relentlessly assaulting them. These Green Berets of the ancient world demonstrate guerrilla-style combat skills that would have been welcome at the Special Forces center at Fort Bragg.

Generally, a spirit of masculine regeneration permeates the rebel army as thousands of ex-slaves joyously throw off their shackles and claim independence. "I'd rather be here, a free man among brothers, facing a long march and a hard fight, than to be the richest citizen of Rome, fat with food he didn't work for and surrounded by slaves," Spartacus tells them. As they prepare for the final battle, he proclaims to his followers, "We've fought many battles and won great victories. . . . I know that, as long as we live, we must stay true to ourselves. I do know that we're brothers, and I know that we're free." A famous scene at the end of the film highlights the importance of the rebels' manly bond. When the victorious Crassus, fearful of the slave leader's legacy, tells the survivors that he will spare their lives if they identify Spartacus, they rise to their feet in unison shouting, "I'm Spartacus," to protect him. It is an emotional affirmation by this masculine band of brothers.

Finally, the vigorous sexuality of Kennedy's masculine mystique permeates *Spartacus*. Throughout the film, the healthy, manly sexual appetite of the rebellious gladiators is highlighted. At the Capua gladiator school, visiting Roman matrons drool over a lineup of masculine specimens as the sexual power of these physically imposing fighters is on full display. When the gladiators train and fight successfully, they are rewarded with slave women who are brought to their cells to spend the night. Yet despite such eroticized images, Spartacus resists being reduced to mere animal physicality. Even though intensely aroused by the beauty of Varinia, the young woman who is brought to pleasure him in his cell, he refuses to engage in barnyard rutting. "Go away, I'm not an animal," he tells her.

The film also contrasts the wholesome sexuality of Spartacus and his followers with the decadent, perverse sexual urges of the powerful classes in Rome. Aristocratic Roman matrons ask that the gladiators be minimally clothed—just enough to "preserve modesty," as one of them coyly expresses it—during their brutal fight to the death, while the masters of the school seek voyeuristic gratification by gathering lasciviously around a ceiling grate to watch when Varinia is brought to Spartacus's cell. Roman sexual depravity appears most dramatically, however, in the bisexuality of the haughty Crassus, an urge that scandalized, indeed horrified, American audiences in the early 1960s. In the movie's "snails and oysters" scene, Crassus attempts to seduce the handsome slave Antoninus in a bathhouse before he flees to join the rebellion. The libertine Roman leader tries to convince the young man that any kind of physical pleasure is good, regardless of moral considerations. As his new body slave washes him in the bath, Crassus inquires seductively if Antoninus likes eating both snails and oysters, or if he considers the eating of one to be moral and eating the other to be immoral. When the slave hedges, Crassus observes, "Taste is not the same as appetite, and therefore not a question of morals. . . . My taste includes both snails and oysters." This dramatic scene highlights the lewd sensuality of the Romans and contrasts it with the upright, straightforward sexual energy of the manly rebels. As *Time* observed in a review of *Spartacus,* Laurence Olivier's Crassus is "a voluptuary of power, a moral idiot whose only feelings are in his skin."[23]

Ultimately, President Kennedy's favorable public reaction to *Spartacus* cemented its identification with the Cold War sensibility and assertive masculinity of the New Frontier. The president, noted Red Fay, was an attentive viewer of the movie on that cold winter evening in February 1961. He was riveted to the screen, and during the show remarked favorably on the acting and characters. "I was conscious of his total absorption despite the occasional nervous gestures," said Fay. "Sometimes he tapped his teeth lightly with his index finger, or brushed the hair off his forehead with the full palm of his hand. But always those heavy-lidded eyes were intent on the film." When it ended, JFK engaged Fay in a spirited conversation. "He thoroughly enjoyed *Spartacus*," reported his old friend. "His intimate knowledge of the history of the period and his comments on various leaders of that time made the characters in the film come alive almost as contemporaries." Kennedy would list *Spartacus* as one of his favorite movies, a recommendation that, in the words of one film critic, made for "the single most important endorsement" of the film as it began its stratospheric climb toward popularity and profit.[24]

On his way out of the theater, JFK stopped to pick up a brochure created by Universal Pictures, titled *Spartacus, Rebel Against Rome*. Given the president's voracious appetite for history, it seems likely that he read this paean to New Frontier masculinity. The booklet presented Spartacus as "one man . . . who led an inspired crusade for freedom against the most powerful state on earth" and performed "a miracle of leadership engineering. He was a slave, with no organized government behind him, no trained soldiers at his beck and call, no stores of weapons and food upon which to draw . . . and in his humanity and intelligence far above the status of a slave." The rebel leader, the brochure continued, eschewed any form of bureaucracy because "the cement that held them together was not the carefully planned campaign of a regular government but the hatred of their lot, hatred of their oppressors, the desire for freedom. . . . Spartacus supplied the spark, the brains, the sustained counsel that almost succeeded." He was a man with a charismatic "personality and genius for leadership" whose crusade for liberty almost toppled the might of Rome, a sentiment that must have appealed mightily to JFK.[25]

In many ways, the JFK-style masculine mystique of this popular movie was also realized in two of its leading male characters. Spartacus and Antoninus, partners in the slave rebellion, engage the viewer's sympathy through much of the film as they struggle against the cynical, corrupt voluptuaries among their Roman foes. The two rebels—one a sensitive warrior who thirsts for knowledge, and the other an intellectual who wants to fight for freedom—present heroic studies in contrast. Yet they converge as two halves of the masculine mystique. Portrayed by the actors Kirk Douglas and Tony Curtis, these manly figures appeared as ancient applicants for positions in the New Frontier.

As a charismatic young actor in the late 1940s and the 1950s, Kirk Douglas made an indelible presence on the silver screen. With his deeply cleft chin, sharp features, wavy hair, clenched-teeth voice, firm jaw, and muscular body, he exuded an intense, straining physicality that threatened to erupt at any moment. Douglas made a string of films that highlighted this powerful screen presence as he played tough figures—boxers, sailors, soldiers, policemen, cowboys, artists—who confront obstacles and struggle to overcome them and impose their will on the world. In pre–World War II films, Hollywood's leading men had often been elegant, debonair, understated, yet outlandishly idealized and heroic figures whose film characters came from the same mold. By the 1950s, however, male movie stars increasingly projected harder, more realistic, antihero characteristics that were more Humphrey Bogart than Cary Grant. Douglas personified this new type as he dominated the screen with a passionate, physically imposing, deeply masculine style. It would make him one of the biggest movie stars in Hollywood by the late 1950s.

Douglas had been born in upstate New York to a poor immigrant family of Russian Jews. His family lived in near poverty, and he worked as an errand boy and stole food from the local grocery when he was hungry before finagling entrance into St. Lawrence University. Holding down several jobs to get through school, he starred on the wrestling team, became head of the drama club, and was elected president of the student body. He earned a scholarship to the prestigious American Academy of Dramatic Arts in New York and then won a couple of minor Broadway roles. After serving in the navy during World War II, Douglas returned to the stage and secured small parts in several Hollywood movies.[26]

Douglas finally got his big break when he won the lead role in *Champion* (1949). Based on a Ring Lardner short story, this film tells the story of a boxer who ruthlessly battles his way to the top with little sense of ethics or gratitude. Douglas's bravura performance led to a nomination for an Academy Award as best actor. Over the next decade, Douglas starred in a series of popular movies that made him one of the biggest stars of the silver screen, including a tormented police officer in *Detective Story* (1951), a hard-driving movie producer in *The Bad and the Beautiful* (1952), a roustabout sailor in the lavish Walt Disney production *20,000 Leagues Under the Sea* (1954), the agonized genius Vincent van Gogh in *Lust for Life* (1956), the tough but compassionate French army colonel in *Paths of Glory* (1957), and a lethal Norse warrior in *The Vikings* (1958). As a leading student of his career has noted, this intense, intelligent actor was "particularly effective in parts dealing with hard, ruthless men."[27]

Douglas established an image as the vibrant tough guy of physical strength and emotional resilience who never hesitated to stand up for himself and what he believed in. This sensibility seemed ingrained both in his hyper, passionate nature—his college training as a wrestler underlined his rugged physicality and competitive spirit—and in the strong movie characters he played. In a 1954 piece titled "Hollywood's Muscle Men and Pin-Up Pretties," the fan magazine *Movieland* described Douglas as "the man who's been a Hollywood favorite since he bared his chest in *Champion*." His friend John Wayne took him aside after his role of Vincent van Gogh in *Lust for Life* and said, "How dare you play a weakling, an artist who commits suicide?" When Douglas protested that it was all just make-believe, Wayne replied passionately, "Tough guys like us have an *obligation* to keep up that image for the audience." Douglas acknowledged his inspiration from Teddy Roosevelt's famous praise for the strenuous life and the man who "is actually in the arena; who knows the great enthusiasm, the great devotion; who at best knows in the end the triumph of high achievement; and who, at the worst, fails while doing greatly, so that his place shall never be with those cold and timid souls who know neither victory nor defeat."[28]

Douglas polished his vigorous, masculine image. He went big-game hunting in Africa for three weeks in the early 1960s at the invitation of *True*, the men's adventure magazine. There he discovered a natural aptitude for shooting: "I shot everything—guinea fowl, gazelles, impalas, oryx, zebra, leopard, a 1,200-pound eland, the largest of the antelopes. I tracked them, killed them, skinned them. Once I got started, it mushroomed. I experienced a feeling of power," Douglas reported. The local tribesmen inducted him into their tribe, gave him a shield and spear, and dubbed him Killer Douglas. In Hollywood, the actor gained a reputation for making himself heard and brooking no insults. Otto Preminger, the powerful producer, was notorious for bullying rages that sent underlings running and left many actors cowering. But not Douglas. "Once, he raised his voice in a nasty way toward me," the actor noted. "I walked over to him, nose to nose. In a very low voice, I said, 'Are you talking to me?' That was the end of it. He never insulted me again." Some people, however, disliked Douglas's forceful personality. When one of his early movies became successful, the columnist Hedda Hopper snipped, "Now that you've got a big hit, you've become a real son of a bitch." He replied airily, "You're wrong, Hedda. I was always a son of a bitch. You just never noticed before." Even Douglas's good friend Burt Lancaster introduced him for an award by saying, "Kirk would be the first person to tell you he's a very difficult man. I would be the second."[29]

Douglas's masculine manner was enhanced by his reputation as a sex symbol. The actor's physical allure was obvious, with one film historian describing him as "an icon of fifties male beefcake." The passionate young actor became noted for a long series of affairs with a wide variety of women, including some of Hollywood's leading actresses. These occurred, by his own admission, both during his bachelor days and during his two marriages. "Sex is a powerful drive and it rears its ugly—or beautiful—head at unusual times. For a man, anyway, it has something to do with proving himself," he mused. "Man is not a monogamous animal. You get lonely, far from home, from family. I've been guilty, during my marriage, as much as anyone else. Maybe more." He dated or had trysts with a long string of actresses and celebrities including Ann Sothern, Marilyn Maxwell, Joan Crawford, Rita Hayworth, Patricia Neal, Gene Tierney, Evelyn Keyes, Irene Wrightsman, Ava Gardner, Marlene Dietrich, and Pier Angeli. Douglas's philandering ranged more widely. While in the Bahamas shooting Disney's *20,000 Leagues,* for example, in the evenings he would go to Nassau to throw dice at the craps table. One night he saw a beautiful blond woman sitting nearby, whispered in her ear to meet him at his car in space 402 in the parking lot, and when she appeared took her to his hotel room for the night. While in Jamaica for the same film, he often saw attractive young women dancing and singing calypso songs and, he said, regularly "would take them up to my bungalow."[30]

Douglas gained a reputation as a determined individualist willing to buck the power of the studio system. As a rising star, he increasingly bridled at film studios' contractual authority, an arrangement that forced actors to do films and then manipulated profits into studio coffers. So in 1955 he revolted and founded Bryna Productions, a personal company named after his mother, and began securing, developing, and completing film projects. It was partly a matter of profits, of course, but also a matter of creative control. He insisted on having a bigger say in the making of movies. "I insist on being heard," he declared. "I don't object if they [producers and directors] don't accept my suggestions. All I ask is that they listen to me. . . . Of course, they have the last word. Forming my own company gave *me* the last word."[31]

It was Douglas's involvement in a movie project about a slave rebellion in ancient Rome, however, that elevated him to the top of the Hollywood hierarchy. In 1957, he read the novel *Spartacus* by Howard Fast and immediately concluded it would make a great movie. So he bought the rights, and Bryna Productions launched the project with Douglas as both executive producer and star. The undertaking brought Douglas a ton of headaches because numerous problems accompanied the making of this epic film. Troubles began with Fast, whose original screenplay "was awful—sixty pages of lifeless characters uttering leaden speeches," in Douglas's words. Then he had problems with actors. Jean Simmons, who played Spartacus's love interest, required surgery that put her out of commission for many weeks. Laurence Olivier, who played Crassus, was depressed during much of the shooting over the breakup of his marriage with Vivien Leigh, who was suffering from mental illness. Peter Ustinov, owner of the gladiator school, ran wild on the set, inflating his role at every opportunity and mugging and improvising to dominate every scene in which he appeared. Charles Laughton, who played Crassus's senatorial opponent, constantly lobbied for more lines and scenes. Finally, the corpulent actor came to Douglas's dressing room dressed in his toga and carrying a thermos of his favorite beverage—a "bull shot" of beef bouillon and vodka. Drawing himself up, he said imperiously, "I wish to inform you that I have notified my solicitors. I intend to take legal action against you and your company." An incredulous Douglas told him to take a place in line.[32]

If all this were not enough, Tony Mann, the director, was overwhelmed by the scope of the movie after several weeks of shooting, and Douglas had to find a replacement midstream. He chose Stanley Kubrick, an up-and-coming, youthful director who had worked with him earlier on *Paths of Glory,* a critically acclaimed film about World War I. "There were two things I knew about Stanley. First, even though he was only thirty, he had the talent and self-confidence to step in and take over a picture of this size," Douglas later explained. "Second, his self-confidence often bordered on arrogance." But Kubrick, who would go on to become a legend in the movie world, caused his own problems during the filming with his own enormous ego and haughty manner. In fact, many of the cast and crew began calling him "Stanley Hubris" behind his back.[33]

The sheer scope and size of *Spartacus* created its own complications. Cost overruns plagued the project as the epic took over a year of shooting to complete and more than doubled the original budget, making it at the time one of the most expensive movies ever made. The battle scenes required a host of extras. Many were filmed in Spain, with the Spanish army providing over eight thousand men, but the arrangement involved a cash payment to the "charity" of Generalissimo Francisco Franco's wife and an agreement that none of Franco's soldiers be depicted dying on film. For the final crucifixion scene, elaborate directions that indicated moaning, groaning, and writhing were given to the victims on the crosses. But Kubrick, the perfectionist, was unhappy with one figure on a distant cross who wasn't doing anything. He angrily sent an assistant to investigate, but there was still no response. When the assistant returned, Kubrick confronted him, and the assistant replied wearily, "It's a dummy, a mannequin." The cast exploded in laughter.[34]

But the biggest difficulty Douglas faced with *Spartacus* concerned the Hollywood blacklist. During the anti-Communist crusades of the 1950s, a number of screenwriters and actors had been ostracized and denied work by the studios when their Communist sympathies had become public knowledge. Thus the involvement of Howard Fast, whose avowed Communism and refusal to testify before a congressional committee had landed him in jail in the early 1950s, immediately raised hackles. Then Douglas chose Dalton Trumbo, perhaps the most famous and talented of the blacklisted screenwriters, to rewrite the script. Douglas hid this controversial decision by having Trumbo work under the pseudonym Sam Jackson but then decided to confront the blacklist by giving Trumbo screen credit under his own name. This move sparked great controversy.[35]

This blockbuster movie was finally completed, however, and the character of Spartacus powerfully projected Douglas's masculine image to the American public. The passionate, charismatic leader of the slave rebellion against Rome seemed to capture perfectly Douglas's persona of the man's man searching for deeper knowledge. The actor once described his understanding of the famous character he played: "Spartacus is an animal at the start, illiterate, evolving into a man reacting against circumstances, then acting on his own ideas and becoming a leader." In other words, he is a heroic figure who fights the restrictions binding him and marshals his talents and resources to create a genuine life. This character suggested an inspiring example for men mired in a stifling atmosphere of bureaucracy, suburban family, and feminine influence in late postwar America.[36]

As played by Douglas, Spartacus dominates the screen as a ferocious warrior for liberty. He demonstrates his physical courage at the opening of the film when, in chains, he attacks an abusive guard at the Thracian mine and hamstrings him with his teeth. In the gladiator arena, he fights with fierce intensity, and when the revolt explodes at the training school, he drowns a domineering trainer in a vat of soup and stabs a soldier in the throat. But Douglas's Spartacus is no mere physical brute. As the rebellion gathers force and attracts escaped slaves from all over Italy, he evolves into a strategic thinker as he organizes thousands of motley followers into an effective force and skillfully formulates battle plans. Spartacus evolves into a military maverick and political tactician who consistently outmaneuvers the Romans against all odds. Moreover, lamenting his lack of education, he desperately seeks knowledge about every aspect of the world around him.

Most important, Douglas's Spartacus emerged from a mold of the cold warrior battling for freedom. When the Roman state moves to crush the uprising, the rebel leader captures a pursuing army and sends its general back with a message: "Tell them we want nothing from Rome. Nothing except our freedom!" When he shares a last private moment with Varinia, his pregnant wife, before the climactic battle, Spartacus tells her, "I pray for a son who'll be born free." Even after being defeated, the unbowed leader declares, "Just by fighting them, we won something. When just one man says, 'No, I won't,' Rome begins to fear. And we were tens of thousands who said no." The film continually juxtaposes the freedom-loving slave leader with Crassus, the dictatorial opponent determined to crush him. The general and consul ruthlessly seeks to destroy Roman traditions and consolidate power in his own hands. "This republic of ours is something like a rich widow," his senatorial opponent, Gracchus, says sardonically. "Most Romans love her as their mother, but Crassus dreams of marrying the old girl—to put it politely." But Crassus's military victory rings hollow. When a youthful Julius Caesar asks the consul if he fears the slave leader, he confesses, "Not when I fought him; I knew he could be beaten. But now I fear him, even more than I fear you." Crassus ultimately loses his masculine competition with Spartacus.

As *Spartacus* soared in early 1961, Douglas made common cause with President John F. Kennedy. The actor/producer deeply appreciated JFK's public endorsement of the film and understood its importance. When Bobby Kennedy once kidded Douglas that his brother had really made *Spartacus* with his much-publicized attendance, Douglas happily acknowledged, "Yes, he did," and expressed his gratitude that JFK "became a number one fan of the movie." In fact, Douglas had a personal and political connection with the president that stretched back several years and granted him membership in the Kennedy Circle. The actor had first met JFK in the mid-1950s at a party held at the home of Charles Feldman, a prominent Hollywood agent. Feldman "pointed out a slim, handsome fellow in his thirties. The girls seemed to be taken with him," Douglas noted, and then heard Feldman comment, "He's going to be President of the United States." In 1960, Douglas helped raise funds for the Massachusetts senator and campaigned for him during the presidential contest. They even had a common girlfriend, the actress Gene Tierney, whom both men had dated in earlier years.[37]

Douglas, because of his close association with Frank Sinatra and the Rat Pack, also looked favorably on Kennedy. The actor described Sinatra as "one of my best friends in the business," they had homes near each other in Palm Springs, and their paths crossed frequently in the world of Hollywood moviemaking. Douglas visited Las Vegas in the late 1950s when the Rat Pack was performing and became the object of one of their pranks. Sinatra and Dean Martin insisted that the actor use the new sauna room at the Sands. So he took off his clothes, went into the steam room, sat down, and saw through the mist a beautiful young girl sitting next to him, completely naked. Instead of being nonplussed, Douglas chatted with her for a while and then walked out. He saw Sinatra and Martin waiting to enjoy his flustered state and cash in on their practical joke, but Douglas said casually, "That's a real nice guy in there," and sauntered off. Douglas and Sinatra also shared a hatred of the blacklist. Sinatra had hired a blacklisted screenwriter in 1960 for his new film, *The Execution of Private Slovik*, but then released him when an angry Joseph Kennedy gave him an ultimatum over his son's campaign. The singer railed about the "right-wing bastards" who had cornered him but urged Douglas to stand firm with Trumbo and *Spartacus*. "They're going to try to do this to you, too," Sinatra angrily told his friend. "You can't let them win. Somebody has got to kick 'em in the balls until they stay down."[38]

Douglas's politics meshed smoothly with those of the moderate Democrat occupying the White House. "I've always been a strong Democrat—but I don't hate Republicans," he once wrote. "I've never been a Communist, but I don't hate them either. I think that's what America is all about." In later years, while respectfully disagreeing with much of his political agenda, Douglas would maintain a close friendship with President Ronald Reagan and often visit the First Family, both in the White House and in California. This moderate sensibility influenced *Spartacus*. While buying the rights to Howard Fast's novel and hiring Dalton Trumbo, Douglas did not adopt their extreme leftist politics. "I am not a political activist," he explained later. "When I produced *Spartacus* in 1959, I was trying to make the best movie I could make, not a political statement." He saw *Spartacus* as a story about human freedom. It was, he declared in 1960, "an American statement by an American film company about the cause of freedom and the dignity of man." Here was a message guaranteed to elicit a positive response from JFK.[39]

When Kennedy entered the White House, the friendship with Douglas flourished. The actor deeply admired the young leader for his political energy and style. He observed of the president (and the First Lady), "Here was someone vital, full of health, handsome. They were so beautiful, the two of them. The prince and the princess." He believed JFK's election had an electric effect as the youthful leader "got people inspired, excited about their country, motivated. There's no doubt about that." As the New Frontier unfolded, Bobby Kennedy asked Douglas to represent the United States at a film festival in Colombia, and JFK asked the actor to become a "good will ambassador" for the United States, a mission that eventually sent him to destinations such as Turkey, Germany, India, Hong Kong, Greece, Yugoslavia, and the Philippines. Kennedy's warm feelings for Douglas were obvious. The movie he insisted on seeing in the White House titled *Lonely Are the Brave*—the one disparaged by Ben Bradlee as a "brutal, sadistic little Western"—was a Kirk Douglas film.[40]

In early 1963, the president asked Douglas to serve as co-master of ceremonies (with Gene Kelly) at a celebration of the second anniversary of his term in office. After the festivities, Bobby Kennedy invited Douglas to his McLean, Virginia, home for dinner and then said, "Let's drop over to see my brother." So the Douglases became part of an informal party at the White House, along with the English ambassador, David Ormsby-Gore, George Burns, and Carol Channing, where all the attendees gave impromptu vocal performances. Douglas offered a boisterous version of "Red Hot Henry Brown," and later he and his wife followed Jackie to see the famous

Lincoln Bedroom, where they found Rose Kennedy propped up in bed reading a book. The actor and his wife were thrilled by the event. "It was an evening of gaiety, of youth, of a bunch of camp kids sitting around on the floor, drinking beer, everybody getting up to entertain," reported the actor. "Anne and I were awed by the whole evening."[41]

Douglas's friendship with President Kennedy played a key role in launching another project: a movie version of *Seven Days in May*, the popular novel about a right-wing military coup against a sitting U.S. president. After reading the novel, the actor believed it would make a wonderful film, and he came to Washington, D.C., to consult with the writers. Invited to a fancy buffet dinner, he was standing in line with his plate when a familiar voice said, "Do you intend to make a movie out of *Seven Days in May*?" It was JFK. For the next twenty minutes, he bent Douglas's ear with various recommendations about transforming the book into an "excellent movie." The president's intense interest in the fledgling film came from his experience with General Curtis LeMay, who had walked to the edge of insubordination during the Cuban missile crisis, and General Edwin Walker, who had been fired from his command in Europe after being caught indoctrinating troops with John Birch Society materials. According to Arthur Schlesinger, "Kennedy wanted *Seven Days in May* made as a warning to the generals." The president was so enthusiastic that he even permitted filming at the White House and outside on Pennsylvania Avenue for crowd scenes.[42]

In such fashion, Kirk Douglas emerged as a member of the Kennedy Circle whose cinematic endeavors reflected the masculine ideal of the New Frontier. Another major actor in *Spartacus* created a similar image. Both in his film character and in his personal life as a Hollywood star drawn to politics, he exemplified many of the impulses and values of Kennedy's "new generation of men" with their combination of vigor, intellect, and sophisticated energy.

In *Spartacus*, perhaps the most sympathetic character other than the rebel leader is Antoninus, a young poet and teacher who instructs the children of the Roman nobility before fleeing to join the rebellion. He becomes a surrogate son to Spartacus, laboring to become a fighter while also inspiring the insurrectionists with his epic poems and stories. Antoninus symbolizes the other dimension of the New Frontier's male ideal—the worldly, "cultured" figure of intellectual vigor—alongside Spartacus's physical prowess and courage. The actor who played this inspiring figure, Tony Curtis, also joined his good friend Kirk Douglas as a keen Hollywood supporter of President John F. Kennedy.

Curtis came to the cast of *Spartacus* in a curious fashion. He was under contract to Universal but wanted to escape, and working in this movie would be another step toward filling his quota for the studio. So he called Douglas, an old friend, and campaigned for a role. "I'm kind of hurt there's no part in it for me. Don't you love me anymore?" Curtis asked, jokingly. "It doesn't have to be a big part. A couple of scenes will be enough to get rid of one of my commitments to Universal." All the characters had been filled, but Curtis was so insistent that Douglas and Trumbo took the minor role of Antoninus and expanded it to become the best friend and emotional support for Spartacus. Given Curtis's status as a major Hollywood star, it was a smart move that added even more popular appeal to the film.[43]

Curtis had been born in the Bronx, New York, as the oldest of three sons to Hungarian Jewish immigrants. With their father scratching out a living as a tailor and their mother suffering from schizophrenia, the children spent time at an orphanage at one point. Curtis joined a local gang, played hooky from school, and shoplifted from local stores. After graduating from high school, he enlisted in the navy following Pearl Harbor and served in the submarine force in the Pacific. While on active duty, Curtis and his shipmates had one movie aboard ship, *Gunga Din*, and the crew watched it so often that they learned by heart the dialogue and the characters. The young New Yorker developed an uncanny impersonation of Cary Grant and would amuse his shipmates with it. As Curtis noted, Grant "was the personification of what a man should be. Cary could be funny, sure, but he could also be smart, or tough. . . . But he had manners, too. He would light a woman's cigarette for her, and his clothes were always impeccable."[44]

After the war, Curtis attended the City College of New York and then studied acting. A talent agent was struck by his good looks and signed him to a contract with Universal Pictures, and he arrived in Hollywood in 1948 at age twenty-three. He gained small parts in several movies and then moved upward into starring roles in B-grade adventure movies during the early 1950s, marrying the beautiful actress Janet Leigh in the process. Curtis got his big break when Burt Lancaster chose him to co-star in his hit film *Trapeze* (1956), and he went on to star in films such as *Sweet Smell of Success* (1957), *Kings Go Forth* (1958), where he worked with Frank Sinatra, and *The Defiant Ones* (1958), for which he earned an Academy Award nomination for his portrayal of a white racist convict handcuffed to an African American escapee played by Sidney Poitier. His most memorable performance came in the delightful *Some Like it Hot* (1959), alongside Jack Lemmon and Marilyn Monroe. He played a musician who, forced to hide from gangsters after witnessing the St. Valentine's Day Massacre, impersonates a woman in an all-girl band while also presenting an homage to Cary Grant as a fake millionaire out to seduce Monroe.

As he climbed the Hollywood hierarchy, Curtis emerged as a genuine movie star and male sex symbol. His striking good looks—thick dark hair, luminous blue eyes, effortless charm—made him a favorite in movie fan magazines from early in his career. In 1954, *Modern Screen* magazine named Curtis the third most popular actor in Hollywood after Rock Hudson and Marlon Brando. He generated a particular appeal for young women. As early as 1950, while promoting a film, he walked onstage and "the audience of teenage girls, preconditioned by the massive doses of fan magazine publicity, suddenly exploded into a stomping, shrieking near riot," according to one account. Curtis described public appearances in the 1950s where hundreds of girls surrounded him "screaming like I was Frank Sinatra" or where he was hustled from his limousine and there was a roar as "girls started tugging at me." The actor appeared on *The Ed Sullivan Show*, and when the host introduced him, "the girls in the audience all began screaming."[45]

Curtis embraced his heartthrob image and became one of the legendary Lotharios in the movie capital. He had a host of affairs with Hollywood actresses, including Marilyn Monroe and several of his leading ladies. By his own admission, he also ran wild with countless "beautiful girls who were extras and bit players" in his movies, consorting with them in the backseat of his car, in his dressing room, or in a friend's house off Laurel Canyon. "I somehow felt my contract said I could get laid anytime I wanted," he said in jest. "All I needed was a girl who would agree and a place to do it." Billy Wilder, who directed him, joked that the actor was "a man who just liked to wear too-tight pants." Curtis later confessed, "There's no question about the fact that I was driven to conquer every woman I met. I liked to think of myself as quite a ladies' man, and I felt compelled to prove it."[46]

As his star rose in the late 1950s, Curtis also forged links to members of the Kennedy Circle. He met Frank Sinatra and Dean Martin in movie circles, and they quickly became friends. "I became an honorary member of Frank's Rat Pack: I never went on stage with Frank, Dean, Sammy, Joey Bishop, or Peter Lawford, but anytime they had a get-together, I was invited," Curtis noted. "Whenever these guys got up to any kind of mischief, I was there." The youthful actor particularly admired Sinatra as a man who was "independent, a free spirit who never spent time worrying about what other people thought of him." Curtis often visited Sinatra's house to watch movies, listen to music, play with the singer's elaborate electric trains, and socialize. They went out to dinner in Los Angeles or traveled to Vegas to play blackjack or craps. They also shared a penchant for beautiful young women, habitually gathering a bevy of showgirls for late-night parties in Sinatra's suite at the Sands hotel. Curtis, with his good looks and elegant yet mischievous manner, would also become associated with the cult of the secret agent when he earned a television role in *The Persuaders!*, an English television show co-starring Roger Moore. The protagonists, in Curtis's words, were "two millionaire playboys who roamed Europe fighting bad guys. It was similar to James Bond, but perhaps a little more realistic."[47]

Curtis developed a close friendship with Hugh Hefner, frequently visiting the Playboy Mansion, where, in his words, "I met some very friendly Playboy bunnies and I had not even the slightest pangs of guilt about having sex with them." In August 1961, he displayed his sartorial taste in "Tony Curtis: A Fashion Profile" for *Playboy*, where he presented his thoughts on the well-dressed male and resisted the "womanization" of American culture. He insisted that men not allow women to pick out their clothes for them. "Women have managed to invade practically every other area of our lives; I think we should all get together and keep clothes-buying one of those rare moments when a man can relax in a man's world," he said. A few months later, it was announced that Curtis would play Hefner in a forthcoming movie about the life of the *Playboy* publisher. He spent much time over the next few years observing and communicating with Hefner before the project quietly faded away.[48]

Not surprisingly, given his immersion in the world of the Rat Pack, Hugh Hefner, and James Bond, Curtis projected a sophisticated masculine style. He was a skilled artist—one of his paintings was acquired by the Museum of Modern Art in New York—and dressed with impeccable style. As a young female screenwriter testified after going to lunch, "Tony ordered many different good wines, knowledgeably," and was dressed elegantly as a "contemporary Beau Brummel [*sic*]." Curtis, of course, had always wanted to be Cary Grant, and his young guest thought the idea was not so far-fetched. "I joined with Tony in thinking that might be possible, as he was almost as handsome—and cleverer than anyone imagined."[49]

By 1960, Curtis had become a huge movie star. According to one observer, in this period "the most beautiful couple, the reigning King and Queen of Hollywood, were Tony Curtis and Janet Leigh." They became a fixture on the social scene in the movie capital, part of "the Hollywood establishment," and hung out with influential figures such as Debbie Reynolds, Frank Sinatra, Gene Kelly, Danny Kaye, and Henry Fonda. Soon the couple began throwing huge parties at their own mansion on Summit Drive for the movie elite, events that put the couple on magazine covers throughout the country. As Curtis observed, this torrent of publicity presented "Janet and me as the fabulous, ideal first couple of Hollywood. There was no bigger pair. . . . No other husband-and-wife team came close to us until Richard Burton and Elizabeth Taylor, but that was ten years later."[50]

When Curtis joined the all-star cast of *Spartacus,* he brought a powerful masculine star power to the project. But like everything else involved with this epic film, he soon experienced a share of misadventure. He ruptured his Achilles tendon while playing tennis at Douglas's house and had to shoot many scenes masking the cast on his leg. Nonetheless, Curtis kept a sense of humor about this huge, unwieldy movie as problems with finances, personnel, and control mounted. During one particularly chaotic day, he got a huge laugh on set when he wisecracked, "Who do I have to screw to get *off* this movie?" Curtis also managed to maintain his legendary love life, conducting a steamy affair with Mamie Van Doren, the blond bombshell actress who was shooting another movie on the Universal lot.[51]

When *Spartacus* went into movie theaters around the country, viewers saw in Curtis's character of Antoninus several key characteristics of the Kennedy masculine ideal. The handsome young slave has fled the bonds of slavery and determines to become an independent, self-respecting man by fighting in the slave rebellion. Strikingly handsome, with his tousled, curly black hair, slim physique, and luminous blue eyes, Antoninus displays great bravery and determination in becoming a soldier for freedom. When he first appears at the rebel camp and Spartacus asks about his background, the young slave answers meekly, "I taught the classics to the children of my master." The slave leader mocks Antoninus, seeing little value in his skills as a teacher, singer of songs, and magician. But Antoninus persists and soon wins the respect, and eventually the affection, of the rebel chief.

In fact, Antoninus triggers an epiphany in Spartacus, who hears with wonderment the poet recite a poem to dozens of slaves gathered around a campfire: "When the blazing sun hangs low in the western sky, when the wind dies away on the mountain, when the song of the meadowlark turns still, when the field locust clicks no more in the field, and the sea foam sleeps like a maiden at rest, and twilight touches the shape of the wandering earth, I turn home." Deeply affected, the leader confesses that he cannot read but wants to know everything about the world around him: "Why a star falls and a bird doesn't. Where the sun goes at night. Why the moon changes shape. I want to know where the wind comes from." With newfound respect, he tells Antoninus, "You won't learn to kill. You'll teach us songs." Soon, the young intellectual becomes close friends with Spartacus and takes on a crucial task: becoming the "eyes" for his illiterate leader as he reads documents from pirates and Roman officials. In a rebel army full of ferocious fighters and heroic soldiers, the talented, sophisticated Antoninus rounds out the masculine ideal of the warrior-thinker.

Curtis's crucial role in *Spartacus* is fully revealed at the end of the movie. After defeating the rebel army, Crassus rounds up several hundred survivors and crucifies them along the main road leading into Rome. Sadistically, however, he pulls Spartacus and Antoninus from the line and pits them against each other in a fight to the death, trying to disprove "this myth of slave brotherhood." Turning the emotional tables, however, each seeks to kill the other in order to spare him an agonizing death on the cross. Spartacus's superior gladiatorial skills prevail, and he mortally wounds his young disciple. As the rebel leader holds the dying poet in his arms, the younger man whispers, "I love you, Spartacus, as I loved my own father." With tears rolling down his face, the older man replies, "I love you, like my son that I'll never see. Go to sleep." The masculine bond between the two heroes of *Spartacus* could not have been stronger.

Tony Curtis also shared with Douglas strong personal and political ties to John F. Kennedy. The Hollywood star clearly identified personally with the young politician and his charismatic style. The young actor had met JFK in the 1950s on one of the latter's trips to Los Angeles, and they became friends. "Jack was a big fan of Hollywood movies, and of the beautiful women who starred in them," Curtis noted. He also became friends with Joe Kennedy and would occasionally pal around with the older man, taking him to movie premieres and introducing him to Hollywood starlets, whispering, "He's John Kennedy's father," and watching their eyes widen. Curtis and his wife, Janet Leigh, held several fund-raisers for the Kennedy campaign in 1960 at their mansion on Summit Drive—one writer described it as "one of the West Coast glamour way-stations" for the candidate—and then, after the election, hosted a victory luncheon for Jacqueline Kennedy at the behest of Peter Lawford, another friend.[52]

In early January 1961, Curtis was at Joe Kennedy's house in Palm Beach, Florida, when JFK called. His father talked for a few minutes and then told Curtis, "The president sends you his best wishes." After a couple more minutes, Joe said that his son wanted to read him a draft of his inauguration speech and motioned Curtis to come stand next to the phone. He held out the receiver, and they soon heard a familiar voice say, "Ask not what your country can do for you; ask what you can do for your country." In Curtis's description, "The words were absolutely electric; they gave me goose bumps, and I told the president-elect so."[53]

Curtis was invited to the inauguration festivities for Kennedy in January 1961. At one of the big parties after the swearing-in ceremony, the actor was moving through the crowd with his wife when a voice said, "Tony, Tony." It was JFK, who came over for a chat. The president told him that he had recently screened a Curtis movie and one scene was "the funniest thing we ever saw. I just wanted to tell you that." Curtis thanked the president and later recalled, "I knew I wasn't likely to ever get a compliment to top that." Seven months later, in the *Playboy* article that showcased his wardrobe, Curtis was asked about his own male sartorial ideal. The actor replied that one model was Cary Grant and the other was President Kennedy.[54]

Thus the most popular movie of the early 1960s, and its two protagonists, contributed much to the shaping of John F. Kennedy's crusade for a revived manliness. The Spartacus syndrome of physical heroism, individual initiative, and cultural aspiration, all harnessed in the cause of freedom, used the magic of the movies and the skills of Kirk Douglas and Tony Curtis to bring the Kennedy Circle's masculine ideal to life. When the president left the White House on that cold February evening in 1961 for an entertainment respite at the Warner Theatre, he saw a Hollywood vision of manly insurrection and stylish revolt that mirrored his own endeavors.

But if President Kennedy's masculine crusade received historical support from a tale of a long-ago rebellion against ancient Rome, it also received reinforcement from a vision of the future. The race into space presented a new kind of frontier for the vigorous exploits of manly young Americans. JFK became one of the biggest supporters, and beneficiaries, of this adventure.

ELEVEN

MERCURY MACHO:
ALAN SHEPARD AND JOHN GLENN

O n the morning of September 12, 1962, President John F. Kennedy rose to address some forty thousand people assembled in the Rice University football stadium. It was an oppressively hot and muggy day in Houston, Texas, with temperatures already in triple digits, and observers marveled that JFK remained cool and unruffled while others were suffering mightily. According to several observers, people were wilting in the intense heat, especially those sitting in the blazing sun on the speaker's platform. But the president seemed unfazed, appearing "fresh and relaxed," even "chipper" throughout the proceedings. Over the previous two days, Kennedy had inspected the NASA facilities at Huntsville, Alabama, to see an enormous booster rocket and examined the Launch Operations Center at Cape Canaveral, Florida. The following day, he would view the new Manned Spacecraft Center in Houston and then go on to St. Louis, Missouri, to visit McDonnell Aircraft Corporation where Mercury and Gemini spacecraft were developed and built. Now, however, on a blistering Houston day, Kennedy delivered one of the most eloquent speeches of his presidency.[1]

In sweeping and lyrical language, the president unfolded a rationale for the United States' venture into outer space, an enterprise that he had accelerated shortly after assuming office. It was perhaps JFK's greatest clarion call for Americans to embrace the New Frontier. Space exploration, he insisted, was less a matter of economic advantage or scientific achievement than an expression of mankind's curiosity and insatiable appetite for discovery. Leaving Earth's atmosphere for the far reaches of space, he claimed, was "one of the great adventures of all time" and a test of America's grit and determination to be the leading nation in the world. "The exploration of space will go ahead, whether we join it or not, and no nation which expects to be the leader of other nations can expect to stay behind in the race for space," he declared. "Yet the vows of this nation can only be fulfilled if we in this nation are first, and therefore we intend to be first."

With soaring rhetoric, Kennedy connected the space program to the frontier spirit of his administration. His famous pledge to get the country moving again involved facing, and overcoming, daunting challenges, and the venture into space epitomized it. "But why, some say, the moon? Why choose this as our goal?" he asked rhetorically. "And they may well ask, why climb the highest mountain? Why, 35 years ago, fly the Atlantic?" The British explorer George Mallory, he noted, when asked why he wanted to climb Mount Everest, had replied, "Because it is there." For Kennedy, the implication was clear. "Well, space is there, and we're going to climb it, and the moon and planets are there, and new hopes for knowledge and peace are there," he proclaimed. "And therefore, as we set sail we ask God's blessing on the most hazardous and dangerous and greatest adventure on which man has ever embarked."

The president's justification for sending Americans into space resonated with the language of masculine revitalization. In words redolent of male vigor, assertion, and toughness, he claimed that "the United States was not built by those who waited and rested and wished to look behind them. This country was conquered by those who moved forward—and so will space. . . . We must be bold." This quest demanded qualities of bravery, intelligence, and determination, and Kennedy assured listeners that Americans meant to lead it. Then he came to the most stirring passage of the speech. "We choose to go to the moon in this decade and do the other things," he declared, "not because they are easy but because they are hard, because they will serve to organize and measure the best of our energies and skills, because that challenge is one that we are willing to accept, one that we are unwilling to postpone, and one which we intend to win." JFK underlined the significance of the space program. "I regard the decision to shift our efforts in space from low to high gear as among the most important decisions that will be made during my incumbency in the office of the Presidency," he declared.[2]

President Kennedy, in Ted Sorensen's assessment, came to see the conquest of space as the quintessential expression of "the New Frontier spirit of discovery." Just as clearly, this venture embodied the president's masculine mystique with its stress on toughness, virility, sophistication, and a potent combination of action and intellectualism. The astronauts, as the journalist Tom Wolfe observed, embraced a grueling training regimen and took life-endangering risks for a powerful personal reason. As they prepared to blast off into unknown vistas, the stakes for "the brotherhood of the right stuff" involved "nothing less than manhood itself. . . . Manliness, manhood, manly courage . . . A man either had it, or he didn't!" Space, in other words, emerged as perhaps the most prominent arena for the regeneration of masculine vitality that JFK had made the emotional engine of his administration. It became manifest in the Mercury and Apollo programs, undertakings that he boosted powerfully within a few weeks of taking office in early 1961.[3]

As a senator in the 1950s, John F. Kennedy had shown only a casual interest in space exploration. Like many, he was dismayed by the Soviet Union's successful launch of the *Sputnik* craft in 1957 and subsequently voted in favor of establishing the Senate Special Committee on Space and Aeronautics in 1958 and then the National Aeronautics and Space Administration (NASA) in 1959 and 1960. The young politician, preoccupied with foreign affairs, viewed the space race primarily in the context of the Cold War. He worried that Soviet advances in rocketry could lead to more powerful nuclear-tipped missiles and produce an advantage in the global struggle. According to Sorensen, Kennedy believed that America's lagging space effort symbolized "everything of which he complained in the Eisenhower Administration: the lack of effort, the lack of initiative, the lack of imagination, vitality, and vision; and the more the Russians gained in space during the last few years in the fifties, the more he thought it showed the Eisenhower Administration's lag in this area damaged the prestige of the United States abroad."[4]

During the 1960 campaign, JFK came to embrace the space program as a key element in his agenda of national revitalization. In his acceptance speech at the Democratic convention in Los Angeles, he declared, "The New Frontier is here whether we seek it or not . . . [in] uncharted areas of science and space." The Democratic platform accused the Republican administration of remaining "incredibly blind to the prospects of space exploration. It has failed to pursue space programs with a sense of urgency at all close to their importance to the future of the world." During the campaign, the Democratic candidate contended that the United States had to correct the notion that it was standing still while the Soviet Union was on the march. "We are in a strategic space race with the Russians, and we are losing," he argued in a public letter. "Control of space will be decided in the next decade. We cannot run second in this vital race. . . . This is the new age of exploration; space is our great New Frontier."[5]

Upon assuming office in January 1961, Kennedy made several moves to enhance the space program. It did not take much to show progress. NASA had begun Project Mercury in 1959 as a basic program to launch a human being into space, orbit Earth, investigate his ability to perform basic tasks in a weightless environment, and return him safely to Earth. By the summer of 1960, NASA had begun advance planning for Project Apollo with the goal of a lunar landing mission. But President Eisenhower, along with his advisers, remained unconvinced about the value of manned spaceflight and offered little support for these undertakings. Kennedy was more receptive, however. Shortly after taking office, he assigned Vice President Lyndon Johnson to be chair of the National Aeronautics and Space Council and made him the responsible figure for space issues in his administration. Johnson enthusiastically embraced the task. He also appointed James E. Webb, a former head of the Bureau of the Budget and the number two official at the Department of State for Dean Acheson in the Truman administration, the new director of NASA. Both Johnson and

Webb advocated an accelerated space program, and Kennedy responded by approving a NASA budget increase of 10 percent to fund development of more powerful booster rockets.[6]

On April 12, 1961, however, a dramatic incident galvanized Kennedy into action. On that day, the Soviet cosmonaut Yuri Gagarin, launched from a site in central Asia, became the first human being to enter space and successfully orbit Earth. This achievement marked a tremendous propaganda triumph for the Soviet Union as American political figures and media reacted with a concern that rivaled that of the *Sputnik* launch in 1957. "The fact of the Soviet space feat must be faced for what it is, and it is a psychological victory of the first magnitude for the Soviet Union," editorialized *The Washington Post*. Kennedy, who had presented himself as a vigorous, youthful leader determined to get the country moving again, viewed it as a disturbing political setback.[7]

The new president quickly called a meeting of his top space and science advisers in the White House Cabinet Room two days later. The group discussed possible scenarios for American advancement in this area as Kennedy, restless and tightly focused, asked his usual barrage of questions and, in the words of one attendee, impatiently ran his hand through his hair and "tapped the bottoms of his upper front teeth with the fingernails of his right hand." The discussion eventually alighted on the possibility of a manned mission to the moon, where the experts agreed that the country had a decent chance to surge in front of its rival. According to Sorensen, this proposal caught JFK's attention because it embodied his rhetoric about "striving to get this country moving again . . . about crossing 'new frontiers.'" He commented to the group as he left, "There's nothing more important." Later that evening, Kennedy called Sorensen into his office and expressed his excitement about a manned lunar mission, sensing that it "could galvanize public support for the exploration of space as one of the great human adventures of the twentieth century." The adviser emerged and told Hugh Sidey, the *Time-Life* reporter who was waiting to interview the president, "We're going to the moon."[8]

Kennedy unfolded this new vision of space in a special message to Congress on "urgent national needs" on May 25, 1961. In a speech that was nationally televised and often described as his second inaugural address, he told Congress that "extraordinary challenges" faced the United States and laid out initiatives concerning civil defense, economic revitalization, military modernization, and enhanced assistance to countries threatened by Communist expansion. The president outlined his most expansive proposal at the end of the speech, when he noted that in the ongoing battle "between freedom and tyranny" the exploration of space had emerged as a critical consideration. It was now "time for this nation to take a clearly leading role in space achievement, which in many ways may hold the key to our future on earth." But it was more than a race, Kennedy emphasized; it was an expression of the energy and sense of discovery of a democratic society: "We go into space because whatever mankind must undertake, free men must fully share." In a ringing phrase, he declared, "I believe that this nation should commit itself to achieving the goal, before this decade is out, of landing a man on the moon and returning him safely to earth." In the best spirit of the New Frontier, he argued that there was no sense in embracing this difficult task "unless we are prepared to do the work and bear the burdens to make it successful." But Kennedy was convinced Americans were up to the challenge and "will move forward, with the full speed of freedom, in the exciting adventure of space."[9]

Congress embraced Kennedy's proposal, and over the next few weeks both the Senate and the House of Representatives easily passed authorization bills for nearly $1.8 billion to accelerate the American space program. By 1963, under prodding from the White House, the NASA annual budget would grow to $5.7 billion, an increase of over 300 percent. The agency charged ahead with Project Mercury and launched Project Gemini, an intermediate effort aimed at testing more powerful boosters and conducting rendezvous activities while in orbit. NASA also intensified planning for Project Apollo, the program that would actually take a man to the moon by the end of the decade. This tremendous mobilization saw the agency's workforce increase from about 10,000 when Kennedy took office to around 30,000 by 1963, while the contractor workforce at companies such as McDonnell Aircraft and Grumman Aerospace increased from 35,000 to around 200,000 during this same period. NASA also began to build the new Manned Spacecraft Center in Houston, Texas, as the central facility for its operations, with launch sites designated in Florida, Mississippi, and Louisiana and another development center in Huntsville, Alabama.[10]

The national press was swept up in the excitement. *Newsweek* ran a cover story titled "Journey to the Moon: U.S. Timetable" that surveyed the nation's halting steps toward space exploration and then laid out the steps in "the big push" toward a lunar landing. It looked at the technology—ever larger Saturn super-rockets, the Apollo spacecraft—and explained how a lunar journey would proceed from launching a five-stage rocket and escaping the atmosphere, to cruising toward the moon and orbiting it and setting down, to returning and reentering Earth's atmosphere and splashing down. *Newsweek* sketched out for readers what life would be like on Apollo during the eleven-day journey as astronauts performed a variety of technical tasks in a weightless environment, ate specially dehydrated food, and slept on staggered schedules. It described the "bleak domain" awaiting on the lunar northern latitudes as astronauts, wearing special moon suits, would conduct scientific experiments, collect samples, and explore in a setting where there was "no oxygen, no water, no wind, no clouds, no rain, no atmosphere to screen out solar radiation and meteors." After several days, the magazine concluded, the three sojourners into space would return from this "awesome adventure."[11]

In fact, enthusiasm for space became so intense that it caused something of a crisis among journalists. As Project Mercury moved forward, magazines and newspapers inundated the public with stories that were not only informational but celebratory. Occasionally, reporters wrote about problems besetting the enterprise: NASA mismanagement, shoddy workmanship, pork-barrel politics, and great danger facing astronauts in manned missions. Far more often, however, the press was swept up in the excitement of space exploration and emphasized the heroism of venturing into dangerous environments, the human drama of conquering nature, and the mystery of discovering unknown dimensions of life on Earth. With the media moonstruck by the NASA undertaking, questions began to arise. *Newsweek,* for example, asked, "Reporter, dramatist, apologist, educator? What is the role of the newspaper and television men assigned to the space beat?" It noted reporters' struggles with conveying complicated science, the public's ravenous desire for information, and the danger attending coverage of a launch and flight that could blow up at any moment with disastrous consequences. Most of all, the journalist faced a central conundrum: the temptation "to function as rooters for 'The Team'—a role abhorrent to most newsmen."[12]

Life magazine overcame such qualms and took the lead in promoting the space program to the American public. In 1959, the magazine had signed a special contract with NASA, paying $500,000 for exclusive access to the personal stories of the astronauts and promising to portray "one of the most absorbing, dramatic, human stories of our time." *Life* became the leading chronicler of, and cheerleader for, the space program with its adventurous agenda, heroic astronauts, and connection to JFK's New Frontier. It presented breathtaking color photographs and breathless reports, supporting editorials and the astronauts' first-person accounts of their ventures into space. The arrangement with *Life* had a special resonance for President Kennedy, who saw Henry Luce's *Time-Life* empire as the "key to the independent center" in American politics and believed it to be "the most influential instrument in the country."[13]

In the *Life* chronicle of America's space program, several themes dominated. It argued for the necessity of the manned moon program as, first, a matter of national defense: "If we are to win the cold war, we must overtake the Soviet lead in space." Second, it contended that the program embodied the sense of exploration and discovery that compelled the American "to explore every unknown, scale every unattained summit." Third, for *Life* the space program expressed a yearning for knowledge: "Man's everlasting curiosity, his eternal need to penetrate all unrevealed why's and wherefore's, propels him to the moon." In 1963, the magazine compared the space program to the early modern age of exploration that led to the discovery of the New World. "The U.S. commitment to space seems a natural undertaking for the American people, who are a venturesome lot," it contended. "Man's eternal thirst for knowledge, the call of human adventure. That is the Promethean impulse which now beckons."[14]

With this outpouring of support for the space program, increasing attention fell on the crucial figures in this venture: the astronauts of the

Mercury program. At the center of a torrent of publicity, they captured the public imagination as *the* heroes of the New Frontier. Seven in number—Alan Shepard, Gus Grissom, John Glenn, Scott Carpenter, Walter Schirra, Donald Slayton, Gordon Cooper—these space pilots had been chosen after an extremely rigorous screening process in the waning days of the Eisenhower presidency. Now they appeared in a powerful new spotlight, radiating the youthful, full-blooded, masculine vigor of the new president and the Kennedy Circle. As one writer noted pointedly, they bore "little resemblance to the humdrum Average Man." The seven young men about to ride the first American rockets into space displayed in abundance the characteristic qualities of New Frontier masculinity.[15]

We Seven, a 1962 compilation of *Life* magazine pieces, portrayed the astronauts as the heroic centerpieces of the space program. "What kind of man could manage to be part pilot, part engineer, part explorer, part scientist, part guinea pig—and part hero—and do equal justice to each of the diverse and demanding roles that was *[sic]* being thrust upon him?" it asked. "What kind of man would be strong enough physically to sustain the tremendous stresses and strains of a flight through space, and then be wise enough—and strong enough in other ways—to sustain the pressures of public adulation when he returned home? And what kind of man, above all, would be best qualified to help set the rare standards of courage and stamina, skill and alertness, vision and intelligence that would be needed to lead him and his colleagues to the moon?" For *Life,* the answer was obvious. Such men would be "daring and courageous," "cool and resourceful under pressure," "with nerves of steel," "in their physical prime," and "devoid of emotional flaws which could rattle them or destroy their efficiency when they found themselves in a crisis."[16]

A host of publications and commentators followed this lead by delineating the courage, daring, and coolness of the seven Mercury astronauts. They were described as "premium individuals . . . a bright, balanced, splendidly conditioned first team, willing—eager, in fact—to undertake an assignment most men would find unthinkable." Stories noted that as military test pilots, they had "developed an unfailing instinct for making calm, steely, split-second decisions at high speeds and high altitudes." They were willing to "undertake an assignment most men would find unthinkable."

Newsweek observed, "Something in their lean, crew-cut good looks showed they bore a special stamp setting them apart." As the picture of "physical well-being" and "made of the sternest stuff emotionally," the group splendidly reflected "NASA's astronaut image: personable, emotionally resilient, activity-minded rather than passive."[17]

The raft of stories about the Mercury astronauts also made clear that they possessed technological expertise as well as physical courage, abundant intelligence as well as derring-do. It was no accident that the Mercury program rejected a great many accomplished test pilots, such as Chuck Yeager, because of a key flaw. The American astronaut—the male hero of the age—needed a college degree. In an account of the astronauts' training, *Newsweek* disclosed that their regimen consisted of not only intense physical workouts but rigorous, daunting intellectual demands: "a tremendous maze of technical material . . . briefcases stuffed with reports to be read and memoranda to complete . . . a thick Familiarization Manual from McDonnell Aircraft." Their training headquarters was "oddly reminiscent of a college campus," while the astronauts were all "trained engineers, and take an understandably lively interest in their space mission."[18]

Finally, accounts of the Mercury Seven showed them to be rugged individualists who exemplified a pioneering spirit of discovery and conquest. These accomplished and courageous men were eager to explore and subdue the greatest new frontier of them all, outer space. Even though supported by a large team deploying a vast technological array of machinery and computers, they represented the crucial human factor. "While the entire mission can be controlled automatically from the ground, there are over-ride controls that put the astronaut in charge," noted one article. *Time* described the astronauts as "individualists all," while even skeptics of the space program granted that this enterprise provided a special allure: "Where man can go to see and feel with his own sensory organs, to experience with his own mind and nerves and muscles, he should and will go." Rhetoric and imagery connected the astronauts to the spirit of Kennedy's New Frontier. The *New York Times* described these young men as "the young pioneers of the space frontier," while others praised their "frontiersman's drive to stake out new territory" and labeled them the "Daniel Boones of space."[19]

Thus the astronauts appeared before the American public as the crème de la crème of American manhood. As a NASA official explained about the selection process, "We looked for real men and valuable experience." Loudon Wainwright, who covered the Project Mercury flights for *Life,* told readers his primary impression from observing the group at length: they were "better than you at almost everything. Shepard golfs better, Glenn sings better, Schirra water skis better, Grissom and Slayton hunt and fish better, Cooper drives faster better, Carpenter plays the guitar better." In the words of *We Seven,* they were "seven highly motivated individuals, each of whom . . . was determined to make good. Each of the men was, and is, an explosive bundle of personal pride, professional convictions, and private idiosyncrasies." An air force doctor who cared for the astronauts described each of his charges as "a superman. No one else in the world could have gone to bed that night, had a sound sleep, and then gotten up bleary-eyed the next morning when I went in to wake him and acted just as if he were going out duck-hunting or starting on a fishing trip."[20]

The sophisticated energy of Kennedy's New Frontier also encapsulated an additional quality in the astronauts: a manly, virile sex appeal. Their attractive image included a significant portion of macho sexual power. This was suggested in the massive 1962 reception for the astronauts at the Astrodome when NASA moved its headquarters to Houston, Texas, an event that featured a performance by the famous stripper Sally Rand. It was suggested in *Life* magazine stories that often contained shirtless, beefcake photographs of the astronauts in training. It was suggested in the atmosphere in towns near Cape Canaveral, where many of these hotshot test pilots indulged in sexual escapades with female groupies—some were overheard saying, "Three down, four to go"—that finally brought a stern warning from the most straitlaced of the group.

Thus the daring, courageous, physically fit, manly Mercury astronauts provided another bracing antidote to flabby organization men and deskbound bureaucrats. Among these pioneering figures, two quickly emerged as the natural leaders of the group. Intensely ambitious, and supremely self-confident, they became bitter rivals to be the first man into space before their tense relationship ripened into respectful friendship. In many ways, the two astronauts differed profoundly—one a cool, cocky character given to sardonic gibes and fast living, the other a sentimental, pious man given to public statements about God, country, and family. One observer termed them "the bad boy and the altar boy." But they shared something important: the courageous, assertive, high-achieving energy so central to the masculine ethos of John F. Kennedy's administration. Whether preparing to leave Earth for unknown vistas at the space facility in Florida, talking to the press about their role in this mind-boggling adventure, or visiting the White House to receive awards and mingle with the president, these two modern heroes reflected the spirit of a new age in America. As photographers snapped endless photographs and optimistic rhetoric flowed, they represented the space explorer as manly, rejuvenated New Frontiersman.[21]

On the morning of May 5, 1961, Alan Shepard walked toward the Redstone rocket sitting on the launchpad at Cape Canaveral with a tiny space capsule perched atop it. NASA personnel had been working tirelessly for months to prepare this unprecedented flight, and now, after several days of delay, the weather had finally cleared and allowed it to go forward. Shepard would be the first American astronaut to blast off from Earth and enter outer space. Outfitted in a silvery fabric-and-rubber space suit and wearing an oversize helmet with large visor while carrying a portable air conditioner in his right hand, he stopped to gaze up at the enormous missile that would propel him into unknown territory. Then Shepard continued with steps "that were long and brisk—as if to steel him against the nervousness which would be normal in any man who was about to be shot off this earth."

Conveyed to the top of the framework, Shepard squeezed into the small capsule and a seat that had been contoured to his body. He laughed at the prank played by one of the other astronauts who, knowing Shepard's special affinity for sports and women, had taped onto the control panel a sign reading, "No handball allowed in this area," along with a pinup from a girlie magazine. The launch was expected to begin within an hour, but the NASA staff, deeply concerned that any small glitch would endanger the mission and Shepard's life, confronted one small difficulty after another for over four hours. The wait was so long that he finally had to urinate inside his space suit because he feared that his bladder would burst. Finally, an exasperated Shepard exclaimed over the radio, "I'm cooler than you are. Why don't you fix your little problem and light this candle?"[22]

Shepard had gained the coveted spot as the first Mercury astronaut into space as the culmination of a legendary career. In the prime of life at age thirty-seven, he sported a no-nonsense crew cut and featured prominent teeth that were slightly askew and large, intense blue eyes that could quickly change focus from a dazzling smile to an infamous stare that caused others to blanch. Shepard had grown up in New Hampshire and entered the U.S. Naval Academy in June 1941 at the age of seventeen. During World War II, he served in the U.S. Navy before being admitted to flight school. Over the next fifteen years, the young navy pilot was posted around the world. He then graduated from the U.S. Naval Test Pilot School and participated in tests for high-altitude performance, in-flight refueling systems, and carrier landings. This fearless, confident, high-achieving pilot soon gained a reputation for being able to fly anything, and many navy observers commented that he was the best aviator they had ever seen. Nominated as one of 110 candidates for NASA's new Project Mercury, he surprised few of his colleagues when he was chosen for one of the seven coveted spots.[23]

Shepard was intensely competitive. He wanted to be the first and the best at whatever he did, and as a hotshot navy pilot he worked so relentlessly to top any competitors that some saw him as "cutthroat." During preparation training as a Mercury Seven astronaut, he excelled at the rigorous physical and mental tests, and his competitive drive caused him to refer to himself as "the world's greatest test pilot." When he was chosen to go into space first, an observer noted, he "had become the man, the flyboy he always wanted to be. . . . He knew he had won."[24]

An air of cool detachment and supreme confidence, even arrogance, marked Shepard's personality. When he wanted something, he usually got it, and he carried himself with a certain icy reserve and sense of superiority. His self-assurance became legendary. When asked at a press conferences to describe his attitude about heading into uncharted space, he replied matter-of-factly, "It's a matter of confidence. I don't know where the confidence begins, but it's there." This self-assurance made its mark.

The Mercury astronauts, *Life* reported, who "have learned to rate each other's contribution to the team realistically, rank Shepard high on their own private lists." In the words of one, "He's tough and he's firm, and he's usually right." A NASA official told *Newsweek* when the first astronaut was waiting to blast off, "He was cooler out there than we were in here."[25]

In fact, Shepard carried a reputation as a cocky daredevil who lived fast and flouted the rules on more than one occasion. In his early career, the flier flirted with a court-martial for "flat-hatting" when he swooped under a bridge, buzzed a crowded beach, and zoomed low over a parade field filled with navy officers. Shepard loved to drive his beloved white Corvette very fast at every opportunity and relaxed by smoking cigars and downing martinis after a strenuous day of Mercury training. This accomplished test pilot "was stylish and cool and cocky . . . a cynical, smart-ass fighter jock," said one observer. "Shepard was the military version of what Elvis was to music, what James Dean was to Hollywood, what Kerouac was to literature." *Life* described him as "a cool customer and a hot pilot."[26]

Shepard provided a tonic for his arrogant self-confidence with a strong dose of charm, sophistication, and intelligence. Usually, he held others at a distance while coolly studying the situation and keeping his own counsel. But when Shepard so desired, he displayed a captivating personality. A dapper dresser who held himself gracefully, he demonstrated "an easy charm" and spoke out with "poise, authority, and often humor," noted *Life* of this personal dichotomy. He became adept at handling the press. Before his flight, he led reporters on a tour of a missile factory and dazzled them with his insightful, amusing commentary as he confidently strode through the facility in rolled-up shirtsleeves with a cigarette dangling from his lips. When a reporter asked if the press would be invited on the first space shot, he replied, "Yes, in the nose cone!"[27]

As the Mercury mission developed in the early 1960s, Shepard became noted for his sense of humor. Full of sarcastic gibes and sardonic putdowns, he responded when reporters asked him how he was chosen as an astronaut, "They ran out of monkeys." He liked to play pranks on his fellow astronauts, once telling Deke Slayton right before the group entered their first press conference that he had a food stain on his bow tie. Slayton spent much of the session worrying about this faux pas, glancing down frequently but unable to see the bow tie tucked up under his chin. When they came offstage, Shepard confessed, "There's nothing on your tie, Slayton—gotcha."

Shepard's humor also could be lighthearted, even quirky. During the period of Mercury training, he became enamored of José Jiménez, the Hispanic character created by the comedian Bill Dana, and his routine about a reluctant astronaut. Jiménez, a small, self-deprecating Hispanic man, had supposedly been chosen as the first man to go into space but was extremely apprehensive. When asked about the forthcoming flight, he recounted that his preparation consisted of crying a lot and then added in a meek, quivering accent, "Plees, don't let them send me up." Shepard became a huge fan of Dana's album containing these astronaut skits, and when the comic appeared at a nightclub in Florida where the astronauts were training, Shepard actually went onstage to play straight man (although he laughed throughout). Shepard: "Is that your crash helmet?" Jiménez: "Oh, I hope not." Shepard: "Has NASA provided something to break your fall?" Jiménez: "Oh jess, the state of Nebada." Shepard's love of Jiménez's character soon spread to the other astronauts, and he became the unofficial mascot for the Mercury Seven. When Shepard was sitting in his capsule preparing to blast off, Slayton came over the radio and said, "José? Do you read me, José?" When Shepard replied in the affirmative, Slayton said, "Don't cry too much, José."[28]

The first astronaut into space was athletic, having been a member of the varsity rowing team at the U.S. Naval Academy before taking up golf, water-skiing, ice-skating, and handball. In fact, he had mastered the difficult trick of water-skiing barefoot, a feat he liked to demonstrate at every opportunity. At the same time, Shepard's "alert intelligence" surfaced whenever he talked about "anything having to do with the technical and engineering aspects of Project Mercury—he is animated and well informed." With a bachelor of science degree from Annapolis and much experience with sophisticated aircraft, Shepard constantly picked the brains of the Mercury technicians and learned their language to inquire about capsule designs, flight plans, and rocket stages.[29]

A long-standing reputation as a womanizer rounded out Shepard's macho profile. While at the U.S. Naval Academy, he had habitually "gone over the wall" at night to meet young women before sneaking back to quarters. At ease around females, he had a natural social grace and easily attracted them with his panache and charm. Shepard married Louise Brewer in 1945, became the father of two daughters, took in an orphaned niece whom they raised as their own, and remained devoted to his family throughout his life. The marriage would last fifty-three years. Yet Shepard apparently had few qualms about sleeping with a host of attractive women in far-flung postings around the globe as a naval pilot. He had a knack for entering a bar or a party, sweeping the crowd for the prettiest girl in the room, and effortlessly picking her up by the end of the evening. Many of his friends considered his skirt chasing to be a compulsion, but one observer linked it to "new icons of masculinity . . . with raw sexual energy" such as Marlon Brando, James Dean, and Elvis Presley.[30]

Shepard continued his philandering as an astronaut—as did others among the Mercury Seven—in the rollicking setting of Cocoa Beach, Florida. This "harlot of a town," as a visiting journalist described it, stood near Cape Canaveral, where the astronauts and the NASA workforce had moved their operation in the summer of 1960. Cocoa Beach began to boom, and nightclubs such as the Starlight, the Carnival Club, and the Koko sprang up almost overnight. Drinking and carousing in the evenings with the astronauts—no families had accompanied them to the training site—became a common scene as a surfeit of attractive women proved eager to cavort with these virile space-age celebrities. Shepard emerged as the leading Lothario of the group. As always, he moved smoothly and discreetly with his many flings but once crossed the line into a danger zone. During a trip to San Diego on a NASA jaunt with the Mercury Seven, Shepard showed up at the door of a fellow astronaut's cabin and announced, "I think I got myself in trouble." He had gone drinking across the border in Tijuana, picked up an attractive young woman at a bar, and when they were alone, he saw flashes from a camera. The next day, a West Coast newspaper contacted NASA and disclosed its plan to run the compromising photographs. Shepard's colleague rushed into action and spent several hours pleading and pulling strings successfully to get the story killed and avoid scandal. But the wayward Romeo learned no lessons. Subsequently, when his savior stood up and lectured the group about the need to avoid women, Shepard angrily told him to keep his morality to himself. Defending the creed of the "fighter jock away from home," he argued that having female acquaintances was fine as long as it did not impair your work or embarrass the project. Four of the astronauts backed Shepard, and only one supported the moralist in the group.[31]

Alan Shepard, in other words, radiated the vigorous, confident image of the Kennedy masculine ideal. In the best spirit of the New Frontier, Shepard titled his 1962 reminiscence of the Mercury program "The Urge to Pioneer" and explained his strong desire "to do something no one else has ever done—the urge to pioneer and to accept a challenge and then try to meet it." His success in that endeavor, the astronaut continued, boosted his self-confidence: "Every man needs that." Shepard was the prototypical Kennedy male clad in a space suit.[32]

On May 5, 1961, as millions of viewers watched on television, Shepard blasted off from the launching pad at Cape Canaveral and was soon traveling at a speed of over forty-five hundred miles per hour. He became the first American to leave Earth's atmosphere as the separation rockets fired and the capsule separated from the booster. Shepard then navigated the Mercury capsule for several minutes in zero gravity as he looked through his periscope to observe the Florida Keys, north up the Carolina coast to Cape Hatteras, and across Florida to Tampa Bay and Pensacola. After several minutes, the retro rockets fired to begin braking for a return to Earth, and the pilot used his hand controller to get the blunt end of the capsule at the correct angle for reentry. As the g-forces pushed him back into his seat with ten times the force of gravity and the capsule rolled very slowly in a counterclockwise direction, Shepard calmly reported on conditions back to Earth. A small stabilizing parachute opened at twenty-one thousand feet and the main chute at ten thousand feet before the capsule splashed down in the Atlantic near the Bahamas. Shepard was quickly located by a navy helicopter, which lowered a sling for him to exit the floating capsule, and he was whisked to a nearby aircraft carrier, the U.S.S. *Champlain*, where he trotted easily across the deck to the applause of hundreds of sailors.[33]

In Shepard's account of the flight published in *Life*, two themes dominated. First, he explained his intense effort before blastoff to control his emotions and focus his energies to meet an array of pressing demands.

"I began to feel some small effects of the tension that was growing everywhere around me," he noted of the days leading up to the launch. "There were moments when the stomach began to churn around a bit." While he focused on established procedures to calm his mind, he realized that his position might be perilous. "I had made all the financial arrangements possible in case anything happened," he admitted. With butterflies in his stomach and adrenaline pumping at the countdown, he reminded himself, "Okay, buster, you volunteered for this thing. Now it's up to you to do it." He made himself relax and his pulse and blood pressure elevated only slightly. Shortly after takeoff, however, when he entered supersonic speed, the vibrations became so severe that he decided not to report them because "it might have sent everybody on the ground into a state of shock. . . . My mind had probably been made up unconsciously in advance to handle things alone if I could and call for help only if I couldn't." Shepard presented his own profile in courage.[34]

Second, America's first astronaut underlined how he flew the spaceship manually. Directors of Project Mercury wanted to see if a human pilot could control the capsule in space, so control was turned over to him partway through the flight. Switching over to manual control, he found that he could control both the pitch and the yaw of the craft. "Finally, I took over control of the roll motion of the capsule and was flying Freedom 7 on my own," he wrote. The recent Russian cosmonaut, Shepard noted pointedly, had no control over his capsule and "was a passenger all the way." "I was able to stay on top of the flight by using manual controls," he reported. For a nation that prided itself on the efficacy of individual agency and action—and for a Kennedy administration that prided itself on opening avenues for the masculine individual—it was a revealing moment.[35]

Following his successful flight, Shepard became an instant national hero. "While the whole nation watched with a gripping sense of personal and emotional involvement, Shepard soared off into space for the most grueling ride any American has ever taken," one magazine claimed. "The nation caught Shepard's spirit of confidence." *Newsweek* agreed that America's first astronaut had "rallied the nation." Shepard arrived in Washington, D.C., was paraded up Pennsylvania Avenue before one of the biggest crowds ever to assemble in the national capital, and then deftly handled numerous questions at a mammoth press conference. The next day, in New York, he rode in a huge ticker-tape parade up Broadway as thousands lined the street cheering. *Life* put him on its cover seated on his backyard patio over the caption "Shepard relaxes with his fan mail." In the inside story, Shepard exulted, "We'd brought off a good one, right out in the open where the whole world could watch us take our chances."[36]

President Kennedy became closely associated with the man and the achievement. Like millions of Americans, he stood transfixed in front of a television set watching Shepard's flight, even interrupting a national security staff meeting to take in this pioneering event. Kennedy had been deeply worried about the possibility of disaster with this initial mission— he had even tried to dampen coverage of it—and was tremendously relieved when it was a triumph. But even more, as a strong advocate of the space mission, JFK was thrilled with the success of the flight. Indeed, Shepard's success helped inspire the president's message to Congress on May 25, 1961, calling for an American moon mission. According to one report, Kennedy's decision showed that the gloom "cast by Major Yuri Gagarin's spectacular trip around the world, had been dispelled in part by Comdr. Alan Shepard's flight."[37]

Shepard met Kennedy for the first time on the day of the flight after his splashdown. The delighted astronaut reported, "I was even more thrilled at that moment in talking to him than I had been after the flight." A couple of days later, the president presented him with the Distinguished Service Medal from NASA in a Rose Garden ceremony. Kennedy seemed unusually skittish—Shepard sensed he was somewhat in awe of Project Mercury— and when the medal was handed to him, it fell out of the case and onto the ground. Without missing a beat, Kennedy, who was in the middle of a sentence referring to the coveted award, quipped, "Which came to me from the ground up," and went on with his remarks. But then the president forgot to actually pin on the medal, and the First Lady had to remind him to do it. Said Shepard, "He was as nervous as me. . . . [I]t's perhaps the first real indication that I had in an indirect way of how much he was impressed with the program."[38]

Then Kennedy ushered Shepard and the other six astronauts into the Oval Office along with a few NASA officials and several political leaders.

Kennedy listened raptly as Shepard described his flight and seemed interested in every detail. Then the conversation turned to a controversy among the scientists in the space program: Could humans really perform successfully in space, and were they really needed when computers and sophisticated technology could run flights automatically? Every one of the astronauts maintained that a man could operate with great effect in a spacecraft and, in fact, his presence was necessary in order to achieve successful space missions. Shepard spoke strongly and offered his own successful flight as proof. The president asked questions and seemed receptive to the argument for human agency. Then, before the parade up Pennsylvania Avenue, a delighted JFK, on the spur of the moment, took Shepard on an unscheduled visit to a meeting of the National Association of Broadcasters. Shepard received a tremendous ovation, and a crush of reporters and politicians reacted similarly at a Capitol Hill news conference a bit later.[39]

Shepard became friends with President Kennedy, and over the next few years they talked on numerous occasions about the goals and procedures of the space program. JFK was always "extremely interested in it, and even in some of the details of how the flight controllers reacted, how they responded, what their jobs were, and so on," the astronaut reported. Shepard believed that JFK's strong endorsement of Project Mercury and then the lunar mission came partly from a commitment to besting the Russians and partly from a belief that space exploration offered a unique opportunity for "successful demonstration of man's capability." The president established a personal bond with the astronauts and enjoyed their company and the accompanying conversations. The common bond, noted Shepard, was that they were prepared to "recognize a challenge and [were] willing to meet the challenge." With the astronauts, observed a presidential aide, JFK "had found exactly the type of men he needed as allies in his pursuit of new frontiers. . . . He had a great admiration for heroes; anybody who excelled at what they did."[40]

Thus Alan Shepard became a great national hero in the spring of 1961 as an embodiment of the Kennedy male spirit. But he was soon eclipsed. His great rival among the Mercury astronauts would gain even greater public acclaim some ten months later. This subsequent space explorer, as the first American to orbit Earth while the nation watched spellbound, created an even larger and brighter image of the vigorous, challenge-seeking American man as he fled suburban comfort and bureaucratic conformity to confront the test of the new frontier in space.

On April 9, 1959, the Mercury Seven astronauts huddled nervously backstage before walking stiffly onto a stage in Washington, D.C., taking their seats behind a long table, and facing the bright glare of television lights. NASA had called a press conference to introduce the group to the nation, and after some introductory remarks they rose, one at a time, as their names were called out. They received a standing ovation from the horde of reporters filling the room, and then the questions began. It quickly became apparent that the astronauts, for all of their technical expertise, personal courage, and prime physical conditioning, were unprepared to deal with the press. With mock-ups of an Atlas rocket and Mercury capsule propped up in front of them, they were expecting questions about their backgrounds as fliers or the nature of pending spaceflights. They were surprised when journalists only wanted to know what kind of men they were. How did they feel about the prospect of going on a dangerous mission? Did their wives and children support this endeavor? Did religion play a role in their lives and shape their attitudes toward this undertaking? The astronauts either fumbled the questions or answered in clipped, slightly impatient sentences that reflected the cool, laid-back jauntiness of the fighter pilot.

Except one. John Glenn, when his turn came, gave expansive answers that quickly turned into mini-speeches about God, family, and country. He spoke at length about the importance of his wife and children supporting him 100 percent. He explained his deeply held religious beliefs, contending that "a power greater than any of us" gave individuals certain abilities and they were obligated to use them. He proclaimed his love of country and the importance of the space program to the future well-being of the United States. He compared Project Mercury to when "the Wright Brothers stood at Kitty Hawk with Wilbur and Orville pitching a coin to see who was going to shove the other one off the hill down there. I think we stand on the verge of something as big and expansive as that was fifty years ago." As the other astronauts looked on in amazement—they rightly concluded that he was "eating this stuff up"—he utterly charmed the room. Sensing the public's yearning for heroes, and deploying his infectious grin, boyish good looks, and compelling sincerity, Glenn walked out of the press conference and into the public limelight as the most popular member of the group. He became the "God and country" astronaut.[41]

Glenn came to Project Mercury from an all-American background in New Concord, Ohio. He imbibed the stern Presbyterianism of his family, went through the local schools, played football, and married his high school sweetheart. Glenn enrolled in Muskingum College, where he majored in science and learned to fly after signing up for a pilot training course for course credit. He enlisted in World War II as a Marine Corps aviator and eventually flew fifty-seven combat missions in the South Pacific. In the Korean War, he flew ninety-three combat missions and earned the nickname Ol' Magnet Tail because of a penchant for attracting anti-aircraft fire as he was hit on seven separate occasions. In the mid-1950s, Glenn became a test pilot and flew the navy's newest jets at high altitudes, assessing their various capabilities and setting the transcontinental speed record in 1957. Given his illustrious flying record, no one was surprised when NASA chose him to join the Mercury Seven.[42]

Following the 1959 news conference, Glenn quickly became the face of the space program. With a stocky, muscular build at five feet ten inches and 180 pounds, the marine colonel had thinning red hair already leaning to baldness, a ruddy complexion with freckles, a ready smile, and an utterly sincere manner. Sentimental to the core, he "clouded up" listening to good music and got a lump in his throat when seeing the American flag and hearing "The Star-Spangled Banner." A jovial storyteller and convivial friend, he eagerly joined in party singing with a good tenor voice. Introspective and thoughtful, he wrote poetry. Glenn was intensely devout and proudly wore his family values on his sleeve. Completely devoted to his wife, Annie, and two children, he reveled in family life and never attracted the slightest hint of scandal. According to a friend, "John tries to behave as if every impressionable youngster in the country was watching him every moment of the day."[43]

But behind the wholesome image, Glenn exhibited an intense ambition and powerful drive to succeed. This marine test pilot fully shared the competitive, aggressive qualities of the "fighter jock"—assertively masculine, fiercely competitive, supremely self-confident, and instinctively daring. Of all the astronauts, he followed the most rigorous training regimen, running two miles every morning before breakfast, lifting weights daily, and embracing a strict diet of healthy foods. The press noticed Glenn's "headlong drive to excel." "People are afraid of the future, of the unknown," Glenn told a reporter. "If a man faces up to it and takes the dare of the future, he can have some control over his destiny. That's an exciting idea to me, better than waiting with everybody else to see what's going to happen." This led him to an elevated view of what the first American astronauts should be. Glenn saw the Mercury Seven "as the first of a new and even heroic breed of men who have the enormous responsibility of serving as symbols of the nation's future."[44]

Glenn's wholesome, idealistic, vigorous persona made him an ideal representation of the modern masculine ideal. *Life* portrayed the Ohio astronaut as "an engaging, relaxed, American male in the full prime of life." It stressed his great powers of concentration and conviction and explained that he drove himself relentlessly because he believed that "discomfort, even when it is painful, is easily endured if the goal is worthwhile." Two weeks before his flight, *Life* put him on its cover under the headline "Making of a Brave Man."[45]

In the media portraits presented to the public, Glenn appeared as both a physical specimen and highly intelligent. Beefcake shots abounded as he was photographed variously running on the beach in shorts and T-shirt or even shirtless; scantily clad as he disrobed on a navy destroyer after being pulled from the water in the *Friendship 7* capsule; and relaxing after his splashdown, lying shirtless in bed. At the same time, the marine colonel was depicted in his room after a rigorous day of training "reading technical books and papers on space" with great stacks of material surrounding him.[46]

Glenn's full-blooded masculinity made for a Boy Scout version of the Kennedyesque masculine mystique. This was reinforced by his unquestioned position as the dominant male head of his household. For all his devotion to wife and family—in a fashion, this cut across the grain of the Lothario image common in New Frontier circles—the astronaut made clear his sense of masculine mastery. Glenn was the only astronaut not to bring his family within commuting distance of the Mercury headquarters at Langley Air Force Base in Hampton, Virginia, instead keeping them in a suburb of Washington while he took a room for himself in the officers' quarters. While reluctant to pull his children out of their schools, he also wanted no distractions from his training schedule. A journalist for *Life*, while at the Glenn home for an interview, noticed a revealing confirmation of this masculine domination. On the hallway wall hung two framed sheets of writing: "one a magazine page which listed a number of rules to be followed by the properly subservient wife, the other a formal letter calling for closer attention to the rules." The latter was signed, "John H. Glenn, Jr., the Absolute Ruler." From such sources emerged a picture of Glenn as the authoritative, physically honed, mentally focused male who had roused his energies to succeed in a great pioneering quest.[47]

After the Mercury Seven astronauts were chosen, John Glenn and Alan Shepard quickly emerged as the two leading figures in the group. They presented an interesting contrast. Shepard was the cool, cynical, wisecracking, Corvette-driving test pilot with a cocktail in his hand, a cigarette dangling from his lips, and a pretty woman on his arm. Glenn was the churchgoing patriot and family man with the inviting grin, freckles, wholesome sentiments, and tiny Prinz automobile that got forty miles to the gallon. While the two respected each other as skilled fliers, not surprisingly a gap of understanding separated them. Glenn mystified Shepard with his corny jokes, talk of teaching Sunday school classes, and unbending morality. Glenn found Shepard to be enigmatic. "One side of him was cool, competent, and utterly baffling, the other ready to cut up, joke and have fun. He could defuse a tense situation with a wisecrack, and he had a way of being able to relax everyone around him and make them perform better," Glenn wrote later. "There was a part of him, however, that didn't like the restrictions that came with being a public figure."[48]

In particular, the two clashed over the issue of womanizing. Cocoa Beach, with its smorgasbord of sexual temptations that attracted many of the astronauts, horrified Glenn. He objected both on moral grounds and out of concern for the public image of the space program. He offered several muted warnings that were ignored. The situation finally came to a head with the infamous incident in San Diego. Glenn was the colleague Shepard contacted to get him out of trouble when a newspaper photographer caught him in a compromising position with a woman. After killing the story, the Ohioan got mad and, in his own words, called the astronauts together and "read the riot act, saying that we had worked too hard to get into this program and that it meant too much to the country to see it jeopardized by anyone who couldn't keep his pants zipped." Shepard was the one who led the others in telling Glenn he was "foisting my view of morality on everybody else, and that I should mind my own business."[49]

Yet Glenn and Shepard, while rivals with radically different personalities, were not exactly opposites. Both men loved the thrill of high-level flying, were driven to perform great feats, and had a powerful competitive impulse to win at anything they did. As one observer of the Mercury Seven concluded, "They were more like twins—the bad son and the good son, yin and yang." And each was fully confident he would be chosen for the honor of being the first American to go into space.[50]

Thus the NASA decision to pick Shepard left Glenn thunderstruck, then angry and depressed. It was the first contest he had ever lost in his adult life, and he took it hard. He wrote a letter to NASA administrators, arguing that his chastisement of the other astronauts over philandering had made him unpopular (they had been given a vote on who each believed should go first other than himself, and Shepard had won). After his appeal failed, Glenn fell into a brief depression but then buckled down and loyally worked with Shepard as his backup. As the two men trained, ate, and studied together for hundreds of hours, they slowly put their differences aside and somewhat grudgingly developed a genuine friendship. In a fashion, they even grew close. Glenn was the astronaut who put the "No handball allowed in this area" sign and the girlie picture in Shepard's capsule as he entered to prepare for the first flight, a lighthearted act that released some of the tension of the moment.[51]

Fate, however, had saved Glenn for an even greater feat of early space exploration. Following a second, brief suborbital flight by Gus Grissom on July 21, 1961—it ended rather unhappily when, after splashdown, emergency bolts fired and blew the hatch off, filling the capsule with water and almost causing Grissom to drown—Glenn began to prepare for his own pioneering launch. On February 20, 1962, he blasted into space in Mercury's first attempt to orbit Earth as millions of Americans watched on television holding their breaths. He circled the globe three times over a period of nearly five hours, and the flight proceeded smoothly. At one point, Glenn discovered that Shepard had played his own good-natured gag, putting a toy mouse with gray felt and pink ears (it was based on a José Jiménez routine where Bill Dana lamented the fate of experimental mice sent into space) in the equipment bag that floated up when opened. Glenn performed his tasks efficiently as he circled the globe, noting, "Weightlessness is a wonderful feeling—you can get addicted to it." He also triggered a great mystery by reporting the presence of thousands of luminous, yellow-green "fireflies" swirling around the capsule, a phenomenon only later discovered to be tiny bits of frozen condensation on the capsule exterior that broke off as it moved through different temperature zones.[52]

Two crises welled up, however, to put the *Friendship 7* flight at risk. First, the capsule's automatic guidance systems malfunctioned, and Glenn took the controls to fly the capsule manually on its final two orbits. Much more dangerously, about midway through the mission, on-board warning systems indicated that the heat shield on the large, blunt end of the capsule might be coming off, a development that would cause it (and him) to incinerate at a temperature of ninety-five hundred degrees when reentering the atmosphere. Controllers kept the news from Glenn and tried to remain casual as they asked a series of questions trying to confirm or deny the problem. He soon caught on, however, and became aware of the life-threatening difficulty. When Glenn began his reentry into Earth's atmosphere, his nerves and those of NASA experts were on edge while radio contact was lost for several minutes as the capsule plunged back toward Earth. In his words, "Flaming pieces of something started streaming past the window. I feared it was the heat shield. Every nerve fiber was attuned to heat along my spine; I kept wondering, 'Is that it?' . . . The fiery glow wrapped around the capsule, with a circle the color of a lemon drop in the center of its wake." But the astronaut bravely rode out the mission as the heat shield remained sufficiently in place to avoid disaster. According to a NASA official, "Glenn faced his moment of truth inside a fireball." When communication was reestablished, Glenn confirmed that it had been "a real fireball" and admitted after landing, "There were some moments of doubt." *Friendship 7* splashed down right on target, and the capsule and astronaut were quickly picked up and hoisted onto the deck of the destroyer U.S.S. *Noah*. A jubilant Glenn was given a physical exam and debriefed over the next several hours. On a written evaluation form that asked if he noticed any unusual activity during the mission, he answered jauntily, "No, just a normal day in space."[53]

Glenn's successful flight brought a euphoric reaction from the public. Throughout the nation, he was proclaimed as an American hero and became an instant symbol of national pride. A tidal wave of congratulatory letters and telegrams engulfed NASA offices at Cape Canaveral and a host of magazines, newspapers, and public figures trumpeted his achievement. "Colonel Glenn gave Americans their most spirit-lifting day since 1945," said one publication, while a *Time* cover story asserted that his flight "put the U.S. back in the space race with a vengeance and gave the morale of the U.S. and the entire free world a huge and badly needed boost." In another cover story, *Newsweek* concluded that Glenn's achievement "lifted the self-doubt that had plagued the United States since the first Sputnik flashed through the night skies of October 1957." New York City held a ticker-tape parade even larger than the one for Shepard, which *Life* chronicled with color photographs of Glenn and his wife riding through a snowstorm of shredded paper that almost blotted out the view, under the headline "Shower of Glory for a New American Hero."[54]

Glenn strode forward as a triumphant symbol of the modern, invigorated American male idealized in Kennedy's New Frontier. Stories on the *Friendship 7* flight depicted its pilot as a determined, skilled, sophisticated man who heroically overcame the most daunting of challenges. *Time* presented him as "a latter-day Apollo, flashing through the unknown," and claimed that he "seemed almost destined for last week's time of triumph." *Newsweek*, in its cover story, described the astronaut as "one self-reliant, modest, and courageous man." Another publication proclaimed "this awesome and historic moment when he rode his upside-down volcano to a long-awaited date with space" and noted that Glenn and his wife, when they talked on the phone shortly before blastoff, followed the same farewell routine as when he left to fight in World War II and the Pacific. He said, with forced casualness, "Well, I'm going down to the corner store to buy some chewing gum." She replied tearfully, "Well, don't take too long." The columnist James Reston, writing in *The New York Times*, concluded, "Glenn himself is almost as important as his space flight, for he dramatized before the eyes of the nation the noblest qualities of the human spirit."[55]

In particular, Glenn's manual control of the space capsule symbolized a triumph of the individual man in a mechanical age. "By taking over the controls himself and proving that man can 'fly' a capsule through space, Glenn struck a blow for man's genius and versatility," *Time* claimed. For *Life*, the lesson of *Friendship 7*'s successful voyage was that "it would have been impossible without the intervention of the man in the capsule." Added another publication, Glenn demonstrated that a "trained and attentive pilot can be superior to the best-made robot mechanisms in the world. The machine faltered, never Glenn." *Newsweek* characterized Glenn's mission as "the ageless human drama of the individual—solitary, questing, vulnerable—facing the unknown." The astronaut himself insisted that while some of the work in space could be done with instruments, "Only man himself . . . has the imagination, curiosity, and flexibility to notice the smaller facts and take advantage of the unexpected things that crop up. That is why man is needed in space."[56]

In the aftermath of *Friendship 7*, Glenn cemented his national hero status when he was invited to address a joint session of Congress. He gave a bravura performance. Loud cheers and applause, and even a few tears, followed his declaration of love for America, his "hard-to-define feeling deep inside when the flag goes by," and his abiding devotion to his family. Glenn's "unabashed, star-spangled sincerity evoked the pride of the nation," said one account. He captured the spirit of the New Frontier as his words "conjured up a vision not of stellar space but of the tough unity of westward-moving wagon trains." He brought the house down with a self-deprecating story of how Caroline Kennedy met him and the other astronauts at the White House, looked disappointed, and asked plaintively, "Where's the monkey?" When Glenn finished, the audience shot to its feet, applauding wildly, "full of a cleansing, rejuvenating pride in the man, his family, the nation which bore him—and his triumph."[57]

President Kennedy, even more than with Alan Shepard, publicly embraced Glenn as a living, breathing embodiment of the New Frontier. After the successful flight of *Friendship 7*, JFK called Glenn while he was aboard the U.S.S. *Noah* to say how much it "meant to him personally and to the country." Later he went down to Cape Canaveral to present the astronaut a NASA medal. As he came down the ramp from Air Force One and walked toward Glenn, the band started playing the "Marines' Hymn." The president leaned over and asked the astronaut what he usually did for this song, and the marine officer replied that he stood at attention. Glenn was deeply moved as JFK stopped and stood at attention until the song finished. During his remarks, the president praised the astronaut for his "unflinching courage." Glenn noticed that as their personal relationship grew over the years, Kennedy's attitude toward the space program evolved. Originally, the astronaut concluded, JFK had seen Project Mercury largely as a matter of Cold War competition with the Russians. But gradually he came around to endorsing it for reasons of "research and exploration" on their own terms—the scientific discoveries that might be made and the human challenges that could be met.[58]

As Glenn drew closer to Kennedy, the astronaut and his family went to Hyannis Port in early summer 1962 as guests for the weekend and had a wonderful time water-skiing, yachting, and swimming. The hosts included not only JFK and Jackie but also Robert and Ethel Kennedy, who were becoming very good friends of the Glenns'. President Kennedy, the consummate politician, not only admired the astronaut but sensed that he might have a future in the electoral arena. After talking with Glenn in the Oval Office following his successful spaceflight, JFK remarked to an aide, "That character takes a good picture from any angle, he ought to go into politics." Later, Jackie Kennedy told the astronaut that her husband had believed he might have a future in politics and expressed a hope that he "would be interested in continuing public service." Once, JFK gently approached Glenn on the subject, inquiring if he was a Republican or a Democrat, and when the astronaut diplomatically replied that he was an independent, they both laughed.[59]

Throughout their many interactions and discussions, one factor stood out. Glenn observed that JFK, when they met right before his flight on *Friendship 7*, had spoken to him "as one 'guy' to another, if you will." When they talked after his successful mission, the astronaut noted that Kennedy was very interested in his war record and his combat experiences in World War II and the Korean conflict. He asked about the nature of the wartime dogfights and inquired about the experience of blasting off atop a rocket and navigating a small capsule around Earth. "He wanted to know about things that occurred on a space flight—what I saw, what things looked like, how I felt during re-entry, was it hot or not, how did it feel when it banged down on the water, how did it feel when I got out," Glenn reported. "He seemed to be more interested in what had occurred on a personal experience basis rather than the scientific details of the event. What did it feel like to me as a man?"[60]

This manly connection between the heroic astronaut and the youthful president, in fact, loomed large in the culture of early 1960s America. John Glenn came out of Project Mercury as America's greatest hero of the age. Courageous and intelligent, competitive and modest, patriotic and determined, this hardy individual had tested himself as few others ever would and had emerged completely triumphant. Beckoned to the side of President Kennedy, he personified the masculine vigor that the young president had brought into the political arena. JFK, in turn, seemed to draw energy and inspiration from the daring feats of Glenn and his fellow astronauts and presented them as striking symbols of regeneration. Pushing the boundaries of space, Kennedy contended, encapsulated everything he believed that the country, and its men, should be doing.

For President John F. Kennedy, the epic spaceflights of Alan Shepard and John Glenn fit seamlessly into his crusade on behalf of the masculine mystique. As Glenn discerned, the president's original Cold War rationale for the space program was rooted in ideology. "If the world is to judge us by our exploits in space, let's be first," he told a NASA official early in his presidency. "He felt that pre-eminence in space was important to any country that hoped to be a leading country in the world." As the Mercury space program took off in the summer and fall of 1961, however, it gradually took on a deeper meaning for the leader who trumpeted the adventures awaiting Americans on the New Frontier. Colleagues, observers, and family members noticed the change. Robert Kennedy observed that his brother increasingly compared this enterprise "to the explorers in our own country, Lewis and Clark. . . . I think that made a profound impression on him." Hugh Sidey, the journalist who often talked to the president about the NASA programs, reported that JFK compared his role to that of "Isabella to Columbus. . . . I think without question that Kennedy saw this as one of the great epics of mankind, one of the great adventures." Arthur Schlesinger Jr. believed that for Kennedy space "was the last frontier and part of the general human process by which you move ever forward. I think the conquest of space, the exploration of space, was in his mind the ultimate objective." Jacqueline Kennedy reported that her husband became so enveloped in the space program that he kept "exciting new plane and rocket models in his office to show [his son]."[61]

Space scientists who spoke with Kennedy corroborated this impression. The NASA administrator Robert C. Seamans noted that JFK came to believe "it's important that this country show real leadership in this area. . . . We're a rich country and we ought to be doing more." Dr. Wernher von Braun, a prominent rocket scientist who played a leading role in NASA's space program, talked with Kennedy at length on several occasions and reported that the president "took a great personal interest in every detail of the program" and "found it difficult to understand why some people couldn't see the importance of space. . . . [T]his was a challenge as great as that confronted by the early explorers of the Renaissance. . . . He wanted to rejuvenate the country—give the nation new goals, new ideals, new objectives that the youth of America and the rest of the world could believe in." Moreover, von Braun related, Ted Kennedy told him that "the Kennedy brothers had one favorite topic when they were among themselves, and that topic was space flight!"[62]

JFK's broadening interest became evident during his NASA meetings, when he bombarded engineers and astronauts with questions that expressed a keen interest in details. According to von Braun, "He was intensely interested in seeing things, in understanding for himself how big or how complex things were. He would interrupt you with a question: 'What is this black tube sticking out of the second stage?' He seemed to evaluate things on the basis of what he could really see with his own eyes." Robert

Gilruth noticed that JFK drew upon his own military background. "He had been a naval officer and did know something about navigation and guidance for ships and this is somewhat similar. He was interested in the kind of sextant one would use in space."[63]

But overshadowing Kennedy's interest in technical details and mission strategy was his full embrace of the masculine individualism of the Mercury astronauts. Publicly, he described them as men of a "new generation" who would compete in "a race for the mastery of the sky." While awarding NASA's Distinguished Service Medal to one of their number in 1963, JFK argued that in America's "rather settled society," the Mercury astronauts "demonstrated that there are still great frontiers to be crossed." In private discussions, Kennedy reflected that it was not abstract science that drew people to the space program but the human factor. To those who contended that technological advances were the real goal of space exploration, he replied, "Well, that's all very well, but I don't really know that there are many people for whom it's significant to have these kinds of scientific exploits, but I do know that they find the manned lunar landing and the manned program to have great significance."[64]

Kennedy accorded great respect to the astronauts and established an atmosphere of manly camaraderie. He awarded them medals, escorted them to various occasions, and invited them frequently to the White House for lunches, parties, and informal chats about the space project and their experiences. JFK established a real bond with the group. "Kennedy identifies enthusiastically with the astronauts, the glamour surrounding them and the courage and skill it takes to do their jobs. He knows them quite well by now and recognizes them individually with ease," noted Ben Bradlee. "He called Shepard and Glenn 'the personality boys.'" (Bradlee also related that at one gathering the president, with his irrepressible eye for women, commented "two or three times that evening that he finds Rene Carpenter [spouse of the astronaut Scott Carpenter] the most attractive of the wives.") Kennedy revealed his fellow feeling with the Mercury astronauts after Gordon Cooper's flight in 1963 when the group and their wives visited the Oval Office for a photograph. Everyone gathered around the famous rocking chair in a semicircle, but JFK and the First Lady stood with the others. The president had Cooper sit in his chair.[65]

JFK made clear that the astronauts, perhaps more than any other figures during his administration, demonstrated the qualities of courage, competition, mental acuity, and physical prowess that he so valued, embodied, and promoted. The two heroic figures of the space program, Shepard and Glenn, entered the Kennedy Circle. Alan Shepard became proud of his personal friendship with President Kennedy and used it on several occasions to lobby for enhancements to the space program. He was even approached by the Democratic Party in his native New Hampshire to run for the Senate, but he rejected the notion. John Glenn became even closer to John F. Kennedy and his administration. He not only visited the president at the White House but socialized with the Kennedys. The president's vision and charisma, said the astronaut, "could move millions to contribute to something I thought was vital—a democracy of energized participation." Glenn soon became involved in Democratic politics, campaigning actively for Robert F. Kennedy during his run for the White House in 1968 and eventually serving as a U.S. senator from Ohio from 1974 to 1999.[66]

The cult of the astronaut in the early 1960s became the climax of JFK's crusade for masculine regeneration. Alan Shepard, with his pioneering blast into space, was the first to illuminate this link, but John Glenn, with his dramatic orbiting of Earth, surpassed him to become its greatest symbol. When New York City hosted Glenn's enormous ticker-tape parade in early March 1962, thousands of buttons were produced. They featured the smiling face of the astronaut, around which curled a caption reading, "Astronaut John Glenn: The New Frontier Man of the Year." Around the same time, *Life* published a photograph that illuminated the masculine mystique even more vividly. It pictured President Kennedy and Glenn riding together in the backseat of an open limousine as it traveled from Cape Canaveral to Patrick Air Force Base a few miles away. Smiling broadly at the cheering crowds lining the road, the two men gave them a confident, even phallic, thumbs-up sign. Said the caption, "Two exuberant young Americans share the country's joy." This triumphant scene provided an indelible image of Kennedy's masculine mystique.[67]

EPILOGUE

The Masculine Mystique

News of John F. Kennedy's assassination on November 22, 1963, hit American society like a thunderbolt. As details about the deadly shooting during a presidential political swing through Dallas, Texas, spread throughout the country, stunned disbelief gave way to horror and then grief. Millions of sorrowful citizens, even if they were not supporters of the president, asked themselves how a youthful, vibrant leader could be struck down in his prime in such a senseless manner. For many, it was only Mrs. Kennedy's televised arrival back in the national capital later that evening, her pink suit still stained with her husband's blood, as the president's coffin was silently loaded from Air Force One into a waiting hearse, that confirmed the nightmare had been real. The newly sworn-in president Lyndon B. Johnson's sober remarks into a battery of microphones at the airport—"We have suffered a loss that cannot be weighed. . . . I will do my best. That is all I can do"—provided a jolting reminder that an inevitable transfer of political power accompanied the emotional trauma of this event. Kennedy's state funeral, a few days later, a dignified yet heart-wrenching ceremony, prompted an emotional outpouring of mourning by the entire nation.

Within a matter of weeks, the martyred president's historical legacy began to take shape. It first appeared in a compelling trope fostered by

Jacqueline Kennedy that was adopted by the media and much of the public. In an interview with the journalist Theodore White for a special edition of *Life* magazine, the former First Lady disclosed that her late husband had been very fond of the Broadway musical *Camelot* and especially liked the concluding lyrics from the title song: "Don't let it be forgot, that once there was a spot, for one brief shining moment that was known as Camelot." Mrs. Kennedy added, "There will be great presidents again, but there will never be another Camelot." This comparison seemed to capture JFK's idealism, grace, wit, and determination to embrace the future, and it quickly took root in American memory. For many citizens, the late president survived as an inspiring symbol of the New Frontier, an urbane, confident, even dashing political figure who had appealed to the better instincts of the American people and achieved a political apotheosis as a martyr to idealistic reform. The arc of Kennedy's reputation bent steadily upward as Americans (especially progressives) recalled his invocation of national self-sacrifice in his inaugural, his cool handling of the Cuban missile crisis, his rhetorical defense of international freedom in Berlin, his sympathetic phone call to Martin Luther King Jr. during the civil rights crisis, his call for a nuclear test ban treaty, and his promotion of service and economic development with the Peace Corps. Overall, his stylish embodiment of American vigor and idealism created a kind of mythology that gained fervent approval from millions.[1]

But another factor also influenced the formation of cultural memory. For many in the aftermath of Dallas, in more subtle but equally powerful ways, memories of Kennedy's masculine mystique lingered. The vigorous manly impulse that had permeated both the content and the style of his administration seemed to hang in the air, palpable but no longer quite real. For the tribunes of the New Frontier, the resulting tension and sense of loss was acutely painful. Joseph Alsop, the influential columnist and Kennedy supporter, captured this sentiment in a revealing observation. "The Washington landscape seemed to me littered with male widows," he observed in the days after JFK's assassination. A presidential aide had told him, "You know, Joe, when the President died, I suddenly realized that I felt about him as I've never felt about another man in my life." Alsop's mournful words highlighted an important aspect of JFK's death: the demise of the alpha male in an administration overflowing with them. They invoked a darker theme in the original Camelot story that saw the dissolution of a kingdom due to infidelity and a circle of knights left mourning for their lost king. The fate of Kennedy's masculine mystique, in fact, revealed much about the youthful leader's impact on American values.[2]

As the years passed, it became clearer that JFK's deepest emotional needs and desires—the assertive individualism, youthful vigor, and sexual energy that found expression in his masculine agenda—in a certain sense held him prisoner. The handsome, charismatic, beguiling young man who survived in American memory as a legendary hero was, in fact, a tragically flawed leader whose essential impulses undermined many of his best intentions. If Nixon Agonistes was an insecure, awkward, paranoid figure who desperately pursued an archaic creed of the self-made man to the point of self-destruction, Kennedy Adonais was an elegant, attractive, tough-minded man's man whose masculine strivings produced several consequences that were equally corrosive.

In personal terms, Kennedy's relentless, indiscriminate sexual adventurism, quite apart from any judgments about moral turpitude, raised deeply troubling questions about protection of the presidency and national well-being. Potential problems regarding his personal conduct—revelations of his constant philandering, disclosure of venereal disease (which his medical records strongly suggest), blackmail from unscrupulous consorts, breaches of national security protocols during secret trysts with women—hung over JFK like a cloud. His behavior was so reckless that it threatened not only his own personal integrity but that of his administration. Had he lived longer and won a second term as president, the odds are high that it would have erupted in scandal and threatened his leadership of the most powerful nation in the world.

Less melodramatically, aspects of Kennedy's assertive masculinity also proved problematic in public policy, particularly in foreign affairs. JFK's obsession with counterinsurgency as an expression of masculine vigor helped lead the United States into the morass of the Vietnam War, which even before his death had begun to overwhelm the limitations of this strategy. Its bumbling application with regard to unseating Fidel Castro helped produce the Cuban missile crisis, a confrontation that took the United

States (and the world) catastrophically close to the brink of nuclear war before the president moved to defuse it. Kennedy's soaring, competitive race-into-space rhetoric inspired a great spasm of national pride that produced the glory of the moon landing in 1969 but then fizzled out as the expenditure of billions of dollars seemed to bring few lasting effects. Similarly, his manly crusade with the Peace Corps proved strikingly ineffective in combating Communist inroads around the world, producing neither affection for the United States in less developed countries nor concrete advances in comparison with later realpolitik calculations that undermined and then brought down the Communist empire in the 1970s and 1980s.

But the most profound consequences of Kennedy's masculine mystique played out in the broader realm of American culture and society, where several difficulties emerged. First, the image of Kennedy Adonais moved the cult of charismatic personality to the forefront of modern American political life. The result, while edifyingly glamorous in the short run, proved unhappy in the long run. After Kennedy, enormous pressures built to shape the modern political leader—and an appreciation of him—as a handsome, virile leading man symbolizing an array of values and emotions in the drama of national life. This notion of the leader as movie star steadily permeated both political parties. With its stress on attractive features, a charismatic personality, and a manly ethos, the politics of celebrity threatened to overwhelm policy formulation and debate over political issues while highlighting the allure of personal imagery. After Kennedy, the politician as celebrity became the ideal and increasingly the norm.

Second, JFK's crusade for regenerated, vigorous manhood helped unleash social forces that proved dangerously unruly. The standard historical narrative holds that the early years of the 1960s were marked by the idealistic reforms of the New Frontier, and it was only after the president's assassination in Dallas and the escalation of the Vietnam War that wholesale cultural and political rebellion exploded to throw the country into upheaval. But in fact, JFK and the Kennedy Circle did much to promote the crisis of American life that erupted later in the decade. Their disdain for the stultifying impact of bureaucratic organizations, the debilitating effects of suburban consumerism, and the priggish traditions of bourgeois self-restraint powerfully influenced the dissenting spirit of the late 1960s. The Kennedy ethos, with its antibourgeois sophistication and admiration for the superior intelligence, drive, and physical appeal of "the best and the brightest," in David Halberstam's famous phrase, promoted the dominance of Ivy League elites during the New Frontier. But this quasi-aristocratic impulse spilled over its bounds and helped ignite the countercultural insurrections that divided the country a few years later.

In this later, more radical atmosphere, the high-flying spirit of the New Frontier with its cool pragmatism crashed and burned, as did many of the New Frontiersmen themselves, such as Robert McNamara, who in 1966 confronted a crowd of anti-Vietnam protesters at Harvard and was reduced to shouting from the hood of his car, "I was tougher than you then, and I'm tougher today." Thus Kennedy's disdain for bureaucracy and middle-class conventions and his crusade for invigorated masculinity helped unleash subversive social forces that soon whirled out of control, making the age of Kennedy a seedbed for later rebellion. So while it is ludicrous to imagine JFK standing at the barricades in 1968, fresh off his yacht, alluringly tanned and chic in his sunglasses, chinos, deck shoes, and pastel polo shirt, screaming slogans against the establishment, his ghost hovered over the proceedings. Many of the youthful rebels, and their middle-aged supporters, who railed against "the establishment" in the late 1960s and early 1970s, had been unmoored from it by the restless energy of Kennedy's earlier campaign for manly regeneration.[3]

But perhaps the most lasting impact of Kennedy and his masculine mystique lay in its legacy for men and women, the family, and their connection to the larger society. JFK's ethic of manly assertiveness, sexual prerogative, and family indifference helped unravel many traditional social ties rooted in domestic life. According to his sophisticated new ideal, the alpha male dominated all and recognized few restraints, including the obligation to repress his impulses in the interest of family well-being. Disdainful of bureaucratic labor and the plodding organization man, Kennedy and his circle encouraged modern males to transcend the traditional ideal of provider and embrace hip new guidelines promoting excitement, adventure, and conquest, both socially and sexually. They urged young men to seek their own fulfillment and circumvent suburban conformity, family togetherness, consumer comfort, and female aspiration in order to confront and overcome fresh challenges. Theirs was a world where a few women might volunteer for the Peace Corps or fill minor positions in government, but the manly endeavors of military counterinsurgents, international secret agents, maverick novelists, heroic astronauts, and hip entertainers dominated the game. The New Frontier clearly established an arena for masculine action.

As the intoxicating effects of Kennedy's masculine mystique began to wear off, however, an awareness of its shortcomings became more acute. In the years after the young president's tragic death, it would become increasingly evident that families (let alone a society) full of fledgling Frank Sinatras, Norman Mailers, James Bonds, Alan Shepards, and Jack Kennedys functioned, at best, erratically. A revealing, and rather ironic, indication of the disturbing cultural impact of the masculine mystique came near the end of the Kennedy era. Betty Friedan's landmark book, *The Feminine Mystique,* published in 1963 shortly before JFK's death, was dedicated, significantly, to "all the new women, and the new men." She famously denounced "the problem with no name" that beset modern women—a cultural mind-set in postwar America that urged the education of women and then bound them in the home, demanding devotion to child-raising duties and housekeeping while denying them a place in the workplace and a larger arena of experience. *The Feminine Mystique* eloquently called for expanding the scope of female activity beyond the confines of the family and the domestic scene. In particular, it urged women to enter the workforce and demanded equal opportunity when they did so. The book became a bible for modern feminism as its illumination of women's second-class status helped trigger the crusade for women's liberation that marched across the landscape of American society over the next decade.[4]

In one important sense, Friedan's call for women's liberation ran against the grain of the New Frontier's masculine agenda. JFK and the Kennedy Circle, after all, championed an expansive creed of male assertion and authority that sent men off unencumbered by domestic ties to confront a world of challenge and adventure. Friedan and other feminists, however, insisted that male domination of society thwarted women's opportunities at every turn, imprisoning them in unsatisfying lives that were lived secondhand in service to children, husband, and home. It was women, not men, who needed to escape the home and find genuine identity and self-fulfillment. The implication was clear. On the hypermasculine New Frontier, women had neither the protection of traditional paternalism—moral authority rooted in the domestic realm of the family—nor a genuine place outside it in the world of work. Instead, they drifted in a kind of "no woman's land" and too often appeared as merely playthings. In other words, for many women seeking liberation, the Kennedyesque male ideal represented the worst kind of male chauvinism. Feminists in the 1960s revolted not only against a long tradition of male privilege but against the supercharged version of it represented by JFK's masculine mystique.

Yet Friedan's crusade for feminine liberation also offered a fascinating parallel to Kennedy's crusade for masculine regeneration. The two movements shared much. *The Feminine Mystique* contended that male dissatisfaction and female dissatisfaction in the postwar world were linked. Like women, Friedan argued, men were locked in lonely, isolated roles and "weren't really the enemy—they were fellow victims, suffering from an outmoded masculine mystique that made them feel unnecessarily inadequate when there were no bears to kill." This recognition of the constraints imposed on men by postwar social conventions echoed Arthur Schlesinger's famous "Crisis of American Masculinity" article and reflected the broad sense of uneasiness and malaise that beset men in the 1950s. But JFK's masculine revival movement, of course, did not reject the masculine mystique but intensified it by indentifying new challenges to face, new frontiers to cross, new bears to kill.[5]

Friedan, again like Kennedy and his circle, vilified postwar middle-class conventions—suburban life, family togetherness, mass consumption, the deadening effects of traditional social roles—that they believed sent modern individuals into an emotional dead end. They attacked the same target from opposite directions. JFK and his cohort denounced the male version of this trap: the organization man trudging through the benumbing maze of modern bureaucracy. Friedan and her supporters decried the female version: the modern housewife imprisoned in the "comfortable concentration camp" of the suburban home. "The American spirit fell into a strange sleep, men as well as women," insisted *The Feminine Mystique*, as people retreated to the suburbs and "the warm brightness of home" and the "hopeless conformity" of the family. Friedan lamented "the personal emptiness which sends many men and women into psychotherapy" and denounced a system where daily work had become an exercise in meaningless routine. Women became trapped in the drudgery of housework and child raising, which created a "deadly sameness of their lives" and inspired "a dull and lifeless look" and "lack of vitality." Similarly, American men fell into a snare with their labor "on the assembly lines or in the corporation offices: work that does not fully use a man's capacities [and] leaves in him a vacant, empty need for escape."[6]

Friedan, like Kennedy and his circle, finally zeroed in on a problem with identity fashioned by this social system. JFK and his acolytes focused on a weakened male spirit produced by the bureaucratic ethos and consumer comforts. The feminist writer agreed but rooted the problem in the female version of this anemic identity. The "apathetic, dependent, infantile, purposeless being, who seems so shockingly nonhuman when remarked as the emerging character of the new American man," she wrote, "is strangely reminiscent of the familiar 'feminine' personality as defined by the mystique." This "passive non-identity," Friedan contended, characterized stunted individuals, both male and female, who had renounced "active aims, ambitions, [and] interests of one's own." Thus both Kennedy and Friedan reflected a restless ferment among affluent Americans, arguing that postwar American life had shortchanged individuals who sought genuine identity and meaningful experiences.[7]

Finally, the Kennedy Circle and Friedan launched movements for revitalization that located social salvation in a vision of individual self-fulfillment. For JFK and the New Frontiersmen, emotional rescue lay in the cool masculine banter of the Rat Pack, the manly daring of a secret agent or an ancient gladiator, the intense experience of a maverick novelist or journalist, the sexual conquests of a sophisticated playboy, the tough-minded tactics of a Green Beret, or the courageous exploration of an astronaut. For Friedan and her followers, salvation for educated and well-heeled women came when they moved to "break out of the housewife trap" and find deliverance through "fulfilling their own unique possibilities as separate human beings." In her words, bored mothers and unfulfilled housewives who had exhausted the mundane possibilities of the PTA, shopping, and child rearing must "exercise their human freedom and recapture their sense of self. They must refuse to be nameless, depersonalized, manipulated and live their own lives again according to a self-chosen purpose." In such fashion, the male president and the influential female writer swept through American society in tandem, overturning the stultifying tradition of bourgeois self-restraint and defining a new nirvana of emotional self-realization for affluent men and women.[8]

Fairly soon, however, a powerful backlash developed against the male agenda of the Kennedy era. It came from two directions. On one side, by the late 1960s increasingly angry feminists (while carefully tiptoeing around the martyred figure of JFK himself) were launching attacks from the left that condemned its powerful sense of male entitlement as reactionary. On the other side, traditionalists began mounting an even stronger defense of family values that denounced both JFK's masculine mystique and Friedan's feminism for undermining bourgeois civilization. Both campaigns steadily increased in intensity. As the glamour of the New Frontier faded in the face of debilitating war, racial violence, political upheaval, gender tensions, cultural clashes, and economic decline, the cool, sophisticated manliness of JFK, Frank Sinatra, James Bond, the Playboy Philosophy, the Mercury astronauts, and the Green Berets seemed increasingly anachronistic if not downright dangerous.

Thus by the early twenty-first century, the image of the Kennedyesque male survives mainly as a poignant figure from the past. His commanding, glamorous presence might be viewed with a touch of wistfulness, perhaps, but also considerable discomfort and disapproval. Nothing better illustrates this historical fact than the television series *Mad Men*, which ran from 2007 to 2015 to tremendous popular approval and critical acclaim. In this period drama set in the early 1960s, its protagonist, Don Draper, fully exercises the social and personal imperatives of the forceful, adventurous male fully in tune with the spirit of the New Frontier. A handsome, ambitious, and virile masculine figure, he has vaulted to prominence as a high-achieving advertising executive at a Madison Avenue firm. With a beautiful wife and children ensconced in the tony suburbs of New York, he nonetheless philanders compulsively with a series of fetching females who serially swoon into his arms and land in his bed. Confidently confronting life through a haze of cigarette smoke while navigating rivers of martinis, Draper moves deftly through a male atmosphere of challenge and achievement. He stands astride his world as a vigorous, elegant, ironically intelligent, and commanding presence who leads other men and awes most women.[9]

A certain glamorous sense of nostalgia pervades *Mad Men*. It evokes a world gone by, one that fascinated with its sleek style and elegance, uninhibited enjoyment of cigarettes and alcohol, sexual escapades, and challenges to conformity. The show captured the look and feel of the early 1960s with its IBM Selectric typewriters, women adorned with beehive hairdos and encased in rigid foundation garments, men in slim suits with white shirts and slender ties, houses and apartments styled in ersatz colonial or mid-twentieth-century modern, a world of cocktail parties and casual affairs and 1950s-style conformity beginning to come apart. It is the world of Kennedy and his circle where a young, hip generation of Americans, led by vigorous and irreverent males, is undermining an aging, looming authority structure. Seminal events in the Kennedy presidency frame *Mad Men*'s narrative: the 1960 election, the October 1962 Cuban missile crisis, the November 1963 assassination. The show's characters are shown watching Jackie Kennedy's famous tour of the White House in February 1962, while Don's wife, Betty, mirrors the First Lady with her slim, fashion-model good looks, fluency in Italian, Bryn Mawr background, equestrian skills, and haute couture wardrobe. Don is a Kennedyesque figure with his striking good looks, self-confidence, stylish appearance, voracious sexual appetite, and cool, pragmatic pursuit of achievement. As one of the show's writers disclosed, they "fashioned Don Draper in the JFK mold."[10]

Mad Men generated a certain nostalgic, wistful appeal. But only up to a point. Ultimately, the world of Don Draper, which is to say the world of John F. Kennedy and masculine power, evoked discomfort, disapproval, and occasionally pity among modern viewers. Viewed half a century later, the treatment of women in the *Mad Men* milieu was cringe inducing as they are relegated to doing menial tasks, subject to a constant stream of salacious comments, made to suffer small daily indignities, and cut off from genuine opportunity and advancement. Women are clearly second-class citizens in the manly corporate world of Sterling Cooper. On the erotic front, things are no better. Here it is not so much the casual sex that rankled as the cavalier treatment of women as sexual playthings. Draper, in good JFK fashion, hops from bed to bed with various paramours with only slight interest in them as human beings. Women are dominated and then discarded. On the broader social front, a casual disregard for the family looms in the background as men's traditional loyalties to the breadwinner ethic play a clear second fiddle to the desires and needs of the moment.

The portrait of Don Draper was equally unsettling to modern eyes. The montage that opens every episode of *Mad Men* suggested it: a faceless, animated man in a suit and tie falls, first through his office, then down the side of a skyscraper, tumbling and unable to find firm footing. Indeed, this stylish alpha male is roiled with uncertainty and angst beneath that cool, confident exterior. Ironically intelligent, creative, and occasionally sensitive while pursuing an elusive happiness, Draper finds that many of his conquests, both in his career and with women, ring hollow. For most viewers in the early twenty-first century, Draper's powerful masculine mystique—despite occasional pangs of nostalgia—ultimately appeared as a poignant, futile series of gestures that fail to provide genuine meaning in his life. This unhappy scene prompted sympathy for those whom he dominates, but equally a sense of tragic loss for the man himself. *Mad Men*'s masculine mystique of the early 1960s, so powerfully symbolized by the young leader in the White House, seems anything but fulfilling. It was entirely appropriate that November 22, 1963, is the date when Draper's private life crumbles as his wife sues for divorce and his family stability dissolves.

Thus the Kennedy assassination, a tragedy of Shakespearean proportions, left important consequences in its wake. But one must penetrate the idealistic fog of Camelot that enveloped the former president to get a clearer view of them. In an immediate sense, JFK's death cut down a vibrant young leader in the prime of his life, leaving behind a devastated widow with young children, a traumatized citizenry, and a terrible sense of historical incompleteness. In a broader sense, it did much more. The man who died in Dallas was not only a dynamic political figure with great gifts but a cultural figure who was a product of his time, reflecting at the same time some of its greatest yearnings and its greatest flaws. Mortally wounded along with JFK was an intensely male cultural style that would soon prove unsatisfying to just about everyone, from the politically correct Left to the family-values Right, from resentful working-class males to frustrated suburban housewives, from rebellious student radicals to pious churchgoers.

But in the halcyon days of the early 1960s, the cultural crusade for masculine regeneration had provided the essence of the youthful president's appeal and significance. Reflected in JFK's vigorous, stylish public persona, it had spoken eloquently to many of the underlying concerns of his age and become an inspiration for millions of citizens. So to those who cherish an idealized, progressive image of John F. Kennedy and bemoan his philandering, or decry his adventurism in Cuba, or besmirch his passion for the Green Berets, or disparage the cool pragmatism of his domestic policies, or belittle his soaring rhetoric on the conquest of outer space, let the word go forth from this time and place. None of these were uncharacteristic departures, or aberrations in judgment, or betrayals of deep-rooted principles. They were central to the man's makeup, both personally and politically. Kennedy and his masculine mystique gave Americans exactly what they asked for.

NOTES

In the following notes, JFK stands for John F. Kennedy. JFKL stands for the John F. Kennedy Library in Boston. OH stands for Oral History, a collection of transcribed interviews with JFK associates, friends, and family at the JFKL.

Introduction: Kennedy Adonais

1 Jill Abramson, "Kennedy, the Elusive President," *New York Times*, Oct. 22, 2013.
2 Caitlin Flanagan, "Jackie and the Girls," *Atlantic*, July/Aug. 2012, 133–42.
3 Jeff Greenfield, *If Kennedy Lived: The First and Second Terms of President John F. Kennedy* (New York, 2012), offers an example of the attempt to posthumously capture JFK for the Left, while Ira Stoll, *JFK, Conservative* (Boston, 2013), offers an example of a similar conservative hijacking.
4 Garry Wills, *Nixon Agonistes: The Crisis of the Self-Made Man* (1970; New York, 1979), 549, 546.
5 I have explored the development of this cultural revolution in a series of biographies of key figures in it: *The People's Tycoon: Henry Ford and the American Century* (New York, 2005), *Self-Help Messiah: Dale Carnegie and Success in Modern America* (New York, 2013), *The Magic Kingdom: Walt Disney and the American Way of Life* (New York, 1997), and *Mr. Playboy: Hugh Hefner and the American Dream* (New York, 2008).
6 Percy Shelley, *Adonais: An Elegy on the Death of John Keats* (1821).
7 For treatments of JFK's political and policy advisers, see David Halberstam, *The Best and the Brightest* (New York, 1972); Robert Dallek, *Camelot's Court: Inside the Kennedy White House* (New York, 2013).

One: The Crisis of Masculinity in 1950s America

1 Arthur Schlesinger Jr., "The Crisis of American Masculinity," *Esquire*, Nov. 1958, 63–65. On Schlesinger's life and career, see John Patrick Diggins and Michael Lind, *The Liberal Persuasion: Arthur Schlesinger Jr. and the Challenge of the American Past* (Princeton, N.J., 1997); James Chace, "The Age of Schlesinger," *New York Review of Books*, Dec. 21, 2000.

2 J. Robert Moskin, "The American Male: Why Do Women Dominate Him?," *Look*, Feb. 4, 1958, 77–80.

3 George B. Leonard, "The American Male: Why Is He Afraid to Be Different?," *Look*, Feb. 18, 1958, 95–104; William Attwood, "The American Male: Why Does He Work So Hard?," *Look*, March 4, 1958, 71–75.

4 Attwood, "Why Does He Work So Hard?," 75.

5 Amram Scheinfeld, "The American Male," *Cosmopolitan*, May 1957, 23–25. See also pp. 26–29, 31–32, 39–43, and 58–61.

6 Louis Lyndon, "Uncertain Hero: The Paradox of the American Male," *Woman's Home Companion*, Nov. 1956, 41–43, 107; Lemuel C. McGee, "The Suicidal Cult of 'Manliness,'" *Today's Health*, Jan. 1957, 28–30; Margaret Mead, "American Man in a Woman's World," *New York Times Magazine*, Feb. 10, 1957, 11, 20–23; Helen Mayer Hacker, "The New Burdens of Masculinity," *Marriage and Family Living*, Aug. 1957, 227–33.

7 For stimulating discussions of movies and masculine crisis in the 1950s, see Steven Cohan, *Masked Men: Masculinity and the Movies in the Fifties* (Bloomington, Ind., 1997); James Gilbert, *Men in the Middle: Searching for Masculinity in the 1950s* (Chicago, 2005), 164–88.

8 Attwood, "Why Does He Work So Hard?," 71.

9 William H. Whyte, *The Organization Man* (New York, 1956), 143, 149; McGee, "Suicidal Cult of 'Manliness,'" 28.

10 Hacker, "New Burdens of Masculinity," 229.

11 David Riesman, *The Lonely Crowd: A Study of the Changing American Character* (New Haven, Conn., 1950), 20, 22, 25, 45; see also pp. 129–30. James Gilbert, in *Men in the Middle*, 54, shrewdly observes that Riesman's *Lonely Crowd*, while purporting to be a study of "the American character," in fact focuses exclusively on men and constitutes "a male declension narrative."

12 Riesman, *Lonely Crowd*, 25, 136; Leonard, "Why Is He Afraid to Be Different?," 97; Hacker, "New Burdens of Masculinity," 229.

13 Whyte, *Organization Man*, 4, 13, 6–7, 3, 10, 358–59, 392–93, and more generally, pt. 7, "The New Suburbia: The Organization Man at Home."

14 Lyndon, "Uncertain Hero," 41, 43, 107; Attwood, "Why Does He Work So Hard?," 72.

15 See David Potter, *People of Plenty: Economic Abundance and the American Character* (Chicago, 1954). The kitchen debate is described in Stephen J. Whitfield, *The Culture of the Cold War* (Baltimore, 1991), 72–74; Elaine Tyler May, *Homeward Bound: American Families in the Cold War* (New York, 1988), 16–18.

16 Attwood, "Why Does He Work So Hard?," 72–73; K. A. Cuordileone, *Manhood and American Political Culture in the Cold War* (New York, 2005), 104, 172.

17 Riesman, *Lonely Crowd*, 116, 78, 127; Whyte, *Organization Man*, 18.

18 Dorothy Barclay, "Trousered Mothers and Dishwashing Dads," *New York Times*, April 28, 1957; Attwood, "Why Does He Work So Hard?," 78; Richard Gehman, "Toupees, Girdles, and Sun Lamps" *Cosmopolitan*, May 1957, 39–43.

19 "The Shoulder Trade," *Time*, Aug. 2, 1954, 62–68. See also Scheinfeld, "American Male," 24; Gilbert, *Men in the Middle*, 152–53; Riesman, *Lonely Crowd*, 292–97; Steven Gelber,

"Do-It-Yourself: Constructing, Repairing, and Maintaining Domestic Masculinity," *American Quarterly* 49, no. 1 (March 1997): 66–112.

20 See Robert L. Griswold, "The 'Flabby American,' the Body, and the Cold War," in *A Shared Experience: Men, Women, and the History of Gender,* ed. Laura McCall and Donald Yacovone (New York, 1998), 326–27; John B. Kelly, "Are We Becoming a Nation of Weaklings?," *American,* March 1956, 28–29, 104–7; and Jean Mayer, "Muscular State of the Union," *New York Times Magazine,* Nov. 6, 1955, 17.

21 Hanson Baldwin, "Our Fighting Men Have Gone Soft," *Saturday Evening Post,* Aug. 8, 1959, 13–15, 82–84.

22 For an interesting cultural critique of *The Seven Year Itch,* see Cohan, *Masked Men,* 61–68.

23 Hacker, "New Burdens of Masculinity," 228.

24 Gehman, "Toupees, Girdles, and Sun Lamps," 40; Lyndon, "Uncertain Hero," 107.

25 Moskin, "Why Do Women Dominate Him?," 80, 77.

26 Ibid., 7; Lawrence K. Frank, "How Much Do We Know About Men?," *Look,* May 10, 1955, 57–58.

27 Amory Clark, "The American Male: His Sex Habits," *Cosmopolitan,* May 1957, 32; Moskin, "Why Do Women Dominate Him?," 77, 79; Frank, "How Much Do We Know About Men?," 57–58; Barclay, "Trousered Mothers and Dishwashing Dads." See also Hacker, "New Burdens of Masculinity," 229–30.

28 Moskin, "Why Do Women Dominate Him?," 80, 78.

29 Philip Wylie, *Generation of Vipers* (1942; Champaign, Ill., 2012), 201, 212–13; Philip Wylie, "The Abdicating Male," *Playboy,* Nov. 1956, 23–24, 50, 79; Philip Wylie, "The Womanization of America," *Playboy,* Sept. 1958, 51–52, 77–79; Philip Wylie, "The Career Woman," *Playboy,* Jan. 1963, 117–18, 154–56. On Wylie's life and writings, see Robert Barshay, *Philip Wylie: The Man and His Work* (Washington, D.C., 1979).

30 Moskin, "Why Do Women Dominate Him?," 80; Hacker, "New Burdens of Masculinity," 231; Clark, "His Sex Habits," 31–32.

31 Frank, "How Much Do We Know About Men?," 57–58; Moskin, "Why Do Women Dominate Him?," 80; Wylie, "Career Woman," 156; Hacker, "New Burdens of Masculinity," 231–32.

32 Attwood, "Why Does He Work So Hard?," 74.

33 Max Eastman, "Let's Close the Muscle Gap!," *Reader's Digest,* Nov. 1961, 122, 124, 125.

34 R. M. Marshall, "Toughening Our Soft Generation," *Saturday Evening Post,* June 23, 1962, 13; Baldwin, "Our Fighting Men Have Gone Soft," 13, 15, 82.

35 For perceptive and divergent analyses of *North by Northwest* that differ in part from my reading of the film, see Cohan, "The Spy in the Grey Flannel Suit," in *Masked Men,* 1–33; Richard H. Millington, "Hitchcock and American Character: The Comedy of Self-Construction in *North by Northwest,*" in *Hitchcock's America,* ed. Richard H. Millington and Jonathan Freedman (New York, 1999), 135–54.

36 For useful discussions of *The Ugly American,* see Cuordileone, *Manhood and American Political Culture in the Cold War,* 220–22; Robert D. Dean, *Imperial Brotherhood: Gender and the Making of Cold War Foreign Policy* (Amherst, Mass., 2001), 172–79; John Hellman, *American Myth and the Legacy of Vietnam* (New York, 1986), 15–38.

37   William J. Lederer and Eugene Burdick, *The Ugly American* (New York, 1958), 12–14, 69, 84, 205, 80–83, 199–204.

38   Ibid., 43–47, 206, 110–14.

39   Ibid., 93–94, 105, 108, 266–70.

40   Arthur Schlesinger Jr., *The Vital Center: The Politics of Freedom* (New York, 1950), 163, 147, 28, 46.

41   Arthur Schlesinger Jr., *A Thousand Days: John F. Kennedy in the White House* (New York, 1965), 116, 739–40, 113–14. The italics in this paragraph are mine.

42   Schlesinger, "Crisis of American Masculinity," 64–65.

Two: Style Makes the Man: Candidate John F. Kennedy

1   "The Fascinators," *Cosmopolitan,* May 1957, 52.

2   *New York Times,* Jan. 23, 1959, 23; JFK to Burdick, March 11, 1959, "B" folder, Senate Files, Correspondence, 1953–1960, box 458, JFKL; JFK, "Speech at the Cow Palace, San Francisco, CA," Nov. 2, 1960, at http://www.presidency.ucsb.edu. For a thorough look at JFK and *The Ugly American,* see Joan Iversen, "The Ugly American: A Bestseller Reexamined," in *John F. Kennedy: The Promise Revisited,* ed. Paul Harper and Joann P. Krieg (New York, 1998), 153–68.

3   On JFK's life and career, see Robert Dallek, *An Unfinished Life: John F. Kennedy, 1917–1963* (Boston, 2003), which is probably the most comprehensive and balanced biography of many that are available.

4   See David Nasaw, *The Patriarch: The Remarkable Life and Turbulent Times of Joseph P. Kennedy* (New York, 2012).

5   Joseph Kennedy, as described by JFK's friend Lem Billings, quoted in Peter Collier and David Horowitz, *The Kennedys: An American Drama* (New York, 1984), 58.

6   The Kennedy family friend Robert Downes quoted in ibid., 59; "The Senator Is in a Hurry," *McCall's,* Aug. 1957, 125, 118.

7   Collier and Horowitz, *Kennedys,* 188; Rose Kennedy quoted in Garry Wills, *The Kennedy Imprisonment: A Meditation on Power* (1981; Boston, 2002), 40; Charles Spalding quoted in Dallek, *Unfinished Life,* 31; "Election Night Tension Inside Kennedy House," *Life,* Nov. 21, 1960, 36. The same point about "terrific" was made in "Out Front," *Time,* Dec. 2, 1957, 19.

8   Nasaw, *Patriarch,* 374–75; JFK quoted in a 1960 interview, in Dallek, *Unfinished Life,* 30–31; "Senator Is in a Hurry," 118; "The Senator Women Elected," *Cosmopolitan,* Dec. 1953, 83.

9   On JFK's schooling, see Dallek, *Unfinished Life,* 36–39, 45–46, 54–55, while Wills, *Kennedy Imprisonment,* 72–76, offers an insightful discussion of his aristocratic cast of mind.

10   For the fullest account of JFK and the PT-109 incident, see Joan Blair and Clay Blair Jr., *The Search for JFK* (New York, 1976), 267–311. On PT-109 and JFK's early political campaigns, see Dallek, *Unfinished Life,* 30–31.

11   Dallek, *Unfinished Life,* 78, 154.

12   Ibid., 46; Seymour Hersh, *The Dark Side of Camelot* (Boston, 1997), 22–23; Thomas Reeves, *A Question of Character: A Life of John F. Kennedy* (New York, 1991), 83.

13 "The Senate's Gay Young Bachelor," *Saturday Evening Post,* June 13, 1953, 26–27, 123–29.

14 Ibid., 26.

15 Ibid., 123.

16 Ibid., 123, 127.

17 Ibid., 26, 124, 27.

18 See Dallek, *Unfinished Life,* 199, 210; Reeves, *Question of Character,* 198–99. Wills offers a harsher verdict on JFK's authorship in *Kennedy Imprisonment,* 134–38.

19 JFK, *Profiles in Courage* (1956; New York, 1964), 21, 22, 23, 24, 38, 201, 205, 36–37, 39.

20 Ibid., 40, 64, 84, 101, 103, 108, 122, 126–27, 129.

21 Ibid., 259, 266.

22 "Democratic Hopefuls," *Time,* Nov. 28, 1958; Andre Fontaine, "Senator Kennedy's Crisis," *Redbook,* Nov. 1957, 49.

23 "Senator Is in a Hurry," 45; "Senator Women Elected," 81; Russell Turner, "Senator Kennedy: The Perfect Politician," *American Mercury,* March 1957, 33, 36, 37; Richard Rovere, "Kennedy's Last Chance to Be President," *Esquire,* April 1959, 65; Douglass Cater, "The Cool Eye of John F. Kennedy," *Reporter,* Dec. 10, 1959, 28; "Out Front," 20; Tris Coffin, "Young Man in a Hurry," *Progressive,* Dec. 1959, 11.

24 Cater, "Cool Eye of John F. Kennedy," 27–28; "This Is John Fitzgerald Kennedy," *Newsweek,* June 23, 1958, 30; Coffin, "Young Man in a Hurry," 14, 12.

25 Cater, "Cool Eye of John F. Kennedy," 29; John Fischer, "The Editor's Easy Chair: Hard Questions for Senator Kennedy," *Harper's,* April 1960, 23.

26 "Life Goes Courting with a U.S. Senator," *Life,* July 20, 1953, 96; "This Is John Fitzgerald Kennedy," 30; "Senator Women Elected," 83.

27 "Senator Women Elected," 85; Turner, "Perfect Politician," 38; "Out Front," 18; "Senator Is in a Hurry," 119, 123; Fontaine, "Senator Kennedy's Crisis," 121.

28 "Senator Is in a Hurry," 45; Rovere, "Kennedy's Last Chance to Be President," 65; "Out Front," 18; "Senator Women Elected," 83; "This Is John Fitzgerald Kennedy," 32; Coffin, "Young Man in a Hurry," 11, 18.

29 "Senator Women Elected," 81, 82.

30 "Out Front," 17; Coffin, "Young Man in a Hurry," 11.

31 "Senator Is in a Hurry," 123; *Life,* April 21, 1958, cover and 41.

32 See Nasaw, *Patriarch,* 144–47, 241–42, 379–80, 610–11, on Joseph Kennedy's womanizing.

33 Reeves, *Question of Character,* 87–88; Blair and Blair, *Search for JFK,* 545–48; Tip O'Neill, *Man of the House: The Life and Political Memoirs of Speaker Tip O'Neill* (New York, 1987), 87; Gloria Emerson, interview with Seymour Hersh, quoted in *Dark Side of Camelot,* 22.

34 Dallek, *Unfinished Life,* 194–95; Fontaine, "Senator Kennedy's Crisis," 121.

35 Eric Sevareid, "Junior Executives Reach the Top," *Boston Globe,* Aug. 7, 1960.

36 JFK, "Are We Up to the Task?," Jan. 1, 1960, in JFK, *The Strategy of Peace,* ed. Allan Nevins (New York, 1960), 199–202.

37 JFK, "Message to the Nation's New Voters," Oct. 5, 1960, at Gerhard Peters and John T. Woolley, The American Presidency Project, http://www.presidency.ucsb.edu.

38 JFK, "Speech Before VFW Convention, Detroit, MI," Aug. 26, 1960, at Peters and Woolley, The American Presidency Project.

39 JFK, "Speech Before American Legion Convention, Miami Beach, FL," Oct. 1960, at Peters and Woolley, The American Presidency Project.

40 JFK, "Speech at the Cow Palace, San Francisco, CA," Nov. 2, 1960, and "The Presidency in 1960—National Press Club, Washington, D.C.," speech, Jan. 14, 1960, both at Peters and Woolley, The American Presidency Project; "Democrats," Time, Nov. 14, 1960, 23.

41 "Remarks of Senator John F. Kennedy, Al Smith Dinner, October 22, 1959," National Archives, at media.nara.gov/media/images.

42 JFK, "The Global Challenge," Jan. 1, 1960, speech in Strategy of Peace, 7; JFK, "Speech Before VFW Convention, Detroit, MI," Aug. 26, 1960, "Text of a Speech Delivered in Alexandria, VA," Aug. 24, 1960, "Speech Before American Legion Convention, Miami Beach, FL," Oct. 1960, and "Excerpts of Remarks at City Hall, Springfield, MA," Nov. 7, 1960, all at Peters and Woolley, The American Presidency Project.

43 "Candidate in Orbit," Time, Nov. 7, 1960, 26; "The Election," Time, Nov. 16, 1960, 3, 6.

44 Richard Schickel, Intimate Strangers: The Culture of Celebrity in America (New York, 2000 [1985]), 4, 54; Joseph Kennedy quoted in Collier and Horowitz, Kennedys, 235.

45 Charles Spalding quoted in Blair and Blair, Search for JFK, 548; JFK, "A Force That Has Changed the Political Scene," TV Guide, Nov. 14, 1959, 6–7.

46 "This Is Kennedy," Newsweek, Oct. 10, 1960, 26; "Candidate in Orbit," 26; Gary A. Donaldson, The First Modern Campaign: Kennedy, Nixon, and the Election of 1960 (Lanham, Md., 2007), viii.

47 William Costello, "Nixon on the Eve: Candidate in Search of an Identity," New Republic, Nov. 7, 1960, 17–21.

48 New York Times, Oct. 8, 1960.

49 Costello, "Nixon on the Eve," 21; "Candid Camera," Time, Oct. 10, 1960, 20; Theodore White, The Making of the President, 1960 (New York, 1961), 316; "TV Debate Backstage: Did the Cameras Lie?," Time, Oct. 10, 1960, 25; "Stormy K . . . and Television: How Much Influence on the Voters?," Newsweek, Oct. 10, 1960, 28; "Candidate in Orbit," 29.

50 Kempton quoted in Wills, Kennedy Imprisonment, 16; Beverly Smith, "Campaigning with Kennedy," Saturday Evening Post, Oct. 29, 1960, 79.

51 White, Making of the President, 1960, 361; "This Is Kennedy," 26; "Candidate in Orbit," 26.

52 George Reedy, interview with Thomas C. Reeves, quoted in Question of Character, 202; Maxine Cheshire, Maxine Cheshire, Reporter (Boston, 1978), 54; Dallek, Unfinished Life, 375, 768; James Giglio, The Presidency of John F. Kennedy (Lawrence, Kans., 1991), 270–71.

53 Arthur Schlesinger Jr., Kennedy or Nixon: Does It Make Any Difference? (New York, 1960), 4, 11, 15, 17, 18.

54 Ibid., 23–24, 25, 19–20, 28, 13, 24, 22, 4, 25, 33, 27.

Three: Hollywood Cool: Frank Sinatra and the Jack Pack

1 The fullest treatment of JFK's inaugural can be found in Todd S. Purdum, "From That Day Forth," *Vanity Fair,* Feb. 2011.

2 On the Rat Pack, see Richard Gehman, *Sinatra and His Rat Pack* (New York, 1961); Shawn Levy, *Rat Pack Confidential* (New York, 1998); Max Rudin, "Reflections on the Rat Pack," *American Heritage,* Dec. 1998, 52–65.

3 Among many biographical treatments of Sinatra, see James Kaplan, *Frank: The Voice* (New York, 2010) and *Sinatra: The Chairman* (New York, 2015); Anthony Summers and Robbyn Swan, *Sinatra: The Life* (New York, 2005); Bill Zehme, *The Way You Wear Your Hat: Frank Sinatra and the Lost Art of Living* (New York, 1997); Kitty Kelley, *His Way: The Unauthorized Biography of Frank Sinatra* (New York, 1986); Leonard Mustazza, ed., *Frank Sinatra and Popular Culture: Essays on an American Icon* (Westport, Conn., 1998).

4 See Richard Abowitz, "Once in a Lifetime: The Significance of Sinatra," *Gadfly,* March 1998; Francis Davis, "Swing and Sensibility: Frank Sinatra," *Atlantic,* Sept. 1998; "Frank Sinatra," *Telegraph,* May 16, 1998.

5 Thomas M. Pryor, "Rise, Fall, and Rise of Sinatra," *New York Times Magazine,* Feb. 10, 1967, 17.

6 "The Kid from Hoboken," *Time,* Aug. 29, 1955, 52.

7 Gehman, *Sinatra and His Rat Pack,* 22–25. Sinatra quoted in Louis Larkin, "Sinatra: 'Why They Hate Me,'" *Redbook,* Aug. 1959, 92.

8 Gehman, *Sinatra and His Rat Pack,* 169–71.

9 E. J. Kahn, "The Fave, the Fans, and the Fiends," *New Yorker,* Nov. 2, 1946, 35–48; Deborah Kerr quoted in Isabella Taves, "Frank Sinatra," *Woman's Home Companion,* May 1956, 39; Robert George Reisner, "The Word on Frank Sinatra," *Playboy,* Nov. 1958, 62; Sinatra quoted in Tom Waits, "It's Perfect Madness," *Observer,* March 19, 2005.

10 George Jacobs and William Stadiem, *Mr. S: My Life with Frank Sinatra* (New York, 2003), 75; Reisner, "Word on Frank Sinatra," 86; Janet de Cordova quoted in "Remembering Frank," *New York Social Diary,* Dec. 12, 2007.

11 The quotations are from Larkin, "Sinatra: 'Why They Hate Me,'" 94; "Kid from Hoboken," 52; Frank Coss, "Frank Sinatra: Mr. Personality," *Metronome,* Dec. 1957, 15. For an academic treatment of Sinatra's masculinity, see Karen McNally, *When Frankie Went to Hollywood: Frank Sinatra and American Male Identity* (Urbana, Ill., 2008).

12 For an insightful, more theoretical reading of *The Tender Trap* and *Pal Joey* that differs somewhat from mine, see McNally, *When Frankie Went to Hollywood,* 148–69.

13 See Nick Tosches, *Dino: Living High in the Dirty Business of Dreams* (New York, 1992), for an impressionistic but insightful biography of Dean Martin.

14 On Davis's career, see his two volumes of memoirs titled *Yes I Can* (New York, 1965) and *Why Me?* (New York, 1989). Biographies include Wil Haygood, *In Black and White: The Life of Sammy Davis Jr.* (New York, 2003); Gary Fishgall, *Gonna Do Great Things: The Life of Sammy Davis Jr.* (New York, 2003).

15 See James Spada, *Peter Lawford: The Man Who Kept the Secrets* (New York, 1991); Patricia Seaton Lawford, *The Peter Lawford Story,* with Ted Schwarz (New York, 1988).

16 On Bishop's life, see Michael Seth Starr, *Mouse in the Rat Pack: The Joey Bishop Story* (New York, 2002); Levy, *Rat Pack Confidential*, 75–81.

17 Frank Sinatra, "The Way I Look at Race," *Ebony*, July 1958, 34–38, 40, 42–44. For various accounts of the Rat Pack Summit shows, see Gehman, *Sinatra and His Rat Pack*, 71–74; Levy, *Rat Pack Confidential*, 99–115; Rudin, "Reflections on the Rat Pack," 55, 57–59; Robert Legare, "Meeting at the Summit: Sinatra and His Buddies Bust 'Em Up in Vegas," *Playboy*, June 1960, 34–37, 48, 97–100. It should be noted that the Rat Pack's attempts to parody racial prejudice and defuse racial tension occasionally veered into a tastelessness that makes modern observers cringe. For example, when Davis was performing, one of the Rat Pack would heckle from the wings, "Hurry up, Sammy, the watermelon is getting warm."

18 Legare, "Meeting at the Summit," 99; Gehman, *Sinatra and His Rat Pack*, 35.

19 Levy, *Rat Pack Confidential*, 95; Legare, "Meeting at the Summit," 34, 48.

20 For an insightful critique of *Ocean's Eleven* that, once again, differs somewhat from mine, see McNally, *When Frankie Went to Hollywood*, 172–74.

21 "The Jack Pack, 1958–1960," in www.pophistorydig.com; Michael O'Brien, *John F. Kennedy: A Biography* (New York, 2005), 750; Rudin, "Reflections on the Rat Pack," 61; Levy, *Rat Pack Confidential*, 72.

22 Red Fay quoted in Nigel Hamilton, *JFK: Reckless Youth* (New York, 1992), 767; Thomas Broderick, OH, 16–17; William DeMarco, OH, 10; *Boston Globe*, Sept. 28, 1960.

23 Lawford quoted in Levy, *Rat Pack Confidential*, 72.

24 Kenneth O'Donnell and David F. Powers, *Johnny, We Hardly Knew Ye: Memories of John Fitzgerald Kennedy*, with Joe McCarthy (New York, 1976), 18; Wills, *Kennedy Imprisonment*, 22; Judith Exner, *My Story* (New York, 1977), 106, 148.

25 Jacobs and Stadiem, *Mr. S*, 120–21; Ronald Brownstein, *The Power and the Glitter: The Hollywood-Washington Connection* (New York, 1990), 159.

26 Jacobs and Stadiem, *Mr. S*, 126, 129–31.

27 See Rudin, "Reflections on the Rat Pack," 57–58, 61.

28 Brownstein, *The Power and the Glitter*, 155–56.

29 Rudin, "Reflections on the Rat Pack," 61; Gehman, *Sinatra and His Rat Pack*, 53.

30 Sammy Davis Jr., *Hollywood in a Suitcase* (New York, 1980), 83–84.

31 Rudin, "Reflections on the Rat Pack," 61, 63; Davis, *Why Me?*, 108; FBI Frank Sinatra File no. 105-0-23367, Freedom of Information release, reports dated March 29, April 1, and July 26, 1960, 105–6, 110–11, 121.

32 Exner, *My Story*, 63–64, 106, 111, 148, 177–78.

33 Russell Baker, "Daring Democratic Drama Opens to Big Stretches of Empty Seats," *New York Times*, July 12, 1960; Levy, *Rat Pack Confidential*, 163–64; Davis, *Hollywood in a Suitcase*, 84.

34 Davis, *Hollywood in a Suitcase*, 84; Rudin, "Reflections on the Rat Pack," 60; Levy, *Rat Pack Confidential*, 164–65; Spada, *Peter Lawford*, 230.

35 "The Birth of Cool Politics," *Los Angeles Times*, Aug. 13, 2000; Exner, *My Story*, 162–65; Levy, *Rat Pack Confidential*, 164; Spada, *Peter Lawford*, 229.

36 Thomas Rees quoted in Brownstein, *The Power and the Glitter*, 147; "Hollywood Wing in Kennedy Drive," *New York Times*, Sept. 8. 1960; "Birth of Cool Politics"; Spada, *Peter Lawford*, 232–33, 225.

37 Spada, *Peter Lawford*, 226; Brownstein, *The Power and the Glitter*, 158–59; Jacobs and Stadiem, *Mr. S*, 144.

38 Levy, *Rat Pack Confidential*, 155; Davis, *Why Me?*, 117; "Happy as a Clan," *Time*, Dec. 5, 1960, 62; Spada, *Peter Lawford*, 231.

39 Brownstein, *The Power and the Glitter*, 152, 154–56, 147, 153.

40 Ibid., 145, 149; Gehman, *Sinatra and His Rat Pack*, 11–12.

41 The full story of the inaugural is told in Purdum, "From That Day Forth."

42 Purdum, "From That Day Forth"; Levy, *Rat Pack Confidential*, 176–77.

43 Purdum, "From That Day Forth"; "Sinatra Is Sartorial Star," *Washington Post*, Dec. 31, 1960.

44 Levy, *Rat Pack Confidential*, 177–78; Brownstein, *The Power and the Glitter*, 161; Gehman, *Sinatra and His Rat Pack*, 85.

45 Davis, *Yes I Can*, 556, 570; Levy, *Rat Pack Confidential*, 154–55, 175–76; Davis, *Why Me?*, 132.

46 Levy, *Rat Pack Confidential*, 177–78, 189, 213; Kelley, *His Way*, 286, 291; Brownstein, *The Power and the Glitter*, 157–59; "The Hollywood Set and the Kennedy Family," *U.S. News & World Report*, Oct. 16, 1961, 60; "Kennedy Speaks in Los Angeles," *New York Times*, Nov. 19, 1961.

47 Spada, *Peter Lawford*, 254–55; Lawford, interview with Kitty Kelley, quoted in *His Way*, 269.

48 Kelley, *His Way*, 290–91; Gehman, *Sinatra and His Rat Pack*, 185–88; Levy, *Rat Pack Confidential*, 156–58, 191; John Seigenthaler, OH, 176.

49 "Most," 17; "Sinatra Show Set for Kennedy Inauguration," *Los Angeles Times*, Jan. 15, 1961; Ruth Montgomery, "'Rat Pack' in the White House?," quoted in Arnold Shaw, *Sinatra: Twentieth-Century Romantic* (New York, 1968), 276; "Hollywood Set and the Kennedy Family," 60.

50 Brownstein, *The Power and the Glitter*, 162–65.

51 Ibid., 165; Spada, *Peter Lawford*, 292–94; Campbell verifies the end of her relationship with JFK but claimed that contact did not cease until June 1962, in Exner, *My Story*, 251–52; Jacobs and Stadiem, *Mr. S*, 164–65; Levy, *Rat Pack Confidential*, 214–15, 220.

52 Brownstein, *The Power and the Glitter*, 167.

53 Rudin, "Reflections on the Rat Pack," 52.

Four: Existential Tough Guy: Norman Mailer

1 Schlesinger, *Thousand Days*, 62–63.

2 Norman Mailer, "Superman Comes to the Supermart," *Esquire*, Nov. 1960, 123.

3 Schlesinger, *Thousand Days*, 116.

4 Mailer, "Superman Comes to the Supermart," 124. See Peter Schwenger, *Phallic Critiques: Masculinity and Twentieth-Century Literature* (London, 1984), for a discussion of the "virility school" in modern American literature.

5 On Mailer's life, see Hilary Mills, *Mailer: A Biography* (New York, 1982); J. Michael Lennon, *Norman Mailer: A Double Life* (New York, 2013); Peter Manso, *Mailer: His Life and Times* (New York, 1985). The last is a collection of reminiscences (from taped

interviews) from Mailer and some two hundred of his friends, family, colleagues, and associates.

6 Norman Mailer, *The Naked and the Dead* (New York, 1948).

7 David Dempsey, "The Dusty Answers of Modern War," *New York Times Book Review*, May 9, 1948; Mailer, 1980 interview, with Hilary Mills, quoted in her *Mailer*, 106.

8 Norman Mailer, *The Barbary Shore* (New York, 1951); "The Last of the Leftists?," *Time*, May 28, 1951, 61; Norman Mailer, *The Deer Park* (New York, 1955); Dudley Nichols, "Secret Places of the Groin," *Nation*, Nov. 5, 1955, 393; Orville Prescott, "Books of the Times," *New York Times*, Oct. 14, 1955, 25; William Hogan, *San Francisco Chronicle*, Oct. 13, 1955, 23; C. J. Rolo, *Atlantic*, Nov. 1955, 97; Dachine Rainer, "Fattening for the Slaughter," *New Republic*, Oct. 31, 1955, 25; John Brooks, *New York Times Book Review*, Oct. 16, 1955, 5; Richard Chase, "Novelist Going Places," *Commentary*, Dec. 1955, 583; Malcolm Cowley, *New York Herald Tribune Book Review*, Oct 23, 1955, 5.

9 For an anthology of pieces in this new genre, see Tom Wolfe and E. W. Johnson, eds., *The New Journalism* (New York, 1973); an analysis of it can be found in Marc Weingarten, *The Gang That Wouldn't Write Straight: Wolfe, Thompson, Didion, and the New Journalism Revolution* (New York, 2006). See the following Mailer articles: "The Meaning of Western Defense," *Dissent* (Spring 1954): 157–65; "What I Think of Artistic Freedom," *Dissent* (Spring 1955): 98, 192–93; "Reflections on Hipsterism," *Dissent* (Winter 1958): 73–81; "Advertisements for Myself on the Way Out," *Partisan Review* (Fall 1958): 519–40.

10 Tom Carson, "Mailer's Mark," *American Prospect*, Oct. 29, 2013.

11 Mailer, *Advertisements for Myself*, 17, 21.

12 Ibid., 213, 18, 189, 197, 199, 205, 206–7, 204.

13 Ibid., 283–84, 304, 388.

14 Ibid., 19–20, 265, 311–12, 408, 472.

15 Ibid., 92, 234, 222.

16 Mailer quoted in "The Playboy Panel: The Womanization of America," *Playboy*, June 1962, 44, 49, 50, 139.

17 Ibid., 142–43.

18 Mailer, *Advertisements for Myself*, 339. The essay had originally been published in *Dissent* in 1957.

19 Mailer, *Advertisements for Myself*, 354, 355, 340–41.

20 Ibid., 339, 347, 351, 344, 354, 355.

21 Ibid., 362; Mailer quoted in Lennon, *Norman Mailer*, 230.

22 Mailer, *Advertisements for Myself*, 362, 22; Mailer quoted in "The Playboy Panel: Sex and Censorship in Literature and the Arts," *Playboy*, July 1961, 98.

23 Mailer, *Advertisements for Myself*, 314, 347, 355.

24 James Finn, "Virtues, Failures, and Triumphs of an American Writer," *Commonweal*, Feb. 12, 1960, 551; Gore Vidal, "The Norman Mailer Syndrome," *Nation*, Jan. 2, 1960, 15; Benjamin De Mott, "Reading They've Liked," *Hudson Review* (Spring 1960): 146; Irving Howe, "A Quest for Peril," *Partisan Review* (Winter 1960): 146; Ned Polsky, "Reflections on Hipsterism," *Dissent* (Winter 1958): 79; De Mott, "Reading They've Liked," 145; Howe, "Quest for Peril," 143; Finn, "Virtues, Failures, and Triumphs of an American Writer," 552; John Chamberlain, "About Us Squares," *National Review*,

Nov. 1959, 494; George Steiner, "Naked but Not Dead," *Encounter*, Dec. 1961, 67; Alfred Kazin, "How Good Is Norman Mailer," *Reporter*, Nov. 26, 1959, 40–41; Vidal, "Norman Mailer Syndrome," 16.

25 Clay Felker, interview in Manso, *Mailer*, 299–300.

26 Ibid., 300, 301–2.

27 Lerner, Peretz, and Felker, interviews in ibid., 300–302.

28 Felker and Adele Morales Mailer, interviews in ibid., 302–3.

29 Schlesinger and Felker, interviews in ibid., 302–3; Mailer, "Superman Comes to the Supermart," 124.

30 Mailer, interview with Brian Lamb about his book *Oswald's Tale*, *Booknotes*, C-SPAN, June 25, 1995.

31 Ibid.

32 Mailer, 1961 interview with *Mademoiselle*, in *Conversations with Norman Mailer*, ed. J. Michael Lennon (Jackson, Miss., 1988), 50; Mailer, interview in Manso, *Mailer*, 305–6.

33 Mailer, "Superman Comes to the Supermart," 119.

34 Ibid., 120.

35 Ibid., 121.

36 Ibid., 122; Mailer, interview in Manso, *Mailer*, 305.

37 Mailer, "Superman Comes to the Supermart," 122, 124, 123.

38 Ibid., 122–23.

39 Ibid.

40 Ibid., 123.

41 Ibid., 123–25; Norman Mailer, *The Presidential Papers* (New York, 1963), 26–27.

42 Mailer, "Superman Comes to the Supermart," 122–27.

43 Ibid., 125, 127.

44 Mailer, 1961 *Mademoiselle* interview, 50; Mailer, *Presidential Papers*, 60.

45 Felker, interview in Manso, *Mailer*, 304–5.

46 Schlesinger, *Thousand Days*, 116; Schlesinger, interview in Manso, *Mailer*, 303; Jacqueline Kennedy to Norman Mailer, Oct. 24, 1960, Mailer Papers, Harry Ransom Center, University of Texas at Austin. See also Lennon, *Norman Mailer*, 270–71.

47 Pete Hamill, interview with Hilary Mills, quoted in her *Mailer*, 213.

48 For extensive treatments of the 1960 stabbing incident, see ibid., 222–28; Lennon, *Norman Mailer*, 280–93.

49 Mailer, *Presidential Papers*, 183, 74, 86.

50 Ibid., 66.

51 Ibid., 183, 1–2, 2–3, 4, 7.

52 Ibid., 130, 77–78, 171.

53 Ibid., 5, 22–23, 90–91.

54 Richard Gilman, "Why Mailer Wants to Be President," *New Republic*, Feb. 8, 1964, 23; Garry Wills, "The Art of Not Writing Novels," *National Review*, Jan. 14, 1964, 31.

55 *Mailer, Presidential Papers*, 130, 199–200, 4, 134, 183.

56 Manso, *Mailer*, 306; "Playboy Interview: Norman Mailer," *Playboy*, Jan. 1968, 74; 1999 Mailer interview for the French documentary film *Mailer's America*, quoted in Lennon,

Norman Mailer, 274; Jennifer L. Farbar, "Mailer on Mailer," *Esquire,* June 1986, reprinted in Lennon, *Conversations with Norman Mailer,* 342.

57 Mailer, *Advertisements for Myself,* 17.

Five: Secret Agent Men: Ian Fleming and James Bond

1   Fleming related this story in an interview for Geoffrey Hellman in his "Bond's Creator," *New Yorker,* April 12, 1962, 33–34.

2   See ibid.; Christopher Moran, "Ian Fleming and the Public Profile of the CIA," *Journal of Cold War Studies* (Winter 2013): 142; John Pearson, *The Life of Ian Fleming* (New York, 1966), 296–97.

3   Pearson, *Life of Ian Fleming,* 297; Skip Willman, "The Kennedys, Fleming, and Cuba: Bond's Foreign Policy," in *Ian Fleming and James Bond: The Cultural Politics of 007,* ed. Edward P. Comentale, Stephen Watt, and Skip Willman (Bloomington, Ind., 2005), 178–79; Evan Thomas, *The Very Best Men: Four Who Dared: The Early Years of the CIA* (New York, 1995).

4   "Diversification: Bond, Rum, and Agatha," *Time,* June 21, 1968, 33; Raymond Mortimer, review of *On Her Majesty's Secret Service, Sunday Times* (London), March 30, 1963.

5   On Fleming's early life, see Pearson, *Life of Ian Fleming;* Andrew Lycett, *Ian Fleming: The Man Behind James Bond* (Atlanta, 1995). The quotations are from Hellman, "Bond's Creator," 33; "Playboy Interview: Ian Fleming," *Playboy,* Dec. 1964, 98.

6   See Pearson, *Life of Ian Fleming,* 76–96; Lycett, *Ian Fleming,* 101, 119; "Playboy Interview: Ian Fleming," 100; Willman, "Kennedys, Fleming, and Cuba," 181–82.

7   On Fleming's wartime service, see Lycett, *Ian Fleming,* 101–58; Pearson, *Life of Ian Fleming,* 75–120.

8   Pearson, *Life of Ian Fleming,* 122, 134.

9   Lycett, *Ian Fleming,* 67–68, 75, 81–82, while the description comes from "Playboy Interview: Ian Fleming," 97.

10 Ibid., 16, 31, 102–3, 33; Lycett, *Ian Fleming,* 183, 198.

11 Pearson, *Life of Ian Fleming,* 31, 117–19; Lycett, *Ian Fleming,* 87.

12 Pearson, *Life of Ian Fleming,* 17, 30, 67, 160; Lycett, *Ian Fleming,* 28, 85–86, 279–80, 285, 322–25, 407–8.

13 Pearson, *Life of Ian Fleming,* 60, 68–69; Lycett, *Ian Fleming,* 151.

14 Lycett, *Ian Fleming,* 170–71, 34–39, 51, 65, 85, 94, 113, 217; Pearson, *Life of Ian Fleming,* 150–55.

15 Lycett, *Ian Fleming,* 154, 217.

16 Pearson, *Life of Ian Fleming,* 167; "Playboy Interview: Ian Fleming," 100.

17 Ian Fleming, *Casino Royale* (1953; Las Vegas, 2012), 12, 29, 30, 52–53, 44.

18 Ibid., 32–33, 50.

19 Ibid., 27, 97, 90, 146.

20 "Playboy Interview: Ian Fleming," 100; Fleming quoted in Hellman, "Bond's Creator," 32; Ian Fleming, "Intrepid: Silhouette of a Secret Agent," *Sunday Times Magazine,* Oct. 21, 1962; Fleming, *Casino Royale,* 22. See also Anthony Cave Brown, *The Last Hero: Wild Bill Donovan* (New York, 1984).

21 "Playboy Interview: Ian Fleming," 100; Fleming, *Casino Royale*, 49, 56, 62, 68, 113, 125, 132, 178.

22 Ian Fleming, *Moonraker* (New York, 1955), 3–5; Fleming, *Casino Royale*, 6, 8; Ian Fleming, *For Your Eyes Only* (1960; New York, 2003), 4; Ian Fleming, *Goldfinger* (1959; Las Vegas, 2012), 2, 7, 13; Ian Fleming, *Thunderball* (New York, 1961), 15; Ian Fleming, *On Her Majesty's Secret Service* (New York, 1963), 2, 12, 11, 15–17; Ian Fleming, *Diamonds Are Forever* (New York, 1956), 6. Kingsley Amis, writing under the pseudonym "Lt.-Col. William 'Bill' Tanner," amusingly surveyed many of Bond's habits in *The Book of Bond: Every Man His Own 007* (New York, 1965). See also Michael Denning, "Licensed to Look: James Bond and the Heroism of Consumption," in *The James Bond Phenomenon: A Critical Reader*, ed. Christoph Lindner (Manchester, U.K., 2003), 56–75.

23 Ian Fleming, *Live and Let Die* (1954; Waterville, Maine, 2006), 159, and *Goldfinger*, 279. 237.

24 Fleming, *Goldfinger*, 169, 162; Bond in "The Living Daylights" in *Octopussy*, quoted in Jeremy Black, *The Politics of James Bond: From Fleming's Novels to the Big Screen* (Westport, Conn., 2001), 83–84.

25 Paul Johnson, "Sex, Snobbery, and Sadism," *New Statesman*, April 5, 1958, 430–31; Bernard Bergonzi, "The Case of Mr. Fleming," *Twentieth Century*, March 1958, 220–28; "Old Tricks," *Times Literary Supplement*, April 11, 1958, 193; "New Novels," *Listener*, April 23, 1953, 695; Anthony Boucher, "Dr. No," *New York Times*, July 6, 1958; Robert Hatch, "Excitement from England," *Nation*, June 21, 1958, 566–67; Sergeant Cuff, "Dr. No," *Saturday Review*, Aug. 16, 1958, 38; Robert R. Kirsch, "The Book Report," *Los Angeles Times*, Aug. 28, 1957; James Sandoe, "Book Reviews," *New York Herald Tribune Book Review*, July 6, 1958.

26 These figures come from a chart detailing sales of the Bond novels, and a discussion of it, in Lindner, *James Bond Phenomenon*, 16–17.

27 Kingsley Amis, *The James Bond Dossier* (New York, 1965), 28, 15.

28 Lycett, *Ian Fleming*, 367; *Jacqueline Kennedy: Historic Conversations on Life with John F. Kennedy* (interviews with Arthur Schlesinger Jr. in 1964) (New York, 2011), 42–43; Theodore Sorensen, *Kennedy* (New York, 1965), 388.

29 Christopher Hitchens, "Great Scot," *Atlantic Monthly*, March 2004. On JFK's enthusiasm for Buchan, see Evan Thomas, *Robert Kennedy: His Life* (New York, 2000), 40, 119. For two other insightful evaluations of Buchan, see Stella Rimington, "John Buchan and the Thirty-Nine Steps," *Telegraph*, Jan. 11, 2011; Roger Kimball, "Catching Up with John Buchan," *Fortnightly Review*, June 2012.

30 John Buchan, *Pilgrim's Way: An Essay in Recollection* (Cambridge, Mass., 1940), 212, 127, 49–50, 289–90. See also the discussion in Wills, *Kennedy Imprisonment*, 75–76; Kimball, "Catching Up with John Buchan," last page; Michael O'Brien, *John F. Kennedy: A Biography* (New York, 2005), 795–96.

31 See Laurence Leamer, *The Kennedy Men, 1901–1963* (New York, 2001), 185, 223; Barbara Leaming, *Mrs. Kennedy: The Missing History of the Kennedy Years* (New York, 2001), 9.

32 On Bond's background, see his "Obituary," written and published by M. in *The Times* when it was believed the secret agent had been killed, in Ian Fleming, *You Only Live Twice* (New York, 1964), 223–37.

33 Fleming, *Thunderball*, 145; comment on Bond is in his "Obituary," in Fleming, *You Only Live Twice*, 225; JFK's attitude toward military bureaucracy as discussed in Dallek, *Unfinished Life*, 92–94.

34 The quotation on Bond is from his "Obituary," in Fleming, *You Only Live Twice*, 225; Fleming's comment is in "Playboy Interview: Ian Fleming," 106.

35 Allen Dulles, OH, Dec. 5 and 6, 1964, 1–2.

36 Ibid., 16; Peter Grose, *Gentleman Spy: The Life of Allen Dulles* (Boston, 1994), 162–67, 430, 451; Allen Dulles, "Our Spy-Boss Who Loved Bond," *Life*, Aug. 1964, 19; Allen Dulles, "The End of James," in *Great Spy Stories from Fiction*, ed. Allen Dulles (New York, 1969), 362.

37 Grose, *Gentleman Spy*, 492; Dulles, "End of James," 360–61; Dulles, "Our Spy-Boss Who Loved Bond," 19. For a look at the Dulles-Fleming friendship, see Moran, "Ian Fleming and the Public Profile of the CIA," 140–44.

38 Hugh Sidey, "The President's Voracious Reading Habits," *Life*, March 17, 1961, 55–57.

39 Pearson, *Life of Ian Fleming*, 298; Lycett, *Ian Fleming*, 383.

40 Fleming quoted in "007 in Depth: William Plomer Interviews Ian Fleming, 1962," jeremyduns.net/2010/08/23/007-in-depth-william-plomer-interview; Hellman, "Bond's Creator," 34; Thomas, *Very Best Men*, 166; June 1962 exchange of letters between Fleming and Robert Kennedy, quoted in Willman, "Kennedys, Fleming, and Cuba," 190. The originals are held by the Lilly Library in Bloomington, Indiana.

41 Ben Macintyre, *For Your Eyes Only: Ian Fleming and James Bond* (London, 2008), 105; cartoon in *New Yorker*, Sept. 21, 1963, 37; Jeff Smith, "Creating a Bond Market," in Lindner, *James Bond Phenomenon*, 221, which cites documents from the United Artists Collection in the Wisconsin Center for Film and Theater Research; Vincent Canby, "Longevity—the Real James Bond Mystery," *New York Times*, Oct. 16, 1983.

42 Lycett, *Ian Fleming*, 387–89; Black, *Politics of James Bond*, 91–93.

43 "Dr. No," *Film Daily*, March 19, 1963, 7; Brendan Gill, "Yes to No," *New Yorker*, June 1, 1963, 65.

44 Klaus Doss, "Screening Geopolitics: James Bond and the Early Cold War Films, 1962–1967," *Geopolitics* (Spring 2005): 271; "No, No, a Thousand Times No," *Time*, Oct. 19, 1962, 63.

45 Ian Fleming, *From Russia with Love* (1957; New York, 2010), 95; "From No to Yes," *Newsweek*, April 13, 1964, 93; "From Russia with Love," *Variety*, Oct. 14, 1963; Hollis Alpert, "Thrice Over Lightly," *Saturday Review*, April 18, 1964, 29; Benjamin C. Bradlee, *Conversations with Kennedy* (New York, 1975), 221, 227.

46 Lycett, *Ian Fleming*, 418; Moran, "Ian Fleming and the Public Profile of the CIA," 140; Dulles, "Our Spy-Boss Who Loved Bond," 19.

47 Ian Fleming, *The Spy Who Loved Me* (1962; New York, 2003), 110; Ian Fleming, *The Man with the Golden Gun* (New York, 1965), 77–78, 176; Fleming to Krock, quoted in Moran, "Ian Fleming and the Public Profile of the CIA," 124.

48 John Ranelagh, *The Agency: The Rise and Decline of the CIA* (New York, 1987), 352–53.

49 Thomas, *Very Best Men*, 207; the Colby quotations come from William Colby and Peter Forbath, *Honorable Men: My Life in the CIA* (New York, 1978), 180.

50 Harris Wofford, *Of Kennedys and Kings: Making Sense of the Sixties* (New York, 1980), 358; Richard Reeves, *President Kennedy: Profile of Power* (New York, 1993), 72.

51 Ranelagh, *Agency,* 312, 352, 353; Thomas, *Very Best Men,* 95–97, 179–80, 240, 245; Bissell quoted in an interview with Leonard Klady, "007: Bonding Fact and Fiction," *Los Angeles Times,* July 26, 1987. In part, these authors draw upon Bissell's later testimony before a Senate committee, quoted and discussed in U.S. Senate, *Alleged Assassination Plots Involving Foreign Leaders: An Interim Report of the Select Committee to Study Government Operations with Respect to Intelligence Activities* (Washington, D.C., 1975), 181–84.

52 Evan Thomas has perceptively portrayed these CIA figures in *Very Best Men,* 75–86, 130, 192–202, 245, 289.

53 Sorensen, *Kennedy,* 388; Thomas, *Robert Kennedy,* 151–52. The fullest, if rather extreme, argument that JFK's Cuba policy embodied a James Bond fantasy can be found in Willman, "Kennedys, Fleming, and Cuba," 178–201.

54 The *Pravda* piece is reprinted in Black, *Politics of James Bond,* 82; the *Izvestiya* piece is quoted in "Books of Human Bondage," *Time,* April 13, 1962, 41.

55 Ralph G. Martin, *A Hero for Our Time: An Intimate Story of the Kennedy Years* (New York, 1983), 567, which quotes from Martin's interview with Chuck Spalding.

56 Ralph G. Martin, *Seeds of Destruction: Joe Kennedy and His Sons* (New York, 1995), 449–50, based on a memorandum to the author from Frank Cormier's wife, Andrea; Thurston Clarke, *JFK's Last Hundred Days: The Transformation of a Man and the Emergence of a Great President* (New York, 2013), 185–86; Gerald Blaine, *The Kennedy Detail: JFK's Secret Service Agents Break Their Silence* (New York, 2010), 130–31. See Cormier's UPI story, "Kennedy Acts Role of the Straight Man to Aide's Clowning," *New York Times,* Sept. 22, 1963, and then his later recollection of the episode in "Significance Found in Presidential Trivia," *Los Angeles Times,* April 14, 1979.

Six: A Philosophy for Playboys: Hugh Hefner

1 Photographs, inaugural ball tickets, and Hefner's commentary on the JFK inaugural are in Hefner Scrapbook no. 66. This scrapbook, as well as all others mentioned in the endnotes for this chapter, is located at the Playboy Mansion West in Los Angeles, California.

2 Ibid.

3 Hugh Hefner, interview with the author, Nov. 11, 2004.

4 See Watts, *Mr. Playboy,* 49–58.

5 *Playboy* (undated first issue; actually Dec. 1953), 3.

6 Bob Norman (a pen name for Burt Zollo), "Miss Gold-Digger of 1953," *Playboy,* Dec. 1953, 6–8; Burt Zollo, "Open Season on Bachelors," *Playboy,* June 1954, 37–38; Shepherd Mead, "The Sorry Plight of the Human Male," *Playboy,* Nov. 1955, 46–48, 59–61; Shepherd Mead, "The Handling of Women in Business," *Playboy,* Jan. 1957, 53–54; Shepherd Mead, "Beware of Hasty Marriage," *Playboy,* Sept. 1962, 119–20, 205.

7 "Dear Ann and Abby: Move Over for the Masculine Point of View," *Playboy,* Dec. 1958, 25–28; Jay Smith, "A Vote for Polygamy," *Playboy,* July 1955, 15–16; William Iversen, "I Only Want a Sweetheart, Not a Buddy," *Playboy,* July 1960, 57, 75; William Iversen, "Love, Death, and the Hubby Image," *Playboy,* Sept. 1963, 93–94, 192–98, 200–204, 206–10, 212–15.

8 See the following in *Playboy*: Philip Wylie, "The Abdicating Male," Nov. 1956; Wylie, "Womanization of America"; Wylie, "Career Woman"; "Playboy Panel: The Womanization of America."

9 "An Impolite Interview with Hugh Hefner," *Realist,* May 1961, 11, 14.

10 Hefner speaking on 1958 David Susskind television show, the transcript of which was later reprinted in *Mademoiselle* (Oct. 1963), 113; "An Impolite Interview with Hefner," 9–10; Hefner quoted in *Project '62: Playboy of the Modern World* (1962), a Canadian Broadcast Company documentary film.

11 Watts, *Mr. Playboy,* 107–22.

12 Ibid., 109–11, 114–18.

13 "What Is a Playboy?" ad, *Playboy,* April 1956, 73, and then repeated in many issues thereafter.

14 Watts, *Mr. Playboy,* 79, 123–36; Hefner, interview with the author, Nov. 8, 2012.

15 Watts, *Mr. Playboy,* 82, 105–6, 151–52.

16 Hefner in "Playbill," *Playboy,* Dec. 1958, 3; Hefner, interview with author, Jan. 3, 2004; Hefner in *Project '62;* Hefner quoted in Hal Higdon, "Playboying Around the Clock with Hugh Hefner," *Climax,* Feb. 1962, n.p.; Hefner quoted in *Project '62.*

17 On the politics of Hefner and *Playboy* in the 1950s, see Watts, *Mr. Playboy,* 137–42.

18 Ibid., 80–81, 103–4, 138.

19 Ibid., 158–60.

20 Ibid., 156–58.

21 Ibid., 160–62.

22 Hefner, interview with the author, Nov. 8, 2012; Hefner Scrapbook no. 64 for photographs and descriptions of the "Irwin Corey for President" rally and party in 1960.

23 Ralph Ginzburg, "Cult of the Aged Leader," *Playboy,* Aug. 1959, 59–60, 96–98.

24 Reisner, "Word on Frank Sinatra," 62–66, 84–88; "Playboy Interview: Frank Sinatra," *Playboy,* Feb. 1963, 35–40.

25 Hefner Scrapbooks nos. 65 and 67; Hefner, interview with the author, Nov. 8, 2012. See Hugh M. Hefner and Bill Zehme, *Hef's Little Black Book* (New York, 2008), 32, on Sinatra's mixed emotions about Hefner and *Playboy.*

26 Hefner, interview with the author, Nov. 8, 2012; Hefner Scrapbook no. 64.

27 Legare, "Meeting at the Summit," 34–37, 48, 97–100; Hefner interview with author, Nov. 8, 2012. Even many years later, Hefner's magazine continued its fascination with Sinatra and his cronies. See David Halberstam, "Sinatra at Sunset," *Playboy,* April 1998, 76, 154–57; George Jacobs and William Stadiem, "Sinatra and the Dark Side of Camelot," *Playboy,* June 2003.

28 "Playboy Panel: The Womanization of America," 43–50, 133–36, 139–44; "Playboy Panel: Sex and Censorship in Literature and the Arts," 27–28, 72–76, 88–99; Norman Mailer and William F. Buckley, "The Role of the Right Wing in America Today," *Playboy,* Jan. 1963, 110–12, 165–70, 172–74; "Playboy Interview: Norman Mailer," 69–84.

29 Hefner, interview with the author, Nov. 8, 2012; Mailer's attendance at Playboy Mansion party as documented in Hefner Scrapbook no. 75; Norman Mailer, "Ten Thousand Words a Minute," *Esquire,* Feb. 1963, 109–20, republished in his *Presidential Papers,* 213–67.

30 Hefner, interview with the author, Nov. 8, 2012; "Playbill," *Playboy,* March 1960, 6;

Hugh Hefner memo titled "Chronology for Ian Fleming/James Bond/Sean Connery," Oct. 12, 1990, Hefner Papers.

31 "Playbill," *Playboy*, April 1963, 8. The *Playboy* serializations included "The Hildebrand Rarity," March 1960; *On Her Majesty's Secret Service*, beginning in April 1963; *You Only Live Twice*, beginning in April 1964; *The Man with the Golden Gun*, April 1965. See also "Playboy Interview: Ian Fleming" and "Playboy Interview: Sean Connery," *Playboy*, Nov. 1965.

32 "Playbill," *Playboy*, March 1960, 6; Hefner, "Chronology for Ian Fleming/James Bond/ Sean Connery"; Patrick O'Donnell, "James Bond, Cyber-Aristocrat," in Comentale, Watt, and Willman, *Ian Fleming and James Bond*, 59; Fleming quoted in *The Rough Guide to James Bond* (London, 2002), 67.

33 Hefner, interview with the author, Nov. 8, 2012.

34 Ibid.

35 Ibid.

36 Ibid.

37 Watts, *Mr. Playboy*, 174–80.

38 "The Playboy Philosophy," pt. 2, *Playboy*, Jan. 1963, 42, 49.

39 Ibid., 49–50.

40 "The Playboy Philosophy," pt. 3, *Playboy*, Feb. 1963, 43–46.

41 Ibid., 44, 45, 47.

42 "The Playboy Philosophy," pt. 13, *Playboy*, Dec. 1963, 105, 104, and pt. 3, 46, 44.

43 Walter T. Ridder, "The Kennedys: Tastemakers in the White House," *Show Business Illustrated*, Oct. 31, 1961, 25–26, 86.

44 Hefner, interview with the author, Nov. 8, 2012; photograph and description of Joseph Kennedy's visit to Chicago in Hefner Scrapbook no. 70.

45 Cartoon from *Los Angeles* magazine, May 1962, in Hefner Scrapbook no. 73.

46 Watts, *Mr. Playboy*, 350.

47 Hefner's comment about "the Playboy President" came in his interview with the author, Nov. 2012.

Seven: Vigor and Virility: President John F. Kennedy

1 "The 35th," *Time*, Jan. 27, 1961, 11; "A New Hand, a New Voice, a New Verve," *Life*, Jan. 27, 1961, 17.

2 JFK, "Inaugural Address, 20 January 1961," JFKL; Sam Rayburn quoted in "John F. Kennedy: He Brought Youthful Energy to Washington," *Time*, Jan. 2, 1962, 8.

3 "The Take-Over Generation," *Life*, Sept. 14, 1962, 2.

4 "A Family Man with a Big Job to Do," *Life*, Nov. 21, 1960, 33, 37.

5 "Forceful and Diverse," *Newsweek*, Dec. 26, 1960, 15.

6 Joseph Kraft, "Kennedy's Working Staff," *Harper's*, Dec. 1962, 36; "Kennedy's 'Best Men' Move into Power," *Life*, Feb. 17, 1961, 104, 106, 109.

7 Kraft, "Kennedy's Working Staff," 35; "Kennedy's 'Best Men' Move into Power," 109; Laura Bergquist, "Life on the New Frontier," *Look*, Jan. 2, 1962, 18–19.

8 Louis Kraar, "The Two Lives of Robert McNamara," *Life*, Nov. 30, 1962, 99; "Ford's McNamara: Wanted on the New Frontier," *Newsweek*, Dec. 19, 1960, 22.

9   Kraar, "Two Lives of Robert McNamara," 97.

10   Ibid., 96–98, 95.

11   "Ford's McNamara," 20–21; Kraar, "Two Lives of Robert McNamara," 95–98; "The Big Eleven Close Up," *Life*, Jan. 2, 1961, 77; "Vim and Vigah on the New Frontier," *Sports Illustrated*, Aug. 13, 1962, 16–17.

12   "Ford's McNamara," 22; Robert Kennedy quoted in Halberstam, *The Best and the Brightest*, 218; Bradlee, *Conversations with Kennedy*, 230.

13   Robert Manning, "Secretary of Things in General," *Saturday Evening Post*, May 20, 1961, 38–39, 79–81. See also "Meet Mr. Secretary of the Interior," *Field & Stream*, April 1961, 43–45, 99.

14   Dennis Hutchinson, *The Man Who Once Was Whizzer White: A Portrait of Justice Byron R. White* (New York, 1998), 322.

15   "Kennedy's 'Best Men' Move into Power," 100, 115–16; Kraft, "Kennedy's Working Staff," 29–30; Douglass Cater, "A New Style, a New Tempo," *Reporter*, March 16, 1961, 28–29. For another, similar analysis, see "How Kennedy Runs the White House," *U.S. News & World Report*, Nov. 13, 1961, 54–56.

16   "Vim and Vigah on the New Frontier," 16; "The Football Look of Kennedy's Team," *Life*, Nov. 21, 1960, 28–29.

17   JFK, "The Soft American," *Sports Illustrated*, Dec. 26, 1960, 15–17.

18   Ibid., 18–23.

19   "In a Dangerous World, Is American Youth Too Soft?," an interview with Bud Wilkinson, *U.S. News & World Report*, Aug. 21, 1961, 75–77.

20   JFK, "Our Unfit Youth," *Good Housekeeping*, Jan. 1962, 12–15; JFK, "The Vigor We Need," *Sports Illustrated*, July 16, 1962, 12; "The Federal Government Takes on Physical Fitness," jfklibrary.org/JFK/JFK-in-History/Physical Fitness; "The Big Walk: Marines Do It, Bobby Kennedy Does It, 10-Year Olds Do It," *Life*, Feb. 22, 1963, 71–82; "Nip-Ups, Anyone?," *Time*, Feb. 15, 1963, 27; "Physical Fitness on the New Frontier," *U.S. News & World Report*, Feb. 18, 1963,

21   Schlesinger, *Thousand Days*, 3, 731–32; Leonard Bernstein, OH, July 21, 1965, 3.

22   Jack Hamilton, "The Big New Culture Kick," *Look*, Jan. 12, 1962, 57–58; "Versailles-on-the-Potomac," *Esquire*, Jan. 1963, 41; Leslie Judd Ahlander, "Culture Is Breaking Out All Over," *Washington Post*, July 15, 1962.

23   "Arts and Culture in the Kennedy White House," jfklibrary.org.

24   Bernstein, OH, 5–6.

25   Diana Trilling, "A Visit to Camelot," *New Yorker*, June 2, 1997, 65; George Plimpton, "Newport Notes: The Kennedys and Other Salts," *Harper's*, March 1963, 39–47; "Versailles-on-the-Potomac," 43; Schlesinger, *Thousand Days*, 671.

26   JFK, "Remarks at Amherst College, October 26, 1963," JFKL; Schlesinger, *Thousand Days*, 733.

27   Letitia Baldrige Hollensteiner, OH, April 24, 1964, 86.

28   Bernstein, OH, 1–2.

29   Joseph Kraft, "Kennedy and the Intellectuals," *Harper's*, Nov. 1963, 112, 117.

30   Alfred Kazin, "The President and Other Intellectuals," *American Scholar*, Autumn 1961, 504, 507–8, 516; Kennedy's reaction detailed in Schlesinger, *Thousand Days*, 744.

31 Sir Isaiah Berlin, OH, April 12, 1965, 1, 2, 11.

32 Ibid., 5, 9, 10, 18, 21.

33 Schlesinger, "Crisis of American Masculinity," 65.

34 For a fascinating, idiosyncratic look at JFK and the culture of the hat, see Neil Stein-berg, *Hatless Jack: The President, the Fedora, and the History of an American Style* (New York, 2004). On Kennedy's fashion style more generally, see Christian Chensvold, "Jack and John: The Sartorial Dichotomy of JFK," *Ivy Style*, Feb. 3, 2010.

35 "New Fashion Frontier: In the American Manner," *Gentlemen's Quarterly*, March 1962, 87–101, 167–73, esp. 88; John L. Steele, "Well Suited for the White House," *Life*, Oct. 13, 1961, 29–31; "The Well Appointed Wardrobe of President John F. Kennedy," *Esquire*, Jan. 1962, cover and 35–40.

36 For an exhaustive treatment of this film project, see Nicholas J. Cull, "Anatomy of a Shipwreck: Warner Bros., the White House, and the Celluloid Sinking of PT 109," in *Hollywood and the American Historical Film*, ed. J. E. Smyth (Houndmills, U.K., 2012), 138–64.

37 Ibid.; Brian Foy quoted in Robert J. Donovan, OH, June 8, 1983, 35.

38 "PT 109: The Man JFK Picked to Play His Wartime Role," *Look*, June 8, 1963; Bill Da-vidson, "President Kennedy Casts a Movie," *Saturday Evening Post*, Sept. 8, 1962; "20 Years After: PT 109," *Life*, May 17, 1963, 98–99; "On Location with PT 109," *News-week*, July 23, 1962, 70; Bosley Crowther, review of *PT 109, New York Times*, June 27, 1963. For other reviews, see "PT 109," *Variety*, March 14, 1963; "Movie Critics Bomb PT 109 in London," *Los Angeles Times*, July 27, 1963; Morrie Ryskind, "Kennedy Movie: A Question of Taste," *Los Angeles Times*, Feb. 27, 1963.

39 On JFK and civil rights, see Carl M. Brauer, *John F. Kennedy and the Second Recon-struction* (New York, 1977).

40 See the following at the JFKL: "Remarks of Senator John F. Kennedy at Charleston, West Virginia, April 20, 1960"; "Remarks of Senator John F. Kennedy at Wheeling, West Virginia, April 19, 1960"; "Remarks of Senator John F. Kennedy at Glenwood Park, West Virginia, April 26, 1960."

41 Harry M. Caudill, *Night Comes to the Cumberlands: A Biography of a Depressed Area* (Boston, 1962); Schlesinger, *Thousand Days*, 1007.

42 Caudill, *Night Comes to the Cumberlands*, vii, 6–8, 12, 333, 350; Michael Harrington, *The Other America: Poverty in the United States* (New York, 1962), 41.

43 Caudill, *Night Comes to the Cumberlands*, 367–92, xi; William L. Batt, OH, May 10, 1967, 186. See also Carl M. Brauer, "Kennedy, Johnson, and the War on Poverty," *Journal of American History* (June 1982): 98–119.

44 Among the many treatments of the Bay of Pigs, see Jim Rasenberger, *The Brilliant Disaster: JFK, Castro, and America's Doomed Invasion of Cuba's Bay of Pigs* (New York, 2011); Trumbull Higgins, *The Perfect Failure: Kennedy, Eisenhower, and the CIA at the Bay of Pigs* (New York, 1989); Peter Wyden, *Bay of Pigs: The Untold Story* (New York, 1980); Howard Jones, *The Bay of Pigs* (New York, 2008).

45 Sorensen, *Kennedy*, 295–309; Schlesinger, *Thousand Days*, 196.

46 Wofford, *Of Kennedys and Kings*, 361–62.

47 Wills, *Kennedy Imprisonment*, 222–23, 231.

48 Dean, *Imperial Brotherhood*, 184, 292, noting the April 10, 1961, memo in the Schlesinger Papers housed in the JFKL; Wofford, *Of Kennedys and Kings*, 347, 341, 342, 363; Schlesinger, *Thousand Days*, 256; Sorensen, *Kennedy*, 297.

49 Presidential News Conference, April 12, 1961, in Washington, D.C., transcript reprinted in *Kennedy and the Press: News Conferences*, ed. Harold W. Chase and Allen H. Lerman (New York, 1965), 69–70; Schlesinger, *Thousand Days*, 290; Charles E. Bohlen, OH, May 21, 1964, 15, 17.

50 JFK's address before the American Society of Newspaper Editors, April 20, 1961, reprinted in Thomas W. Benson, *Writing JFK: Presidential Rhetoric and the Press in the Bay of Pigs Crisis* (College Station, Tex., 2004), xv–xix.

51 Schlesinger, *Thousand Days*, 292; "Kennedy's World Box Score," *Life*, June 23, 1961, 46; "Kennedy to Castro," *New York Times*, April 21, 1961.

52 The many books examining various aspects of the Cuban missile crisis include Alexander Fursenko and Timothy Naftali, *"One Hell of a Gamble": Khrushchev, Castro, and Kennedy, 1958–1964* (New York, 1997); Michael Dobbs, *One Minute to Midnight: Kennedy, Khrushchev, and Castro on the Brink of Nuclear War* (New York, 2008); David G. Coleman, *The Fourteenth Day: JFK and the Aftermath of the Cuban Missile Crisis* (New York, 2012).

53 Walter Lippmann's column quoted in Ronald Steel, *Walter Lippmann and the American Century* (Boston, 1980), 536; William S. White's column, *San Francisco Examiner*, Oct. 23, 1962; Walter Trohan, "Report from Washington," *Chicago Tribune*, Oct. 27, 1962; Joseph Alsop and Charles Bartlett, "In Time of Crisis," *Saturday Evening Post*, Dec. 8, 1962, 20; Kraft interview, quoted in Collier and Horowitz, *Kennedys*, 300.

54 "When One Man Sizes Up Another," *Newsweek*, Dec. 3, 1962, 23–24.

55 On the Peace Corps, see Schlesinger, *Thousand Days*, 605–9; Gerard T. Rice, *The Bold Experiment: JFK's Peace Corps* (Notre Dame, Ind., 1986).

56 Most of this information and accompanying quotations come from Gerald W. Bush, "The Peace Corps as a Value-Oriented Movement" (Ph.D. diss., Northern Illinois University, 1968), and from the Gerald W. Bush Papers, JFKL. In turn, they are quoted in Dean, *Imperial Brotherhood*, 187–98.

57 "Americans Rate JFK Top Modern President: Kennedy Also Received Highest Average Approval Rating While in Office," www.gallup.com/poll/165902/americans-rate-jfk-top-modern-president.aspx.

58 Laura Bergquist, "JFK One Year Later," *Look*, Jan. 2, 1962, 45; "Both Ike and JFK Hit the 1962 Campaign Trail, and Minnesota Provides a Test of Their Glamour," *Newsweek*, Oct. 22, 1962, 27; William G. Carleton, "The Cult of Personality Comes to the White House," *Harper's*, Dec. 1961, 63–68.

59 "Family Man with a Big Job to Do," 33–34; "Our New First Family," *Look*, Feb. 28, 1961, 3–4, 103–6.

60 "Caroline in the White House," *Newsweek*, May 15, 1961, 65–67; "Family Thanksgiving," *Time*, Dec. 1, 1961, 14; "With the Kennedys on Vacation," *Ladies' Home Journal*, Aug. 1961, 758–66; Igor Cassini, "How the Kennedy Marriage Has Fared," *Good Housekeeping*, Sept. 1962, 68–69, 183–88, 192, 195, 198; *Look*, Jan. 2, 1962, cover photograph, "Uncle Jack," 19–20, and "New Frontierland," 36–37.

61 *Life*, Aug. 16, 1963, cover photo and 26–28.

62 "Both Ike and JFK Hit the 1962 Campaign Trail, and Minnesota Provides a Test of Their Glamour," 26–27.

63 Trilling, "Visit to Camelot," 59, 62; Laura Bergquist Knebel, OH, Dec. 8, 1965, 15–16.

64 "Kennedy Caps Visit with Dip in Pacific," *Los Angeles Times*, Aug. 20, 1962; Scott Harrison, "John F. Kennedy Takes a Swim," LATimes.com, May 13, 2011; O'Donnell and Powers, *Johnny, We Hardly Knew Ye*, 409–10.

65 "Picture of the Week," *Life*, June 2, 1991, 2; *Esquire*, Jan. 1963, foldout cover.

66 Monroe's famous birthday song can be seen on YouTube. JFK biographers who have confirmed Kennedy's affair with Monroe include Dallek, *Unfinished Life*, 580–81; Reeves, *Question of Character*, 317–27; Reeves, *Profile of Power*, 315, 707; Giglio, *Presidency of John F. Kennedy*, 267. Seymour Hersh, in *The Dark Side of Camelot*, 102–6, recounted numerous interviews with figures who confirmed Monroe's sexual relationship with JFK, as did the biographers Anthony Summers, *Goddess: The Secret Lives of Marilyn Monroe* (New York, 1985), and Donald H. Wolfe, *The Last Days of Marilyn Monroe* (New York, 1998), and the Hollywood columnist Earl Wilson, *Show Business Laid Bare* (New York, 1974).

67 See Dallek, *Unfinished Life*, 475–77, 636–37; "Jack Kennedy's Other Women," *Time*, Dec. 29, 1975, 11; Giglio, *Presidency of John F. Kennedy*, 267; Sally Bedell Smith's interviews with Chavchavadze and de Vegh, in *Grace and Power: The Private World of the Kennedy White House* (New York, 2004), 72–73, 152–53, 146–48, 286–88.

68 Traphes Bryant, *Dog Days at the White House: The Outrageous Memoirs of the Presidential Kennel Keeper* (New York, 1975), 35, 38, 37, 24, 22–23.

69 Agents Lawrence Newman, Anthony Sherman, Timothy McIntyre, and Joseph Paolella gave taped interviews to ABC in Dec. 1997 for a shelved news special on JFK's womanizing. These can be viewed at http://www.amazon.com/Survivors-Guilt-Service-Failure -President/dp.

70 See Exner, *My Story*; Nina Burleigh, *A Very Private Woman: The Life and Unsolved Murder of Presidential Mistress Mary Meyer* (New York, 1998). Robert Dallek confirmed Exner's and Meyer's sexual relationships with President Kennedy in *Unfinished Life*, 476–79.

71 Mimi Beardsley, *Once Upon a Secret: My Affair with President John F. Kennedy and Its Aftermath* (New York, 2011). On Beardsley and JFK, see Barbara Gamarekian, OH, June 10, 1964, 15–24; Dallek, *Unfinished Life*, 476; Dallek, *Camelot's Court*, 31–33.

72 Dallek, *Unfinished Life*, 477; Hugh Hefner, interview with the author, Nov. 8, 2012.

73 Schlesinger, *Thousand Days*, 115.

Eight: Celebrity Journalist: Ben Bradlee

1 Bradlee, *Conversations with Kennedy*, 27–28.

2 Ibid., 22; Benjamin C. Bradlee, *A Good Life: Newspapering and Other Adventures* (New York, 1996), 205.

3 Bradlee, *Good Life*, 20–27, 30–34.

4 Ibid., 30, 35–39.

5 Ibid., 43–59.

6 Ibid., 59–60, 62–93.

7   Ibid., 94–111.

8   Ibid., 112–30.

9   Ibid., 133–89.

10 Ibid., 166–71, 172–73, 182–83, 174, 144.

11 Ibid., 84, 130, 145, 73, 149–50.

12 Ibid., 159–64, 174–77.

13 Ibid., 191–203.

14 Ibid., 206–7.

15 Bradlee, *Conversations with Kennedy,* 15, 16.

16 See the photograph of Ben and Tony Bradlee sitting with Jacqueline Kennedy at JFK's announcement of his candidacy, in Jeff Himmelman, *Yours in Truth: A Personal Portrait of Ben Bradlee* (New York, 2012), 77; Bradlee, *Good Life,* 205.

17 Bradlee, *Conversations with Kennedy,* 21–22, 25–26.

18 Ibid., 22, 28, 31–32.

19 "Memorandum for Sen. John F. Kennedy," May 9, 1959, in folder "Ben Bradlee, May 1959–February 1962," JFKL.

20 William L. Jacobs, OH, July 6, 1964, 4–8.

21 Bradlee, *Conversations with Kennedy,* 18–20.

22 Ibid., 31–32.

23 Ibid., 11, 193, 196, 199, 204, 208.

24 "Mr. Kennedy Today—the Change in Him," *Newsweek,* Jan. 23, 1961, 19; "The First Days," *Newsweek,* Jan. 30, 1961, 18; "Fast Action on the New Frontier," *Newsweek,* Feb. 4, 1961, 15; "JFK in the Bully Pulpit," *Newsweek,* June 24, 1963, 27–28.

25 "Anatomy of a Speech," *Newsweek,* Oct. 9, 1961, 15; "Kennedy Closing the 'Kennedy Gap,'" *Newsweek,* Nov. 27, 1961, 15–16; "Kennedy: A Wider Choice," *Newsweek,* Aug. 7, 1961, 13; "In Every Sense, Capitalism on Trial" and "Non-spectation," *Newsweek,* Dec. 18, 1961, 25–26.

26 Bradlee, *Good Life,* 221, 229, 249; Bradlee, *Conversations with Kennedy,* 49.

27 Bradlee, *Conversations with Kennedy,* 152; Bradlee, *Good Life,* 222.

28 Bradlee, interview in 1975, quoted in Himmelman, *Yours in Truth,* 78–79.

29 Bradlee, *Conversations with Kennedy,* 51, 154.

30 Ibid., 73, 127; Douglass Cater, OH, Nov. 17, 1982, 23.

31 Fletcher Knebel, "Kennedy vs. the Press," *Look,* Aug. 28, 1962, 19; Arthur Krock, "Mr. Kennedy's Management of the News," *Fortune,* March 1963, 82, 199.

32 Bradlee, *Conversations with Kennedy,* 18, 132; Berlin, OH, 5.

33 Roger Mudd, *The Place to Be: Washington, CBS, and the Glory Days of Television News* (New York, 2008), 95; Barbara Gamarekian, OH, June 10, 1964, 27–28.

34 Knebel, "Kennedy vs. the Press," 20; Bradlee, *Conversations with Kennedy,* 114–16, 118, 22.

35 James Fallows, "Big Ben," *Washington Monthly,* Nov. 1, 1995, n.p.

36 Bradlee, *Conversations with Kennedy,* 95; David Remnick, "Last of the Red Hots," *New Yorker,* Sept. 18, 1995, 79; Burleigh, *Very Private Woman,* 19–20.

37 McGeorge Bundy memo to Lyndon B. Johnson, quoted in Bradlee, *Good Life,* 263; Remnick, "Last of the Red Hots," 79; Bradlee, *Conversations with Kennedy,* 212–13.

38   Bradlee, *Good Life,* 149–50.

39   Ibid., 70, 163.

40   Michael Lewis, "He Lost It at the Movies," *New Republic,* Nov. 20, 1995, 40; Carl S. Stepp, "Wise Words from Two Old Warriors," *American Journalism Review,* Sept. 1995; Phil Bronstein, "The Newsroom," *New York Times,* Aug. 3, 2012; Remnick, "Last of the Red Hots," 76, 78.

41   "If You Knew Ben Like I Knew Ben," *Weekly Standard,* Nov. 3, 2014, 10; "Ben Bradlee's Charmed, Charming Life," *New York Times,* Oct. 22, 2014.

42   Bradlee, *Conversations with Kennedy,* 55, 187, 100, 147, 144; Wills, *Kennedy Imprisonment,* 20.

43   Bradlee, *Conversations with Kennedy,* 74–75, 76, 62, 126.

44   See portion of Kennedy's Jan. 5, 1960, interview on YouTube, and other portions presented in Himmelman, *Yours in Truth,* 311–14.

45   Bradlee, *Conversations with Kennedy,* 148, 49; Bradlee, *Good Life,* 216–17.

46   Bradlee, *Good Life,* 394, 217.

47   Bradlee, *Conversations with Kennedy,* 187; Smith, *Grace and Power,* 144–45, based on an interview with Tony Pinchot Bradlee.

48   Bradlee, *Conversations with Kennedy,* 196–98; Smith, *Grace and Power,* 363–65.

49   Tony Pinchot interview with Sally Bedell Smith, quoted in *Grace and Power,* 411. Two of Bradlee children's told his biographer about their mother's version of the incident, which she had related to them on several occasions. See Himmelman, *Yours in Truth,* 314–16.

50   Bradlee, *Conversations with Kennedy,* 190, 192; Himmelman, *Yours in Truth,* 315–16, 318; Arthur Schlesinger Jr., *Journals, 1952–2000* (New York, 2007), 387.

51   Smith, *Grace and Power,* 144–45, 365; Bradlee, *Good Life,* 232.

52   Burleigh, *Very Private Woman,* 192, 180; Smith, *Grace and Power,* 233–35. James Truitt first brought the affair to light in a story in the *National Enquirer* and then in subsequent interviews with newspapers such as *The Washington Post.* The affair was then confirmed by Anne Truitt and Tony Pinchot Bradlee.

53   Burleigh, *Very Private Woman,* 35–42.

54   Ibid., 54–71.

55   Ibid., 119–25, 145–46, 149, 203–4.

56   Ibid., 122–23, 163, 175, 222; Smith, *Grace and Power,* 235.

57   Burleigh, *Very Private Woman,* 26. On the influence of Georgetown in the postwar period, see Gregg Herken, *The Georgetown Set: Friends and Rivals in Cold War Washington* (New York, 2014), 7; C. David Heymann, *The Georgetown Ladies' Social Club: Power, Passion, and Politics in the Nation's Capital* (New York, 2003).

58   Burleigh, *Very Private Woman,* 24–25, 187–88, 189, 191.

59   Ibid., 124, 157, 160–62.

60   Ibid., 193–95.

61   Ibid., 221–22, 224; Smith, *Grace and Power,* 254–55.

62   Burleigh, *Very Private Woman,* 194–95, 225; interview with Blair Clark, quoted in Heymann, *Georgetown Ladies' Social Club,* 160.

63   Burleigh, *Very Private Woman,* 218–19; Bradlee, *Conversations with Kennedy,* 213–14.

64 Burleigh, *Very Private Woman,* 230–35. The story of the trial is related on pp. 257–74.

65 Bradlee, *Good Life,* 267–68; Burleigh, *Very Private Woman,* 245–48.

66 Bradlee, *Good Life,* 267–69; Bradlee, *Conversations with Kennedy,* 54. After Meyer's death, the drug guru Timothy Leary, in his memoir *Flashbacks: A Personal and Cultural History of an Era* (New York, 1983), 128–30, 178, and in an article for *Rebel* (an alternative magazine), contended that she had contacted him, experimented with LSD, and wanted to learn how to administer it to "this friend who is a very important man." He hinted that Meyer had taken LSD with President Kennedy. This suggestion seems far-fetched and is impossible to verify.

67 Bradlee, *Good Life,* 269–71; Burleigh, *Very Private Woman,* 285–88.

Nine: Modern Warriors: Maxwell Taylor and Edward Lansdale

1 Donald Duncan, *The New Legions* (New York, 1967), 187–89.

2 "JFK in History: Green Berets," JFKL; "The Presidency: That's the Spirit," *Time,* Oct. 20, 1961.

3 Robert S. McNamara, OH, April 4, 1964, 19.

4 "National Security Memorandum No. 2," Feb. 3, 1961, JFK Papers, Presidential Papers, National Security Files, JFKL.

5 JFK, "Address at the U.S. Military Academy, West Point, 6 June 1962," JFK Papers, Presidential Papers, JFKL; Stewart Alsop, "Kennedy's Grand Strategy," *Saturday Evening Post,* March 31, 1962, 14–16; Roger Hilsman, *To Move a Nation: The Politics of Foreign Policy in the Administration of John F. Kennedy* (Garden City, N.Y., 1967), 53. See Dallek, *Unfinished Life,* 346, for a cogent discussion of JFK's advocacy of a strategy of "flexible response" instead of the earlier one of "massive retaliation."

6 Schlesinger, *Thousand Days,* 340–41; George J. W. Goodman, "The Unconventional Warriors," *Esquire,* Nov. 1961, 130.

7 For details on Taylor's life and career, see his autobiography, *Swords and Plowshares* (New York, 1972); Robert S. Gallagher, "An Exclusive Interview with General Maxwell D. Taylor," *American Heritage Magazine,* April/May 1981, 4–17; John M. Taylor, *An American Soldier: The Wars of General Maxwell Taylor* (1989; Novato, Calif., 2001).

8 Ibid.

9 Maxwell D. Taylor, *The Uncertain Trumpet* (1959; New York, 1960), xi, 17–18, 146, 147–48, 150, 179.

10 JFK to Evan Thomas, Dec. 17, 1959, and JFK to Maxwell Taylor, April 9, 1960, both quoted in Taylor, *American Soldier,* 8. For confirmation of Taylor's influence on Kennedy's thinking about a new military strategy after he assumed the presidency, see Sorensen, *Kennedy,* 626; Schlesinger, *Thousand Days,* 310.

11 JFK to Taylor, April 22, 1961, JFK Papers, Presidential Papers, National Security Files, JFKL; Taylor, *Swords and Plowshares,* 190–91. On Taylor's report, see also Hilsman, *To Move a Nation,* 78–79; Sorensen, *Kennedy,* 298, 301, 304, 308.

12 Taylor, *Swords and Plowshares,* 204–5, 199. On Taylor's special advisory role to the president, see Schlesinger, *Thousand Days,* 297; Sorensen, *Kennedy,* 607.

13 Charles Maechling, "Camelot, Robert Kennedy, and Counter-insurgency: A Memoir," *VQR: A National Journal of Literature and Discussion* (Summer 1999): 5; Hilsman, *To Move a Nation*, 53, 427.

14 National Security Memorandum No. 124, "Establishment of the Special Group (Counter-insurgency)," Jan. 18, 1962, JFK Papers, Presidential Papers, National Security Files, JFKL.

15 Taylor, *Swords and Plowshares*, 200–202, 252–53; "Exclusive Interview with General Maxwell D. Taylor," 10. On Taylor's role in developing counterinsurgency policy, see Schlesinger, *Thousand Days*, 341.

16 Jack Raymond, *Power at the Pentagon* (New York, 1964), 290. This theme is stressed by Halberstam, *The Best and the Brightest*, 162–63.

17 "A Soldier and the White House," *Time*, July 28, 1961, 9–13.

18 Maxwell Taylor, "The American Soldier" (commencement address at the U.S. Military Academy, June 5, 1963), reprinted in full as app. B, in Taylor, *American Soldier*, 404–10.

19 JFK quoted in Taylor, *American Soldier*, 241, and in "Cold War: Chief of Staff," 10; Edward O. Guthman and Jeffrey Shulman, eds., *Robert Kennedy in His Own Words* (New York, 1988), 255; Averell Harriman, OH, June 6, 1965; Maxwell Taylor to Tom Taylor, July 8, 1962, quoted in Taylor, *American Soldier*, 242.

20 Taylor, *American Soldier*, 290; "Exclusive Interview with General Maxwell D. Taylor," 12; Taylor, *Swords and Plowshares*, 259.

21 Taylor, *Swords and Plowshares*, 185; Taylor, *American Soldier*, 241–42.

22 Cecil B. Currey, *Edward Lansdale: The Unquiet American* (Boston, 1988), 4–8, 9–16.

23 Ibid., 17–26.

24 Ibid., 34; Jonathan Nashel, *Edward Lansdale's Cold War* (Amherst, Mass., 2005), 31–34.

25 Nashel, *Edward Lansdale's Cold War*, 77–78, 80–81; Currey, *Edward Lansdale*, 66–67, 136.

26 Currey, *Edward Lansdale*, 83–84.

27 Edward G. Lansdale, *In the Midst of Wars: An American's Mission to Southeast Asia* (1972; New York, 1991), 10; Edward G. Lansdale, "A Political Warfare Lesson," April 1954, quoted in Nashel, *Edward Lansdale's Cold War*, 191.

28 Edward G. Lansdale, "Civic Action" (lecture delivered to the Special Warfare Center at Fort Bragg, Feb. 24, 1961); Edward Lansdale, comments in *Counterinsurgency: A Symposium, April 16–20, 1962*, ed. Stephen T. Hosmer and Sibylle O. Crane (Rand Corporation, 1963), 56.

29 Lansdale's comments in Hosmer and Crane, *Counterinsurgency*, 60; Edward G. Lansdale, "Art of Guerilla War—I," *Christian Science Monitor*, Jan. 18, 1964; Edward G. Lansdale, "Vietnam: Do We Understand Revolution?," *Foreign Affairs*, Oct. 1964, 2.

30 Edward G. Lansdale, "Art of Guerilla War—II," *Christian Science Monitor*, Jan. 20, 1964; Lansdale to Gilpatric, June 19, 1961, memorandum.

31 Lansdale to Gilpatric, "Paper I: Counter-guerilla Training," June 19, 1961, memorandum; "Lansdale's Team Report on Covert Saigon Mission in 1954 and 1955," quoted in Nashel, *Edward Lansdale's Cold War*, 82.

32 Lansdale, "Military Psychological Operations, Part Two," March 29, 1960, quoted in Nashel, *Edward Lansdale's Cold War,* 40; Lansdale, *In the Midst of Wars,* 74–75.

33 See Nashel, *Edward Lansdale's Cold War,* 173–78, for a revealing discussion of Lansdale and *The Ugly American.*

34 See Nashel, *Edward Lansdale's Cold War,* 149–62, for an insightful discussion of Lansdale, Graham Greene, and *The Quiet American.*

35 A. J. Langguth, "Our Policy-Making Men in Saigon," *New York Times Magazine,* April 28, 1968, 102; Jack Lasco, "Our Mysterious Edward G. Lansdale: America's Deadliest Secret Agent," *Saga: The Magazine for Men,* March 1967, 92; Jim Lucas, "Bad News for Red Warlords—Lansdale Heads for Vietnam," *Washington News,* Oct. 14, 1961.

36 Joseph Baker, interview, quoted in Currey, *Edward Lansdale,* 176; Roswell L. Gilpatric, OH, May 5, 1970, 99–100; Nashel, *Edward Lansdale's Cold War,* 72.

37 Nashel, *Edward Lansdale's Cold War,* 163–73; Michael McClintock, *Instruments of Statecraft: U.S. Guerilla Warfare, Counterinsurgency, and Counterterrorism, 1940–1990,* chap. 8, p. 1, at http://www.statecraft.org/chapter 8.html.

38 "National Security Action Memo No. 9," Feb. 4, 1961, JFK to McGeorge Bundy, at http://www.fas.org/irp/offdocs/nsam-jfk/nsam9.jpg; American Officer, "The Report the President Wanted Published," *Saturday Evening Post,* May 20, 1961, 31, 69–70.

39 Halberstam, *The Best and the Brightest,* 124; Gilpatric, OH, 8–9.

40 William Bundy, OH, Nov. 12, 1964, 6; Chester Bowles, OH no. 2, July 1, 1970, 99; Roger Hilsman, OH, Aug. 14, 1970, 22; Nashel, *Edward Lansdale's Cold War,* 86–87.

41 "Memorandum to the President" from Walt Rostow, Feb. 24, 1961, JFK Papers, Presidential Papers, JFKL; Fursenko and Naftali, *"One Hell of a Gamble,"* 144; McGeorge Bundy, OH, March 1964, 29–30; David Martin, "The CIA's 'Loaded Gun,'" *Washington Post,* Oct. 10, 1976.

42 Lansdale, "Civic Action," quoted in Nashel, *Edward Lansdale's Cold War,* 93; Lansdale to Ngo Dinh Diem, Jan. 30, 1961, quoted in Currey, *Edward Lansdale,* 226.

43 Hilsman, *To Move a Nation,* 415.

44 For the text of Lansdale's memorandum, see *United States–Vietnam Relations, 1945–1967* (Washington, D.C., 1971), bk. 11, 1–12. See also Halberstam, *The Best and the Brightest,* 127; Schlesinger, *Thousand Days,* 320, 539–40.

45 W. W. Rostow, *The Diffusion of Power: An Essay in Recent History* (New York, 1972), 264–65; "Summary Record of a Meeting, White House, January 28, 1961," in *Foreign Relations of the United States, 1961–1963,* vol. 1, *Vietnam, 1961* (Washington, D.C., 1988), doc. 3; Currey, *Edward Lansdale,* 224–25; Halberstam, *The Best and the Brightest,* 128–29; Brigadier General Lansdale, "Memorandum for Deputy Secretary Gilpatric," April 25, 1961, in *United States–Vietnam Relations, 1945–1967* (Washington, D.C., 1971), 11:36.

46 JFK to Maxwell Taylor, Oct. 13, 1961, and Taylor's account of the task force's work in Vietnam, both in *Swords and Plowshares,* 225–26, 227–41. The Taylor Report is summarized, along with chunks of quotation, in *United States–Vietnam Relations, 1945–1967,* 11:94–101. For other discussions of the Taylor mission, see Schlesinger, *Thousand Days,* 545; Hilsman, *To Move a Nation,* 422–23, 507, 510–11; Rostow, *Diffusion of Power,* 274–78.

47 Taylor quoted in William J. Rust, *Kennedy in Vietnam* (New York, 1985), 45; Lansdale quoted in Currey, *Edward Lansdale*, 238.

48 Currey, *Edward Lansdale*, 237. See also the description of the Taylor-Lansdale snit in Halberstam, *The Best and the Brightest*, 164.

49 Taylor, *Swords and Plowshares*, 280.

50 Richard Bissell testimony, July 25, 1975, quoted and summarized in U.S. Senate, *Alleged Assassination Plots Involving Foreign Leaders*, 141; Edward Lansdale testimony, July 8, 1975, *United States Senate Select Committee to Study Governmental Operations with Respect to Intelligence Activities* (Washington, D.C., 1975), 3–6.

51 "Memorandum from President Kennedy," Nov. 30, 1961, in *Foreign Relations of the United States, 1961–1963*, vol. 10 (Washington, D.C., 1997), 688–89.

52 "The Cuba Project," Eyes Only of Addressees, Feb. 20, 1962, JFK Papers, Presidential Papers, National Security Files, "Special Group Augmented Jan.–June 1962," box 319, JFKL; "Illumination by Submarine" memorandum by Brigadier General Lansdale, Oct. 15, 1962, JFK Papers, Presidential Papers, National Security Files, "Special Group Augmented Jan.–June 1962," box 319, JFKL; Currey, *Edward Lansdale*, 243–44.

53 "Minutes of Meeting of Special Group Augmented on Operation Mongoose, Oct. 4, 1962," photocopy from the Gerald R. Ford Library.

54 U.S. Senate, *Alleged Assassination Plots Involving Foreign Leaders*, 147–48; Ranelagh, *Agency*, 385–89.

55 JFK, "Letter to the United States Army, April 11, 1962," White House Chronological File, box 5, April 1962 3–15 folder, JFKL.

56 Joseph Kraft, "Hot Weapon in the Cold War," *Saturday Evening Post*, April 28, 1962, 88; Alsop, "Kennedy's Grand Strategy," 16; John Hellman, *American Myth and the Legacy of Vietnam* (New York, 1986), 44–45; "Jungle Faculty," *Newsweek*, March 6, 1961, 33–34. For scholarly analyses of JFK and the Special Forces, see J. Justin Gustainis, "John F. Kennedy and the Green Berets: The Rhetorical Use of the Hero Myth," *Communication Studies* (Spring 1989): 41–53; John Hellman, "The Return of the Frontier Hero: National Purpose and the Legend of the Green Berets," in *American Myth and the Legacy of Vietnam*, 41–69; Richard Slotkin, "Gunfighters and Green Berets: The Magnificent Seven and the Myth of Counter-insurgency," *Radical History Review* (1989): 65–90.

57 Everett H. Ortner, "U.S. Special Forces: The Faceless Army," *Popular Science*, Aug. 1961, 56–59, 172–73; Goodman, "Unconventional Warriors," 129, 131.

58 JFK, "Address at U.S. Military Academy, West Point, June 6, 1962," JFK Papers, Presidential Papers, JFKL; Kraft, "Hot Weapon in the Cold War," 87–88; Will Sparks, "Guerillas in Vietnam," *Commonweal*, June 29, 1962, 344–46.

59 "Jungle Faculty," 33; Goodman, "Unconventional Warriors," 131; "The American Guerillas: How to Multiply Small Numbers by an Anti-Communist Factor," *Time*, March 10, 1961, 19; "The Men in the Green Berets," *Time*, March 2, 1962, 19–20; Kraft, "Hot Weapon in the Cold War," 91, 87–88.

60 Kraft, "Hot Weapon in the Cold War," 88; Goodman, "Unconventional Warriors," 130, 132; "Men in the Green Berets," 19–20; Yarmolinsky quoted in Michael Charlton and Anthony Moncrief, *Many Reasons Why: The American Involvement in Vietnam* (New York, 1978), 60–61.

Ten: The Spartacus Syndrome: Kirk Douglas and Tony Curtis

1 This episode is recounted in Paul B. Fay Jr., *The Pleasure of His Company* (New York, 1966), 108–12; "Kennedy Attends Movie in Capital: Slips Out of the White House to See 'Spartacus' with Sub-cabinet Official," *New York Times*, Feb. 5, 1961.

2 Wills, *Kennedy Imprisonment*, 22; Nasaw, *Patriarch*, 101–55.

3 Wills, *Kennedy Imprisonment*, 22; Blair and Blair, *Search for JFK*, 18; William N. Fraleigh, OH, Nov. 1961; Smith, *Grace and Power*, 60; David Pitts, *Jack and Lem: John F. Kennedy and Lem Billings: The Untold Story of an Extraordinary Friendship* (New York, 2007), 79.

4 Pitts, *Jack and Lem*, 79–80.

5 Blair and Blair, *Search for JFK*, 419–20.

6 Reeves, *Question of Character*, 83; Blair and Blair, *Search for JFK*, 181–82, 550.

7 Blair and Blair, *Search for JFK*, 548–50.

8 Bradlee, interview with Arthur Schlesinger, Aug. 26, 1964, quoted in Himmelman, *Yours in Truth*, 85; "What's Playing at the White House Movie Theater?," *Washingtonian*, Feb. 25, 2011; Barbara Gamarekian, "All the President's Popcorn," *New York Times*, May 23, 1985.

9 Bradlee, *Conversations with Kennedy*, 128, 129, 137; Peter Bowen, "Presidential Projections," *Focus Features*, Sept. 19, 2008; O'Brien, *John F. Kennedy*, 753.

10 Schlesinger, *Journals, 1952–2000*, 137; "The Best Perk in the White House," *Guardian*, June 3, 2004; Bradlee, *Conversations with Kennedy*, 142, 221, 227; Smith, *Grace and Power*, 432–33.

11 Smith, *Grace and Power*, 258, 239; O'Brien, *John F. Kennedy*, 753.

12 Laura Bergquist Knebel, OH, Aug. 1, 1977, 22; Smith, *Grace and Power*, 231; Leaming, *Mrs. Kennedy*, 148–54; "Events: 21 September 1961, Luncheon, Cast of 'Advise and Consent,'" JFK Papers, White House Staff Files of Sandford L. Fox, "Social Events, 1961–1964," JFKL.

13 Stephen B. Armstrong, ed., *John Frankenheimer: Interviews, Essays, and Profiles* (New York, 2013), 149–50; J. Hoberman, "Film: A Co-production of Sinatra and JFK," *New York Times*, Sept. 14, 2003; David Talbot, *Brothers: The Hidden History of the Kennedy Years* (New York, 2007), 148–49.

14 Smith, *Grace and Power*, 388–89.

15 See "The Kennedy Library Remembers Filmmaker Robert Drew," http://archiveblog .jfklibrary.org; Andrea Passafiume, "Primary," http://www.tcm.com/this-month/article .htlm; Jeanne Hall, "Realism as a Style in Cinema Verité: A Critical Analysis of *Primary*," *Cinema Journal* (Summer 1991): 24–50; Richard Krolick, "Cinema Verité, Documentary Television, and How It Grew with Robert Drew," *Television Quarterly* (Spring 1996): 68–75.

16 Andrea Passafiume, "Adventures on the New Frontier," http://www.tcm.com/this -month/article.htlm; Lorraine LoBianco, "Crisis: Behind a Presidential Commitment," http://www.tcm.com/this-month/article.htlm. For an informative overview of Drew's film, with much interview commentary by the filmmaker, see P. J. O'Connell, *Robert Drew and the Development of Cinema Verite in America* (Carbondale, Ill., 2010).

17 See Kirk Douglas, *I Am Spartacus: Breaking the Blacklist, Making a Film* (New York, 2012), for Douglas's personal account of this film project.

18 Martin M. Winkler, "The Holy Cause of Freedom: American Ideals in *Spartacus,*" in *Spartacus: Film and History,* ed. Martin M. Winkler (Malden, Mass., 2007), 165.

19 Kirk Douglas, *The Ragman's Son: An Autobiography* (New York, 1988), 331–32; Winkler, "Holy Cause of Freedom," 168; Jeffrey P. Smith, "'A Good Business Proposition': Dalton Trumbo, *Spartacus,* and the End of the Blacklist," *Velvet Light Trap* 23 (Spring 1989): 92–93.

20 "Cinema: The New Pictures," *Time,* Oct. 24, 1960; "A Mighty Tale Told Large," *Life,* Oct. 24, 1960; Bosley Crowther, "'Spartacus' Enters the Arena," *New York Times,* Oct. 7, 1960; "Spartacus," *Variety,* Oct. 12, 1960, 6; *Hollywood Reporter* and Daughters of the American Revolution quoted in Smith, "'Good Business Proposition,'" 92–93.

21 Maria Wyke, *Projecting the Past: Ancient Rome, Cinema, and History* (New York, 1997), 71–72.

22 "Cinema: The New Pictures"; "Spartacus," *Variety,* Oct. 12, 1960, 6.

23 "Cinema: The New Pictures." See also "The New Movie: Spartacus," *New York Herald Tribune,* Oct. 2, 1960; "Behind the Scenes: Dream Coming True," *Newsweek,* March 9, 1959, 110; Hollis Alpert, "The Day of the Gladiator," *Saturday Review,* Oct. 1, 1960, 32; "Spartacus," *Variety,* Oct. 12, 1960.

24 Fay, *Pleasure of His Company,* 111–12; "John F. Kennedy's Favorite Movies," Miscellaneous Information, www.jfklibrary.org>Research>Ready Reference; J. Hoberman, *The Dream Life: Movies, Media, and the Mythology of the 1960s* (New York, 2003), 36.

25 "Kennedy Attends Movie in Capital"; C. A. Robinson Jr., "Spartacus, Rebel Against Rome," in Winkler, *Spartacus,* 112–23, esp. 113, 114–15, 120.

26 For details on Douglas's life, see Douglas, *Ragman's Son;* Michael Munn, *Kirk Douglas* (London, 1985); Tony Thomas, *The Films of Kirk Douglas* (Secaucus, N.J., 1972).

27 Thomas, *Films of Kirk Douglas,* 61, 21.

28 "Hollywood's Muscle Men and Pin-Up Pretties," *Movieland,* Oct. 1954, 49; Douglas, *Ragman's Son,* 415, 475, 365.

29 Douglas, *Ragman's Son,* 355, 381, 193, 272.

30 Cohan, *Masked Men,* 167; Douglas, *Ragman's Son,* 279, 106–8, 145, 149, 162, 169, 170, 172, 176, 184–85, 192, 246.

31 Douglas, *Ragman's Son,* 257.

32 Douglas, *I Am Spartacus,* 49, 113, 94, 99, 118.

33 Ibid., 104–5, 146; Douglas, *Ragman's Son,* 332–33.

34 Douglas, *I Am Spartacus,* 144–45; Tony Curtis, *Tony Curtis, American Prince,* with Peter Golenbock (New York, 2008), 223.

35 Douglas, *I Am Spartacus,* 125–29, 147, 150–51.

36 Douglas, *Ragman's Son,* 310.

37 Ibid., 334, 366–67; Douglas, *I Am Spartacus,* 76.

38 Douglas, *I Am Spartacus,* 152–55; Douglas, *Ragman's Son,* 241.

39 Douglas, *I Am Spartacus,* 36, 4; Douglas, *Ragman's Son,* 485–89; Douglas quoted in Duncan Cooper, "Who Killed Spartacus?," *Cineaste* 18, no. 3 (1991): 27.

40 Douglas, *Ragman's Son,* 485, 348, 370; Bradlee, *Conversations with Kennedy,* 128.

41 Douglas, *Ragman's Son,* 367–68.

42 Ibid., 349; Talbot, *Brothers,* 148–50.

43 Douglas, *Ragman's Son,* 313–14; Douglas, *I Am Spartacus,* 79–81.

44 For the story of Curtis's life and career, see Curtis, *American Prince;* Tony Curtis and Barry Paris, *Tony Curtis: The Autobiography* (New York, 1993); Allen Hunter, *Tony Curtis: The Man and His Movies* (New York, 1985). The quotation on Grant is from Curtis, *American Prince,* 67.

45 Shana Alexander, "Bee-yoody-ful Life of a Movie Caliph," *Life,* Nov. 30, 1961, 169–70; Curtis, *American Prince,* 115, 164, 170.

46 Curtis and Paris, *Tony Curtis,* 179; Gwen Davis, "Farewell, Tony Curtis," *Vanity Fair,* Oct. 5, 2010; Curtis, *American Prince,* 10–19, 165–66, 261.

47 Curtis, *American Prince,* 145–47, 183–86, 280.

48 Ibid., 168; Robert L. Green, "Tony Curtis: A Fashion Profile," *Playboy,* Aug. 1961, 54; Watts, *Mr. Playboy,* 163–64.

49 Davis, "Farewell, Tony Curtis."

50 Ibid.; Curtis, *American Prince,* 142, 144–45, 153–54; Curtis and Paris, *Tony Curtis,* 117.

51 Douglas, *I Am Spartacus,* 113, 119; Curtis and Paris, *Tony Curtis,* 181.

52 Curtis and Paris, *Tony Curtis,* 189–90; Curtis, *American Prince,* 225–26; Davis, "Farewell, Tony Curtis."

53 Curtis, *American Prince,* 226; Curtis and Paris, *Tony Curtis,* 191–92.

54 Curtis, *American Prince,* 226–27; Curtis and Paris, *Tony Curtis,* 190, 193; Green, "Tony Curtis," 51–54, 92.

Eleven: Mercury Macho: Alan Shepard and John Glenn

1 John M. Logsdon, *John F. Kennedy and the Race to the Moon* (New York, 2010), 149–51. On JFK's appearing remarkably fresh in the heat, see Wernher von Braun, OH, March 31, 1964, 16; Robert C. Seamans, OH, March 27, 1964, 29.

2 "President John Kennedy's Rice Stadium Moon Speech," Sept. 12, 1962, at er.jsc.nasa .gov/seh/ricetalk.htm.

3 Sorensen, *Kennedy,* 525; Tom Wolfe, *The Right Stuff* (1979; New York, 1983), 18, 21.

4 Theodore Sorensen, OH, March 26, 1964, 1. For especially insightful treatment of Kennedy's developing views on space, including during his presidency, see Logsdon, *Kennedy and the Race to the Moon;* James L. Kauffman, *Selling Outer Space: Kennedy, the Media, and Funding for Project Apollo, 1961–1963* (Tuscaloosa, Ala., 1994); Michael R. Beschloss, "Kennedy and the Decision to Go to the Moon," in *Spaceflight and the Myth of Presidential Leadership,* ed. Roger D. Launius and Howard McCurdy (Urbana, Ill., 1997), 51–67; Roger D. Launius, "Kennedy's Space Policy Reconsidered: A Post–Cold War Perspective," *Air Power History* (Winter 2003): 16–29. For a good overview of the American space program, see Walter A. McDougall, *The Heavens and the Earth: A Political History of the Space Race* (New York, 1985).

5 Logsdon, *Kennedy and the Race to the Moon,* 8–12; JFK, "If the Soviets Control Space— They Can Control Earth," *Missiles and Rockets,* Oct. 10, 1960, 12–13.

6 Logsdon, *Kennedy and the Race to the Moon,* 25–31, 39–43, 56, 65–66.

7 Ibid., 69–75; "The Soviet Flight into Space," *Washington Post,* April 13, 1961.

8 On the April 14 meeting, see Hugh Sidey, *John F. Kennedy, President* (New York, 1963), 120–23; Ted Sorensen, *Counselor: A Life at the Edge of History* (New York, 2008), 334–36; Logsdon, *Kennedy and the Race to the Moon,* 75–78.

9 JFK, "Special Message to the Congress on Urgent National Needs, May 25, 1961," at http://www.jfklink.com/speeches/jfk/publicpapers/1961.

10 Logsdon, *Kennedy and the Race to the Moon*, 116, 119–20, 130–31, 144, 146.

11 "Journey to the Moon: U.S. Timetable," *Newsweek*, June 19, 1961, 15, 59–65.

12 Kauffman, *Selling Outer Space*, 52–67; "The Interpreters and the Golden Throats," *Newsweek*, Oct. 8, 1962, 101–4.

13 "The Astronauts' Own Stories Will Appear Only in *Life*," *Life*, Aug. 24, 1959, 98–99. For a full rendering of *Life*'s role in the space program, see Kauffman, "*Life*: NASA's Mouthpiece in the Popular Media," in *Selling Outer Space*, 68–92, while a critical examination of the *Life* decision appears in Robert Sherrod, "The Selling of the Astronauts," *Columbia Journalism Review*, May/June 1973, 16–25. On JFK's view of *Time-Life*, see David Halberstam, *The Powers That Be* (1975; New York, 2000), 352–53.

14 "A Costly Trip to the Moon," *Life*, June 16, 1961, 54; "World Will Be Ruled from the Skies Above," *Life*, May 17, 1963, 4.

15 Neal Thompson, *Light This Candle: The Life and Times of Alan Shepard* (New York, 2004), 203.

16 M. Scott Carpenter et al., *We Seven* (1962; New York, 1990), 6–7.

17 "The Astronauts—Ready to Make History," *Life*, Sept. 14, 1959, 26–27; Carpenter et al., *We Seven*, 8; "How Seven Were Chosen," *Newsweek*, April 20, 1959, 64–65.

18 "A Special Space and Atom Section: The Dawn," *Newsweek*, July 11, 1960, 57.

19 Ibid., 58; "Rendezvouz with Destiny," *Time*, April 20, 1959, 17–18; Carl Dreher, "Martyrs on the Moon?," *Harper's*, March 1963, 37; "The Astronauts," *New York Times*, March 1, 1962; "New Boys and Old," *Newsweek*, March 4, 1963, 50; Dan Q. Posin, "An Eye on Space," *Popular Mechanics*, March 1959, 96; "Men in Space," *New York Times*, April 11, 1959.

20 Charles J. Donlan, NASA official, quoted in Roger D. Launius, "Heroes in a Vacuum: The Apollo Astronaut as Cultural Icon" (paper delivered at Aerospace Sciences Meeting and Exhibit, Jan. 2005), 2; "Beyond and Back with the Astronauts," *Life*, May 17, 1963, 3; Carpenter et al., *We Seven*, 19, 176. Launius, in "Heroes in a Vacuum," 2, 5, asserted that the astronauts represented "the epitome of American masculinity" and appeared as "a virile, masculine representative of the American ideal. Young, in excellent physical shape, engaged in a strenuous and dangerous activity, the astronauts personified youth and vigor." He added, "Perhaps the most striking feature of the first astronauts was their mainstream Euro-American maleness."

21 The quotation is from Thompson, *Light This Candle*, xx.

22 Ibid., xvi–xx; quotations from "Shepard and U.S.A. Feel AOK," *Life*, May 12, 1961, 19, 20.

23 For the story of Shepard's life, see Thompson, *Light This Candle*, an insightful and engaging biography.

24 Ibid., xxiii, 4; Neal Thompson quoted in Nancy Atkinson, "Alan Shepard: Complicated, Conflicted, and the Consummate Astronaut," *Universe Today*, May 5, 2011.

25 Thompson, *Light This Candle*, 212–14; "The Chosen Three for First Space Ride," *Life*, March 3, 1961, 30; Carpenter et al., *We Seven*, 10–11; "Everything A-Okay," *Newsweek*, May 15, 1961, 28.

26 Neal Thompson quoted in Atkinson, "Alan Shepard"; Thompson, *Light This Candle*, xx, xxv, 97–98; "Chosen Three for First Space Ride," 30.

27 Thompson, *Light This Candle*, 6, 239–40; "Chosen Three for First Space Ride," 30.

28 Thompson, *Light This Candle*, 239, 198, 203, 235–38, 290.

29 Carpenter et al., *We Seven*, 11; "Chosen Three for First Space Ride," 30; Thompson, *Light This Candle*, 274.

30 Thompson, *Light This Candle*, 38–40, 163–65.

31 Ibid., 242–46, 253–56, 266–69.

32 Alan B. Shepard, "The Urge to Pioneer," in Carpenter et al., *We Seven*, 66.

33 See Shepard's full account of the flight in Alan B. Shepard, "The Astronaut's Story of the Thrust into Space," *Life*, May 19, 1961, 25–33.

34 Ibid., 26–28.

35 Ibid., 28. See also "Everything A-Okay," 28, for another story stressing the importance of Shepard's actions in piloting the spacecraft.

36 "Shepard and U.S.A. Feel AOK," 18; "Everything A-Okay," 28; Shepard, "Astronaut's Story of the Thrust into Space," 32, 31.

37 "All or Nothing," *Newsweek*, June 5, 1961, 84.

38 Alan B. Shepard, OH, June 12, 1964, 1–2.

39 Ibid., 2–4; Thompson, *Light This Candle*, 312–15.

40 Shepard, OH, 4–5, 12–13; Thompson, *Light This Candle*, 306–7.

41 For accounts of the press conference, see Amy Shira Teitel, "John Glenn: The Man Behind the Hero," *Scientific American*, Feb. 20, 2012, scientificamerican.com; John Glenn, *John Glenn: A Memoir* (New York, 1999), 195–98; Thompson, *Light This Candle*, 198–203.

42 On Glenn's early life, see Glenn, *Memoir*, 3–171.

43 Glenn quoted on his religion in Kauffman, *Selling Outer Space*, 43; his friend quoted in Carpenter et al., *We Seven*, 13.

44 "Chosen Three for First Space Ride," 26; Carpenter et al., *We Seven*, 13.

45 "Chosen Three for First Space Ride," 26; "A Man Marked to Do Great Things," *Life*, Feb. 2, 1962, 36.

46 "We're Going Places No One Has Ever Traveled in a Craft No One's Flown," *Life*, Jan. 27, 1961, 46, 48; "The New Ocean," *Time*, March 2, 1962, 11; "For Those Who Cared Most, the Long Watch at Home," *Life*, March 2, 1962, 37.

47 Carpenter et al., *We Seven*, 13; "For Those Who Cared Most, the Long Watch at Home," 28.

48 Thompson, *Light This Candle*, 214–15; Glenn, *Memoir*, 202, 204.

49 Glenn's version of this incident is told in Glenn, *Memoir*, 220–21.

50 Thompson, *Light This Candle*, 215.

51 Ibid., 286, 289.

52 For Glenn's account of the *Friendship 7* flight, see "John Glenn: Shower of Glory for a New American Hero," *Life*, March 9, 1962, 20–31; Glenn, *Memoir*, 256–76.

53 "John Glenn: One Machine That Worked Without Flaw," *Newsweek*, March 5, 1962, 24; "Glenn: Shower of Glory," 31; Glenn, *Memoir*, 272–73.

54 "Liftoff and Uplift for the U.S.: A World's Hope," *Life*, March 2, 1962, 4; "New Ocean," 11; "Glenn: One Machine That Worked Without Flaw," 19; "Glenn: Shower of Glory," 24–25.

55 "New Ocean," 16, 18; "Glenn: One Machine That Worked Without Flaw," 19; "He Hit

That Keyhole in the Sky," *Life*, March 2, 1962, 20; "For Those Who Cared Most, the Long Watch at Home," 31; James Reston, "Is the Moon Really Worth John Glenn?," *New York Times*, Feb. 25, 1962.

56 "New Ocean," 11; "He Hit That Keyhole in the Sky," 39; "Glenn: One Machine That Worked Without Flaw," 24; "The Flight of Friendship 7," *Newsweek*, Jan. 29, 1962, 72; Carpenter et al., *We Seven*, 27.

57 "Applause, Tears, and Laughter and the Emotions of a Long-Ago Fourth of July," *Life*, March 9, 1962, 34–35; John Glenn, OH, June 12, 1964, 5.

58 "Glenn: One Machine That Worked Without Flaw," 19; Glenn, OH, 1–2, 3, 5–6.

59 Kenneth E. Belieu, OH, March 1, 1977, 14; Glenn, OH, 8, 16–17.

60 Glenn, OH, 2, 22–23.

61 Robert R. Gilruth, OH, April 1, 1964, 2, 9–10; Guthman and Shulman, *Robert Kennedy in His Own Words*, 340; Hugh Sidey and Arthur Schlesinger, interviews with Lawrence Suid in 1987, and Mrs. Kennedy to Robert Seamans, March 14, 1964, all quoted in Lawrence Suid, "Kennedy, Apollo, and the Columbus Factor," *Spaceflight*, July 1994, 228–29, 230.

62 Seamans, OH, 46; von Braun, OH, 9, 20, 17.

63 Seamans, OH, 29; von Braun, OH, 14; Gilruth, OH, 8.

64 JFK quoted in Thompson, *Light This Candle*, xx; JFK quoted in Kauffman, *Selling Outer Space*, 33; Seamans, OH, 36

65 Bradlee, *Conversations with Kennedy*, 191; Shepard, OH, 21.

66 Glenn, *Memoir*, 281.

67 "He Hit That Keyhole in the Sky," 40.

Epilogue: The Masculine Mystique

1 Theodore H. White, "For President Kennedy: An Epilogue," *Life*, Dec. 3, 1963, 158–59.

2 Joseph Alsop, *"I've Seen the Best of It"*: Memoirs (New York, 1992), 464.

3 Robert S. McNamara, *In Retrospect: The Tragedy and Lessons of Vietnam* (New York, 1996), 255.

4 Betty Friedan, *The Feminine Mystique* (1963; New York, 1974).

5 Ibid., 371–72.

6 Ibid., 178–79, 233, 241.

7 Ibid., 275.

8 Ibid., 298. Barbara Ehrenreich, a feminist writing two decades later in *The Hearts of Men: American Dreams and the Flight from Commitment* (New York, 1983), also stresses the links between the rise of feminism in the 1960s and a "male revolt" triggered by dissatisfactions with the traditional "breadwinner ethic."

9 For insightful analyses of *Mad Men*, see Benjamin Schwarz, "Mad About Mad Men," *Atlantic*, Nov. 2009; Katie Roiphe, "The Allure of Messy Lives," *New York Times*, July 30, 2010; Scott F. Stoddard, "Camelot Regained," in *Analyzing "Mad Men": Critical Essays on the Television Series*, ed. Scott F. Stoddard (Jefferson, N.C., 2011); Gary R. Edgerton, "JFK, Don Draper, and the New Sentimentality," *CST Online*, Nov. 2012; Sady Doyle, "Mad Men's Feminine Mystique," *Guardian*, Aug. 15, 2009; Robert S. McElvaine, "Could TV's 'Mad Men' Heal America's Culture Wars?," *Christian Science Monitor*,

Sept. 10, 2010; Jeremy Varon, "History Gets in Your Eyes: Mad Men, Misrecognition, and the Masculine Mystique," in *"Mad Men," Mad World: Sex, Politics, Style, and the 1960s,* ed. Lauren M. E. Goodlad, Lilya Kaganovsky, and Robert A. Rushing (Durham, N.C., 2013), 257–78.

10 The series writer is quoted in Gary R. Edgerton, ed., *"Mad Men": Dream Come True TV* (London, 2011), xxvii.

INDEX

Acheson, Dean, 253, 326
Adams, John Quincy, 51–2
Adams, Sherman, 233
Addison's disease, 2, 46
Adonais (Shelley), 6
Adventures on the New Frontier (documentary), 298
Advertisements for Myself (Mailer), 109–15, 130
Advise and Consent (film), 296
The Age of Jackson (Schlesinger), 11
The Age of Roosevelt (Schlesinger), 11
Alsop, Joseph, 151, 214, 242, 253, 357
Alsop, Stewart, 132, 253, 263, 285
American Journalism Review, 246
American magazine, 23
The American Scholar, 201
"The American Scholar" (Emerson), 269
"The American Soldier" (Taylor), 269
Amis, Kingsley, 145
Andress, Ursula, 154
Angleton, Cicely, 252–3
Angleton, James, 252, 257–8
Apollo spacecraft, 325, 328, 329
Appalachian poverty, 207–9
Appalachian Regional Commission, 208

Area Redevelopment Administration (ARA), 208
"Are We Up to the Task?" (JFK speech), 60
Asquith, Raymond, 147
astronauts
    masculinity perceptions tied to, 333–52, 354–5, 364, 401n20
    selection process for, 331–3, 401n20
    womanizing by, 333, 337–9, 346
The Atlantic, 53
Attolico, Maria, 49
Avedon, Richard, 218

Baker, Bobby, 242
Baldrige, Letitia, 200
Baldwin, Hanson, 23–4, 32
Bancroft, Mary, 150
Barbary Shore (Mailer), 108, 111
Barnes, Tracy, 158
Bartlett, Charles, 157, 214, 250
Bay of Pigs, 127, 158, 209–13, 214, 266, 283
Beardsley, Mimi, 224–5, 242
Beatty, Warren, 205
Belafonte, Harry, 72, 96, 97, 162–3
Bemis, Samuel Flagg, 152

Benton, Thomas Hart, 51–2
Bergquist, Laura, 220, 296
Berle, Milton, 72, 93, 94, 96, 97
Berlin, Sir Isaiah, 201–2, 242
Bernstein, Leonard, 196
Billings, Lem, 47, 58
Birds of the West Indies (Bond), 139
Bishop, Joey, 73, 79–103, 162, 318–19
Bissell, Richard, 157–8, 210, 283
Blackwell, Blanche, 137
Bogart, Humphrey, 79, 259, 295, 306
Bohlen, Charles, 212, 253
Bond, James (author), 139
Bond, James (fictional character)
    Bond girls and, 140, 143–4, 154
    JFK as fan of, 131, 132–3, 145–60, 278
    JFK parallels to, 131, 147–50, 153–60, 210–11
    masculinity perception influenced by, 6–7, 131, 134, 139–60, 177–8, 185, 210–11, 364
    Playboy's serialization of, 163, 177–8, 185
    sex appeal/sexuality of, 7, 140–1, 143–5, 149, 160
Boorstin, Daniel, 64
The Boston Globe, 87
Bowles, Chester, 278
Bradlee, Antoinette "Tony" Pinchot Pittman, 228, 234, 237–9, 243, 245, 257–8, 295
    JFK's attraction to, 249–51, 256
Bradlee, Benjamin Crowninshield, 155
    background of, 229–33, 247
    JFK's friendship with, 6, 227–9, 233–51, 256–9, 294–5, 314
    masculinity perception influenced by, 6, 228–9, 235, 237–40, 244–51, 259
    Meyers's murder and, 256–9
    as *Newsweek* reporter, 227–9, 231–41, 243–9, 258–9
    womanizing by, 245–7
Brando, Marlon, 295, 317, 338
Brandon, Henry, 152
Brewer, Louise, 338
Britt, May, 99
Broccoli, Albert R. "Cubby," 153
Bross, John, 132–3
Bryant, Traphes, 222–3
Bryna Productions, 309
Buchan, John, 146–7, 152
Buckley, William F., Jr., 177

Bundy, McGeorge, 6, 157, 222, 244–5, 267, 278
Bundy, William, 278
Burdick, Eugene, 33–6, 39–40, 149, 215–16, 263, 275
bureaucracy
    masculinity's degeneration via, 5, 12–20, 30–1, 32–6, 49, 51, 59, 62–4, 66–7, 70, 73, 84–6, 90, 103, 105, 109–15, 121–30, 144, 147–9, 155, 164, 172, 179, 181–2, 186–8, 192–3, 200, 206, 215–16, 225, 228, 263–4, 268–9, 272–8, 280, 287–8, 311, 333, 343, 359–60, 372*n*11
    in military, 263–4, 268–9, 272–8, 280, 287–8
    "Social Ethic" associated with, 18–19
    women's degeneration via, 361–4
Burns, James MacGregor, 50
Byron, Jim, 75

Cahn, Sammy, 94, 98
Camelot (musical), 357
Camelot myth, 2–3, 6, 103, 357–8, 366
Campbell, Judith, 69, 92, 94, 101–2, 224, 379*n*51
Canby, Vincent, 153
Carpenter, Scott, 331–4, 354–5
Casals, Pablo, 197, 198, 200
Casino Royale, 139–42, 146
Castro, Fidel, 8, 61, 133, 271
    Bay of Pigs and, 127, 158, 209–13, 214, 266, 283
    Cuban missile crisis and, 153, 154, 213–15, 282, 284, 295, 315, 357, 358, 365, 367
    Operation Mongoose and, 158–9, 283–4
Cat on a Hot Tin Roof (film), 15
Caudill, Harry M., 207–8
Cecil, David, 152
celebrity status
    JFK's, 4, 64–6, 71, 72–3, 86–9, 92–3, 96, 121, 123, 129, 217–22, 239, 294, 359
    masculinity perceptions influenced by, 71, 72–103, 121, 123, 129, 239, 359
    politics influenced by, 121, 123, 129, 239
Central Intelligence Agency (CIA), 33, 135, 139–40, 252–4

Bay of Pigs and, 127, 158, 209–13, 214, 266, 283
covert operations by, 127, 132–3, 156–9, 209–13, 214, 266, 283–4
Lansdale's role in, 262, 272, 275, 278
masculinity perceptions and, 132–3, 150, 156
Meyers's murder and, 257–8
Operation Mongoose by, 158–9, 283–4
Cerrell, Joseph R., 95
Chavchavadze, Helen, 222
Cheshire, Maxine, 69
Chicago Tribune, 172, 214
Churchill, Winston, 152, 201
CIA. *See* Central Intelligence Agency
Civil Rights Acts, 2, 206–7
civil rights movement, 2, 171, 176, 182, 206–7, 238, 298, 357, 364
Clark, Blair, 256
Colby, William, 157
Cold War, 20, 108, 240. *See also* counterinsurgency strategies
Bay of Pigs invasion during, 127, 158, 209–13, 214, 266, 283
Bond stories about, 139–45, 149–50, 154–60
counterinsurgency tactics, 260–8, 272–88, 303, 311–12, 358, 364, 367
cuban missile crisis in, 153, 154, 213–15, 282, 284, 295, 315, 357, 358, 365, 367
JFK influenced by, 2, 3–4, 6, 8–9, 60–1, 126–8, 149–50, 153, 154, 158, 202, 209–15, 260–88, 295, 303, 311–12, 315, 357, 358, 364, 365, 367
masculinity perceptions and, 8, 23–4, 30–6, 39–40, 61–4, 104, 126–8, 202, 259, 262, 263–4, 268–9, 272–8, 280, 284–8, 324–30
space programs as extension of, 325–30, 349, 351, 352, 359
Spartacus parallels to, 300–2, 311–12
Cole, Nat King, 72, 93, 94, 98, 173
Commentary, 126
Commonweal, 285–6
Communism, 171, 297. *See also* Cold War
counterinsurgency tactics and, 260–8, 272–88, 303, 311–12, 358, 364, 367
in Cuba, 127, 153, 154, 158, 209–15, 266, 271, 282–4, 295, 315, 357, 358, 365, 367
economic factors influencing, 20
Hollywood blacklist and, 311, 313

JFK policy influenced by, 2, 3–4, 6, 8–9, 60–1, 126–8, 149–50, 153, 154, 158, 202, 209–15, 260–88, 295, 303, 311–12, 315, 357, 358, 364, 365, 367
masculinity perceptions influenced by, 8, 23–4, 30–6, 181
Peace Corps as weapon against, 8, 128, 215–16, 357, 359, 361
in Southeastern Asia, 272–82, 287, 358
Condon, Richard, 296–7
Connery, Sean, 15, 178
consumer patterns
masculinity's degeneration via, 5, 16–17, 20–5, 27–9, 30–1, 32–7, 49, 62–4, 70, 73, 84–6, 103, 105, 109–15, 121–30, 147–9, 165, 168–71, 176, 180, 191, 194, 207–9, 359–60
women's movement and, 361–4
Conversations with Kennedy (Bradlee), 237–8
Cooper, Gary, 65, 89, 292, 293
Cooper, Gordon, 331–4, 354–5
Corey, Irwin, 173
Corwin, Norman, 97
Cosmopolitan, 31, 53, 55–6
on masculinity perceptions, 14, 22, 25, 27, 29, 53
Costello, William, 66
counterinsurgency strategies, 358
in Cuba, 283–4
flexible response via, 261–8, 278–80, 303, 311–12
ideological approach to, 273–5, 280–1
psychological approach to, 274–5, 277, 281–2
in Southeast Asia, 272–82, 287
by Special Forces, 260–8, 274, 278–9, 284–8, 303, 364, 367
Coward, Noël, 138
Cowen, Jill, 222, 242
Cowley, Malcolm, 108
The Craft of Intelligence (Dulles), 151, 156
Crisis: (documentary), 298
"Crisis of American Masculinity" (Schlesinger), 11–12, 36–8, 362
Crowther, Bosley, 205
Cuba, 8, 61, 133, 271. *See also* Communism
Bay of Pigs in, 127, 158, 209–13, 214, 266, 283
Operation Mongoose in, 158–9, 283–4
Cuban missile crisis, 153, 154, 213–15, 282, 284, 295, 315, 357, 358, 365, 367

culture. *See also* masculinity perceptions
celebrity's influence on, 4, 64–6, 71,
72–3, 86–9, 92–3, 96, 121, 123, 129,
217–22, 239, 294, 359
New Frontier's focus on art and,
196–203, 239, 252
politics-entertainment link in, 86–103,
289–99
shifts in masculinity perceptions in, 4–9,
11–38, 39–41, 73, 84–5, 90, 103, 120–30,
134, 144–5, 161, 163–4, 178–9, 181–3,
185, 186–96, 202, 288
women's ascendancy in, 5, 12–13, 25–30,
31, 34, 37, 106, 111–12, 115, 143–4,
163–8, 171, 176, 180, 182, 185, 252–5,
311, 318–19, 360, 361–4, 367
Cummins, Peggy, 293
Curtis, Tony, 15, 93–4
JFK's friendship with, 6, 321–2
in *Spartacus,* 291, 306, 316, 319–21
womanizing by, 317–18, 320

Dana, Bill, 97, 337
Daughters of the American Revolution,
301
Davids, Jules, 50
Davis, Sammy, Jr., 81
racism and, 83–4, 89–90, 99, 176
in Rat Pack, 73, 79–103, 162–3, 175–6,
179–80, 185, 318–19
Dean, James, 15, 338
Dean, Jimmy, 205
The Deer Park (Mailer), 108, 111, 117
de Havilland, Olivia, 292–3
Democratic convention of 1956, 50, 87
Democratic convention of 1960, 93,
99, 101
Mailer's profile on, 115–21
DesRosiers, Janet, 69
de Vegh, Diana, 222
Diamonds Are Forever (Fleming), 142, 143,
148, 178
movie, 178
Dickinson, Angie, 77
JFK's relationship with, 69, 91, 93, 97
Diem, Ngo Dinh, 276, 280–1
Dietrich, Marlene, 47
Dissent, 126
Dr. No (Fleming), 142, 143
movie, 153–4, 159
Donovan, William "Wild Bill," 135, 151,
271

Douglas, Kirk, 306–7
JFK's relationship with, 6, 291, 312–15
Spartacus by, 289–91, 299–312
womanizing by, 308–9
Drew, Robert, 297–8
Drury, Allen, 296
Duke, Angier Biddle, 96–7
Dulles, Allen, 252, 276, 280
Bond's influence on, 132–3, 150–1,
155–7, 159
Dulles, John Foster, 47, 266
Dye, Peter, 100

Ebbins, Milt, 95
The Ed Sullivan Show, 317
Eisenhower, Dwight, 23, 42, 53, 156, 170,
212, 233
Cold War policy by, 209–11, 262–6, 269,
271, 280
cultural image/era of, 5, 8, 36–7, 47, 59,
60, 62, 84–5, 105, 110–11, 121–3, 127,
129, 174, 179, 183, 184, 186–7, 203,
228, 252, 259
governing style of, 189, 193, 198, 325–6
Eisenhower, Mamie, 198, 203
Ekberg, Anita, 77, 221
Emergence of Lincoln (Nevins), 152
Emerson, Gloria, 58
Emerson, Ralph Waldo, 4, 269
Esquire, 177, 197, 204
Mailer's JFK profile for, 6–7, 104–6,
115–30
masculinity perceptions and, 11, 38, 53,
55, 203, 221, 285
Ewell, Tom, 24
The Execution of Private Slovik (film), 100,
313
Executive Action Capability program
(CIA), 158

Farley, Jim, 119–20
Fast, Howard, 299–300, 309, 311, 314
Fay, Paul "Red," 87, 250, 289–90, 305
FBI, 101–2, 127, 156, 222
Federal Communications Commission,
233
Federal Trade Commission, 233
Feldman, Charles, 293, 313
Feldman, Myer, 256
Felker, Clay, 115–16, 124
The Feminine Mystique (Friedan), 361–4
FitzGerald, Desmond, 158, 284

Fitzgerald, Ella, 72, 94, 96, 98, 173
Fleming, Ian. *See also* Bond, James
  book series by, 6–7, 131, 132–60, 163,
    177–8, 185, 210–11, 278, 364
  CIA's Cuba campaigns and, 132–3
  masculinity perception influenced by,
    6–7, 131, 134, 139–60, 177–8, 185,
    210–11, 364
  Playboy's serialization of, 163, 177–8, 185
  womanizing by, 7, 137–8
flexible response strategies, military,
    261–8, 278–80, 286, 303, 311–12
Fonda, Henry, 96, 183, 296, 319
Formosa, Johnny, 101
Fortune magazine, 18, 28
For Your Eyes Only (Fleming), 142
Franco, Francisco, 197, 310
Frankenheimer, John, 297
Frank, Lawrence K., 26–7, 29–30
Frederica, Queen (of Greece), 150
Freedom 7 (spacecraft), 339–40
Freeman, Orville, 192, 290
Friedan, Betty, 361–4
Friendship 7 (spacecraft), 345, 348–51
From Here to Eternity (film), 74–5, 76
From Russia with Love (Fleming), 142, 149,
    150, 152
  movie, 153, 154–5, 295
Frost, Robert, 196, 199

Gable, Clark, 65, 292, 293
Gagarin, Yuri, 327, 341
Gallico, Paul, 138
Gamarekian, Barbara, 242
Gardner, Ava, 77, 309
Garland, Judy, 75, 77, 81, 93
Gehman, Richard, 25, 90
Gemini spacecraft, 323, 328
Generation of Vipers (Wylie), 28
Gentlemen's Quarterly, 204
Giancana, Sam, 76, 101–3, 224
Gilpatric, Ros, 267, 276
Gilruth, Robert, 353–4
Glenn, Annie, 344, 349–50
Glenn, John, 331–2
  characteristics of, 333–4, 343–6, 401*n*20
  JFK's friendship with, 6, 351–5
  orbital flight by, 343–52, 355
  as senator, 355
  Shepard's relationship with, 333–4,
    346–7
Godfrey, John, 135

Goldfinger (Fleming), 142, 143, 149
Good Housekeeping, 195, 219
Goodwin, Richard, 124
Grace, Princess (of Monaco), 221
Graham, Katharine, 244, 246, 253
Graham, Phil, 242, 244, 253
Grant, Cary, 65, 153, 306, 316–17, 322
Great Depression, 20, 44, 181
"The Greatest Thing in the World"
    (Mailer), 106
Green Berets. *See* Special Forces
Greene, Angela, 293
Greene, Graham, 275, 277
Greenmantle (Buchan), 146
Grissom, Gus, 331–4, 347, 354–5
Grumman Aerospace, 328

Halberstam, David, 360
Hamill, Pete, 125
Harling, Robert, 138
Harper's, 53, 54, 200, 217
Harriman, Averell, 269
Harrington, Michael, 208
Harris, Sam, 204
Harvey, Bill, 158–9
Hayworth, Rita, 78, 81, 309
Hefner, Hugh, 225, 318–19. *See also*
    Playboy magazine
  JFK's influence by, 174–6, 181–5
  masculinity perceptions influenced by,
    6–7, 161, 162–85, 364, 386*n*27
  political perspectives of, 163–4, 170–1,
    173–5, 178–80
Helms, Richard, 158
Hemingway, Ernest, 51, 105–6, 110, 186,
    201
Henderson, Finis, 162
Henie, Sonja, 292–3
Hersey, John, 46
Hilsman, Roger, 263, 267, 278
Hitchcock, Alfred, 32–3
Ho Chi Minh, 276
Hollywood blacklist, 311, 313
Hollywood Reporter, 301
Holmby Hills Rat Pack, 79
homosexuality, 12, 25, 29–30, 144,
    304
Honey Fitz (yacht), 99, 100
Hoover, J. Edgar, 102, 222, 224
Hopper, Hedda, 300, 308
Household, Geoffrey, 138
The House I Live In (film), 84

Houston, Sam, 51–2
Humphrey, Hubert, 40, 53, 236, 297

Intimate Strangers: (Schickel), 64
Izvestiya (Soviet newspaper), 159

Jackson, Andrew, 285
Jacobs, George, 77, 95
Jacobs, William L., 236
Jiménez, José (fictional character), 337
John Quincy Adams (Bemis), 152
Johnson, Alexis, 267
Johnson, Lyndon, 40, 53, 69, 93, 120,
    159–60, 212, 235–6, 281, 356
  as NASA chair, 326
Johnson, Rafer, 216
Josselyn, Irene, 13

Kazin, Alfred, 201
Keats, John, 6
Kefauver, Estes, 50
Kelly, Gene, 72, 96, 97, 319
Kelly, John, 23
Kempton, Murray, 68
Kennedy, Caroline, 3, 57, 218–20, 350
Kennedy, Ethel, 250, 351
Kennedy, Jackie. *See* Onassis, Jacqueline
    Bouvier Kennedy
Kennedy, John F. (JFK). *See also*
    masculinity perceptions
  assassination of, 1–2, 356–8, 365, 366–7
  Bay of Pigs invasion under, 127, 158,
    209–13, 214, 266, 283
  as Bond fan, 131, 132–3, 145–60, 278
  Bradlee's relationship with, 6, 227–9,
    233–51, 256–9, 294–5, 314
  Cabinet appointments by, 188–93
  celebrity status utilization by, 4, 64–6,
    71, 72–3, 86–9, 92–3, 96, 121, 123, 129,
    217–22, 239, 294, 359
  CIA operations under, 33, 127, 132–3, 135,
    139–40, 150, 156–9, 209–14, 252–4,
    257–8, 262, 266, 272, 275, 278, 283–4
  civil rights and, 2, 206–7, 238, 298, 357,
    364
  Cold War/Communism influences on, 2,
    3–4, 6, 8–9, 60–1, 126–8, 149–50, 153,
    154, 158, 202, 209–15, 260–88, 295,
    303, 311–12, 315, 357, 358, 364, 365, 367
  Cuban missile crisis under, 153, 154,
    213–15, 282, 284, 295, 315, 357, 358,
    365, 367

  culture/art as focus of, 196–203, 239,
    252, 289–99
  Curtis's friendship with, 321–2
  documentaries on, 297–8
  domesticity by, 2–3, 217–20
  Douglas's friendship with, 6, 291, 312–15
  education of, 43, 44–5
  fitness campaign by, 8, 23, 194–6
  Fleming's influence on, 6–7, 132–4,
    145–60
  Glenn's relationship with, 6, 351–5
  governing style of, 188–93
  health issues of, 2, 46–7, 145–6, 358
  Hefner's influence on, 6–7, 161, 174–6,
    181–5
  in House of Representatives, 41–2
  inauguration of, 72–3, 97–9, 186–8, 196,
    298, 322
  Lansdale's influence on, 6, 262, 271–84,
    288
  legacy of, 357–67
  Mailer's relationship with, 6–7, 104–6,
    115–31, 294
  media manipulation by, 227–9, 233–51,
    257–9
  Meyers's relationship with, 251–9,
    394*n*66
  military service by, 42, 45–6, 48, 55, 122,
    147–8, 195, 204–5, 247, 297, 354
  Peace Corps founding by, 8, 128, 215–16,
    357, 359, 361
  poverty relief campaign by, 207–9
  presidential campaign of, 39–41, 51–71,
    72–3, 86–97, 103, 227–9, 233–7, 326
  Profiles in Courage by, 39, 50–2, 156, 201
  as senator, 42–3, 46–71, 87–97, 227–9,
    233–7, 325
  sex appeal of, 4, 47–8, 56–9, 68–9, 87,
    91–3, 123–4, 129, 149, 164, 179–80,
    184, 187–8, 203–4, 218, 220–2, 245,
    292
  Shepard's relationship with, 6, 342, 350,
    354–5
  Sinatra/Rat Pack's influence on, 6–7, 71,
    72–3, 86–104, 125, 162–3, 176, 186,
    224, 293–4
  space program under, 323–55, 359, 364
  Spartacus masculinity portrayals and,
    299–306, 311–12, 315, 320–1, 322
  style/personal appeal of, 4–6, 39–71, 96,
    118–24, 129, 134, 148, 153, 160, 164,
    183, 185, 186–8, 201–6, 217–22, 235,

237–9, 241–2, 244–5, 314, 321, 322, 359, 367
  Taylor's influence on, 6, 262, 264–70, 279–82, 288
  vice presidential campaign by, 50, 87
  Why England Slept by, 49
  womanizing by, 3, 7–9, 45, 57–9, 69, 88, 91–2, 94, 118, 149, 160–1, 164, 179–80, 184–5, 222–5, 227, 242–3, 246–59, 292–4, 358, 366, 367, 379n51, 391n66
Kennedy, John F., Jr., 2, 3, 218–20
Kennedy, Joseph, Jr., 42, 184
Kennedy, Joseph, Sr., 41, 150, 183–4, 321
  JFK's political career support by, 42, 44, 50–1, 64–5, 88–9, 93, 100, 205, 313
  womanizing by, 57–8, 247, 291–2
Kennedy or Nixon: (Schlesinger), 70
Kennedy, Patrick (JFK son), 219, 238
Kennedy, Patrick Joseph "P.J." (JFK grandfather), 41
Kennedy, Robert, 43, 93, 100, 146, 159, 174, 192, 196, 212, 243, 250, 312, 314, 355
  Cold War and, 267, 269–70, 283–4
  Mafia investigation by, 101–2, 152–3
  space program and, 351, 353
Kennedy, Rose, 43, 315
Kennedy, Teddy, 225, 250, 353
Kerr, Deborah, 76
Khrushchev, Nikita, 20, 31, 61, 63, 67, 202, 248, 266, 302. *See also* Soviet Union
  Cuban missile crisis and, 213–14, 282, 295
Kilgallen, Dorothy, 222
King, Martin Luther, Jr., 2, 162, 206, 357
Knudsen, Robert, 160
Korean War, 24, 31, 265, 297, 344, 352
Kraft, Joseph, 189, 200, 214
Krim, Arthur, 294, 297
Krock, Arthur, 44, 51, 156, 241, 247
Kubrick, Stanley, 310–11

Ladies Home Companion, 165
Ladies' Home Journal, 219
Lamar, Lucius Q. C., 51
Lancaster, Burt, 308, 317
Landis, James, 50
Lannan, Pat, 292
Lansdale, Edward Geary, 6
  Cold War tactics by, 262, 271–84, 288
Laos, 271, 280, 282
Lardner, Ring, 307
Laughton, Charles, 296, 310

Launch Operations Center, Cape Canaveral, Florida, 323
Lawford, Patricia Kennedy, 81, 87, 89, 92
Lawford, Peter, 220, 222, 293, 296, 321
  in Rat Pack, 73, 79–103, 162, 318–19
Lawford, Victoria Francis, 89
Lawrence, T. E., 146–7, 276
Lederer, William, 33–6, 39–40, 149, 215–16, 263, 275
Leigh, Janet, 88, 93–4, 96, 317, 319, 321
Leiter, Marion, "Oatsie," 132–3, 146
LeMay, Curtis, 315
Lemmon, Jack, 15, 317
Lemnitzer, Lyman, 267
Lerner, Max, 116
Lewis, Jerry, 80
Life, 116, 151–3, 155, 187–8, 204, 205, 213, 218, 219, 221, 301, 357
  on JFK's masculine appeal, 53, 55, 57, 65, 187–8, 218, 219, 221
  on space program, 330–1, 333, 336, 339, 341, 345–6, 349–50, 355
Lincoln, Evelyn, 99, 294
Lippmann, Walter, 56, 151, 214, 244
Live and Let Die (Fleming), 142, 143, 148
Lodge, Henry Cabot, Jr., 39, 42, 43, 48
Lonely Are the Brave (film), 314
The Lonely Crowd: (Riesman), 17–18, 21
Look magazine, 190, 197, 205, 241, 243
  on masculinity perceptions, 13–14, 15–18, 19, 20–1, 22, 26, 28–9, 31, 218–20
Loper, Don, 98
Los Angeles magazine, 184
The Los Angeles Times, 101, 144, 221
Love at First Flight (Spalding), 292
Lownes, Victor, 162, 173
Luce, Clare Boothe, 57, 150
Luce, Henry, 330
Luciano, Lucky, 76
Lytton, Bart, 100

MacArthur, Douglas, 106
Macdonald, Torbert, 295
MacLeish, Archibald, 196
Mad Men (TV show), 364–6
Mafia, 76, 83, 101–3, 224
Magic Mountain (Mann), 138
Magsaysay, Ramon, 272, 276
Mailer, Norman
  background of, 106–15
  JFK profiles by, 6–7, 104–6, 115–30, 294

Mailer, Norman (continued)
  on masculinity, 6–7, 104–6, 109–15, 118–30, 160, 176, 185
  in *Playboy,* 163, 176–7, 185
  stabbing of wife by, 126
The Making of the President (White), 242
Mallory, George, 324
Malraux, André, 197
Maltz, Albert, 100
The Manchurian Candidate (film), 296–7
The Man in the Gray Flannel Suit (Wilson), 19
Mankiewicz, Joseph, 277
Manned Spacecraft Center, Houston, Texas, 323, 329
Mann, Thomas, 138
Mann, Tony, 310
The Man with the Golden Gun (Fleming), 143, 156
Marcello, Carlos, 101
Marine Corps Gazette, 267
Marlborough (Churchill), 152
Marriage and Family Living, 14
Martin, Dean, 73, 79–103, 148, 162, 318–19
Martin, Jeanne, 100
masculinity perceptions
  backlash against New Frontier's, 364, 367
  Bay of Pigs and, 209–13, 214
  Bond/Fleming's influence on, 6–7, 131, 134, 139–60, 177–8, 185, 210–11, 364
  Bradlee's influence on, 6, 228–9, 235, 237–40, 244–51, 259
  bureaucracy's influence on, 5, 12–20, 30–1, 32–6, 49, 51, 59, 62–4, 66–7, 70, 73, 84–6, 90, 103, 105, 109–15, 121–30, 144, 147–9, 155, 164, 172, 179, 181–2, 186–8, 192–3, 200, 206, 215–16, 225, 228, 263–4, 268–9, 272–8, 280, 287–8, 311, 333, 343, 359–60, 372n11
  celebrity's influence on, 71, 72–103, 121, 123, 129, 239, 359
  Cold War's influence on, 8, 23–4, 30–6, 39–40, 61–4, 104, 126–8, 202, 259, 262, 263–4, 268–9, 272–8, 280, 284–8, 324–30
  consumerism's influence on, 5, 16–17, 20–5, 27–9, 30–1, 32–7, 49, 62–4, 70, 73, 84–6, 103, 105, 109–15, 121–30, 147–9, 165, 168–71, 176, 180, 191, 194, 207–9, 359–60
  Cuban missile crisis and, 213–15
  culture/art's influence on, 37–8, 196–203
  Hefner/*Playboy*'s influence on, 6–7, 77, 161, 162–85, 364, 386n27
  in *Mad Men,* 364–6
  Mailer on, 6–7, 104–6, 109–15, 118–30, 160, 176, 185
  media's advancement of, 11–38, 46, 48–9, 52–9, 64–70, 78, 104–6, 110, 115–30, 187–90, 195, 200–1, 204, 213, 214, 218–21, 228–9, 235, 237–51, 259
  political service associated with, 7–9, 37–8, 39–71, 86–93, 93–6, 191, 199, 209–15
  sex appeal's tie to, 5, 7, 47–8, 56–9, 68–9, 87, 91–3, 140, 143–4, 149, 164, 179–80, 184, 187–8, 192, 203–4, 218, 220–2, 304, 333, 345
  shifts in culture and, 4–9, 11–38, 39–41, 73, 84–5, 90, 103, 120–30, 134, 144–5, 161, 163–4, 178–9, 181–3, 185, 186–96, 202, 288
  Sinatra/Rat Pack's contributions to, 6–7, 71, 72–3, 75–103, 125, 148, 175–6, 318–19, 364, 386n27
  space exploration's influence on, 324–52, 354–5, 359, 364
  in *Spartacus,* 299–306, 311–12, 315, 320–1, 322
  style/personal appeal influencing, 5–7, 39–71, 96, 118–24, 129, 134, 140–5, 148, 153, 160, 164, 183, 185, 186–8, 201–6, 217–22, 235, 237–9, 241–2, 244–5, 302–3, 314, 319, 321, 322, 359, 366
  violence, romanticism of, and, 75–6, 107, 114–15, 126, 130, 155
  womanizing's influence on, 3, 7–9, 58–9, 69, 73, 77, 79, 83, 84, 88, 91–2, 140–1, 143–5, 149, 150, 160–1, 222–5, 242–3, 246–51, 258–9, 333, 337–9, 346
  women's ascension influencing, 5, 12–13, 25–30, 31, 34, 37, 106, 111–12, 115, 163–8, 171, 176, 180, 182, 185, 311, 318–19, 361–4
Mattis, Joni, 175
Mayer, Jean, 23
McCalls, 44, 53, 55
McCarthy, Joseph, 2, 3, 171
McCarthy, Shane, 23
McCone, John, 267
McDonnell Aircraft Corporation, 323, 328, 332

McIntyre, William, 223
McNamara, Robert, 6, 190–2, 260, 278, 280, 360
Mead, Margaret, 14, 27
Mead, Shepherd, 165–6
media
  celebrity status championed by, 64–6, 217–21
  journalistic integrity of, 228–45, 248–9, 257–9
  masculinity perceptions advanced by, 11–38, 46, 48–9, 52–9, 64–70, 78, 104–6, 110, 115–30, 187–90, 195, 200–1, 204, 213, 214, 218–21, 228–9, 235, 237–51, 259
  on space program, 327, 329–34, 336, 339–41, 343, 345–6, 349–50, 355
  womanizing's coverage by, 9, 69, 242–3, 248–9, 257–9
Mercury program (Project Mercury), 323, 325, 326–33, 353–4, 359, 364
  inaugural orbital flight in, 343–52, 355
  inaugural suborbital flight in, 334–42, 347, 355
Metronome magazine, 78
Meyer, Cord, 232, 252–3
Meyer, Mary Pinchot, 224, 250
  JFK's relationship with, 251–9, 394n66
  murder of, 256–8
Mike Wallace Interview, The (TV show), 169
Mill, John Stuart, 4, 181
Milton, John, 5
Mr. Standfast (Buchan), 146
Modern Screen, 317
Monroe, Marilyn, 15, 24, 77, 168, 317
  JFK's relationship with, 69, 91, 94, 184–5, 221–2, 294, 391n66
Montgomery, Ruth, 101
Moonraker (Fleming), 142, 143
Moore, Roger, 153, 318
Morales, Adele, 113, 115, 126
Mortimer, Lee, 75
Movieland, 307
Mudd, Roger, 242
Murphy, Audie, 277

Naked and the Dead, The (Mailer), 81, 107–8, 111, 117
NASA (National Aeronautics and Space Administration), 323, 325–54
National Guard, 298

National Review, 129
Nation, 114, 170
Nevins, Allan, 50, 152
New Frontier administration. See Kennedy, John F.
New Hampshire Sunday News, 231
Newman, Lawrence, 223–4
New Republic, 53, 66, 116, 246
Newsweek, 155, 169, 189–90, 205, 214
  Bradlee as journalist at, 227–9, 231–41, 243–9, 258–9
  journalistic integrity of, 228, 234–41, 243–5, 248–9, 257–9
  masculinity perceptions and, 53, 54–5, 65, 67, 68, 219, 220, 285
  on space program, 329–30, 332, 336, 340, 349–50
New Yorker, 46, 76, 138, 169, 244, 246
New York Herald Tribune, 145
New York Journal-American, 222
New York Post, 125
New York Times, 1, 32, 39, 44, 75, 93, 156, 205, 241, 268
  on masculinity perceptions, 14, 22, 23, 67, 153, 213, 246
  on space program, 332, 350
  on Spartacus, 290, 301
New York Times Book Review, 107
New York Times Magazine, 14, 23
Night Comes to the Cumberlands (Caudill), 207–8
Nixon Agonistes: (Wills), 4–6, 358
Nixon, Richard, 2, 20, 97, 236–7
  cultural image/appeal of, 4–6, 59–63, 66–8, 70, 117, 123, 235
Nizzari, Joyce, 162, 175
Norris, George, 51
North by Northwest (film), 32–3
nuclear weapons, 238, 261–6, 285, 325, 357

Ocean's Eleven (film), 85–6, 90, 97
O'Donnell, Kenneth, 6, 88
Official U.S. Physical Fitness Program, 195
Olivier, Laurence, 97, 304, 310
Olympic Games, 31–2
Onassis, Jacqueline Bouvier Kennedy, 57, 98, 100, 117, 125, 146–7, 150, 183, 186, 321, 341, 351, 353, 354, 365
  Bradlees' friendship with, 228, 234, 237–9, 243, 249, 295
  cultural focus as First Lady, 196–200, 202

Onassis, Jacqueline (continued)
  JFK's assassination and, 2, 366
  JFK's domesticity and, 2–3, 217–20
  JFK's womanizing and, 58–9, 222–5,
    249–51, 255
  style/personal appeal of, 203, 239, 314
O'Neill, Tip, 58
On Her Majesty's Secret Service (Fleming),
    142
  movie, 178
Operation Mongoose (CIA), 158–9, 283–4
Organization Man (Whyte), 18, 21
Other America (Harrington), 208

Paolella, Joseph, 223
Peace Corps, 8, 128, 215–16, 357, 359, 361
Peretz, Martin, 116
the Philippines, 271–3, 276, 277
Pickering, Ruth, 252
Pilgrim's Way (Buchan), 45, 146–7, 152
Pinchot, Amos, 251
Pinchot, Gifford, 251
Pinchot, Ruth, 256
Pittman, Steuart, 233
Pius XII, Pope, 44
Playboy Clubs, 173–8, 183–4
Playboy magazine, 319
  Bond books serialized by, 163, 177–8, 185
  consumerism and, 168–71, 176, 180
  Mailer's contributions to, 163, 176–7, 185
  masculinity perception influenced by,
    6–7, 77, 161, 162–85, 364, 386n27
  political slant of, 174–5
  on sexual revolution, 163, 167–8, 180,
    182, 185
Playboy Mansion, 172, 175, 177, 180, 318
"Playboy Philosophy" (Hefner), 180–2, 364
Playboy's Penthouse (TV show), 172–3, 176
Plimpton, George, 199
Plomer, William, 138
Poitier, Sidney, 72, 162, 317
Popular Science, 285
Potter, David, 20
poverty, campaign against, 207–9
Powers, Dave, 6, 223–5, 256, 295
Powers, Gary, 240
Pravda (Soviet newspaper), 159
Preminger, Otto, 296, 308
Presidential Papers, The (Mailer), 126
President's Council on Youth Fitness, 8, 23,
    194–6
Primary (documentary), 297–8

Profiles in Courage (Kennedy), 39, 50–2,
    156, 201
Progressive, 53–4, 56–7
Project Mercury. See Mercury program
"psywarfare," 274–5, 277
PT 109 (movie), 205–6, 297
"Pt 109" (song), 205
PT 109: John F. Kennedy in World War II,
    204
Pursuit of Happiness, The (campaign
    film), 50

Quiet American, The (film), 277
Quiet American, The (Greene), 275, 277

race, 99, 112–13
  civil rights movement and, 2, 171, 176,
    182, 206–7, 238, 298, 357, 364
  Rat Pack themes on, 83–4, 89–90,
    378n17
Rand, Sally, 333
Rash, Lynne, 162
Rat Pack, 80–1, 313
  JFK's association with, 86–103, 125,
    162–3, 179–80
  masculinity perceptions influenced by,
    71, 72–3, 82–103, 125, 148, 162–3,
    175–6, 179–80, 185, 318–19, 386n27
  racial/ethnic themes of, 83–4, 89–90
  womanizing by, 73, 77, 79, 83, 84, 88,
    91–2, 160, 318
Rayburn, Sam, 187
Raymond, Jack, 268
Reader's Digest, 31, 46, 201
Reagan, Ronald, 314
Realist, 126
Rebel Without a Cause (film), 15
Redbook, 53, 58, 76
Reedy, George, 69
Rees, Thomas M., 94
Reporter, 241
Reston, James, 350
Rickles, Don, 76
Riddle, Nelson, 75, 97
Ridgway, Matthew B., 264
Riesman, David, 17–18, 21, 32
Robertson, Cliff, 205
Rogue Male (Household), 138
Rometsch, Ellen, 222
Roosevelt, Eleanor, 93–4, 119
Roosevelt, Franklin D., 41, 86, 96, 135,
    291, 298

Roosevelt, Teddy, 33, 190, 196, 238, 241, 251, 285, 307
Roselli, Johnny, 101
Ross, Edmund G., 51
Rosson, William B., 287
Rostow, Walt, 6, 278, 280–1
Rothermere, Anne, 137–9
Rovere, Richard, 53, 55, 125
Rusk, Dean, 280

Saga: The Magazine for Men, 276
Sahl, Mort, 93, 168
Salinger, Pierre, 6, 116–17, 160, 196, 205, 237, 243
Saltonstall, Jean, 230–2, 245
Saltzman, Harry, 153
Samson Agonistes (Milton), 55
Saturday Evening Post, 172, 277
    on JFK's personal appeal, 48–9, 53, 68, 204–5
    masculinity perceptions and, 23–4, 32, 34, 214, 285–6
Schickel, Richard, 64
Schirra, Walter, 331–4, 354–5
Schlesinger, Arthur, Jr., 116–17, 208, 296
    on JFK, 70, 104, 125, 199, 201–3, 210, 211, 250, 315, 353
    on masculinity, 11–12, 32, 36–8, 105, 263, 362
Seamans, Robert C., 353
Securities and Exchange Commission, 41, 233
Sevareid, Eric, 59
Seven Days in May (film), 315
Seven Year Itch, The (film), 24
Shelley, Percy, 6
Shepard, Alan, 331–2, 352
    characteristics of, 333, 335–8, 401n20
    Glenn's relationship with, 333–4, 346–7
    JFK's friendship with, 6, 342, 350, 354–5
    suborbital flight by, 334–42, 347, 355
Sherman, Anthony, 223–4
Show Business Illustrated, 182–3
Show magazine, 296
Shriver, Sargent, 215–16, 250
Sidey, Hugh, 69, 151, 235, 327, 353
Simmons, Jean, 309
Sinatra, Frank, 297, 313, 317
    JFK's relationship with, 6–7, 71, 72–3, 86–104, 125, 162–3, 176, 186, 224, 293–4
    Mafia ties to, 76, 83, 101–3, 224

    masculinity perception influenced by, 6–7, 71, 72–3, 75–103, 125, 148, 175–6, 318–19, 364, 386n27
    on race, 84, 378n17
    in Rat Pack, 73, 79–104, 125, 162–3, 175–6, 179–80, 185, 318–19
    sex appeal of, 56, 73, 74, 76–8, 83–8
    violent encounters by, 75–6
    womanizing by, 7, 73, 77, 79, 83, 84, 88, 91–2
Sitwell, Dame Edith, 138
Slayton, Donald, 331–4, 336–7, 354–5
Smathers, George, 46, 242, 250
SMERSH, 142, 149
Smith, Al, 62
Smith, Jay, 166
Smith, Jean Kennedy, 97
Smith, Stephen, 97
"Social Ethic," 18–19
Some Like It Hot (film), 15, 317
Sorensen, Ted, 6, 50, 146, 210–12, 325
Soviet Union, 31–2, 194–5. *See also* Cold War; Communism
    Bay of Pigs and, 127, 158, 209–13, 214, 266, 283
    Cuban missile crisis and, 153, 154, 213–15, 282, 284, 295, 315, 357, 358, 365, 367
    space program of, 325–30, 349, 351, 352
space program, 8, 323, 364
    astronaut selection process in, 331–2, 401n20
    as Cold War extension, 325–30, 349, 351, 352, 359
    inaugural orbital flight in, 343–52, 355
    inaugural suborbital flight in, 334–42, 347, 355
    masculine regeneration via, 324–52, 354–5, 401n20
Spalding, Charles, 44, 47, 65, 159–60, 292–3
Spartacus (film), 289–91
    masculinity representations in, 299–306, 311–12, 315, 320–1, 322
    production of, 309–11, 314, 319–20
Special Affairs Staff (CIA), 284
Special Forces (Green Berets), 260–8, 274, 278–9, 284–8, 303, 364, 367
Special Group (Augmented), 158–9, 283–4
Special Group (Counterinsurgency), 267
SPECTRE, 142, 143, 149, 154–5
Sports Illustrated, 192, 194–5
Sputnik spacecraft, 325, 327

Spy Who Loved Me, The (Fleming), 155
Stevens, George, Jr., 205
Stevenson, Adlai, 11, 40, 42, 47, 50, 53, 87,
      93, 119, 157, 170
Story magazine, 106
Stravinsky, Igor, 197, 200
Sunday Times, 138, 152
"Superman Comes to the Supermart"
      (Mailer), 6–7, 104–6, 115–30
Swanson, Gloria, 44, 57, 291–2
Symington, Stuart, 40, 53, 93, 120

Taft, Robert A., 51
Tansill, William R., 50
Taylor, Maxwell, 6
   Cold War strategies of, 262, 264–70,
      279–82, 288
Third Hour, The (Household), 138
Thirty-Nine Steps, The (Buchan), 146
Thunderball (Fleming), 142, 143
Tierney, Gene, 293, 296, 313
Time-Life, 327, 330
Time magazine, 75, 78, 144–5, 169, 172,
      231, 235, 301, 304
   on JFK's presidency, 101, 151, 154, 187,
      219, 222, 268, 285
   masculinity perceptions and, 17, 22, 53,
      55, 56, 65, 69, 219, 285
   on space program, 332, 349–50
Today's Health, 14, 17
Tracy, Spencer, 65, 292, 293
Trafficante, Santo, 101
Trilling, Diana, 198, 220
Trohan, Walter, 214
True magazine, 308
Truitt, Anne, 252–3, 255, 257
Truitt, James, 252, 258
Truman, Harry, 47, 87, 179, 186, 198, 203,
      231, 252
Trumbo, Dalton, 300, 311, 313, 314, 316
Turnure, Pamela, 69, 222
TV Guide, 65, 173

Udall, Stewart, 192, 208
Ugly American, The (Burdick/Lederer),
      33–6, 39–40, 149, 215–16, 263, 275
   film, 295
Uncertain Trumpet, The (Taylor), 265
University of Alabama, 298
"The Urge to Pioneer" (Shepard), 339
U.S. News & World Report, 101
U.S.S. *Champlain* (aircraft carrier), 339

U.S.S. *Noah* (destroyer), 349, 351
U.S.S. *Philip* (destroyer), 230
Ustinov, Peter, 310

Van Doren, Mamie, 320
Variety, 99, 155, 301–2
Vidal, Gore, 114, 183, 296
Vienna Summit, 214, 248
Vietnam, 271–7, 278, 280–2, 287
   War, 358, 359
Village Voice, 109, 117, 126
Vital Center, The (Schlesinger), 11, 36–7
von Braun, Wernher, 353

Wagner, Robert, 120
Wainwright, Loudon, 333
Walker, Edwin, 315
Wallace, George, 298
Walton, William, 132, 250, 296
Warner, Jack, 205–6
Washington Post, 69, 197, 231, 242, 246,
      253, 258, 327
Wayne, John, 300, 307
Wear, Priscilla, 222, 225, 242
Webb, James E., 326–7
Webster, Daniel, 51–2
We Seven (Life), 331, 333
What About Communism? (Schlesinger), 11
White, Byron "Whizzer," 192–3
White, Theodore, 68, 125, 242, 357
White, William S., 214
Why England Slept (Kennedy), 49
Whyte, William H., Jr., 18–19, 21, 32
Wilder, Billy, 24, 318
Wilder, Thornton, 199
Wilkinson, Charles B. "Bud," 195
Williams, Tennessee, 15
Wills, Garry, 4–6, 129, 247, 358
Wilson, Sloan, 19
Wilson, Woodrow, 4
Winchell, Walter, 76
Wofford, Harris, 210–11
Wolfe, Thomas, 106, 109, 325
womanizing, 137–8, 308–9, 317, 320
   by astronauts, 333, 337–9, 346
   by Bond, 140–1, 143–5, 149, 160
   by JFK, 3, 7–9, 45, 57–9, 69, 88, 91–2, 94,
      118, 149, 160–1, 164, 179–80, 184–5,
      222–5, 227, 242–3, 246–59, 292–4,
      358, 366, 367, 379*n*51, 391*n*66, 391*n*69
   by Kennedy, Joseph, Sr., 57–8, 247,
      291–2

masculinity perceptions influenced by, 3, 7–9, 58–9, 69, 73, 77, 79, 83, 84, 88, 91–2, 140–1, 143–5, 149, 150, 160–1, 222–5, 242–3, 246–51, 258–9, 333, 337–9, 346
media's portrayal of, 9, 69, 242–3, 248–9, 257–9, 366
national security concerns over, 101–2, 222, 224, 358, 379n51, 391n69
by Rat Pack, 73, 77, 79, 83, 84, 88, 91–2, 160, 318
Woman's Home Companion, 14, 19, 25, 76
women's ascension, 360
bureaucracy as limit to, 361–4
conservative backlash against, 364, 367
fictional women and, 143–4
Mailer on, 106, 111–12, 115
masculinity's degeneration due to, 5, 12–13, 25–30, 31, 34, 37, 106, 111–12, 115, 163–8, 171, 176, 180, 182, 185, 311, 318–19, 361–4

political culture and, 252–5
sexual revolution and, 29–30, 163, 167–8, 180, 182, 185
World War II, 13, 20, 26, 85–6, 105, 164, 170, 181, 188, 190, 192, 193, 229, 230–1, 252, 264, 271, 298, 307, 316, 335, 344, 352
Fleming's service in, 135–6, 141
JFK's service in, 42, 45–6, 48, 55, 122, 147–8, 195, 204–5, 247, 297, 354
Wylie, Philip, 28–9, 30, 166–7

Yarborough, William, 261
Yarmolinsky, Adam, 287
Yeager, Chuck, 332
Young Melbourne, The (Cecil), 2, 45, 152
Young, Terence, 153
You Only Live Twice (Fleming), 142

Zollo, Burt, 165